D1518154

PASSING THE TEST

BATTLES AND CAMPAIGNS

The Battles and Campaigns series examines the military and strategic results of particular combat techniques, strategies, and methods used by soldiers, sailors, and airmen throughout history. Focusing on different nations and branches of the armed services, this series aims to educate readers by detailed analysis of military engagements.

SERIES EDITOR: Roger Cirillo

AN AUSA BOOK

PASSING THE TEST

COMBAT IN KOREA
April–June 1951

Edited by
William T. Bowers and
John T. Greenwood

THE UNIVERSITY PRESS OF KENTUCKY

Published by The University Press of Kentucky

Scholarly publisher for the Commonwealth,
serving Bellarmine University, Berea College, Centre
College of Kentucky, Eastern Kentucky University,
The Filson Historical Society, Georgetown College,
Kentucky Historical Society, Kentucky State University,
Morehead State University, Murray State University,
Northern Kentucky University, Transylvania University,
University of Kentucky, University of Louisville,
and Western Kentucky University.
All rights reserved.

Editorial and Sales Offices: The University Press of Kentucky
663 South Limestone Street, Lexington, Kentucky 40508-4008
www.kentuckypress.com

15 14 13 12 11   5 4 3 2 1

Unless otherwise indicated, all photographs are from the
National Archives and Records Administration, Record Group 111.

Library of Congress Cataloging-in-Publication Data

Passing the test : combat in Korea, April–June 1951 / edited by William T. Bowers
and John T. Greenwood.
    p.   cm. — (Battles and campaigns)
 Includes bibliographical references and index.
 ISBN 978-0-8131-3452-9 (hardcover : alk. paper) —
 ISBN 978-0-8131-3453-6 (ebook)
 1. Korean War, 1950–1953—Campaigns. 2. Strategy—History—20th century.
3. United Nations—Armed Forces—History—Korean War, 1950–1953. 4. United
States—Armed Forces—History—Korean War, 1950–1953. 5. Korea (North)—
Armed Forces—History—Korean War, 1950–1953. 6. China—Armed Forces—
History—Korean War, 1950–1953. I. Bowers, William T., 1946– II. Greenwood,
John T.
 DS918.P37 2011
 951.904'24—dc23
                            2011023322

This book is printed on acid-free paper meeting
the requirements of the American National Standard
for Permanence in Paper for Printed Library Materials.

Manufactured in the United States of America.

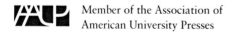
Member of the Association of
American University Presses

A NOTE ON THE TEXT

Sadly, Col. William T. "Tom" Bowers, U.S. Army (retired), passed away in September 2008, just as the University Press of Kentucky published *The Line: Combat in Korea, January–February 1951*, the first volume of his trilogy on the U.S. Army's combat operations in Korea from January to early June 1951. Fortunately for us, he had completed preliminary drafts of the text and maps for the second and third volumes, and the second volume was nearly ready for submission to the press. Following Tom's death, Dr. Roger Cirillo called on me, an experienced Army historian and editor and a former colleague of Tom's at the U.S. Army Center of Military History, to complete what work remained on the second volume and to coordinate with the press throughout the editorial and publication process. Late in 2009 the press published the second volume, *Striking Back: Combat in Korea, March–April 1951*.

Upon publication of *Striking Back,* Dr. Cirillo asked me to finish the work on the third volume, titled *Passing the Test: Combat in Korea, April–June 1951*, and to see it through the publication process. This I did beginning in early 2009. With the publication of *Passing the Test*, Tom's personal and professional commitment to preserving the actions and sacrifices of the American soldiers of the Korean War in their own words is finally concluded. These three volumes will remain a fitting tribute to William T. "Tom" Bowers as an American soldier and a U.S. Army historian.

John T. Greenwood
Editor

CONTENTS

Preface ix

Note on Maps xv

List of Abbreviations xviii

1. The War before the Communist Spring Offensive of 1951 1

2. Battles along the Outpost Line: 32d Infantry Regiment, 19–23 April 1951 13

3. Caught in a Chinese Ambush: Battery B, 999th Armored Field Artillery Battalion, 22–24 April 1951 39

4. Tanks above Kap'yong: Company A, 72d Tank Battalion, 23–24 April 1951 59

5. Artillery in Perimeter Defense: 92d Armored Field Artillery Battalion, 22–24 April 1951 88

6. Hill 628: 8th Ranger Infantry Company (Airborne), 23–25 April 1951 117

7. Gloster Hill: 1st Battalion, Gloucestershire Regiment (the Glosters), 22–25 April 1951 143

8. Action along the No Name Line: U.S. IX Corps 180

9. Anything but Peaceful Valley: 15th Field Artillery Battalion, 16–18 May 1951 223

10. The Battle below the Soyang River: Company C,
    72d Tank Battalion, 16–18 May 1951   244

11. The Supply Battle of the Soyang River: U.S. X Corps,
    10 May–7 June 1951   285

12. Task Force Gerhart: Company B, 72d Tank Battalion,
    24 May 1951   297

13. Task Force Hazel: 7th Reconnaissance Company,
    24–25 May 1951   331

Conclusion   376

Notes   383

Bibliographical Essay   415

Index   425

Photo gallery follows page 214

PREFACE

Much can be learned about war from studying the thirty-eight months of fighting in Korea, from June 1950 to July 1953. Military operations ranged from rapid advances and withdrawals and amphibious landings and evacuations, all reminiscent of World War II, to static operations interrupted by set-piece battles and vicious raids that recall the battles on the Western Front during World War I. The weather was often as brutal as the fighting: summers hot and humid, winters frigid with icy Siberian winds. The rugged terrain challenged even those who thought they were in good physical condition. Before Korea, U.S. strategic planners, and indeed most people in the United States, believed that such a war would never be fought again, and certainly not in Korea. Consequently, preparations were few, and the individuals who actually had to fight the battles paid the price.

This book, the third in a series on the Korean War, takes a close look at some of the fighting that occurred during the Chinese Communist Spring Offensive from late April to late May–early June 1951. This volume focuses mostly on combat at the lowest levels: battalion, company, platoon, squad, and individual soldiers. Although the spotlight is on tactical operations and frontline fighting, each combat action is placed in its own unique context, so that the reader is aware of the way in which events and decisions in Korea influenced what happened on the battlefield.

Most of the material for this book is drawn from interviews conducted by U.S. Army historians soon after a combat action occurred, in some cases within hours or a few days. Additional information comes from official records, such as unit journals and periodic reports, and from unit and individual award recommendations, which included eyewitness accounts of heroic actions.

Army historians had to overcome many problems to collect the combat interviews that form the basis for this book. They worked on tight deadlines because the interviews and after-action summaries were needed not only to capture the historical record while events were still fresh, but also to provide information to other American units about enemy and friendly operations, namely which tactics and methods the enemy was using and which procedures and tactics seemed to be effective or were failures in fighting the enemy. There were many combat actions, and little time was available to conduct interviews and compile the reports, which in most cases included maps, photographs, and a narrative summary. Sometimes historians could not visit units until long after a battle had ended. Often the key individuals necessary to provide a complete understanding of the fight were not available for interviews because they were dead, ill, wounded, on leave, or on rotation, or for other reasons. The ideal was for the historian to walk the battlefield with the participants so that the resulting interviews, maps, and photographs brought the action to life. But this could not always be accomplished because of time limitations or because the former battlefield at that point lay in enemy territory. Accounts by different participants were sometimes contradictory, even about such routine matters as orders, indicating that the confusion of combat remained after the fighting ended. Other statements were vague about the most recent actions or seemed to focus on one specific incident, indicating perhaps that the trauma produced by the immediate presence of danger and death in combat still lingered.

The combat interviews used in this volume were based mostly on the notes that the combat historians and their enlisted assistants took during individual and group interviews. Following these sessions, the historians and their assistants compiled, edited, typed up, and revised copies of their refined and combined notes, which were then used to complete the studies and were attached to them as supporting documents. Only in some rare instances did the interviewees personally review, edit, and authenticate their comments in the transcripts prepared by the military historians. Because the interviews used in chapter 2, "Hill 902," and in chapter 3 fall into this category, they are the only ones in the book that appear as first-person accounts. The interviews were not tape-recorded and transcribed because the military history detachments at the time lacked such equipment. This particular shortcoming was clearly recognized, and Army military history detachments in subsequent conflicts have always gone to the field fully equipped and trained to conduct recorded interviews.

Despite occasional shortcomings, these interviews provide a unique picture of the fighting in Korea that is not distorted by years of veterans' gatherings and reading other accounts. When soldiers describe what they saw and heard, it becomes clear that most narrative histories of the war fail to capture the confusion, uncertainty, fear, hardships, incompetence, dedication, professional skill, determination, and heroism that were an everyday occurrence in most combat actions. When the interviews are compared with unit records, it appears that, on occasion, higher headquarters had an incomplete and erroneous understanding of what had actually happened. Taken as a whole, the interviews provide an explanation of why the U.S. and UN forces prevailed in the difficult war that was fought in Korea. In most cases soldiers and their leaders found a way eventually to overcome all problems and to succeed on the battlefield.

This volume could be divided into three unequal sections. The first, covering the Communist Spring Offensive and the run-up to it, consists of chapters 1–7. As in the two previous volumes, chapter 1 provides the context for the following chapters, which focus on specific combat actions. It clearly spells out both U.S. and UN strategy and operations and those of the Communist Chinese and North Korean forces, which were then preparing what they called the first phase (or "impulse") of the Fifth (Spring) Offensive. Chapters 2 through 7 recount the actions of U.S. and British Commonwealth forces immediately before and during the Chinese and North Korean offensive (22–30 April 1951). Chapter 2 examines in detail three intense actions of elements of the 32d Infantry Regiment, 7th

Infantry Division, to defeat enemy probing attacks and then to hold the initial attacks of the Chinese and North Koreans that opened the night of 22–23 April. Chapter 3 follows the operations of Battery B, 999th Armored Field Artillery Battalion, in its efforts to support the Republic of Korea (ROK) 1st Division during the opening days of the Spring Offensive. Support of allied forces of the United Nations Command (UNC) is also the theme of chapters 4 and 5. The story of Company A, 72d Tank Battalion, 2d Infantry Division, and the 1st Royal Australian Regiment (RAR) in support of the ROK 6th Division is the focus of chapter 4. The classic fight of the well-prepared 92d Armored Field Artillery Battalion to hold the flank of the 1st Marine Division after the ROK 6th Division collapsed is told in chapter 5. The difficult combat operations of the 8th Ranger Infantry Company (Airborne) in the 24th Infantry Division's sector are recounted in chapter 6. Chapter 7 tells the tragic story of the 1st Battalion, the Gloucestershire Regiment, 29th British Independent Infantry Brigade Group, which was overrun and largely captured while stubbornly holding Hill 235 to retard the Chinese offensive.

The renewal of the Chinese offensive is the subject of the second section of the book, chapters 8–11. Chapter 8 examines three actions on the U.S. IX Corps's sector that were intended to stabilize the front and push back against the anticipated renewal of the Chinese Spring Offensive. After regrouping and resupplying, the Chinese launched the second phase of their Spring Offensive (16–23 May 1951). Chapters 9 through 11 focus on U.S. and UN actions to counter this phase of the offensive with planned fighting withdrawals intended to slow and inflict heavy casualties on the attackers. Chapter 9 follows plans and operations of the 15th Field Artillery Battalion, and chapter 10 retraces the hard combat of Company C, 72d Tank Battalion, 2d Infantry Division, south of the Soyang River. Chapter 11 tells the story of how logistical support was organized for UNC forces in X Corps during the fighting south of the Soyang River.

By the last week of May, even before the second phase of the Chinese Spring Offensive was clearly spent, the UNC and Eighth U.S. Army launched their counteroffensive, which is the focus of the third section of the book. Chapters 12 and 13 examine the Eighth U.S. Army's plans and operations for the UN counteroffensive of late May. In the X Corps, Task Force Gerhart and the hard fight of the 72d Tank Battalion up Route 24 to retake the road and the crossings of the Soyang River at Umyang-ni are the subject of chapter 12. At the same time, IX Corps formed Task Force Hazel, drawn mostly from the 7th Infantry Division's 7th Reconnaissance Company, which pushed through heavily defended enemy territory to Ch'unch'on as a prelude to the push north to secure the important road network west of the Hwach'on Reservoir. The conclusion summarizes the results of the Communist Spring Offensive and the United Nations' counteroffensive operations and their effect on the rest of the Korean War.

With the exception of the first chapter and the conclusion, which were researched and written by Dr. Roger Cirillo (Lt. Col., U.S. Army, retired), director of the Book Program of the Association of the United States Army (AUSA), the narrative is carried by the interviews, set off by brief remarks in italics to set the stage and link the interviews together. Minor editing was done to the interviews to remove repetitious and extraneous material not key to understanding the action, such as the repeated use of the military ranks of the interviewees and complete unit designations. Obvious typographical and grammatical errors were corrected so that the reader is not constantly distracted, and occasional changes to punctuation have been made for the sake of clarity. All of the interviews contained numerous references to map coordinates from the Army Map Service's 1:50,000 Korean War–era topographical maps (AMS L751 series) to locate the combat actions. These references are meaningless without the access to the actual maps themselves. Such references have been either deleted when they have no relevance to the story or replaced with ellipses (. . .) or with recognizable geographical descriptions of the locations set off in brackets. In no circumstances has the content of the basic interviews been otherwise changed. In addition, the full names of Army personnel who were killed in action or died of wounds received during these actions but who were not identified by name in the reports have been identified in the text. The Korean War Casualty Files of the U.S. Army Adjutant General's Office, which are now accessible on the Internet at the National Archives and Records Administration's Access of Archival Databases (http://aad.archives.gov/aad), were used to obtain these identifications. Chapter notes at the end of the book provide information for further research and study.

A number of individuals were of great assistance during the preparation of this book. Roger Cirillo initially proposed the project as a way not only to preserve the Korean War combat interviews, but also to provide an opportunity for a wider audience to become acquainted with their worth as a valuable source of information on the Korean War and on combat in general. Bob Wright, Mary Haynes, and Jim Knight provided expert assistance and cheerful encouragement and support, and Tom Bowers conducted research in the archives and library of the U.S. Army Center of Military History (CMH). John Elsberg, Steve Hardyman, Sherry Dowdy, and Beth Mackenzie, all of CMH, helped him gain a better understanding of the cartographic support needed so that the combat interviews could be understood. David Rennie turned rough and incomplete sketches into maps. At the National Archives, Tim Nenninger, Rich Boylan, and Mitch Yockelson, all of the Modern Military Branch, provided invaluable assistance in tracking down unit records and award recommendations. Richard Sommers, Dave Keough, and the staff of the U.S. Army Military History Institute, U.S. Army History and Education Center (AHEC), at Carlisle Barracks, Pennsylvania, also provided invaluable advice and assistance. I would also like to extend a special thanks to Stephen M. Wrinn and Ila McEntire at the University Press of Kentucky, and to Ann Twombly, their freelance copyeditor, for making this manuscript into a book. While these individuals contributed immeasurably to this book, the editors alone are responsible for any errors in fact or omission that might appear.

NOTE ON MAPS

A number of the maps used in this work were rough sketches drawn by soldiers as they recounted their experiences during the Korean War. As such, the maps employ a variety of symbols for terrain and military operations. To ensure clarity, notations have been added to some sketches. Whenever possible, the standard military and topographical symbols shown below have been used, along with common abbreviations. Numbers on all contours are in meters.

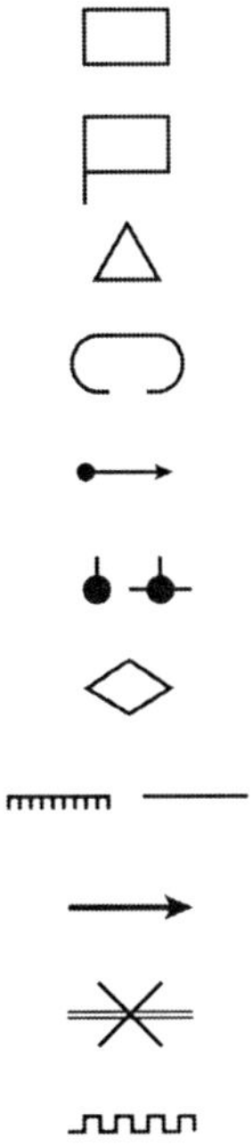

▭	Unit symbol (enemy shown in gray or labeled)
⊏⊐	Headquarters or command post
△	Observation post (OP)
�	Position area
•→	Machine gun or automatic weapon
● ●	Mortar or gun
◇	Tank, self-propelled weapon
ᴨᴨᴨᴨ ——	Front lines
→	Route or direction of attack
✕	Road block
⊓⊔⊓⊔	Trenches, fortified positions

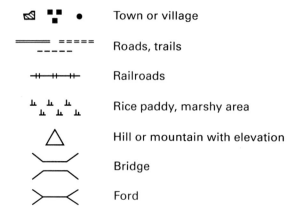

Town or village

Roads, trails

Railroads

Rice paddy, marshy area

Hill or mountain with elevation

Bridge

Ford

The following symbols placed in boundary lines or position area ovals or above the rectangle, triangle, or circle enclosing the identifying arm or service symbol indicate the size of military organizations.

●	Squad
●●	Section
●●●	Platoon
I	Company, troop, battery
II	Battalion, cavalry squadron
III	Regiment, group, combat team
X	Brigade
XX	Division
XXX	Corps
XXXX	Army
XXXXX	Army Group

Examples are given below. The letter or number to the left of the symbol indicates the unit designation; that to the right, the designation of the parent unit to which it belongs. Letters or numbers above or below boundary lines designate the units separated by the lines. Unit designations sometimes are shown as 3/A/9 (3d Platoon, Company A, 9th Infantry Regiment) or as 1–9 (1st Battalion, 9th Infantry Regiment).

A ⊠ 137   Company A, 137th Infantry

⊡ 8   8th Field Artillery Battalion

⊠ 5   Command post, 5th Infantry Division

137
—III—   Boundary between 137th and 138th Infantry
138

For those readers who are interested in viewing or using the Army Map Service's original topographical maps from the Korean War era, many of the L552 series of 1:250,000 maps and L751 series of 1:50,000 maps are now digitized and available online at the Korean War Project (www.koreanwar.org/index.html).

ABBREVIATIONS

AA	Antiaircraft
AAA	Antiaircraft Artillery
Abn	Airborne
AFA	Armored Field Artillery
AOP	Aerial Observation Post
A&P	Ammunition and Pioneer
AR	Automatic Rifle
ARCT	Airborne Regimental Combat Team
Arty	Artillery
ASP	Ammunition Supply Point
AT	Antitank
AUV	Armored Utility Vehicle
AW	Automatic Weapons
BAR	Browning Automatic Rifle
BCT	Battalion Combat Team
Bde	Brigade
BIB	British Independent Infantry Brigade
BN or bn	Battalion
Btry	Battery
BUNBN	Belgian UN Battalion
CCF	Chinese Communist Forces
CG	Commanding General
CINC	Commander-in-Chief
CO	Commanding Officer or Company
COY	Company (usually British)

CP	Command Post or Check Point
CPVA	Chinese People's Volunteer Army
DSC	Distinguished Service Cross
EUSAK	Eighth U.S. Army Korea
FA	Field Artillery
FDC	Fire Direction Center
FDLS	Forward Defended Localities
Fd Regt	Field Regiment
Fd Sqn	Field Squadron
FECOM	Far East Command (U.S.)
FO	Forward Observer
FWD	Forward
G-1/S-1	Personnel Officer
G-2/S-2	Intelligence Officer
G-3/S-3	Operations Officer
G-4/S-4	Supply Officer
H	Hussars
HE	High Explosive
HMG	Heavy Machine Gun
HQ	Headquarters
HRS	Hours
IP	Initial Point
I&R	Intelligence and Reconnaissance
KIA	Killed in Action
KMAG	Korean Military Advisory Group
KSLI	King's Shropshire Light Infantry
LD	Line of Departure
LMG	Light Machine Gun
MASH	Mobile Army Surgical Hospital
MG	Machine Gun
MIA	Missing in Action
MLR	Main Line of Resistance
MMG	Medium Machine Gun
MP	Military Police
MSR	Main Supply Road
NCO	Noncommissioned Officer
NF	Royal Northumberland Fusiliers

NK	North Korea
NKPA	North Korean People's Army
OP	Observation Post; Outpost
OPL	Outpost Line
OPLR	Outpost Line of Resistance
PEFTOK	Philippine Expeditionary Force to Korea
PLA	People's Liberation Army (Chinese Communist)
POL	Petroleum, Oil, and Lubricants
POW or PW	Prisoner of War
RA	Royal Artillery
RAR	Royal Australian Regiment
RCT	Regimental Combat Team
RE	Royal Engineers
Recon, recce, rcn	Reconnaissance
ROK	Republic of Korea (South Korea)
R&R	Rest and Recreation
RUR	Royal Ulster Rifles
SA or S/A	Small arms
SCR	Signal Corps Radio
SOP	Standard Operating Procedure
TF	Task Force
TK	Tank
TO/E	Table of Organization and Equipment
UN	United Nations
UNC	United Nations Command
VT	Variable Time Fuse
WIA	Wounded in Action
WP	White Phosphorous

RANKS

Pvt.	Private
PFC	Private First Class
Cpl.	Corporal
Sgt.	Sergeant
SFC	Sergeant First Class
M. Sgt.	Master Sergeant
1st Sgt.	First Sergeant

Lt.	Lieutenant
2d Lt.	Second Lieutenant
1st Lt.	First Lieutenant
Capt.	Captain
Maj.	Major
Lt. Col.	Lieutenant Colonel
Col.	Colonel
Gen.	General
Brig. Gen.	Brigadier General
Maj. Gen.	Major General
Lt. Gen.	Lieutenant General

Chapter 1

THE WAR BEFORE THE COMMUNIST SPRING OFFENSIVE OF 1951

The military situation in Korea had already seen four major turning points by April 1951. On 25 June 1950 the North Korean People's Army (NKPA) attacked a peaceful Republic of South Korea (ROK). When the United Nations (UN) Security Council called on its member nations to assist the Republic of Korea two days later, it was the first time the United Nations committed armed forces of its members to oppose aggression against a peaceful nation. The piecemeal commitment of U.S. and UN forces in an attempt to stabilize the military situation before restoring captured territory to the control of the legal government came without the benefit of a declaration of war by any of the UN member nations participating. Unofficially, the fighting in Korea came to be called a police action, or the Korean Conflict.[1]

During July and into August 1950, the ROK army, along with the forces of the newly form United Nations Command (UNC), primarily U.S. Army units from the Eighth U.S. Army in Japan, were thrown back from the 38th parallel to the tip of the Korean peninsula, where they formed a defensive perimeter near the port of Pusan. The U.S. and UNC units that held the Pusan perimeter against a determined North Korean onslaught and retained a foothold on the Korean peninsula won the initial turning point in the conflict. Appointed the United Nations commander in chief on 8 July, General of the Army Douglas MacArthur, commander in chief, U.S. Far East Command (FECOM), launched Operation Chromite in mid-September, an amphibious landing by X Corps to

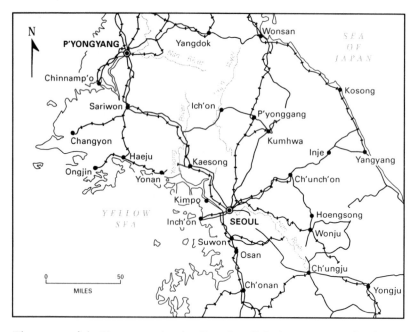

The center of the Korean peninsula. (Based on U.S. Army Center of Military History map.)

the rear of the enemy at the port of Inch'on. In a stroke, this sent the enemy reeling as the Eighth Army, under the command of Lt. Gen. Walton H. Walker, simultaneously broke out from the Pusan perimeter, driving northward to link up with X Corps near Seoul. By early October UN forces had crossed the 38th parallel into North Korea, and X Corps again landed from the sea at Wonsan, on the northeast coast, on 25 October. Chromite and the crossing into North Korea formed the second great turning point, promising to unify Korea under a democratic banner.

In October and November Communist China entered the war by infiltrating seven field armies of the Chinese People's Volunteer Armies (CPVA) into North Korea. Though some units of the CPVA, or Chinese Communist Forces (CCF), had been engaged by late October, MacArthur banked on rapidly closing in on the Yalu River on the Chinese-Korean border and his own overwhelming airpower to deter a mass entrance of China's forces into the war. Britain gave political intelligence to all concerning the Chinese threat to enter the war, and Chinese propaganda broadcasts warned of the dangers of crossing the 38th parallel, but MacArthur discounted these warnings. He believed that UN airpower would nullify any intervention of the "Chinese volunteers." MacArthur personally flew on aerial reconnaissance of the rough topography at the Yalu. From the terrain he could see across the river, he believed that China's forces could not cross en masse without being canalized between the hills and limited to a few crossing points. Clearly, he believed his calculation and assessment of a military risk of closing the borders of North Korea was justified. This was shaped by his view of airpower. He concluded that the political threats of CCF intervention on a large scale would be militarily fruitless. The result of his taking this risk would soon be apparent.[2]

On 24 November the Eighth Army launched its major offensive toward the Yalu River against light to negligible resistance. The Eighth Army noted about 30,000 CCF troops in its sector, X Corps fewer than 8,000. Though great numbers of Chinese were known to be north of the Yalu, U.S. field commanders believed that their "massive compression envelopment" would clear North Korea, and only Chinese reinforcements scattered to NKPA units would intervene. At every level the commanders seemed intent on taking the risk, seeing a massive Chinese intervention as unlikely, especially because of the strength of the UN air forces. MacArthur's own confidence confirmed this view.[3] This concluded the second turning point.

Attacking in great strength in late November, Chinese Communist forces split the Eighth Army on the west side of Korea and the U.S. X Corps, which had been operating independently to the east. The CCF appeared first in scattered battalion- and regiment-sized counterattacks, but by late November both Walker and MacArthur recognized that a massive Chinese intervention and offensive were under way. UN forces withdrew under heavy threat of annihilation that was due to superior numbers, though Walker later noted that his attack precipitated a counteroffensive of about 200,000 men that would have doubled had the Chinese finished their deployment before attacking. In this manner, "develop[ing] the situation was indeed, most fortunate."[4] MacArthur's risk and

Walker's offensive brought on "a new war" and the third turning point.

The Chinese intervention changed the entire strategic situation. MacArthur viewed this as a new war that was unwinnable without aerial attack into China at the enemy's bases and the possible use of Nationalist Chinese troops on the mainland to refocus the Chinese army's offensive onto its own ground. Denied both options by President Truman, who was heavily besieged by Allied demands not to expand the war, MacArthur told Walker to withdraw, keeping the Eighth Army intact. With no victory possible, MacArthur noted that Korea was not worth holding. Walker's death in a jeep accident on 23 December permitted a change in leadership. Both the Eighth Army and its commander had been fought to exhaustion in six months of hard campaigning.[5] The fourth turning point came with the arrival of another Eighth Army commander.

The new commander, Lt. Gen. Matthew Bunker Ridgway, attempted to counter enemy moves with local counterattacks when possible. He noted that Chinese Communist logistics brought offensives to a halt after a number of weeks.[6] Taking advantage of fresh troops, an influx of UN support, and MacArthur's authority, he counterattacked, seeking not so much to take ground as to inflict heavier casualties on the enemy after the Chinese offensives slowed or during lulls. Ridgway stopped the enemy and slowly moved north in a series of small operations, but to uncertain advantage. The names of these operations echoed Ridgway's aggressive temperament. Thunderbolt (January), Roundup and Killer (February), Courageous, Ripper, and Tomahawk (March), and Rugged, Swing, and Dauntless (April) soon topped the operations plans issued as names, not the usual numbers.[7]

The UN now sought no liberation of North Korea. The Western allies were concerned about the Communist threat in Europe. Korea, though a valuable symbol that demonstrated the West's determination to halt the spread of aggression, was not seen as the sole battleground between the Free World and Communism. The West also clearly signaled an unwillingness to fight to a military conclusion in Asia. This changed policy led to MacArthur's relief for not supporting it publicly and his replacement by Ridgway.[8]

The new Eighth Army commander was Lt. Gen. James A. Van Fleet, like Ridgway a fighting commander, but who lacked Ridgway's public persona and fine-tuned sensitivities to public relations. His arrival in Korea on 14 April 1951 signaled no immediate change in the ground fighting.[9] Moreover, as Ridgway had been kept informed by MacArthur concerning Washington's policies, Ridgway knew of Washington's concern for substituting diplomacy for a battlefield victory and did not question the policy in public or private. "Van" immediately received ironclad instructions governing his conduct of operations. These included both specific tactical practices as well as plans restricting major operations and the destruction of or heavy casualties for large units.

Ridgway had detailed these policies already for his division and corps commanders in a full-day conference in March 1951. Ridgway banned the use of any directive to hold a terrain feature or line "at all costs," reserving that authority to himself as Army commander until he had visited the ground and seen its justification.[10] Ridgway, with MacArthur's concurrence, summarized his policy, "that 'terrain, as such, means nothing to me, except as it facilitates the destruction of hostile forces and the conservation of our own.'"[11] Thus, "We shall make optimum use of offensive action to inflict maximum personnel and material losses on hostile forces with minimum losses to ourselves, both consistent with the maintenance intact of all major units, and to the utmost possible extent, retaining the initiative."[12] In every case, he would use movement forward as a way to prompt engagements, "subject to enemy reactions and our own logistics."

Moreover, he struck a note that would be amplified by Van Fleet upon his assumption of command in mid-April. Ridgway had stated, "If compelled to a period of relatively static warfare, we shall seek to fit our coordinated firepower to the terrain by offensive maneuver, whenever wherever we can."[13] Recognizing that the enemy would attempt to resume offensive operations, Ridgway expressed confidence in the Eighth Army's arrival "at the stage where the combination of leadership and battle-seasoned troops will permit us to invite [enemy] penetrations for the purpose of containing and destroying them."[14]

Van Fleet assumed command fully in accord with Ridgway's tactics and stressed that artillery should be used to the greatest possible extent. The "Van Fleet Day of Fire," as planners referred to his guidance, multiplied by five the former daily allocation of artillery rounds to units for planning purposes. Units were thus allocated 250 rounds of 105mm howitzer ammunition for a twenty-four-hour period, rather than the previous 50. Units with larger calibers, such as 155mm or 8-inch howitzers, received between 200 and 250 rounds per tube per day.[15]

The Van Fleet allocation of artillery ammunition and repetitive limited objective attacks with closely tied flanks became a standard. The climb north followed phase lines with names such as Utah, Kansas, and Wyoming, each with the intent of facilitating a tightly tied-in move to grind up the enemy with massed fires and coordinated assaults.

Ground war's key elements, terrain and weather, had a heightened influence in Korea. The terrible winter that hardened rice paddies like steel gave way to a warmer spring that left paddies muddied and filling with water from the increasing rains of late April and early May, which would turn roads to slurry with the passage of a few vehicles. The Korean peninsula is unrivaled even by Italy in being scored by sharp mountains and valleys. Most roads fell into the "fair-to-poor" range of condition for both usage and further improvements. The great mountains blended into lower highlands of steep hills cut only by meandering trails, streams, or dirt roads. Each was a tactical puzzle and granted defenders complex advantages. The high North Taebaek Range of mountains lay astride the objectives designated for the Eighth Army.[16]

By the last ten days of April, Ridgway's original plans to go north to the "Iron Triangle" area, formed by the villages of Ch'orwon, P'yonggang, and Kimwha (Chorwon, Pyonggang, and Kumhwa during the war period),[17] and the Ch'orwon valley to its east had drawn to a close. Enemy resistance had stiffened in the Iron Triangle. The CCF showed sensitivity to covering its own lines of communication because the central Chinese supply point was in the Iron Triangle. The Ch'orwon valley would be a fight postponed, and both Ridgway and Van Fleet now waited for the Chinese to make the first major move while still slowly advancing. Earlier, during the March conference, Ridgway had noted that friendly retrograde movements to meet attacks in overwhelming numbers would be considered, and that the Eighth Army had initiated a coordinated plan on a very close-hold basis. The Eighth Army had stressed maximum coordination between the corps, delay on every possible enemy avenue of advance, and the use of every possible barrier, obstacle, and defensive technique available to halt and destroy an enemy advance.[18]

Ridgway and MacArthur expected another major Chinese offensive, probably in April. On 12 April the Eighth Army planned for such a contingency by issuing operations plan Audacious, which set withdrawal lines named Delta, Golden, and Nevada, accounting for withdrawals both holding on to Seoul (Golden) and withdrawing completely south of it (Nevada). As part of this plan both the U.S. 1st Cavalry and 2d Infantry Divisions were to be held in reserve and used as counterattack forces.[19]

Intelligence predicted a major Chinese attack. The classic indicators were present beginning early in April. These included repair and construction of roads in the enemy forward area, drops in refugee travel after a surge in refugees, and radio silence among units in contact. In addition, the most important indicator was the fading away of enemy resistance.[20]

While the U.S. Fifth Air Force, with attached UN air squadrons, pounded airfields and prevented the Chinese and North Korean air units from moving south, they also hit road termini, railroads, and bridges. Despite these attacks, the CCF managed to slowly build up stocks for offensive action, using some trucks but mostly carts and wheelbarrows to move supplies. Night movement to survive was imperative; during daylight vehicles hid under bridges, in woods, and in tunnels. Submerged bridges were also used for crossing streams and shallow rivers. Companies and regiments stocked only seven days' rations.[21]

The Chinese had developed a well-practiced drill in evading reconnaissance. S. L. A. Marshall, one of the war's analysts, described the Chinese infiltrating into North Korea as "a phantom which cast no shadow."[22] Having moved and survived four full offensives by this time, the Chinese were practicing experts. With bad weather, fog, and the lack of the large modern army's telltale trail of thousands of vehicles, mountains of supplies, and a distinct communications signature, the Chinese seemed almost universally absent despite the presence of numerous prisoners and occasional radio use. Van Fleet wanted deep patrolling, sending large bands or company-sized units aggressively into the enemy's rear, but the range of such patrols was limited to a night's march in and out, no more than six miles.

The Chinese withdrew two-thirds of their divisions to assembly areas at least a full day's march in the rear, and thereafter extending deeper. This created a porous front: deep and large incursions were resisted lightly, and regular patrolling failed to uncover the enemy situation in the classic mode, that is, locations, size of units, and activity.[23] This approach followed a technique described in a captured document dated 17 March called "Flexible Warfare," which defended against the enemy through movement. A "roving defense," whose "roving motion" kept forces moving around, either attacking or defending, was a way of sapping an enemy's strength. These tactics conserved CCF strength for a more opportune time when the spring mud would hamper UN counterattacks.[24]

The Eighth Army's slow, cautious advance toward the Kansas Line, a terrain-based objective designed to coordinate the corps advance and minimize risk, mirrored the Chinese withdrawal. The U.S. I Corps straddled the main enemy avenues of approach southward. Throughout late March and early April, the corps moved toward the Imjin River and its crossings, noting stiffening resistance from mid-April onward.[25]

Van Fleet and his commanders carefully watched their front. G-2 reported on 18 April, "Concerning the expected forthcoming 'Fifth Phase' Offensive, a survey of all sources has failed to indicate conclusively any specific date or period of the initial attack—although most indications favor the period 20 April through 1 May."[26] A louder warning was sounded on 20 April, after a thorough review of Chinese tactics and the anticipated attack noted: "The similarity between the enemy's tactical and logistical pattern during the period preceding the 12th of February attack and the

current situation is unmistakable. In view of the enemy forces available, this similarity strengthens the possibility of offensive enemy
action in the near future."[27]

By 21 April the UN line units had reconnaissance extended
north of the river and, in the west, north to the Hwach'on Reservoir.
Enemy prisoners of war continued to report that an enemy offensive
was imminent, but no likely date could be confirmed.[28]

Ridgway had not intended to press hard into an enemy trap, as
had happened in November. If firepower could not stop the inevitable counteroffensive, falling back and firing masses of artillery
from line to line would create the attrition battle he wanted. By
mid-April, as General Van Fleet took over, he knew he was taking
command of an army on the eve of a Chinese-initiated offensive. He
and his men—indeed, like all of United Nations Command—were
ready for the inevitable attack.

Likewise, the Chinese were ready. Having received their attack
directive from Mao Zedong himself, the Chinese army would attack along a front of more than fifty miles, seeking multiple penetrations. Marshal Peng Dehuai's plan followed the major avenues used
by the NKPA in the June 1950 advance.[29] This leaned the offensive
toward the center and west of the peninsula, the main effort falling
in the Ch'orwon–Uijongbu (Route 33) and the Kumhwa–Uijongbu
(Route 3) corridors that led directly toward Seoul, both of which
had been considered possible main invasion routes since Ridgway's
arrival.[30] Astride the rough mountains to the west, additional Chinese crossed the Imjin River toward the second major invasion corridor leading from Kaesong toward Seoul along the P'yongyang–Seoul
capital-to-capital approach. While further operations in the east
solidified a firing line under pressure, the two great "impulses"
(phases) that the Chinese planned followed the Ch'orwon and Imjin
crossings, as most Chinese divisions piled on the American divisions
rather than the ROK corps, already weakened by lengthy battle.
The Americans blocked the key avenues and constituted the key
enemy objectives. Peng intended to slip into Seoul and trap as many
UN soldiers north of the Han River as possible, repeating the 1950
tactic that had failed to trap the ROK, falling back from the invasion from the north.[31]

The Fifth Offensive followed the pattern of all the previous Chinese Communist army offensives in that it was exceptionally well prepared and well coordinated. Already behind their delay-and-screening force, the main body waited to attack Van Fleet's army at the time and place of its choosing. Stockpiled ammunition and rations for a week were distributed. Troops were briefed on the importance of their offensive and its plan, as part of the standard Communist political indoctrination, a "method of building up the individual's sense of duty in the operation." Only the exact date and hour of attack were withheld.[32]

American tactics conformed to the uniqueness both of the ground and the enemy. U.S. divisions most often occupied ground exceeding twice that normally held in a planned defense.[33] Initially overwhelmed by larger numbers on an extensive front, Ridgway's and later Van Fleet's commanders concentrated forces in the attack, calling for heavy fires and, when available, air support. Because the enemy often resorted to night action to avoid concentrated observed artillery fires, American units dug in on dominant ridges at night in battalion or larger perimeters, often lit by flares or illumination rounds fired by artillery or air dropped, or eventually bathed in the eerie, dim light of powerful searchlights whose beams were bounced off low-hanging clouds forward of friendly positions. In daylight the units came off their positions to clean up the valleys and low ground along the advance to the next dominant hill mass or ridge. In retrograde, the reverse would be true, the tactics and techniques the same.[34] April and May operations saw both tactical versions used.

Chinese Communist Party Chairman Mao, his troops having lost headway with their Fourth Offensive in March 1951, wanted to undertake a major offensive before UN firepower and numbers could stalemate the front north of the 38th parallel. In a new assault he hoped to finish off the ROK army's fighting capability as well as "wipe out another 10,000 of the American troops." Chinese intelligence concluded that MacArthur might launch another amphibious end run toward Wonsan and that large numbers of reinforcements would be available to both the ROK and U.S. forces by April's end. Mao, who oversaw Peng's operations in detail, ordered him to continue refusing combat and encourage UN advances to keep them from digging in. Peng expected to launch his own attack by 20 April if the enemy moved rapidly, and in May if the Eighth Army's attacks slowed. High on Peng's task list for the offensive approved for April was to instill confidence in his troops to "make sure our troops will no longer fear fighting in daytime combat."[35]

The central theme of Peng's operations was a mirror image of Ridgway's own tactics. Ridgway, who demanded that no units be sacrificed and ground given when pressed by numbers, was countered by Peng's concept that destroying enemy divisions would prevent MacArthur and Ridgway from regaining the offensive. He wanted to "carve up the enemy forces into many pockets and wipe them out one by one." Key among his targets was the concentration of troops in the vicinity of the Kumhwa-Kap'yong sector, which he wanted to cut in two, and then isolate the surrounded units and annihilate them. Peng's "instructions on Command and Tactics for the [Fifth Phase] Offensive" were published on 11 April, the same day MacArthur was relieved of command.[36] Peng's optimism was abundant. "We are determined to eliminate three U.S. divisions (excluding one regiment), three British and Turkish Brigades, and the ROK 1st and 6th Divisions."[37]

His first attack would take out the ROK 6th Division, the U.K.'s 27th Brigade, the U.S. 3d Infantry Division, and the Turkish Brigade, and another field army would take out the U.K.'s 29th Brigade and then outflank the U.S. 24th and 25th Infantry Divisions from the south. The army crossing the Imjin would penetrate to Uijongbu and cut off the Ch'orwon–Uijongbu corridor (Route 33) as a withdrawal route paralleling Route 3, the Kumhwa–Uijongbu corridor.

Peng's offensive would be phased in two movements, or "impulses." The Chinese inability to issue both food and ammunition forward during offensive operations required a pause that played into Ridgway's and Van Fleet's hands. It allowed them to use their reserves to launch a counteroffensive after the initial enemy offensive ended.

As the attack day came closer, the Eighth Army carefully watched its front for what it already termed the Fifth Phase Offensive. Until darkness fell, 22 April was another day of limited contact. Four hours of artillery preparation preceded the Chinese attacks.

The command assessment by midnight outlined the essence of the Chinese plan: "The attack is designed to initially throw UN Forces off balance in the central sector and then with the forces available in the west launch a strong attack against the west flank of UN forces."[38] The story of how some U.S. and UN units fought in the Chinese Spring Offensive follows.

Chapter 2

BATTLES ALONG THE OUTPOST LINE

32d Infantry Regiment, 19–23 April 1951

The enemy's Spring Offensive fell unevenly across the UN front. The Chinese and North Koreans planned to hit hard at the weakest and most vulnerable areas and at those UN units defending key terrain covering their main objective, the South Korean capital of Seoul. In other sectors the Communist attacks were designed to deceive or fix units in position so that UN forces could not be shifted to reinforce threatened points. In these areas, the assault forces were weaker and less capable. This was the situation in the U.S. 7th Infantry Division sector, which elements of the North Korean 45th Division, a new and poorly trained formation, and the North Korean 12th Division, a veteran but severely understrength unit, were assigned to attack.

The U.S. 7th Infantry Division, X Corps, held a ten-mile line running eastward from the right edge of the Hwach'on Reservoir to the ROK 5th Division, above the town of Inje. The 7th Division had two regiments online, the 17th Infantry on the left and the 32d Infantry on the right. The terrain in the 32d Infantry's sector was mountainous; there were no roads and only a few difficult trails. The 32d was prepared for the expected attack, its patrols to the front for early warning and strong positions located on commanding terrain.

Combat Outpost: Company B, 32d Infantry Regiment, 19–22 April 1951

Members of Company B, 32d Infantry Regiment, which held a

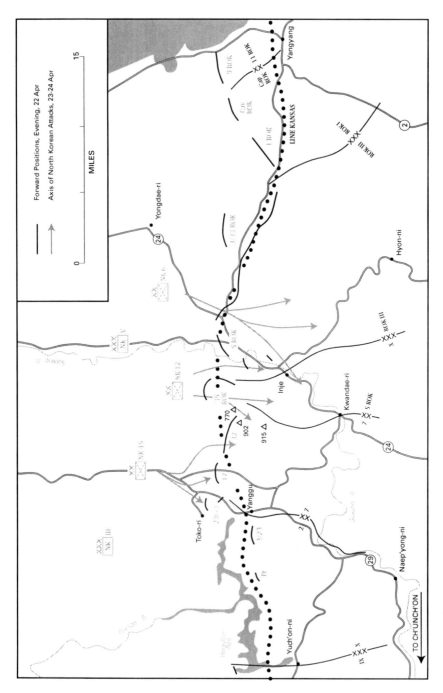

The eastern front, 22–24 April 1951. (Based on U.S. Army Center of Military History map.)

combat outpost north of Line Kansas, provided an account of the
North Korean 45th Division's initial attack.

At 0700, 19 April 1951, Company B, 32d Infantry Regiment,
7th U.S. Infantry Division, jumped off from Hill 915 [about four
miles northwest of Inje] to seize the high ground to the NE approximately 6,000 meters away. Advancing in platoon columns,
this objective was secured at 1200 hours without enemy resistance.
Upon seizing the objective, a squad patrol was sent 1,500 meters
forward to Hill 770 to check and clear the area of enemy. Hill 770
was the highest ground in the area and commanded the approaches
to the right and the left of the battalion sector. Prior to reaching Hill
770, the squad was fired on by an undetermined number of enemy
using automatic weapons, and was ordered by the squad leader to
return to the company perimeter, arriving at approximately 1400.
At 1500 hours, the battalion commander, Lt. Col. Gillis, ordered
Company B to seize Hill 770 utilizing one platoon to make the attack. Capt. Cecil G. Smith, commanding officer, Company B, ordered the 2d Platoon under the command of 1st Lt. Freemont
Piercefield to perform the mission. The platoon advanced via a
ridgeline by leapfrogging the squads toward the objective. The position was secured without enemy resistance at approximately 1700
hours.

The platoon was ordered by Lt. Piercefield to dig in and secure
the hill. Two- and three-man foxholes were dug in perimeter defense. A fence composed of fallen trees and brush was constructed
around the perimeter. The strongest emphasis was placed on the
approaches from the north and northeast. The brush fence was approximately twenty yards away from the top of the hill. To insure an
adequate warning of approaching enemy, three M-1948 parachute
flares were emplaced and the approaches into the position were
booby-trapped with fragmentation and phosphorous hand grenades.
The grenades were attached to the base of the fence and rigged with
pieces of wire, shoe strings, and heavy weeds as trip wires. Each
foxhole in the platoon perimeter was constructed with a lean-to
over the position. On top of the lean-to a poncho was laid out and
covered with pine brush. This camouflaged each position, and the
shadows cast by the overhead cover would tend to confuse the enemy

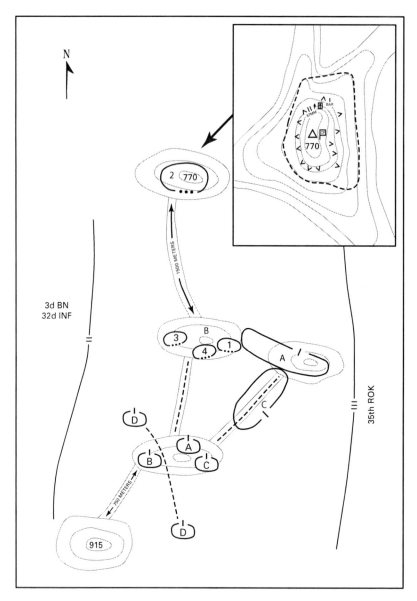

First Battalion, 32d Infantry and Company B: the situation on 22 April 1951. (Based on map in CMH manuscript, U.S. Army. Not to scale.)

as to the actual position during daylight hours. Camouflage was vital because the area had been burned over and little natural cover remained. The platoon was equipped with one SCR300 radio and one sound-powered phone.[1] The phone was tied into the company communications net on the reverse side of the hill. The construction of the defense positions on 19–20 April was covered by patrols operating 1,500 yards to the north and the northeast. The patrols went out at 0800 each morning and returned at 1200 hours. Defensive fires from 4.2-inch mortars and artillery were registered on the two ridgelines to the north and the northeast. The fires were available on call to the platoon commander. All remained quiet through the night of 21 April.

At approximately 0310, 22 April, Sgt. Robert E. Workman, BAR [Browning automatic rifle] man, 2d Platoon, who had been on guard in his area on the forward slope, saw a flare go up in front of his position. The source of the flare was not certain since the ROK unit on the right and the artillery had been firing flares intermittently throughout the night. After a period of about a minute the whole platoon was alerted by voices and rattling of ammunition boxes in front of the position. The voices were obviously officers giving instructions to their men prior to the assault. From a distance of six feet a group of twelve to fifteen enemy closed in on Sgt. Workman. He opened fire killing six or eight and wounding an undetermined number. The enemy opened fire with burp guns and small arms from positions farther down the hill. After a period of three to five minutes of fighting, the enemy opened fire with a Russian BAR and a machine gun. The enemy continued to move toward the position. The platoon started throwing fragmentation and white phosphorous grenades. At this time Cpl. Joseph J. Sapuppo called for the 60mm mortars to fire at his direction. Due to the limited target area and ammunition supply, only one mortar was fired. The rounds were laid in front of the position with such accuracy that the enemy became demoralized and started to withdraw. The mortar fire was brought within fifteen yards of the foxhole positions on the forward slope. During the withdrawal the mortar fire was placed at twenty-five yard intervals down the hill. The enemy attempted to take cover by hitting the ground, but round after round landed in the enemy group. The enemy was subjected to the mortar fire until they were four hundred yards in front of the friendly positions. The mortars stopped firing at approximately 0530, and the platoon remained in their foxholes until about 0645 hours.

The firing of the mortars was accomplished by Cpl. Sapuppo. The sound power phone failed, and fire commands were relayed by voice through the machine gun position to the platoon command post and then to the mortar crew.

At 0645 two-thirds of the platoon returned to the reverse side of the hill for chow, the other one-third remaining in position on alert for a possible counterattack. After chow, at approximately 0730, the platoon went out in front of the position to pick up the "loot" and found maps, a picture of Joe Stalin, a chart of the five-year plan, and propaganda leaflets. A North Korean payroll was also picked up along with various small arms and burp guns. The remainder of the day was spent in improving emplacements, setting out more trip flares, and sniping at suspected targets to the front.

About 1900, 22 April, SFC Lewis E. Spencer, the platoon sergeant, called in two 4.2-inch and one 105mm concentration for registration of defensive fires to be used during the night if needed. Everything remained quiet until 2330, when a rustle was heard in front of the position. It was thought to be the wind blowing loose leaves and twigs that had not been burned by previous artillery and mortar fires. About five minutes later a trip flare was set off. The enemy started firing burp guns and small arms, which went over the heads of the platoon members. The platoon then returned the fire with small arms and burp guns, which they had taken previously with the idea that the enemy would possibly think they were firing on their own troops. This firing continued for approximately twenty minutes.

After a lull of about three minutes the enemy was seen moving up the hill. Cpl. Sapuppo called for the 4.2-inch concentration that had previously been registered. Immediately following the concentration, the enemy, estimated to be of two platoons in strength, opened up again with all their weapons.

During the hail of fire, four North Koreans had managed to creep into the platoon position under the cover of their own fire.

One North Korean of very large build, screaming and laughing hysterically, jumped upon the parapet of the foxhole in which Cpl. Sapuppo and PFC Kenneth L. Daywalt, an ammo bearer, were housed. The North Korean opened fire with a burp gun, but the weapon jammed after firing a single shot that tore the right sleeve of Daywalt without injuring him. Daywalt, being somewhat smaller than his opponent, attempted to take the weapon away from the enemy soldier by pulling at the weapon in a tug-of-war fashion. In the meantime Sapuppo was trying to maneuver so as to shoot the enemy with a .45 caliber pistol and still keep the three other North Koreans from coming into the position. Daywalt's gun had been kicked out of reach during the encounter so he was relying upon his wits to help overcome his assailant. As the tug-of-war continued, Daywalt suddenly let go of the burp gun, causing the enemy soldier to fall backwards off-balance out of the foxhole. As the enemy fell, Daywalt kicked him in the mouth with his heel, causing him to scream, which led the other platoon members to believe that one of their buddies had been bayoneted. The North Korean jumped up and started to run. Sapuppo handed Daywalt a .45 caliber pistol, and he dropped the enemy with the second shot. Sapuppo opened up with his light machine gun and riddled the enemy soldier with tracer bullets, causing him to roll down the hill. The other three North Koreans, who had been in the platoon area, disappeared, and it is not known whether they were casualties or not.

At approximately 2400 Cpl. Sapuppo called again for a concentration of 4.2s, and the enemy began a rapid withdrawal. After the enemy had retreated 250 yards from the position, Sgt. Snowden Dale Burnett called in artillery fire. The enemy troops started to scatter in all directions. Artillery and mortars continued to place harassing fire on the areas that had been previously registered.

Throughout the entire fight only four to six members of the platoon were actively engaged in the action, these being those on the forward slope. The remainder of the platoon stayed in their foxholes and kept a constant vigil to keep the enemy from enveloping the position.

The following day twenty-seven bodies were found in front of the position, and blood stains on the ground showed that an undetermined number of wounded had been carried off. The 2d Platoon suffered no casualties in this action.[2]

Hill 902: 3d Battalion, 32d Infantry Regiment, 22–23 April 1951

The North Korean attack on Company B's 2d Platoon came before the main attacks of the Spring Offensive began the night of 22–23 April. It is possible that the 2d Platoon's camouflage work succeeded, and the enemy were unaware that they were moving against a strongly defended position. On the left of the 1st Battalion, the 3d Battalion, 32d Infantry Regiment, held a number of dominant terrain features. A combat historian with the 2d Historical Detachment, Headquarters, Eighth U.S. Army, Korea (EUSAK), Capt. Pierce W. Briscoe, studied the action and described the situation.

On 22 April 1951 the 32d Infantry Regiment was in position on Line Kansas. The 3d Battalion, 32d Infantry Regiment, held Hill 902. Company K was on the peak of Hill 902, and Company L extended to the south and southwest. Company I occupied an OPLR [outpost line of resistance] position some 2,000 yards northwest of Company K and north of the MLR [main line of resistance].

From 17 April, when Company K took Hill 902, until 22 April, the 3d Battalion dug defensive positions. Light probing attacks by the enemy were repelled. Defensive positions were not exceptionally well dug because it was expected that a general attack would be made to Line Wyoming. Nevertheless, a few flares and booby traps were placed 500 to 600 yards to the north and northwest, the most likely avenues of approach. The ridgeline to the northwest was very steep and offered a good field of fire for machine guns.

On 22 April a Company K patrol of platoon strength proceeded 2,000 to 3,000 yards to the northwest and reported at least 300 enemy in that area. The patrol did not engage the enemy, but called for an air strike since artillery was outranged. Although the air strike was promised, it never materialized.

G-2 information on enemy intentions was not available. However, the battalion felt generally that an enemy attack would be made soon. Some junior officers questioned the soundness of Com-

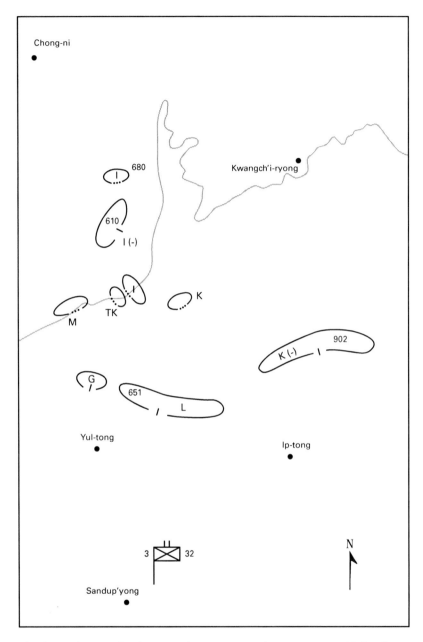

Chong-ni

680

Kwangch'i-ryong

610

I (-)

TK

K

M

K (-)

902

G

651

L

Yul-tong

Ip-tong

3 ⊠ 32

N

Sandup'yong

Third Battalion, 32d Infantry and Company B: the situation on 22 April
1951. (Based on maps in CMH manuscript, U.S. Army. Not to scale.)

pany I's OPLR position. They felt that the nature of the terrain would prevent Company I from accomplishing its mission.

About 1600, 22 April, 1st Lt. Harry W. French, platoon leader, 2d Platoon, Company K, was instructed to outpost two squads approximately 1,500 yards northwest of the company position. The mission of the outpost was to protect Company I's route of withdrawal should Company I be forced to withdraw. Lt. French protested that this would weaken his platoon position on Hill 902, as well as the position of the entire company. His platoon had a frontage of 1,000 yards. Fifty-yard gaps already existed between foxholes. With two squads on outpost, Lt. French felt that he would not be able to fill adequately his position between the 1st Platoon on the right and the 3d Platoon on the left. French sent the 2d and 3d Squads to establish an outpost under command of M. Sgt. Clarence Matthews.[3]

Members of M. Sgt. Matthews's outpost describe their actions upon receipt of the order.[4]

SGT. WILLIAM R. MANNING, SQUAD LEADER, AND PFC MARVIN F. LOTTMAN, ASSISTANT SQUAD LEADER, BOTH OF THE 2D SQUAD, 2D PLATOON: A runner from the platoon CP notified us at 1600 that our 2d squad was to meet M. Sgt. Matthews, Platoon Sergeant, 2d Platoon, on top of Hill 902 to go on an outpost mission. Our mission was to set up an outpost in the right rear of Company I to our left front, to cover them in case they were pushed off the OPLR and had to withdraw. We had four BARs, twelve M-1 rifles, one carbine, and four .45 caliber pistols. Each man also carried three fragmentation grenades. The ammunition supply was approximately three bandoliers per man and one belt full. BAR men had twelve magazines each and two BAR bandoliers extra.

CPL. JACK A. FAZZINO AND PFC BILLY L. McFADIN, RIFLEMEN, 2D PLATOON: M. Sgt. Clarence Matthews, Platoon Sergeant, 2d Platoon, led the two squads from Hill 902, marching out in single file, the 3d Squad in the lead. No enemy resistance was encountered en route to the position. Immediately three-man foxholes were dug in. Booby traps, composed of fragmentation hand grenades, were tied knee-high across possible avenues of approach about fifty yards out around the perimeter. Approximately thirty to forty grenades were set out. All defense measures were completed by 2000 hours.

SGT. MANNING AND PFC LOTTMAN: While we were digging in, Sgt. Matthews spotted four enemy approximately 400 yards down the ridgeline to our right front. We fired on them and knew that we hit one because he screamed. Another group of approximately six came out of hiding in the same vicinity and ran down the ridgeline toward the valley. About this time one of the booby traps in the rear of the position exploded. It was set off by a carrying party from the company who were bringing us mail, PX rations, and beer. Matthews had previously informed the company not to do this, as he knew we would have all approaches to our position booby-trapped. No one in the carrying party was hurt.

CPL. FAZZINO AND PFC MCFADIN: Sgt. Matthews then told Sgt. Charles Crawford, 3d Squad leader, to take one man with him and contact Company I on the left front. On the way out a trip flare, which Company I had previously set out for their defense, was set off by Crawford. Elements of the company opened fire, but neither man was hurt. Crawford made contact with Company I and returned to the outpost, informing Matthews. It was a bright moonlight night.

SGT. MANNING AND PFC LOTTMAN: Both squads pulled guard duty with six men on duty at all times. At approximately 2230 we received one mortar round from our own lines that killed Pvt. William Lees, one of the BAR men.[5] Lees was approximately ten feet from his position relieving himself. It was evidently a short round.

At midnight Sgt. Crawford came up to tell Sgt. Manning to be sure his squad was awake. At approximately 0100 we could hear Company I being fired on on our left front. An occasional banzai was also heard. This continued with a lull every now and then until about 0300.

As noted, Company I manned a forward outpost. An after-action report describes their situation.

At 0630 on the morning of 21 April, Company I, 32d Infantry, set out from 3d Battalion Headquarters with the mission of establishing an OPLR on Hill 610 in front of the main lines. The company passed through L Company lines at 0830 hours and entered the valley located between the MLR and Hill 610.

The 1st and 2d Platoons were given the mission of taking the hill, and they converged on the point of Hill 610 from the south and southwest. Small arms fire was encountered by both platoons near the crest of the hill. SFC Wallace Miller and SFC Charles Girtz led the 2d Platoon over the hill, and while the platoon was reorganizing preparatory to moving forward again, the two sergeants continued forward on their own and "banzaied" the next hill. After gaining control of Hill 610, the company moved forward to patrol the ridge-line to the north. Hill 680 was taken after a brief skirmish, and succeeding hills were taken in a like manner.

At approximately 1400 the company returned to Hill 610 to establish an OPLR. Half of the 3d Platoon was sent to the valley floor to establish a roadblock, along with a platoon of tanks from the 32d Tank Company. The 81mm mortar platoon of M Company was located at the base of Hill 610 inside the protective line formed by the roadblock. The remainder of I Company was set in a tight perimeter defense on the crest of Hill 610. At approximately 1600, Capt. Byron D. Meadows, commanding officer, Company I, received orders to outpost Hill 680. The remaining half of the 3d Platoon was sent to Hill 680 to establish this outpost.

There was no activity on the night of the 21st, nor on the following day. The night of the 22d passed without incident up to approximately 2400 hours. At that time Cpl. Robert Wright, who had one of the squads on Hill 680, reported small arms fire off to the left front. This was the first indication of enemy activity.[6]

It also remained quiet at the main Company K position on Hill 902 until about 0300 hours. Company K's 2d Platoon leader, 2d Lt. Harry W. French, describes the situation.

At 0300, 23 April 1951, a burst of burp gun fire awakened me. I left the platoon CP and went along the line of the 1st and 4th Squads to see if everything was all right. After checking positions, I sent my assistant platoon sergeant, SFC Rathal, to check the right flank of the 1st Squad. I then reported to the company commander, Lt. J. P. Kingston, at the company CP. He asked if everyone in my

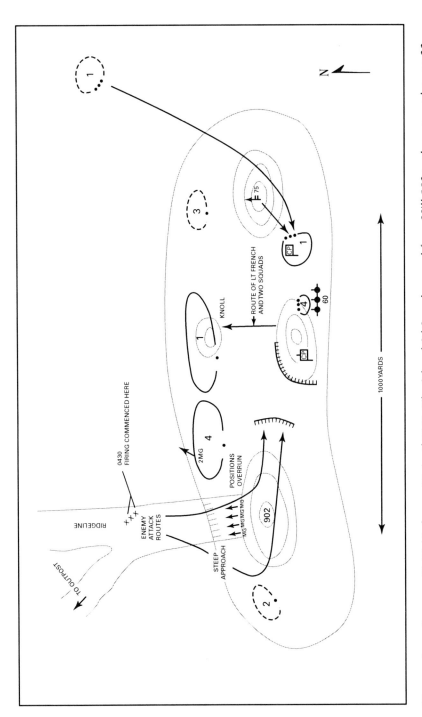

The attack on Company K, 32d Infantry, 23 April 1951. The 2d and 3d Squads moved from Hill 902 to the outpost late on 22 April. (Based on maps in CMH manuscript, U.S. Army. Not to scale.)

squads was awake. I asked about my two squads on the outpost, and he said, "there's nothing we can do for them now."

It was now approximately 0400. Lt. Kingston sent a runner to the 75mm crew and the 1st Platoon to tell them to come to the company CP. Sensing an attack from the northwest, these units were to be used as a defense for the CP. Kingston then called for mortar and artillery fire on the ridgeline to the northwest. The 32d Heavy Mortar Company plus one battery of the 48th Field Artillery Battalion were in support of the battalion in this area. The 4.2-inch mortars had been previously registered on avenues of approach on the ridgelines by the forward observer with the company. The field artillery could not be used as a direct support because of the steepness of the terrain.

It was now 0430, and there had been no firing by the enemy since 0300. At 0430 firing commenced from the ridgeline in front of the machine gun positions. All types of fire were received—small arms, burp gun, automatic rifle, and antitank. Someone told me that Sgt. [SFC] George H. Allen Jr. [killed in action 23 April 1951], Squad Leader of the 4th Squad, had been hit.[7] I took the platoon medic to Sgt. Allen's foxhole and found that he had been hit in the right arm and was bleeding badly. I told the medic to help him as much as possible and to take him to the company CP. My two squads continued to fire on the northwest approaches to the position.

Approximately fifteen minutes later the entire left flank of the company was overrun. The penetration came in the former area of the 2d Squad. I then brought my two squads, fifteen men, to the CP. The enemy continued his attack toward the CP but was stopped approximately fifty yards away by the CP defenders.

I then took my two squads and started for a knoll north of the CP. My idea was to get flanking fire on the enemy and to possibly draw some of his fire away from the CP defense perimeter. About fifteen yards out I saw an enemy soldier aiming at me from the left. Cpl. John H. Beebe [killed in action 13 June 1951], a BAR man, seeing the enemy also, fired and saved my life.[8]

About this time the assistant platoon sergeant shouted, "Lt. French, come back." I thought he said, "go forward." We continued toward the knoll. After reaching the knoll we regrouped and started to banzai toward the enemy position. We met them starting another attack. Firing as we advanced and yelling "banzai," we drove them back approximately seventy-five yards. We then returned to the company perimeter around the CP.

After staying in the perimeter for approximately ten minutes, Lt. Kingston ordered me to attack again. This attack was to be in conjunction with the men in the perimeter around the CP, approximately one hundred in all. These were composed of the headquarters personnel, the 60mm mortar section, and members of the 1st Platoon.

I said, "All right men, let's go get 'em. Let's see you all fight." Screaming and hollering, firing as we ran, we pressed forward. The enemy began to withdraw to the opposite side of the knoll to the northwest. The company then occupied the knoll and held it for approximately one hour. At approximately 0645 the enemy attacked again and drove the left flank back about seventy-five yards.[9]

SFC Guy E. Woodhouse, the platoon sergeant of Company K's 1st Platoon, describes the action from his perspective.

At approximately 0215, 23 April 1951, I was awakened by a large volume of small arms fire and the yelling of "Banzai." I immediately alerted my platoon to await the outcome of the attack. At approximately 0300 I received a call from the company CP to send two of my squads to the top of Hill 902 because there were about 600 enemy trying to come up the north side of the hill. I moved twelve of my men under Cpl. [Edward D.] Strocky [killed in action 13 June 1951] to the 3d Platoon.[10] I was called upon to move an LMG [light machine gun] to help at about 0400. About 0430 I was called to bring the rest of my platoon of which Lt. Thomas Boyle was platoon leader to the hill. When we had gone about fifty yards, we were caught under fire from two sides by automatic and rifle fire. My platoon leader [Thomas D. Boyle] was killed, and my assistant platoon sergeant wounded.[11] We had an hour-long battle with the enemy with small arms and hand grenades in which we killed twenty-three. During this battle the rest of the company had to withdraw about fifty yards because their supply of ammunition was about exhausted.

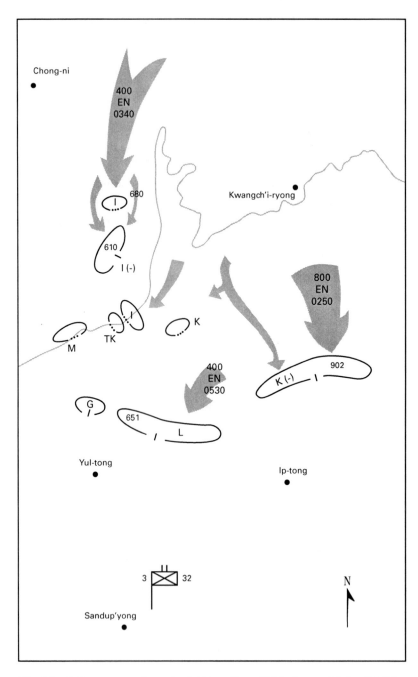

Chong-ni

400
EN
0340

680

Kwangch'i-ryong

610

I (-)

TK

M

K

800
EN
0250

400
EN
0530

902

K (-) — I

G
I

651

I — L

Yul-tong

Ip-tong

3 ⊠ 32

Sandup'yong

N

The North Korean attack on the 3d Battalion, 32d Infantry, 23 April 1951.
(Based on maps in CMH manuscript, U.S. Army. Not to scale.)

The ammo was resupplied, and the company under command of 1st Lt. J. P. Kingston retook the hill. By this time I had the men of my platoon that had gone with me to Hill 902. The enemy was putting up a fierce fight to retake the hill. The enemy's tactics were simple—"Banzai." We pushed on about one hundred yards to a small rise in the ground. The enemy counterattacked, and we had to withdraw about seventy-five yards. We were receiving several casualties. Lt. Kingston gave his attack order. We retook the ground again. We held for about one half hour and had to withdraw again. We had to resupply ourselves again with ammo. We again under the leadership of Kingston banzaied the hill, and this time we held the ground. We finally had Hill 902 secured at about 0930. When it was all over and was summed up, the enemy soldiers were piled up in all of our positions. The enemy dead were estimated at 300 and enemy wounded were estimated at 300.[12]

During the fighting, the executive officer of Company K, 1st Lt. Willard B. Rogers, returned from the rear with a supply of ammunition. Lt. Rogers describes his actions and the situation he found when he arrived on Hill 902.

I left Hill 902 at 1900 hours on 22 April for the vicinity of the battalion CP to take care of the resupply of ammunition for the company. I carried an SCR300 radio with me. At 0230 I received a call from Lt. Kingston, the Company K commander, that the enemy had started their attack. I loaded one hundred Korean Civilian Transport workers, who were with the company, with all types of ammunition and started up the ridgeline to the base of Hill 902. It was approximately 0300.

After having traveled a distance of one and one half hours at a maximum rate of speed, we reached the base of Hill 902. I heard "banzai," and the enemy was seen running down the ridgeline to our left, where part of the 3d Platoon had been located. The enemy made no pretense about being seen and upon seeing the pack train, they opened up with small arms fire. Seeing this, I couldn't take the normal supply route that led up the hill in the general direction of the enemy penetration. I took another route towards the east, and through sheer luck arrived at the company CP.

Upon arriving at the company CP I could see that the only ground held was about a fifty-yard portion extending west. The enemy had actually overrun the left portion of Hill 902, and all that remained of the company was about one and a half platoons. The enemy had approached from the ridge to the northwest, completely overrunning the machine gun positions. Following up the penetration they moved down the ridge to the left where a portion of the 3d Platoon had previously been. They captured three of the platoon members. The rest of this portion of the 3d Platoon withdrew farther down the ridge. One of the younger soldiers in the other position of the 3d Platoon, seeing this action, assumed that the company CP had been overrun. Being panic-stricken, he spread the word throughout the rest of the 3d Platoon that the company CP had been overrun and that the company was withdrawing. This created further panic, and the remainder of the 3d Platoon withdrew in a disorderly manner into the Company L sector, leaving the left flank completely exposed.

I resupplied what was left of the company and then talked via radio with the battalion executive officer, Capt. Irvin B. Bigger. I said, "Sir, I don't want to be dramatic, but things are a bit difficult up here." Bigger replied, "Now son, don't get worried. I know you can handle things up there. Show those sons-of-a-guns what's up. Reinforcements are on the way." This did more to bolster officer morale than any other thing. The attack continued, but what was left of the company held, due entirely to the leadership of Lt. Kingston, the company commander.

The firing continued very heavy, as the enemy had an overabundance of ammunition and was firing at ranges of about seventy-five yards. They were using 82mm mortars, heavy machine guns, anti-tank guns, Russian BARs, and Springfield .22 [caliber] rifles. The enemy was thought to be new troops, as they wore new uniforms, had fresh haircuts, new weapons, and were very young.

To keep a resupply of ammunition to the men, 1st Sgt. John I. Kearley and I distributed it by crawling and running in crouch silhouettes to each position. The men from the 60mm mortar section in the rear of the CP went up on line because their ammunition had been expended. Some of them went into action with .45 caliber pistols and even banzaied, knowing that the situation was practically hopeless.

At 0800 hours reinforcements from Company A arrived together with the battalion commander and his staff. The presence of the battalion commander gave courage to what was left of the company. Lt. Kingston, in conference with the battalion commander, told him that if he would let him put two platoons of Company A in to hold his present positions, he would take the remainder of his men and attack. This plan was agreed on, and the attack started forward toward the northwest. Firing and yelling as they moved, the company pushed the enemy back approximately 150 yards over the ridgeline to the northwest. The fighting ended at approximately 0900.[13]

As Company K was fighting for its life, the outpost under M. Sgt. Clarence Matthews to the northwest on the approach route of the North Koreans also came under attack. Sgt. William R. Manning, Cpl. Jack A. Fazzino, and Pvts. (later PFCs) Billy L. McFadin and Marvin F. Lottman, all soldiers in the two squads manning the outpost, describe what happened.

SGT. MANNING AND PFC LOTTMAN: At 0330 we heard enemy voices about 200 yards to our front. The voices continued to be heard until about 0430; however, there was no firing during this period.[14]

CPL. FAZZINO AND PFC MCFADIN: At approximately 0330 Company K on Hill 902 was attacked, cutting off our OPL [outpost line] and all communications. Sound power wire had been laid out toward our position, but it was never completed due to the shortage of wire in the company.

Nothing happened in front of our position until approximately 0430. At this time the enemy set off one of our booby traps to the right front. Cpl. Ralph G. Jones, a BAR man, opened fire with his weapon, but was killed a few seconds later by return burp gun fire.[15] Pvt. Hiram T. Mabry, his assistant, and Pvt. Kenneth Kramer took over the BAR and kept on firing.[16]

SGT. MANNING AND PFC LOTTMAN: At 0445 the enemy, strength unknown, started firing flares and approached the position, setting off a grenade booby trap and hollering "banzai." Pvt. Mabry started firing his BAR and hollering "banjo." Some enemy small arms fire was being received. The enemy fell back from our fire for a short distance, and we could hear them talking again.[17]

CPL. FAZZINO AND PFC MCFADIN: M. Sgt. Matthews sent Sgt. Crawford to tell PFC Carlton in a foxhole to the right to join Mabry and Kramer. He was to give supporting rifle fire. By this time some enemy had approached the position close enough to throw grenades into it. One grenade landed in the BAR position, killing Mabry and wounding Kramer in the head.[18] Matthews then sent Crawford to Cpl. Looney's foxhole and told him to bring his BAR over to a position below Matthews. Looney in moving over was shot in the knee, but continued on toward the position without the weapon. Pvt. McFadin picked up Looney's BAR and carried it into position. Looney, though wounded badly, again took over the weapon. Men who were wounded stayed in their foxholes and handed ammunition to the others. The outpost held off the enemy for approximately one hour.

At approximately 0630 Sgt. Crawford called to M. Sgt. Matthews that ammunition was running low and that seven members of the group had been wounded. Matthews ordered us to withdraw back of the ridgeline, two at a time, wounded first. Those not wounded were to fire as they withdrew to cover the wounded. Matthews, seeing the wounded, and knowing the situation in the rear, then said, "Let's make a last stand here." At this moment, as Matthews started to fire his carbine at an enemy soldier, a burp gun opened fire from down the ridgeline, and one bullet hit him between the eyes, killing him instantly.[19] Pvt. McFadin was also wounded in the foot by the same burst. Seeing that Matthews was dead, Sgt. Crawford said, "Let's get the hell out of here, fast." Crawford jumped out of his foxhole and was followed by the wounded. The rest of the squads followed, firing as they withdrew, all proceeding up the ridgeline toward Hill 902.

On a knoll along the ridgeline to Hill 902, a North Korean had set up a machine gun. He fired on the group. Dispersing, they immediately proceeded down the ridgeline to the right and across the valley to Company L's positions. The group continued through friendly harassing artillery and mortar fire without further casualties. Not knowing whether Company L was still in its positions or whether the North Koreans had taken the ridge, Sgt. Crawford told us to make sure our weapons were fully loaded because we were going to banzai the position on top of the ridgeline and try to get across.

We crossed the ridgeline without opposition and proceeded on a trail down to where Company M's 81mm mortar positions had been in the rear of Company L. Following the trail for approximately one-half mile, we came to the position of the 32d Heavy Mortar Company. A medic stationed there attended to the wounded. Two litter jeeps were also at the position and were used to carry the wounded to the 3d Battalion aid station. Those men not wounded stayed at the mortar position to help defend in case of enemy attack.

It was estimated that approximately 300 enemy soldiers attacked the outpost.[20]

The enemy attack also had engulfed the remainder of the 3d Battalion. A narrative of the action, prepared as part of a recommendation for award of the Presidential Unit Citation, puts the assault on Company K in perspective and describes the fighting throughout the 3d Battalion Sector.

In the pre-dawn of 23 April 1951, the enemy sledgehammer fell. At 0250 an enemy attacking force of undetermined strength struck a heavy blow against the perimeter of Company K, 32d Infantry Regiment. By 0400 hours the attack had reached a savage pitch, and it was estimated that an entire enemy battalion had concentrated its forces in a breakthrough attempt in the K Company sector on Hill 902. By 0455 the right flank of the company had been penetrated by the sheer weight of the attacking force. The situation was critical. A breakthrough at that point would have crippled friendly operations in the entire sector of the front. Men of Company K clung doggedly to their positions and launched counterattacks. Scores of enemy dead littered the command post area. Company K refused to break under the onslaught, and because the enemy was hurling themselves into their midst and had penetrated their right flank, moved to reverse slope positions.

At 0340 Company I, outposting Hills 610 and 680, was attacked on Hill 680 by an enemy force estimated to number over
400. The small group of men on the hill continually exposed themselves in moving to positions where they could deliver maximum
volume of fire to the assaulting troops. The enemy was repulsed in
his repeated attempts to storm the hill in frenzied banzai attacks. By
0400 the enemy had deployed his forces and was maintaining heavy
pressure on three sides of Hill 680. At 0405 the outpost, its mission
accomplished, began moving off Hill 680 and joined other elements
of the company outposting Hill 610. By 0545 the enemy, moving
against the hill mass from three sides, was making a determined
effort to dislodge Company I from Hill 610. In an outpost action
unparalleled in any campaign, Company I not only blunted the assault of the numerically superior attacking force, but at 1030 hours,
launched a vicious counterattack into the enemy's midst.[21]

   *Company I's After-Action Report adds additional details of
their fight.*
   At approximately 0300, enemy troops were seen and heard approaching Hill 680. The enemy repeatedly tried to storm the hill in
frenzied banzai attacks and was repulsed. SFC Daniel F. Benton of
the 3d Platoon was instrumental in repulsing the attacks. Braving
heavy enemy fire, he exposed himself continually in order to rally
the eleven men on the post. Although mortally wounded, he continued to direct the men in the defense of their position.[22] His bravery
was an inspiration to every man present. On the fourth charge by
the enemy, Cpl. Wright, seeing that his men had no ammunition,
gave the order to withdraw and return to the company perimeter.
   In the meantime, the roadblock in the valley was hit by a full-
scale attack at approximately 0330 hours. Cpl. Karl Olga and PFC
Cook first observed a column of enemy moving down the ridgeline
toward their outpost on the right flank of the roadblock. Their firing dispersed the group initially, and Cook killed two enemy within
ten feet of his position. A grenade attack by the NKs [North Kore-
ans] was beaten off by the 3d Platoon and the tankers. Sgt. Campbell of the attached 57mm recoilless rifle squad continually exposed

himself to fire point-blank at the enemy as they charged the positions.

SFC James Green, the 3d Platoon leader, directed the 81mm mortar fire. This firing was done at minimum range. Green directed Cpl. Germano and one squad around to the right flank as a stop-gap to any enemy attempting to infiltrate through the valley below L Co.

Back on Hill 610 Capt. Meadows oriented the platoon leaders on the situation. The 1st Platoon under M. Sgt. Preston was directed to retake Hill 610 at 0530. The attack was to be preceded by a heavy concentration of mortar and artillery fire.

At 0530 the 1st Platoon started off Hill 610 headed for Hill 680. As they reached the low point in the ridgeline and were starting to ascend Hill 680, the enemy attacked the group in force. Sergeant Preston set down a base of fire to cover his own men while he withdrew the platoon to its old positions on Hill 610. One squad led by Sgt. Tilbert failed to return. Preston immediately called for close supporting mortar and artillery fire. Under cover of this protecting fire, the squad [Tilbert's] was able to break through.

The enemy by this time was probing Hill 610. Intense fire from our own troops and from supporting weapons kept the enemy from massing his forces. Small groups of the enemy tried to flank the company but were beaten off. At approximately 1000 hours, there was only sporadic firing, and the 1st Platoon retook all the ground down to the low point in the ridgeline. Enemy dead and equipment littered the area. At this time orders were received by Capt. Meadows not to attempt to retake Hill 680.[23]

The narrative of the 3d Battalion's action resumes with the attack on Company L.

At 0530 hours the right flank of Company L came under attack and by 0600 the company was heavily engaged. The enemy had hit a veritable stone wall. Troops of Company L clung stubbornly to their positions, battling fiercely. In thirty minutes, the assaulting forces had not only been stopped but had been beaten off.

The machine guns, mortars, and recoilless rifles of Company M engaged the enemy in a manner that will forever remain a bright spot in the history of the role of heavy weapons companies in the Korean campaign. Gunners remained in positions until guns were destroyed or the enemy assault had been stopped. Often firing at minimum ranges, the company, with elements supporting each of its line companies, maintained continuous and effective fire that contributed immeasurably to the ultimate success of the operations of the 3d Battalion. Hundreds of enemy dead littering the approaches were mute proof of the accuracy, foresight, and battle effectiveness of Company M.

Elements of Companies K and M that had been attached to Company L were relieved from attachment and rejoined Company K to launch a coordinated attack against strongly held enemy positions on the crest of Hill 902. Attacking uphill through heavy fire, Company K, knowing the urgency of reaching the dominating heights, never faltered. Enemy positions fell to the attacking force, and the tactically important heights of the hill were restored to the 3d Battalion.[24]

Later on 23 April, Company I again engaged the enemy. The action is described in Company I's report.

The Capt. [Meadows] set out to reform the company perimeter on Hill 610. While this was being accomplished, the 57mm recoilless rifle section of the 4th Platoon was engaged in long-range firing on enemy troops retreating along a distant road approximately 1,400 yards across the valley to the northeast. This was the last contact with the enemy until late afternoon.

At 1300 hours the Capt. received word from regiment to extend the company's lines to the left and make contact with the 17th Infantry. In doing this, most of the company was withdrawn from the hill and placed in position along a ridge extending to the west from Hill 610. The 2d Platoon was left on Hill 610, and an outpost from the 3d Platoon was left on the northernmost end of Hill 610 at the highest point. The company CP was moved to a point near the center of the line, and a large store of ammunition was hand-carried by the men to this point. Meadows ordered mortar registration on Hill 680 and also on the north end of Hill 610 in case this point was abandoned.

At approximately 1530 hours a report from S-2 indicated a body of about 600 enemy moving on the ridgeline approximately an hour's march away. At 1630 the first elements of this group struck. The north point of Hill 610 was rendered untenable to the men digging in on the outpost by heavy machine gun fire from Hill 680. Cpl. Wright withdrew his men from under this withering fire to the south end of Hill 610 where the weapons squad of the 2d Platoon was located. The North Koreans charged over the far end of the hill and immediately secured themselves in our old positions.

At this point small arms fire was exchanged between the two groups for approximately an hour. Two squads from the 3d Platoon roadblock joined the fight on the hill at approximately 1730. As darkness began to settle over the hill, the company realized that it was going to be impossible to hold the hill. Even at that time, the enemy was flanking the company's positions on the right flank.

At approximately 1910 the order came from the battalion headquarters for Company I to withdraw from the hill. Meadows began an orderly withdrawal through the draw [gully] to the rear of the company's positions. One squad was left on Hill 610 with Lt. G. H. Marchant Jr., and SFC Charles Girtz to cover the withdrawal from the right flank. As this squad prepared to abandon its positions, a heavy concentration of enemy 120mm mortar landed in its midst. The group managed to escape with no casualties. On the left flank, a squad of the 1st Platoon under Sgt. Wait remained behind to destroy any equipment that could not be carried off the hill.

The company reformed under cover of darkness in the valley below and moved to new positions. The enemy paid heavily in both men and equipment. They abandoned the hill during the night, and the next day approximately two hundred dead were found between Hills 610 and 680.[25]

Meanwhile, on Hill 902 the battalion commander was positioning his men for a renewal of the enemy attack. Lt. Rogers, executive officer, Company K, describes the situation and the actions over the next several days.

The battalion commander then ordered the company to move to the left to cover a frontage of approximately 1,000 yards. This was done in order that two companies would occupy the same amount of ground that Company K had occupied the night before. Company A was assigned Hill 902 extending to the right and east approximately 1,000 yards. Company K tied into the left flank of Company A and extended to the left and west approximately 1,000 yards.

The men dug in deep because no one felt he would survive. At 2400 hours for the next three succeeding nights the enemy would begin singing and having parties to the northwest of our positions. At 0200, on the nose, they would attack but were thrown back because of our strengthened positions. Hand grenades played an important part in the actions because of steepness of terrain. The grenades were dropped straight down steep approaches where rifle fire would have been ineffective.

At 1700 hours, 27 April, the company received orders to withdraw from the hill within a half hour's time. Up until that time each man had said over and over again, "what wouldn't I give to get off this hill." When the orders were received to withdraw, you could have heard a pin drop. The men felt that they were giving up a part of themselves because they had fought so hard to hold it.

The withdrawal was very quiet and dejected. The reason for the withdrawal was an air report of an estimated three enemy divisions moving south in this direction. They were assumed to be heading to take the hill.[26]

The morning after the initial North Korean attack several hundred enemy dead lay scattered across the 3d Battalion sector; a total of 482 were counted in front of Company K's positions on Hill 902, a clear sign of the fierce fighting that had taken place. The executive officer of the 32d Infantry Regiment, Maj. Frederick F. Lash, said that he had never seen so many enemy dead piled up in front of one company position. The main Communist blows, however, had fallen on the ROK divisions to the east and farther west in the U.S. I and IX Corps sectors. The strength of the enemy's attack was forcing a UN withdrawal across the front.[27]

Chapter 3

CAUGHT IN A CHINESE AMBUSH

Battery B, 999th Armored Field Artillery Battalion, 22–24 April 1951

On the far western flank of the UN line along the Imjin River, due north of Seoul, a strong Communist attack hit the ROK 1st Division of the U.S. I Corps hard. One of the best of the ROK army divisions, the South Korean unit was reinforced by the U.S. 999th Armored Field Artillery Battalion, an African American organization. A combat historian, Capt. (later Maj.) Edward C. Williamson, who studied the action of one of the battalion's firing batteries, describes the situation.

In late April 1951 the 1st ROK Division anchored the western end of the U.S. I Corps front on the Imjin River, the MLR being on the south bank with the OPLR north of the river. The 999th Armored Field Artillery Battalion (155mm howitzers, self-propelled) had the mission of giving artillery support to the 1st ROK Division. Its Battery B, under the command of Capt. James Welden, was at the mud hut village of Taech'on, four miles south of the Imjin.

In the vicinity of the settlement of Tuji-ri on the south bank of the Imjin, the commanding terrain feature is Hill 128. From its heights an observer has a clear view of the surrounding country, particularly to the north across the Imjin. Therefore, for that reason Battery B maintained an OP [observation post] on its northern slope.[1]

The forward observer assigned to Hill 128 was Warrant Officer (later 2d Lt.) David R. Reed. Reed describes his actions on 22 April when the enemy attack began.

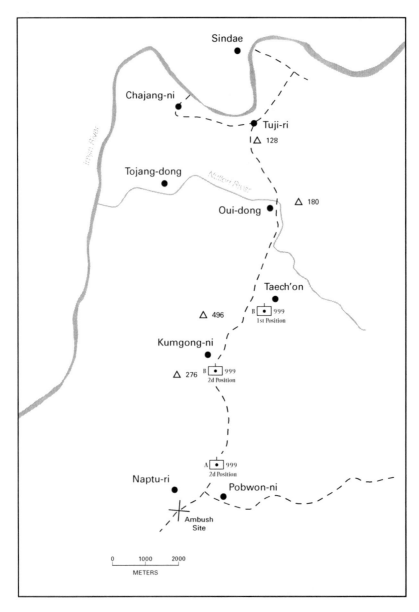

Area of operations, Battery B, 999th Armored Field Artillery Battalion, 22–24 April 1951. (Original map by author, based on map in Army Map Service series L751.)

On 22 April 1951 I received the assignment of being forward observer on Hill 128. That afternoon I left the battery position at Taech'on at 1250. My party consisted of the radio operator, Cpl. Reece Andrews; the jeep driver, Pvt. Thomas McCall; and an ROK soldier attached to Battery B, Kim Yung Man. We carried two radios, one attached to the jeep and one portable. We followed a narrow Korean trail north to the base of Hill 128. There we dismounted and carrying our equipment climbed the hill, arriving at the OP at 1320.

Capt. Deward Sims, Asst. S-3, was holding service practice [live fire training] for the 999th Armored Field Artillery Battalion at the OP; therefore I did not relieve Lt. George A. Buonocore, the Battery B reconnaissance officer, as forward observer until 1500, when the service practice ended. Capt. Sims and the other battalion officers then left the area, and I proceeded to police up around the OP. Andrews and I then checked communications, both wire and telephone, with Battery B, following the battalion SOP of checking in every thirty minutes during the night. Ten soldiers from the 12th Infantry Regiment, 1st ROK Division, were on the hill acting as a guard for our OP.

From 1500 until 2000 there were no unusual incidents. However, at 2000 hours on my extreme right flank (to the east of Lt. Reed), four shells from a 150mm enemy artillery battery exploded. I immediately called battalion headquarters and informed it of what was happening. I was ordered to keep the front under sharp observation and report any more enemy action. During the next three hours an estimated 200 rounds of enemy artillery came in. At 2330 I heard machine guns on my left flank and to the front. From the flashes I estimated that the machine gun on my left flank was on the north bank of the Imjin, three hundred yards downstream from the Chajang-ni ferry site [about 4,000 yards to the west of Hill 128]. The second machine gun was in defilade and firing on the ferry site at Sindae [about 3,000 yards to the north of Hill 128].

Since the machine gun covering the Chajang-ni ferry site was out in the open, I decided to call for a fire mission. At dark, Lt. Joseph V. Spitler, Battery B executive officer, had fired one round of illuminating shell to mark Concentration Point #1; therefore, I determined my data using that concentration. Calling in my fire mission, I commanded, "Fire Mission. From Concentration One add 400 (yards). Enemy machine gun in the open, firing into friendly positions on south bank of Imjin. Request VT [variable time fuse] in fire for effect. Request one round white phosphorous. Will adjust." Unfortunately, the telephone operator at the battery fire direction center failed to record the fire mission correctly and called, "Say again." So I repeated the fire mission. Crouched in my hole, which was covered on the top and front, with the opening on the side, and using only my eyes to observe, I awaited the "On the way." In a few minutes the operator said, "On the way," and a white phosphorous round dropped about 400 yards short of the target. I then commanded, "Add 400, fire for effect." Battery B gave me six rounds, one volley, all at one time. It was a target hit, and the shells fell squarely on top of the machine gun. Then I commanded, "Enemy machine gun destroyed. Cease firing. End of mission."

In the meantime the enemy in a horseshoe formation was pushing back friendly combat patrols across the Imjin River directly in front of me. At 0130, while I was firing in the vicinity of the concentration mentioned, Capt. Nicholson [S-3, 999th AFA Battalion] called and told me to leave my OP. He gave me the coordinates of where I was standing and said that he was going to shoot a fire mission there. I didn't leave, and a battery from the 999th started dropping fire in on the eastern slope. I sent the ten ROK soldiers to the right flank to see if the enemy had succeeded in reaching Hill 128.

Between 0200 and 0230, the ROKs whom I had sent out made contact, and I heard their rifles barking. About that time a machine gun to my right rear opened up firing south. Then Capt. Nicholson phoned and ordered me off Hill 128. Four or five machine guns were shooting nearby as I came off the hill with McCall, Andrews, and Kim. We were joined by an ROK officer and an ROK enlisted man. We got in the jeep and started south toward the MLR. For safety I got the ROK officer to challenge all soldiers before we reached the MLR.

Reed's jeep moved along the dirt trail that runs south from Hill 128 across the valley of the Nullori River. Reed halted the jeep at the new MLR, located on the northern slope of the hill mass south of the Nullori valley. In the village of Oui-dong, he contacted the ROK officer in charge of that sector. Reed continues his account.

We got back to the MLR, and I located the infantry officer in charge of the section. I then set up a temporary OP [about halfway between Hill 128 and the battery position at Taech'on]. We left the jeep standing in the road in case a sudden withdrawal became necessary. Remaining here until daylight, I reestablished wire communications with Battery B. When I contacted the battery commander, Capt. Welden asked me, "Are you on the OP where you were when the enemy attacked?" I replied, "No." He asked, "Are you going back?" I answered, "Yes, sir," and the conversation abruptly ended. That was right at daylight, 0600 hours.

I got in my jeep with my crew and started out. Just 100 yards north of the jeep across the road, Chinese were massed for an attack. I would estimate that they were in regimental strength. Using my field glasses, I could see enemy soldiers on Hill 128. I had McCall stop. I then contacted Capt. Welden by radio, and just as I made contact with him the Chinese started to move across the field in a crouch formation, not firing. McCall quickly turned the jeep around. The time was now around 0630 hours.

I asked Capt. Welden for a fire mission on the massed Chinese. He turned me over to Lt. Buonocore, who said the battery would be unable to fire the mission because it was displacing on battalion orders. As I finished talking with Buonocore, the Chinese opened fire. I got in the jeep, drove back half a mile, and stopped. Here, as McCall was backing the jeep around, a sniper on Hill 180 [about 800 yards to the north] shot one round at him. We withdrew forty yards farther south, stopped ten minutes, and the sniper took another shot. I picked up smoke of the sniper rifle drifting down from the side of Hill 180. The sniper had shot two ROK soldiers previously. I informed an ROK infantry lieutenant of the location of the sniper. We then proceeded north again, and I reestablished my OP [among the buildings of the village of Oui-dong]. Here I sat on the side of a large hole using my field glasses. At about 1300 mortar shells started falling in open ground to my front. From this new OP I was unable to locate the enemy positions; however, I did observe planes attack enemy in the village of Tojang-dong [about two miles west of Oui-dong]. Meantime, ROK and enemy troops were too close together for me to attempt fire missions; therefore I returned to the battery.[2]

Warrant Officer Reed's driver, PFC Thomas McCall, provides additional information about the Chinese attack the night of 22–23 April.

During the night we ordinarily pulled three- to four-hour guard shifts, but the night of 22–23 April we all stayed up. At 2400 we were overrun by Chinese who climbed Hill 128. I saw fifteen. There were no friendly troops in the direction that they were coming, and the ROK lieutenant with us said that they were Chinese. I shot my carbine when the Chinese were sixty yards below us. At 0030 we packed up all our equipment, destroyed our food, emptied the water can, and climbed down the hill. We overloaded our jeep with our weight and equipment and moved south on the trail to Taech'on.

Until 0700 we patrolled up and down the road observing the enemy. At 0700 I was sitting in the jeep, and Lt. Reed said turn the jeep around. I turned it around, and we moved slowly southward. At 0730 the Chinese attacked the 1st ROK Division.[3]

The combat historian Capt. Williamson describes the opening of the Chinese attack and the situation in Battery B of the 999th Armored Field Artillery Battalion as it responded to the attack and eventually pulled back from its initial firing positions.

On 22 April 1951 in the I U.S. Corps zone the 1st ROK Division was on the left flank, having on its right the U.S. 3d Infantry Division. The MLR of the 1st ROK Division was on the south side of the Imjin River with outposts on the north side. At around 2200 the offensive of the Chinese started. Friendly outposts of the 1st ROK Division to the northwest and west of Korangp'o-ri were forced back across the Imjin River before midnight by advancing enemy columns. It was believed that the 19th CCF [Chinese Communist forces] Army Group and possibly the I North Korean Corps were available for employment by the enemy on the I U.S. Corps west flank.

The 999th U.S. Armored Field Artillery Battalion, 155mm self-propelled howitzers, I U.S. Corps artillery, was in support of the 1st ROK Division with Battery B in position at Taech'on. The battery commenced firing at the beginning of the Chinese offensive and was firing continuously, constantly shifting the carriages. From up along the meandering Imjin the men at the gun position could hear the rattle of machine gun fire. Capt. James W. Welden, battery commander, had broken the firing battery down into two platoons. These platoons covered a 1600-mil sector, the right limit being compass 200 and the left limit compass 5000.[4] Firing was mostly VT with some WP [white phosphorus] for adjustment, in volume the greatest number being Platoon Ten Rounds and Platoon Five Rounds.

Mr. (Warrant Officer) David R. Reed, unit administrator, was manning the battery OP on Hill 128 when the battery prepared to march order at 0200 hours; however, the fire missions continued. The weather was clear with the temperature in the fifties so that when the tents were taken down to march order, the stoves were left burning. By 0330 to 0400 the men had become lax and tired from excessive work. One howitzer section chief, SFC Clarence C. Quander, recalled that he was using fifteen men in the 1st Howitzer Section at a time. Some of the men were hauling ammunition while others were helping fire the piece. The Chinese offensive had not affected the morale of the battery, Capt. Welden commenting, "The men weren't scared, not jumpy."

The wheeled vehicles of the battery moved out at 0530, which was daybreak. The guns arrived at the new position near the town of Kumgong-ni at 0815. It took the battery around one-half hour to make the two-mile march between positions. At the new position Battery B fired continuously all day long, the enemy having broken through the MLR and come up on Hill 496, which was to the left front of the battery.

That night as it was getting dark at 1930 the battery adjusted on an enemy machine gun just over the hill [in view about 4,000 yards north of the battery], which had been firing on soldiers from the 1st ROK Division and controlled the pass through which two batteries of the 17th ROK Field Artillery Battalion (105mm howitzers) had to withdraw. Lt. Joseph V. Spitler, battery executive [officer], commanded, "Number Two, Direct Fire, Lay on that point of rise where you see those trees burning." At that command the 2d Section Gunner, Sgt. Willie M. Deramus, boresighted on the fire by placing the sight on deflection 0 and sighting through it on the fire. The 5th Section was also to be ready to fire. Capt. Welden walked out twenty yards to the left flank of the pieces firing, and Lt. Spitler took a position forty yards to the rear of the guns. Cpl. Howe standing near the executive officer's post heard a command for charge 3 white bag and looked up on the hill and saw Chinese passing over it. The first and second rounds of Shell HE, Fuse Quick, hit the forward slope above the target. The charge was dropped to charge 1, and three rounds burst in the area of the machine gun.

At this time, 2015, the 6 x 6 trucks of the [ROK] 17th Field Artillery Battalion were seen coming through the pass, and because of their proximity, the fire mission was called off before going into fire for effect. The success of this fire mission was apparent when the two batteries of the ROK 17th Field Artillery were able to come through the pass. Battery B now settled down for the night, firing mostly H & I [harassing and interdiction fire missions on possible enemy locations] with charge 5 although some charge 3 and charge 1 were used.

At 2300 Lt. Theodore Von Gerichten, a 999th Armored Field Artillery Battalion forward observer, radioed a message to battalion. This message was first picked up by 1st Lt. George A. Buonocore, Battery B reconnaissance officer, who failed to record it correctly after several "say agains." Lt. Spitler now took the mike at Battery B and heard Lt. Von Gerichten say, "The enemy is where I was, and there is a fire fight where I'm going. What do I do now? Over." Spitler forwarded this message back to Capt. Nicholson, S-3, whose reply relayed back to Von Gerichten was, "Get out the best way you can."

At about 0145 the line to the battery OP on Hill 128 went out. Sgt. Curtis Wilcox, communications sergeant, along with Sgt. Herbert Anderson and PFC Lewis, went out on the line taking with them carbines, test phone, and test clips. They found that a tank had broken the line. So they fixed the line and tested back toward the battery only to find the line dead; however, they could get the

OP. Walking back toward the battery they continued to test the line and again found the wire had been broken by tanks. At this break they were successful in getting both the battery and the OP.

At the same time Sgt. Wilcox and his men were trouble-shooting the OP line, Cpl. Howe, wire corporal, and PFC Oscar Lewis were out on the gun line from the battery fire direction center to the guns. While on the line they observed M46 Patton tanks and ROK infantry pulling back.[5] PFC Lewis remarked at this time to Cpl. Howe, "I don't like this. They're leaving; they're leaving us stranded." After getting the gun line back in, the two men returned to the wire tent.

During the morning of the 24th, Capt. James Nicholson, S-3, called Capt. Welden on the telephone and asked him if he was mobile. Welden replied that he had not been told to move; whereupon Nicholson informed him that there was supposed to be a reserve battalion of ROK infantry on his left flank, and he was to send an officer out to contact them. In case the officer failed to contact them, Battery B was to march order and move out. Welden then sent 1st Lt. George A. Buonocore out on this mission.

It was a moonlight night with a full moon. Buonocore proceeded up the road [to the west] in his jeep and saw a few silhouettes whom he surmised to be enemy in front of him. Therefore, he halted his jeep and proceeded on foot, running across a lone ROK soldier when he reached an open area in a valley. The ROK soldier told him that there were Chinese on Hill 276 [about 500 yards south of the road that Buonocore had traveled over]. Both of them now continued forward on foot, and shortly the ROK soldier nudged Buonocore and pointed to two more silhouettes approximately two hundred yards away. Buonocore and the ROK soldier hit the ditch and started back to the jeep. There was no shooting, and they got out of there fast. The reserve battalion was supposed to be 1,000 yards away, and Buonocore had gone 2,000 yards west in the valley without contact. On Buonocore's return Capt. Welden called Capt. Nicholson, who ordered, "move out."

It was now 0230, and Nicholson told Welden to take the battery to Pobwon-ni, which was three miles south of their present area. Before the battery moved out of its position, four mortar rounds, estimated as 60mm to 81mm, fell in the battery area. Lt. Spitler, after giving "Close station March Order," added, "Hurry it up, let's get the hell out of here." The battery moved down the road with no lights, not even blackout, passing by the Battery A position, and 500 yards to the front the men saw machine gun tracers. Capt. Welden called, "Stop the convoy." Mortar and machine gun fire could be seen and heard in the vicinity of Pobwon-ni, and Welden radioed Nicholson to that effect; Nicholson radioed back that was a mistake, the fire was farther up the road.

The time was now 0300, and Battery B moved about 800 yards south down the road to the crossroads near Pobwon-ni, halting there while Welden radioed Nicholson that the message that he had sent the first time was correct. Nicholson radioed back instructions to move to another position to the south.

Since there was automatic weapons firing on the right flank of the column from the town of Naptu-ri, Welden called for two M39 personnel carriers with .50 caliber machine guns mounted to come up to the head of the column.[6] Fortunately, there were no casualties thus far since the fire was falling short. As soon as the M39s got up front, Welden pulled his jeep in behind the first M39, and Lt. Spitler's jeep pulled in behind the second M39. Welden got out of his jeep and mounted the first M39, then called down the column that they were going through.

Cpl. Howe, driving the wire truck back in the column, mashed on the accelerator. The column moved about 200 yards down the road, which ran in a southwest direction, and started receiving crossfire. M. Sgt. [Enoch] Scott, chief of firing battery, stated his belief that a friendly patrol had contacted the enemy, who fired back, giving away their positions and losing the element of surprise. The narrow dusty road, considering Korean roads, was in fairly good condition. The column then started receiving machine gun fire from about six machine guns interspersed with small arms, automatic weapons, and mortars coming from an estimated enemy company.[7]

The convoy continued forward, attempting to break through the enemy ambush. Members of the battery provide details of the confused fighting.[8]

M. Sgt. Enoch Scott, chief, Firing Battery, during a walk over the terrain with Capt. Williamson: I came out of this draw, Battery A was sitting about 400 yards from here [to the north or behind him]. At this point (crossroads) I could see machine gun fire coming from the hill to the left front where a friendly patrol had contacted the enemy. The enemy gave away positions and lost the element of surprise. I was in about the center of the column. . . . The enemy was approximately a company-size unit. The column was closed-up right along here [in the ambush area]. A message came from the front from Capt. Welden to dismount, we were being ambushed.[9]

M. Sgt. Lloyd M. Jenkins, platoon sergeant: I could see two machine guns on the left flank. One was 25 yards away, the other 20 yards. On the right flank were two machine guns, one 50 yards, the other 150 yards. One .30 caliber machine gun was firing green tracers. . . . We moved forward until we passed by a machine gun that was firing from the hill on the left. The second M39 in front of the maintenance jeep exploded and blocked the road. The next M39 pulled up behind it and stopped, followed by the maintenance jeep and the supply truck. Machine gun fire struck the column, but there were no casualties on the M39, the maintenance jeep, and supply truck.

Lt. George A. Buonocore, reconnaissance officer: There was continuous machine gun fire from the last halt. Everybody got out and on the ground in the furrowed land and in a barley field. They were there about twenty minutes. I crawled up along the ditch to see what the possibilities were of getting through. Mortar rounds were falling into the road, and I saw four bursts. That was after 0400 in the morning. I then returned to the rear of the column where most of the men were, and an enemy machine gun was firing from the rear. The men in the battery returned the fire. As long as we were on the vehicles the .50 caliber machine guns were being utilized. Practically everybody was firing his weapon. Each man had about three clips. Some of the men had taken .30 caliber machine gun belts and stuffed them full of carbine ammunition.

M. Sgt. Lloyd M. Jenkins: You could go around to the right, but you would walk right into four machine guns.

M. Sgt. Eldrich J. Henley, Chief of Detail: I was right by
the hill. After I was wounded in the M39, I crawled off and jumped
in the ditch. I was wounded in the thigh and legs by a burp gun.
There were three M39s that stopped. The Chinese were firing on
them with mortars, about five or six rounds. I crawled about five or
six yards up the ditch until my legs gave out. During the time the
Chinese were firing, they were hollering and seeming to have a
party up on the hill.[10]

Cpl. Thomas Meeks, driver, M41 self-propelled howit-
zer:[11] On the night of the ambush, Sgt. Timothy Bell pulled out the
M41 and told me to take it. Although I was the driver, I told him I
didn't feel like driving. When we drove into the ambush, Sgt. Bell
was shot by a machine gun through the shoulder and killed instantly.[12] The tank ran off the road and hit a weapons carrier that had
been knocked out by a mortar and came to a stop right under the
hill. We shot up our carbine ammunition and got off. In climbing on
an M39, I got in head first, and as I was pulling in my legs, a bullet
hit me on the leg. Cpl. Raymond Williams, who was driving the
M39, left the road. As we left the ambush I could see tracers. Later,
I noticed that the teeth on the track of the M39 were bent. PFC
Maurice Henry, who was riding in the hatch with Sgt. Bell, was
killed while attempting to get Sgt. Bell's body out of the hatch.[13]

Cpl. Douglas M. Hackey, motor officer's driver: When
the jeep first stopped, I was driving the maintenance officer's jeep; a
tank in front got hit. I had to stop and couldn't go around. I crawled
in the ditch back to an M39, shooting a .50 caliber machine gun. At
that time the supply truck got hit. That lit up the whole area just
about like daylight. The Chinese started to close in. I shot one at
forty feet who was about to throw a hand grenade at Cpl. Charles
Fleets, who was firing the M39's .50 cal gun on the tank ahead of
me. I told him to jump. The Chinese threw the grenade anyhow;
fortunately Cpl. Fleets had already moved. Sgt. Laws crawled by
saying, "I'm shot, Hack; I'm going on in. They got me." Another
Chinese stood up in front of me. I shot twice. I don't know whether
I hit the Chinese. Then I stood straight up and made a dive into a
ditch. I started crawling in the ditch back to another jeep, B-6 [bum-

per number]. Driving it back to where Sgt. Laws was lying in a ditch, I got out, and told him to bring it in when he got ready to come. I then proceeded to crawl back to Battery A.[14]

CPL. ANTHONY JACKSON, BATTERY COMMANDER'S JEEP DRIVER: Things were real hot that time when [the] battery went around [the] hill. I was in a jeep in back of an M39. When the M39 pulled off the road I pulled right behind it. When it got back on the road, I couldn't get back on; I was going to cross the rice paddy. At that time the enemy dropped three mortars. My jeep jumped out of gear. When the jeep stopped I stepped on the accelerator, I hollered, "Lord have mercy." I wonder if I'm going to make it through here, and I felt around for my rifle; I eased outside the jeep. I looked across the field, and they were coming like flies. When a mortar hit near the jeep, I said, "Lord Jesus, I gotta get through here now." And I left the jeep and began crawling. There was a little ditch there, and I crawled and ran about three-fourths of a mile. It seemed like everything in the column was gone except one M41. The M41 was SFC Quanders's. Just before that an M39 had just thrown off a tent. Things were still hot. I started to jump on the M39. They were going too fast. I still continued running and crawling. As the M41 passed by, I hollered; he wouldn't stop, but it slowed down. I grabbed some man's leg, jumped up on the track, and kept going round and round on the track. Finally I got on.[15]

M. SGT. LLOYD M. JENKINS AND SFC JOSEPH WORD: M. Sgt. Jenkins and SFC Joseph Word started crawling away from the supply truck. It was about 0440. They crawled past the machine gun that was on top of the hill for fifty yards back toward Battery A. They looked and saw incendiary grenades hit the last M39 and then hit the maintenance jeep. They observed on top of the hill, to the right of where the machine gun was, approximately a platoon of guerrillas (civilian clothes) moving to the rear of the machine gun. They were laughing and shouting. Word said, "Let's move out. They're coming after us." Looking back toward the supply truck, they observed two enemy going to the rear of the truck. Jenkins and Word got up and ran for about twenty yards. Two mortars fell short of them while they were running. Stopping, hitting the dirt, and looking back, they saw the supply truck being set on fire by incendiary grenades. Being in the open, they didn't exchange any rifle fire. Then they moved back to Battery A.

Though some soldiers of the battery made it back to the position of Battery A, most of the survivors moved forward when their commander, Capt. Welden, gave the word. Members of the unit continue describing the fight.

CPL. OSCAR O. SPRAGLIN, GUNNER, 5TH HOWITZER SECTION: We were firing Charge 1 Green bag on a hillside about 100 yards away. There were about fifty to seventy-five Chinese on the hill. Shortly after that, it was approximately 0200 hours, our battery executive officer, after giving close station march order, said, "Hurry it up, let's get the hell out of here." At that time we had the gun march ordered ready to pull in line. We then moved down the road south approximately two miles when the convoy stopped. Our battery commander investigated and gave the command, "Ambush, take cover." We hadn't been briefed before. We took cover. After doing so, we received orders to mount on vehicles, that we were going through the ambush. The Korean truck was in front of us. This Korean truck blew up in front of us; a mortar hit it. To avoid running into the Korean truck, we went into the rice field. While going through the rice field, Chinese were jumping up. The driver ran over about four Chinese. We were somewhat crowded on the vehicles. Bullets were hitting close. So I made a jump in the back. Cpl. [Amos] Green was lying in the back, and I jumped on Green. Cpl. Green grabbed me in the collar and was choking me. I gave a yell out, "Green, it's Spraglin; it's Spraglin." Due to the fact that Green was excited from being fired at, Cpl. Green said, "No, it ain't. It ain't you." So, I said again, "Green, it is me."[16]

CPL. AMOS GREEN, NUMBER I MAN ON GUN, 5TH HOWITZER SECTION: So, I looked up and came to my senses and said, "Yes, Sprag, this is you. Lie down." So then we continued to go on.[17]

LT. JOSEPH V. SPITLER, EXECUTIVE OFFICER, BATTERY B: Ours was the fourth vehicle in the column. Cpl. Artie E. Hector was driving. We followed the two M39s and jeep in front of us into a plowed field. Hector said, "I'm hit in the head. You'll have to drive." I said, "This is no time to change now. I don't think you got hit. Keep on going." When we got to the next position Hector took off his hat, looked at it, and said, "I told you I was hit in the head." Sure enough, a machine pistol bullet had grazed the back of his head, leaving a three-inch hole in his helmet.

SGT. ROBERT J. THOMPSON, BATTERY FIRE DIRECTION CENTER: We had just passed the crossroads 500 yards south of Battery A. The Chinese started firing. I was riding [in] the turret of an M39 personnel carrier when the Chinese started firing at us. It all happened so quick, I really don't know what happened. The enemy machine gun started firing. I heard over the little SR 510 radio in the M39, the battery commander tell the S-3 that we were coming through. Halfway through we picked up other fellows and started moving again. An enemy machine gun was firing on our left flank. I swung the machine gun around and fired at it. When we reached the enemy machine gun, I noticed that it had stopped firing. We went through with nobody hurt on our vehicle.[18]

CPL. ROBERT L. HOWE, WIRE CORPORAL: Sgt. Wilcox and I were riding in the ¾-ton wire truck. After the convoy stopped, all the linemen who were riding on B-7 were getting out because the truck was closed in. All of them got out except three men, including one man who rode on the spare tire. This was Pvt. Joe Fields. The captain called down and said we were going through. One M39 and two jeeps were in front of us. I gave the truck all I could and mashed on the accelerator. Halfway through the ambush a mortar hit in front of the weapons carrier, knocking a jeep over in the ditch. Cpl. Jackson in the second jeep took to the rice paddy. One man who had been in the knocked-out jeep, PFC Allen Thompson, was hollering, "Wait for me." I hit the brake in order to stop for him. Someone in the truck hollered to keep going. Then Sgt. Wilcox hollered to PFC Richard Staunton, "Catch another vehicle." I did not pick up Thompson in slowing up for Staunton. I came under machine gun fire. One machine gun was a .30 caliber light.[19]

SGT. CURTIS WILCOX, COMMUNICATIONS SERGEANT, AND CPL. ROBERT L. HOWE, WIRE CORPORAL: Going through the road block,

Cpl. Howe hollered, "I'm shot." Sgt. Wilcox replied, "Keep going, you're not shot." He said, "I'm shot in the leg. I've got to stop. You take over." Wilcox told him, "Keep going. I can't take it here." He said, "You've gotta take it, or I'll stop." By that time we were nearly through the ambush, and Wilcox asked Howe, "How do you feel?" He said, "I think I can make it on." He told Wilcox to feel his leg to see if it was bleeding. Wilcox felt his leg and told him no he didn't feel any blood. Howe said he could carry on. Later they found out the bullet had penetrated through the tire into the side of the vehicle and skinned the shinbone of Cpl. Howe. At the halt the battery commander called the battalion commander and told him they were being ambushed. [The battery commander told Wilcox to go on through the roadblock, which he did.] . . . [Wilcox] hollered, "We're through." After that they picked up seven wounded and carried them to the medics.[20]

M. Sgt. Scott: We contacted the battalion commander and received orders to proceed on. The order [was] passed on to mount up, going through. Enemy small arms, mortar, and automatic weapons were firing on us. The road was under direct fire. Small arms fire was coming from the field left from the road, machine gun fire, too. A .50 caliber machine gun mounted on an M39 manned by Sgt. Frank Catalon fired from right and left. Sgt. Robert Thompson silenced an enemy machine gun on the hill. The emplacement the machine gun was in was built by the ROKs. The machine gun emplacements were old. As we moved off, Sgt. Thompson of the fire direction center was firing. When a mortar hit the ammunition trailer, it exploded and looked like Harlem, New York. I was a good 200 yards past the ammunition trailer when it happened. A Korean army truck, which had latched on the column, got the same mortar treatment. At a distance of 50–75 yards was a Chinese trench. From this point I could see Chinese troops about 100 yards away. I estimate 75–100 Chinese came across the field shooting small arms. Up on the military crest of the hill, a .50 caliber machine gun was shooting. . . . I recall the Chinese in the roadblock were jumping up and down, blowing their whistles, and trying to scare us.

Right along here at this bend in the road [M. Sgt. Scott was then walking the battlefield with Capt. Williamson] an M39 was knocked out, blocking the road. My M39 ran up in back of the knocked-out one and switched to the right. In it one man was wounded; three others not. The wounded man was shot through the right side of the chest by small arms. The knocked-out M39 blocked the bullets, enabling me to pick up wounded. As I picked up PFC Lemmie F. Sanders, he said, "Don't pick me up by my arm; I'm shot in the chest; I'm hurt." Sgt. Thompson spoke to him, "There's no time to investigate. We've got to get you out immediately." I said, "Take it easy, Sanders. You will make it." I grabbed him in the seat of his pants and put him up on the right front of the M39. Then the three other men crawled up themselves. Inside the compartment it was now full, so I started for the back. I went to step up on the trailer tongue to get on the back of the M39 and looked on the other side of the road, seeing two enemy also close enough to get up on the trailer tongue. I got off and hit the ground down on my stomach right in the gulley. I lit those two up. I killed them both to the right rear of the M39. Neither said a word. I ain't heard neither say nothing. I had already given the driver the go ahead sign. The driver took off. Myself, I got up beside the ammunition trailer in a crouch. I stayed alongside the ammunition trailer until I could run up to the coupling and lie across the tongue. That is where I [rode] until the first position we went in. At this point each armored vehicle came around like it was a race track, including the mess truck from right here [indicating the location during the terrain walk]. The moon was shining. You could tell from the ammunition explosion how to pick up a pin. It was really light. We pulled through this ambush right this side of battalion headquarters [where it was then located, not at the time of the action].[21]

SFC FRANK CATALON, CHIEF, HOWITZER SECTION: When the head of the column started to move on through, SFC Catalon was manning the machine gun on the lead M39. He was firing on both sides of the road and down the ditches. They got to the curve. The enemy cut loose with machine pistols—100–150 rounds, 5 or 6 machine pistols. Practically none of the men on the armored vehicles were down behind the armored plate because of the equipment. Cpl.

Jones, the Battery B medic, sitting just behind Capt. Welden, was shot at around 0400 hrs.

After breaking through the ambush site, Battery B went into position near the headquarters of the 999th Armored Field Artillery Battalion. Members of the unit describe their next actions.

LT. SPITLER: When we got down to the next position, we had four guns. We put them into position to fire and put the M39s around for a complete perimeter. We did not have a wheeled vehicle available because the only jeep that got through was taking the wounded men to the medics.

CAPT. WELDEN: Capt. Welden called all the chiefs of section together and had them check all their men to see if they were wounded and bring them over to a central location. Welden walked up to the medics to speed up the ambulance to pick up the wounded. . . . When Welden went to the dispensary he also went up to Lt. Col. Kenneth DeWalt [battalion commander], who told him to move to a position vicinity [Tuman-ni]. . . . Battery B moved into that position at not quite daybreak and set up guns in firing positions with four guns in position. The other two guns were still back in the road-block. The four guns were laid azimuth 6400. They had a roll call there to see who was there.

M. SGT. SCOTT: When we first pulled into position we took care of the wounded, then pulled over the hill farther and withdrew to a second position. At that point the first sergeant and the clerk were in the hospital. All the battery rosters and the personnel records were in the supply truck [that] had been burned. I got a piece of paper and my fountain pen and constructed a battery roster by personnel I physically saw present. Later in the day Mr. Jackson came from battalion and brought me a roster. Immediately after that I had another battery formation and a roll call. We accounted for all of the battery with six killed, twenty-seven hospitalized, and four . . . sent to the dispensary for medical treatment for shrapnel. Cpl. Artie E. Hecter received a bullet through the helmet that ricocheted on the surface of his head and went out the side of the helmet. He never stopped driving except just long enough to go to the dispensary and have a patch put on his head. At the first battery formation following the roadblock, Capt. Welden talked with the men and "built their morale."[22]

A number of soldiers of the battery were left at the roadblock. Some tell their stories, along with the battery commander who returned to the site after daybreak.

SGT. HENRY D. LAWS, MECHANIC: At 0610, Sgt. Laws, who had stayed at the roadblock wounded in the hand and leg all night, got in an M41. An ROK soldier helped Sgt. Laws put Cpl. James D. O'Neal, who had one foot completely blown off, in the M41 and brought him back to the Battery A aid station. He kept the M41 with Battery A and moved out when Battery A march ordered.

SGT. HENLEY: Just before daybreak I saw the Chinese pick up the body of a dead Chinese and carry it off. First thing after daybreak, ROK soldiers from the 12th Regiment, 1st ROK Division, came up and ROK medics bandaged my wounds. Some of the ROKs captured two to three Chinese prisoners on the hill. These Chinese appeared to have been doped. Right after that Maj. Hoagland, battalion executive [officer], and Captain Vetstein, battalion dental officer, loaded PFC Robert Andrews and me on the medical jeep and took us to the battalion aid station.[23]

CAPT. WELDEN. At 0600 Capt. Welden and six men returned to the roadblock in an M39 to get the equipment, the wounded, and the dead out. By this time ROK soldiers had already cleared the enemy from the roadblock; however, there was still machine gun firing from Naptu-ri. Welden and his men hooked the remaining M41 on the back of the M39 and pulled it out by hooking a cable on it. They picked up the rest of the equipment lying strewn around the place and loaded all the bodies. They recovered B1 (jeep), B2 (M-39), B3 (jeep), B8 (¾-ton), B17 (M41), and B21 (M41). Welden saw ten to fifteen Chinese dead. He estimated the battery inflicted 100 killed and wounded. During the ambush it had been impossible to get the wheeled vehicles around. Off the road, they couldn't move because of the dikes and rice paddies. The drivers had to leave them.

Despite the harrowing ambush at the roadblock, Battery B remained an effective fighting organization, providing steady artillery

support to the South Korean forces. Capt. Williamson, the combat
historian, summarizes their experience.

Battery B had seven killed, five died at the roadblock, one on the
way to the hospital, and one in the hospital; twenty-seven were hospitalized and four sent to the dispensary for medical treatment for
shrapnel. Casualties were mostly due to small arms, automatic
weapons, hand grenades, and mortars. Among the dead, Sgt. Luther
Odums was shot, Sgt. Bell was shot through the shoulder, PFC
Maurice Henry was shot through the head, Pvt. James C. Harris
had a hand grenade tear his side off, PFC Nathan Steele was shot in
the head with the bullet coming out through his neck, Cpl. Clemmett Bennett had serious leg and chest wounds, died in the hospital
[25 April 1951]. [The seventh man to die was Cpl. Charles Brown,
a cook.][24]

Seven vehicles were destroyed: two M39s, one 2½ ton truck,
one jeep, and three ammunition trailers. Six vehicles were damaged:
two M41s, two jeeps (including one which ran off the road), two
¾-ton weapons carriers (including one which ran into a ditch and
turned over). . . .

After the roadblock Battery B had to put survey men, cooks,
mechanics, and firemen on the guns. For a short while morale was
not good. The men had been without sleep and they had had a rough
night; to cap it there was a rumor that friendly troops had fired on
them. Capt. Welden called them together and stated, "Someone told
us they were friendly troops that fired on us, but I have been back
up there and dead Chinese were lying there, and the only thing we
have to do is kill a hundred Chinese for every one they got of us."
Capt. Welden's talk succeeded in restoring the morale, although for
seventy-two hours the men had been without sleep.[25]

Chapter 4

TANKS ABOVE KAP'YONG

Company A, 72d Tank Battalion,
23–24 April 1951

In the center of the UN line the ROK 6th Division held the left flank of the U.S. IX Corps, the 1st Marine Division to the east and the 24th Infantry Division of the U.S. I Corps on the west. The Chinese planned to steamroll the South Korean division with a massive attack by two armies and then exploit the gap by driving into the flanks of the adjacent American divisions and following the Kap'yong and Pukhan. Rivers into the UN rear. When the Chinese buildup in front of the 6th Division was detected on 22 April, IX Corps pushed artillery forward to support the ROK units. That night, however, the Chinese attack overwhelmed the 6th Division's two forward regiments and forced its reserve regiment to withdraw. Artillery support units were caught up in the chaotic night retreat. UN commanders scrambled to react to the collapse of the ROK division.

The next day, when it became obvious that the ROK 6th Division could not be reformed and that its ability to stop another enemy attack was negligible, IX Corps pushed more artillery forward and ordered the 27th British Commonwealth Brigade, then in corps reserve, to establish blocking positions along the Kap'yong River. Late on 23 April the 27th Brigade placed the 3d Battalion, Royal Australian Regiment (RAR), and the 2d Battalion, Princess Patricia's Canadian Light Infantry, in forward positions, with the 1st Battalion, Middlesex Regiment, in reserve.[1] Several American units also moved forward to support the 27th Brigade, including Company A, 72d Tank Battalion; elements of the 74th Engineer Combat

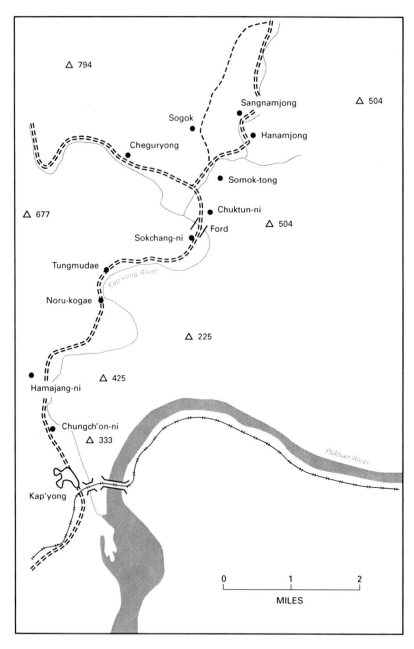

△ 794

Sangnamjong △ 504

Sogok

Hanamjong

Cheguryong

Somok-tong

△ 677

Chuktun-ni

Ford △ 504

Sokchang-ni

Tungmudae

Kap'yong River

Noru-kogae

△ 225

●

△ 425

Hamajang-ni

Chungch'on-ni

△ 333

Pukhan River

Kap'yong

0   1   2

MILES

Area of Operations, 3d Battalion, Royal Australian Regiment, and Company A, 72d Tank Battalion, 23–24 April 1951. (Original map by author, based on maps in Army Map Service series L751.)

Battalion; and artillery and mortar units. The situation is described by commanders and staff officers.

Lt. A. Argent, intelligence officer, 3d Battalion, Royal Australian Regiment (RAR): The 3d Battalion, Royal Australian Regiment, was in reserve in the vicinity of Kap'yong when it was ordered on the afternoon of 23 April to move north four miles. The battalion occupied the high ground northwest of Hill 504 in order to block the valleys to the north and to the northwest. The 2d Battalion, Princess Patricia's Canadian Light Infantry, occupied positions on the high ground east of Hill 677.

The RAR Battalion was in position at 1600, 23 April. The battalion consisted of four rifle companies and one support company, each totaling 120 men.

Company A, 72d Tank Battalion, was in support of the battalion. The RAR Battalion had no artillery support because all field artillery batteries were moving to avoid the danger of being overrun. This included the 16th New Zealand Field Regiment and the 213th Field Artillery Battalion. Communications with Company B, 2d Chemical Mortar Battalion, in support were not operating, and the company [located along the Kap'yong River south of Sokchang-ni] did not fire.[2]

1st Lt. Kenneth W. Koch, commander, Company A, 72d Tank Battalion: On 23 April, Company A (minus the 3d Platoon that was guarding the IX Corps CP), 72d Tank Battalion, was in a bivouac area across the Kap'yong River north of Chungch'on-ni, one mile north of Kap'yong town. That afternoon the company (less the 3d Platoon) was ordered into attachment with the 3d Battalion, Royal Australian Regiment. The company was instructed to take positions in the vicinity of Chuktun-ni in anticipation of an enemy breakthrough in the ROK 6th Division sector. The enemy attack was expected from several avenues of approach: the valley north of Hanamjong and the Sogol valley, converging on Somok-tong generally from the north, and the Cheguryong valley, generally from the northwest.

East of Chuktun-ni, Company D of the Royal Australian Regiment (RAR) took positions in the vicinity of Hill 504; Companies A and C were to the left and slightly north. North of Chuktun-ni and

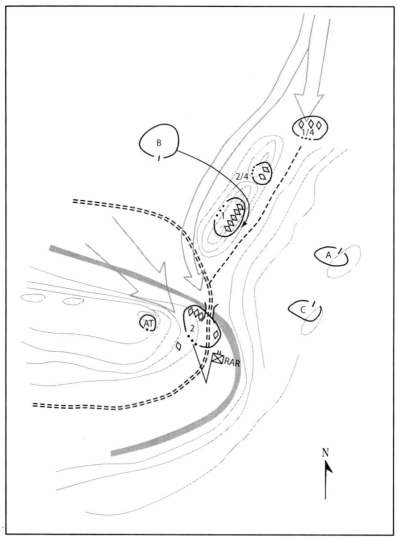

Positions of the 3d Battalion, Royal Australian Regiment, and Company A, 72d Tank Battalion, 23–24 April 1951. (Original map by author, based on maps in CMH manuscript, U.S. Army.)

across the valley from these positions, Company B, RAR, occupied the high ground.

Company A (minus the 3d Platoon), 72d Tank Company, moved north from its bivouac area with the RAR Battalion on the afternoon of 23 April. Lt. Koch placed the 4th Platoon on outpost. He positioned the 1st Platoon on the high ground with Company B, RAR. He situated the 2d Platoon north of Sokchang-ni and south of the river in the vicinity of the RAR Battalion headquarters. Tanks employed by the company were M4A3E8 (Sherman) tanks, 35 tons, each armed with 76mm cannon, one .50 caliber machine gun, and two .30 caliber machine guns.[3]

LT. COL. GEORGE B. PICKETT, ARMORED OFFICER, IX CORPS: Lt. Koch, commander of the tank company, had placed his platoons so that the 4th Platoon was in a blocking position on the only north–south road in the area. The 1st Platoon, Lt. Miller command-ing, was in position on a high ground area [with Company B, RAR] flanking the north–south road on the west and south of the 4th Platoon blocking position. The [remainder of the] RAR Battalion was deployed on the ridge flanking the north–south road on the east. The 2d Platoon and Koch's command tank were deployed at a crossroad to the south of the other tank positions where the north–south road joined the northwest–southeast road. The latter road was being used by elements of the 6th ROK Division as an avenue of withdrawal.[4]

MAJ. THOMAS A. MURPHY, ASSISTANT G-3, IX CORPS: Ele-ments of IX Corps were attacking under Operation Dauntless to Phase Line Wyoming when the enemy began his attack in the IX Corps zone at 2100, 22 April 1951. At 1930, 22 April, the 6th ROK Division came under heavy enemy attack. The division fell back at 1945, but already enemy elements were in the rear of the division. At 2200, the division was withdrawing. At 2300, the division at-tempted to reorganize in the vicinity of Sangnamjong. At 0250, 23 April, the 7th and 19th ROK Regiments were moving back under pressure; there was no indication of the 2d ROK Regiment's loca-tion. At 0415, elements of the division were reported to be south of the British 27th Commonwealth Brigade positions.[5]

MAJ. DON W. BLACK, ASSISTANT S-3, IX CORPS ARTILLERY: At 1005, 23 April, the 213th Field Artillery Battalion was ordered to clear the 1st Marine Division sector and move into position to sup-port the 6th ROK Division and to reinforce the fires of the 16th New Zealand Field Regiment. The battalion could not get clearance on the Marine MSR [main supply road] until 1300. At that time the battalion moved to Kap'yong, then north. At 1600, 23 April, it was realized at IX Corps Artillery headquarters that the 213th Field Artillery Battalion might not be able to remain in the pre-determined positions. Therefore, the battalion was ordered to withdraw south to the vicinity of Kap'yong near the 16th New Zealand Field Regiment if and when it became desirable to do so.[6]

CAPT. BLAINE JOHNSON, ASSISTANT S-3, 213TH FIELD ARTIL-LERY BATTALION: On 22 April the 213th Field Artillery Battalion (105mm howitzers, self-propelled) was supporting the 1st Marine Division in the vicinity of the Hwach'on Reservoir. On 23 April the battalion was sent eleven miles north of Kap'yong to support the 6th ROK Division. The battalion reached the designated position and at 1930 was ready to fire. At that time the 2d Regiment of the 6th ROK Division collapsed; at dark the regiment was withdrawing. At the same time the battalion realized that the front lines had collapsed in that area, corps artillery ordered the battalion by radio to move south to the vicinity of the 16th New Zealand Field Regiment. As the battalion withdrew, it lost one gun, which was run off the road to avoid striking a mass of Koreans.[7]

As the ROK 6th Division and its artillery support withdrew, elements of the British 27th Commonwealth Brigade and Company A, 72d Tank Battalion, came under attack from the closely pursuing Chinese. Members of Company A, 72d Tank Battalion, describe the beginning of their fight with the assault on the 4th Platoon's outpost.

LT. KOCH, COMPANY COMMANDER: Warned that elements of the 6th ROK Division moving south would pass through its positions after dark, the company allowed ROK troops through between 2030 and 2100. ROK soldiers were running. In the rear of the ROKs were lead enemy elements. At 2100 the outpost section of the 4th Platoon was struck from the north by enemy troops who were close behind the withdrawing ROKs. Enemy forces were among the tanks before the tankers realized it. The tank section on outpost, a blocking force operating without infantry, was to withdraw upon enemy approach and tie in with the 1st Platoon and Company B, RAR, on the left, and Company A, RAR, on the right, thereby blocking the approach to Chuktun-ni from the north. At the outbreak of the attack, Lt. [Peter P.] DiMartino, the platoon leader of the 4th Platoon, was killed, and two tank commanders were wounded.[8] Disorganized, the platoon began to withdraw in flight.[9]

PFC LEROY W. RITCHOTTE, GUNNER, 4TH PLATOON: PFC Ritchotte was the gunner of the platoon leader's tank. At 2130, as Ritchotte was getting ready to go to bed, the lieutenant alerted the platoon. At 2200 Sgt. Wells in the next tank fired his .50 caliber machine gun. Lt. DiMartino asked who he was firing at. Wells said there were some Chinese fifty yards ahead of his tank. Lt. Koch, the company commander, then instructed the platoon to be certain before firing that troops from the north were Chinese, not South Koreans.

At about 2200, enemy small arms fire was received from about ten or twenty enemy troops who Ritchotte thought were feeling out the tank positions. Mortar fire was then received by the platoon. Soon after, enemy troops came across the field. Ritchotte fired according to Lt. DiMartino's directions. He fired to the front, then at machine gun nests. During this time, DiMartino was firing his .50 caliber machine gun. The bow gunner was firing, and the driver fired his .45 caliber pistol.

At 2300, Lt. DiMartino ordered the tanks to pull out. Ritchotte started to swing his turret around, but couldn't do so because the ammunition racks were open. Two tanks covered while Ritchotte's tank withdrew, closed the ammunition racks, and turned the turret. Then Ritchotte's tank covered the other two tanks as they withdrew. At this time, DiMartino was struck in the head by a bullet.

Ritchotte went up in the turret, and seeing Chinese in the rear of the tank, he opened up with the .50 caliber machine gun. A shell hit the front of the tank and wounded Ritchotte lightly. Ritchotte told the driver to move out.[10]

PFC BERT TOMLINSON, LOADER, 4TH PLATOON: PFC Tomlinson was the loader in Sgt. Wells' tank. About 2130 or 2200, fifteen or twenty Chinese came across the fields about 150 yards away. Wells observed them through his glasses, then started firing at them.

Tomlinson was busy loading, and he did not see anything. From the amount of ammunition used, he thought there were a great many Chinese.[11]

PVT. ROBERT B. BROWN, GUNNER, 4TH PLATOON: Pvt. Brown was the gunner of Sgt. Williams' tank, which was on the right flank of the platoon. At 2000, 23 April, Chinese feeling forces came behind the ROKs who were withdrawing through the 4th Platoon position. Sgt. Wells first observed Chinese in a rice paddy and put down fire. Then all the tanks fired.

It was quiet until 2100, when enemy mortar fire began to come in. Then Chinese in about battalion strength started coming. Brown fired his .30 caliber machine gun until 2130, when Lt. DiMartino ordered the tanks out. The tanks withdrew, but not according to plan because Wells and Williams were wounded at this time.[12]

Meanwhile, the rest of the company was on alert, and soon the 1st Platoon came in contact with the enemy. Members of the unit describe what happened.

M. SGT. PAUL W. RAGEN, PLATOON SERGEANT, 1ST PLATOON: The 1st Platoon moved into position about 1800. Sgt. Ragen placed the tanks and made sure that infantry were dug in around the tanks. At 2100 Ragen heard small arms and mortar fire to the north about 600 to 700 yards away in the 4th Platoon sector. None fell in the 1st Platoon area. An hour later the 4th Platoon came down the road. At midnight Ragen noticed two or three columns of troops moving south on the road 300 yards away. He inquired of an Australian who they were. The Australian thought the troops were withdrawing Australians. Ragen continued to observe this movement through his glasses. He thought the troops were ROKs with Chinese mixed in. This force continued south and engaged the 2d Platoon from 0100 to 0400, 24 April.[13]

1ST LT. WILFRED D. MILLER, LEADER, 1ST PLATOON: Lt. Miller had been attending an artillery school in the 2d Infantry Division area, and he joined his platoon at 1800 on 23 April. The tanks were already in position. Miller repositioned the tanks and had the tankers improve the camouflage with natural vegetation and brush.

At 1900 a few ROK vehicles withdrew past the 1st Platoon position. At that time, elements of the 213th Field Artillery Battalion were moving north. An hour later, the artillery elements returned and moved south toward the rear. At 2000, foot troops of the 6th ROK Division moved south past Lt. Miller's tanks. By 2030 the ROK soldiers were "pouring through," running. By 2100 the ROK soldiers started to thin out.

At that time, 2100, the 4th Platoon was struck by enemy elements. Miller received instructions by radio not to fire against ROK troops coming through. One tank commander on the radio channel "swore they were Chinese." Shortly after 2100 the 4th Platoon knocked out the lead elements of enemy forces which had reached its position. About 2300 the enemy struck the 4th Platoon on the front and flanks. Miller alerted his crews. He walked east off the high ground to the road. There, he talked with the executive officer of Company B, RAR Battalion, who thought that the troops coming might still be ROKs. Shortly thereafter, the 4th Platoon tanks came down the road. Miller stopped them. The tankers were excited and nervous. Lt. DiMartino was killed; others were wounded. The tankers said that Chinese forces were coming in great numbers.

Lt. Miller put all the wounded on two tanks and instructed them to go to the rear. He ordered the remaining three tanks to turn around and take positions on the road. He waited for the tanks to turn around and come back. He saw the last tank turn around and assumed that the others were behind. He started to lead them up the road.

Seventy-five to a hundred yards ahead Miller saw two columns of figures, one on each side of the road. He signaled to the tank twenty-five yards behind to stop. He did not know whether the troops were ROKs or Chinese. When the figures were twenty-five yards away, they crouched in the ditches. The executive officer of Company B, RAR Battalion, shouted "Come here," in Korean, and at the same time Miller knew that the troops were Chinese. Miller yelled and hit the dirt on the side of the road. The Chinese threw a grenade and opened fire. Miller crawled and ran back to the tank and ordered it to open fire. The tank turned around and moved down the road. Miller ran across the road, across the valley, to the base of the hill, with Chinese soldiers chasing him. At the base of the hill, the headquarters personnel of Company B, RAR Battalion, opened fire on the Chinese, and Miller reached his tank platoon. A firefight at the base of the hill developed. Miller alerted his tankers and waited.[14]

PVT. ROBERT B. BROWN, 4TH PLATOON: [After the 4th Platoon withdrew from its outpost position] Lt. Miller stopped Brown's tank. Williams got out, and Brown took command of the tank. Miller ordered Brown to turn his tank around. As Brown was turning the tank around, Miller and an Australian walked back up the road. Then the Chinese opened up on Miller. As Brown was turning around, enemy troops came out of a house and threw a grenade. Brown could not see where the enemy was, so he waited there about fifteen minutes, then proceeded down the road south and joined the other tanks of the company. Brown stated that the 4th Platoon was somewhat out of control because of the loss of Lt. DiMartino.[15]

As the enemy continued to flow south into the Australian and American positions, Lt. Koch took charge of the leaderless 4th Platoon.

Hearing the 4th Platoon withdraw, Lt. Koch dismounted from his tank, crossed the river, and stopped the tanks. Koch learned that Lt. DiMartino had been killed and that about four men of the platoon were wounded. He instructed the 4th Platoon to dismount the wounded and dead. He reorganized the platoon with Sgt. Rutherford as platoon leader. At this time enemy small arms, automatic weapons, and mortar fire was being received. One 4th Platoon tank was struck by a bazooka round.

As Koch returned to his tank, Sgt. Rutherford moved his tanks down the road about one mile to evacuate the wounded. Koch radioed his executive officer, who was at the company bivouac area in the vicinity of Chungch'on-ni, and instructed him to meet the 4th Platoon tanks, replace the wounded with standby crews, and send the tanks back. The executive officer met the tanks near Hamajang-ni. He evacuated one inoperative tank to the bivouac area and sent four tanks back under the command of Sgt. Ridings. These tanks returned to the vicinity of the 2d Platoon and secured the right flank about 0300.[16]

Other soldiers describe the events surrounding the 4th Platoon's arrival in the rear.

CPL. WILLIAM O. SUITER JR., MEDIC, COMPANY A: During the afternoon of 23 April Cpl. Suiter drove the litter jeep to Lt. Koch's tank and parked there. At 2330 Suiter heard small arms fire from the north. Koch called and told Suiter there were three wounded men across the river. Suiter drove to the river and met the 4th Platoon withdrawing. He met Sgts. Williams and Wells, who had walked out. Lt. DiMartino had been left on the other side of the bridge because the enemy was nearby. Williams and Wells instructed Suiter to hurry to get DiMartino.

As the tanks of the 4th Platoon came by, Suiter yelled to ask where DiMartino was. No one answered. Suiter crossed the bridge and found DiMartino at the side of the road. The lieutenant had a bullet in his head, but he was still alive. Suiter placed him in the jeep and recrossed the bridge. He overtook Wells and Williams and picked them up. Ritchotte dismounted from his tank to assist Suiter in the litter jeep.

Due to Suiter's lack of knowledge of the English or Australian evacuation system, he could not find an aid station until he got to the Indian 60th Field Ambulance. Suiter had put a bandage on DiMartino's head, but Suiter thought the lieutenant was dead before he reached the hospital. Because the road was congested with ROK vehicles and soldiers, it had taken Suiter an hour to get DiMartino to the aid station.[17]

PFC BERT TOMLINSON, 4TH PLATOON: About 2400 Tomlinson helped Wells, who was wounded, out of the tank and into the medical jeep. Sgt. Somerville, helping also, was hit by a mortar, and he got into the medical jeep, too. Lt. Koch ordered the tank back to the 2d Platoon position, and Sgt. Baylor took over Tomlinson's tank. The tank remained in the 2d Platoon area and fired the remainder of the night.[18]

PFC RITCHOTTE, 4TH PLATOON: As the tanks came down the road, Lt. Miller stopped them and instructed them to turn around.

Ritchotte's tank continued to the bridge. There, some men got Lt. DiMartino out of the tank and put him in a jeep. Ritchotte got into the jeep to help and rode back to the medical aid station. PFC Somerville took over the tank.[19]

Men of Company A describe the enemy attack on their 2d Platoon and the Australian battalion headquarters.

LT. KOCH, COMMANDER, COMPANY A: At 2200 enemy forces struck the 2d Platoon from the northwest. These forces had approached directly from the northwest or had moved down from the north, bypassing the 1st Platoon. Following the ROKs closely, enemy troops infiltrated the 2d Platoon area before the tankers became aware of their presence. . . . The main enemy attack on the 2d Platoon commenced about midnight. An estimated enemy force of 300 infiltrated the area with machine guns and bazookas. These troops overran the RAR Battalion headquarters, engaging the Australians and the tanks in a fierce battle. Knocking out an Australian outpost on high ground to the left and rear of the 2d Platoon, the enemy was able to look down on the tanks. A 3.5 [-inch] bazooka round struck Sgt. Mitchell's tank and killed one man [PFC Alban Chmielewski], wounded two.[20]

About 2400, 23 April, Koch ordered the platoon to fire in all directions, to cover each other and to prevent enemy soldiers from getting on the tanks. During the battle which followed, the tankers did not button up. Sufficient moonlight that night enabled the tankers to see the enemy clearly.[21]

SFC WILLIAM A. GOAD, TANK COMMANDER, 2D PLATOON: At 1300, 23 April, the company was sent up as a blocking force and reserve for the Australians. The 2d Platoon moved into position on the river. The 1st Platoon was on a hill, 1,000 yards to the front. Sgt. Goad could not see the 4th Platoon. About 2300 convoys started moving south through the company positions. Then the 6th ROK Division came on the run and in mass formation. These troops cleared the 2d Platoon about 2345, and Chinese were mixed in with them. Goad estimated that 300 to 400 enemy troops and several bazooka teams bypassed the 1st Platoon and infiltrated the 2d Platoon perimeter.

Lt. Koch, Sgt. McClellan, Sgt. Mitchell, and Sgt. Puckett were guarding the left flank and front. Goad was on the right flank and front. The group on the left opened fire. They fired for two hours before the Chinese got to Goad's position about 0200. Then Goad saw three bazooka teams across the river in addition to those inside the perimeter. He opened up with his .30 and .50 caliber machine guns. A group of about 150 enemy troops started to move past his tank. Only about 50 got through. Sometime earlier, the 4th Platoon had fallen back through Goad's position.[22]

SGT. JERARDO RODRIGUEZ, TANK GUNNER, 2D PLATOON: Sgt. Rodriguez was the gunner of Sgt. Puckett's tank. His tank pulled into position between 1900 and 2000, 23 April, and faced northwest, covering the left flank. Between 2300 and 0100, 24 April, Rodriguez heard the enemy attack. Small arms and mortar fire was being received. But nothing came in on Rodriguez's tank. At 0100 Rodriguez saw Chinese all over the perimeter. Rodriguez fired his .30 caliber machine gun at a range from 10 to 75 yards. His loader fired his "grease gun" [nickname for the U.S. M3 machine pistol, .45 caliber]. Rodriguez fired from 0100 to 0300 and again from 0500 to 0700. He expended six boxes (250 rounds per box) of .30 caliber ammunition.[23]

SGT. MANFORD WAYSON JR., TANK GUNNER, 2D PLATOON: [Wayson was then the gunner for the platoon sergeant, 2d Platoon.] Sgt. Wayson's tank moved into position about 1900 or 2000, 23 April, and formed a perimeter with the others. At 2400 the platoon was attacked by approximately 350 Chinese troops who had infiltrated into the perimeter. Wayson estimated about 150 to 200 were killed. The tank on the right of Wayson was hit by a bazooka round. One man was killed, and one was wounded. The wounded man was brought to Wayson's tank and placed in the turret. Therefore, Wayson could not fire his cannon.[24]

PFC WILBERT A. NAASZ, 2D PLATOON: PFC Naasz was the assistant driver and bow gunner of Sgt. Mitchell's tank. From 2300 to 2400, 23 April, Naasz was on guard duty. As he was relieved, enemy small arms fire came in on the platoon. About 0030 Naasz's tank was hit by a bazooka round on the right rear. Sgt. Mitchell and Sgt. Wilson were wounded; PFC [Alban] Chmielewski was killed. After

Naasz and Sgt. Diemond, the driver, gave first aid to the wounded, they began firing machine guns at a range of fifty to one hundred yards against the enemy. They continued firing until daylight.[25]

Cpl. Frederick B. Fowler, 2d Platoon: At 1700, 23 April, Fowler's tank pulled into position on the right flank of the platoon, facing the river. An Australian set up a Bren gun not far to the right of the tank. Between 2330 and 2400 that night Fowler saw ROK troops crossing the bridge about 150 yards to the left front. Between 0030 and 0100 Lt. Koch stopped the 4th Platoon tanks and instructed them to get back to their positions.

About 0200 the Chinese started coming toward the tank from the left flank. A few enemy mortar rounds came in. A bazooka round fell nearby. Then Chinese were observed coming from the left front. At that time, about 0200, the tank fired on the enemy. There was a pause for a short while just before 0430, when the Chinese were observed heading for the hills. Again, the tank fired as the Chinese withdrew to the north. Fowler fired between three to five boxes of machine gun ammunition at a range varying from 15 feet to 300 yards. Firing against the hill, Fowler had to be careful not to fire too high because the Australians were in position there. Fowler fired until about 0600.[26]

While the 2d Platoon and Lt. Koch fought off the enemy, to the north the 1st Platoon listened and watched. Between 0300 and 0400 hours there was a pause in the fighting as the enemy regrouped. Soon after, the attacks resumed, this time against both the 1st and 2d Platoons, as well as the Australians. Members of the 1st Platoon describe the action.

Lt. Miller, leader, 1st Platoon: About 0300 [24 April] Lt. Miller heard bugles, whistles, and yelling. Across the valley the enemy attacked Company A, RAR. At the same time about ten rounds of enemy mortar fire fell in the valley. The enemy attack continued until about 0430. Between 0430 and 0500 enemy troops assaulted Miller's hill. An enemy white phosphorous grenade fell on the southern knob of the hill. There was a short pause. Then Miller distinguished two squads of Chinese twenty-five yards from the knob. These squads assaulted, took the hill. The Australian outpost squad withdrew. Then, as Miller laid down a base of fire with his .50 caliber machine gun, about ten Australians retook the hill.

About 0500 large numbers of enemy forces were seen "flushing down the valley." All the tanks of the 1st Platoon opened fire. The machine guns fired east and southeast into the valley; three tanks fired their cannons to the northwest. This fire continued from 0500 to 0800. When Chinese withdrew toward the north at 0700, the tanks "mowed them down." Between 0800 and 0830 the battle ceased.[27]

SFC Rudolph Triscik, tank commander, 1st Platoon: The tankers, alerted to working with the Australians, knew that the 6th ROK Division was withdrawing. The 1st Platoon placed its tanks in positions with the Australians dug in around the tanks. From those positions, the tankers heard the ROKs moving south on the road fifty yards away. At 2200 small arms and mortar fire was heard from the direction of the 4th Platoon. Firing continued all around the 1st Platoon until about 0430, when the 1st Platoon was attacked. At first the infantry outpost was attacked; then the tankers were able to see Chinese soldiers on the skyline, infiltrating the tank-infantry perimeter. At daylight the tankers could see Chinese troops all around the 1st Platoon positions.

SFC Triscik felt that the presence of the 1st Platoon tanks in that position was a complete surprise to the Chinese, who saw them for the first time at daybreak. The enemy troops then started to get out. Tank gun flashes could have been mistaken by the enemy for 75mm artillery. Shortly after daybreak the Australians flushed out thirty to forty prisoners.[28]

M. Sgt. Ragen, platoon sergeant, 1st Platoon: At 0430 the 1st Platoon was hit by small arms fire from an estimated company-strength force. From that time until 0700 the 1st Platoon engaged the enemy at pointblank range with machine gun and cannon. The platoon quit firing when they could no longer see any enemy. At this time the Australians took about thirty prisoners of war.[29]

PFC Louis Berg, 1st Platoon: On 23 April PFC Berg, the platoon leader's jeep driver, was digging a foxhole near a 1st Platoon tank when Lt. Miller arrived. About 2330 Berg heard firing from the front. Then the noise quieted down, so Berg went to bed. About

0100, when the firing started in the same place, Berg got up and stood guard for Miller's tank. About 0400 hours Berg was in Miller's tank handing up ammunition and fired the coaxial gun. Every once in a while he stuck his head out to observe; each time he did so he saw several Chinese. At daylight, the Chinese started moving back to the hills. Some surrendered.[30]

Attacks were renewed against the 2d Platoon, which had been joined by tanks of the 4th Platoon. Lt. Koch, commander, Company A, explains what then happened.

When the 4th Platoon returned Lt. Koch placed three tanks on the right flank and one tank in the draw. To give these orders it was necessary for Koch to dismount under enemy fire and instruct the tankers by voice. At 0400 a litter jeep gathered a load of wounded and started toward the rear. The enemy, however, had set up a roadblock behind the tank position. Koch ordered Sgt. Rutherford to take two 4th Platoon tanks and eliminate the roadblock. This was done, but Rutherford was wounded, and the turret of the other tank jammed. So Rutherford took both tanks and the litter jeep back to the company bivouac area. The tanks in Koch's immediate area fought until after daylight. At least three enemy bazooka teams were knocked out. Several enemy machine guns were destroyed. Koch estimated that the 2d Platoon killed between 100 and 150 enemy troops.[31]

The IX Corps staff officer who oversaw armored operations, Lt. Col. George B. Pickett, later investigated and prepared a written report of this action. Pickett summarizes the fighting the night of 23–24 April.

The first CCF patrol hit and was destroyed by the 4th Platoon at its blocking positions at 232100 [date and time]. At about 232300 large numbers of CCF heavily attacked the friendly positions. One force struck directly at the 4th Platoon positions. The platoon leader, Lt. [Di]Martino, was mortally wounded. He died almost immediately but not before issuing the order to his platoon to make a fighting withdrawal to previously prepared alternate positions with the 2d Platoon. Three other tank commanders were also seriously wounded in the attack that enveloped the 4th Platoon. However, the platoon was able to withdraw to the positions designated by the platoon leader.

Concurrently with the attack on the 4th Platoon other elements of the advancing CCF circled around the hill mass on the west of the road. These CCF bypassed the 1st Platoon, which could not locate the enemy below because of the lack of any kind of natural or artificial light. This attacking force swept around the hill mass and swung again to the east to strike at the 2d Platoon positions, which he soon surrounded and infiltrated. The enemy then swept on to destroy the RAR Battalion CP that was located well to the rear of the 2d Platoon position.

However, under orders from the company commander the tanks remained in position. During the initial stages of this fight at the 2d Platoon position, tanks from the withdrawing 4th Platoon appeared on the scene, moving south from their former outpost position. The company commander dismounted from his tank, moved under extremely heavy enemy fire to reach the leading tank of the 4th Platoon, and determined the status of the personnel of the 4th Platoon. Upon learning of the heavy casualties in the platoon, he ordered all the wounded and dead, which included four of the five tank commanders, loaded on three of the tanks and ordered the tanks to run the enemy force and return the wounded to the company trains area for treatment. He also instructed the ranking NCO to obtain replacement crews from the company headquarters personnel and return immediately to the scene of the battle.

The company commander placed the remaining two tanks of the 4th Platoon into position with the 2d Platoon, and then, still under heavy enemy fire, returned to his command tank, and continued to direct the action of his company. At one time the enemy succeeded in setting up a machine gun emplacement between the command tank and that of the 2d Platoon leader. This gun was reduced by tank fire. The Chinese attempted to mount the tanks and destroy them with grenades and satchel charges but were destroyed by fire from the tanks. One tank received a direct hit with a 3.5 rocket launcher that killed the loader and mortally wounded the tank commander. However, the position of the tanks was so encircled by this time that it was impossible to evacuate either of these two men or any of the less seriously wounded. The fighting continued with unabated fury until daylight.

At dawn the CCF began to withdraw. As they attempted to pull back along the west of the hill mass around which they had attacked the night before, the 1st Platoon opened fire. This placed the enemy in a crossfire from sixteen tanks, for, by this time, the three tanks of the 4th Platoon had returned to the 2d Platoon positions after fighting back up the entire length of the route. This crossfire into the withdrawing enemy continued until all targets were either destroyed or dispersed. It was later determined that more than 500 enemy were killed in this action.[32]

The fighting the night of 23–24 April encompassed not only American tankers and Australians in the front, but also other UN units, as the enemy pushed into the rear areas. UN soldiers describe the confused fighting and the rapid evacuation of exposed positions.

LT. ARGENT, INTELLIGENCE OFFICER, 3D BATTALION, RAR: Until 0530, 24 April, the battalion fought to keep the Chinese from overrunning the companies and the battalion headquarters. By 0600 the Chinese had surrounded the battalion. At that time the platoon of tanks in the vicinity of the battalion headquarters moved the headquarters to the Middlesex area [near Noru-kogae]. Although the Chinese had established several roadblocks in the rear of the RAR positions, the tanks were able to evacuate the headquarters. Chinese forces had gotten as far as Tungmudae, and from this point succeeded in wounding several members of the Middlesex Regiment. At 0430 a company of the 1st Battalion, the Middlesex Regiment, was sent forward to reinforce the Australians. This company, encountering large numbers of Chinese, joined Company B, 2d Chemical Mortar Battalion, which was withdrawing. Both companies moved east ten miles to Ch'unch'on.[33]

MAJ. WADE H. PADGETT, S-3, 74TH ENGINEER COMBAT BATTALION: Company B and Company C (minus the 1st Platoon), 74th Engineer Combat Battalion, were located forward of the Middlesex Battalion positions. Company B was in support of the British. Company C was building a road from the British area to the 1st Marine

Division area in the vicinity of the 38th parallel. These companies came out with some equipment on 23 [early 24] April and went to the vicinity of Kap'yong.[34]

SGT. HAROLD BURROS, COMPANY B, 74TH ENGINEER COMBAT BATTALION: Sgt. Burros was sergeant of the guard from midnight, 23 April. There were four posts, two men on each post, each post with one .50 caliber machine gun. At daylight, Burros noticed about 300 British and ROK soldiers pulling back. He alerted the guards. When SFC Robinson gave orders to move out of the area, Burros pulled back the security. All men on guard came out with their weapons. The men mounted on trucks and moved out of the area. It was necessary to wait for space on the road because of all the British vehicles traveling south. All the company vehicles were driven out except one which would not start.[35]

SGT. JOHN L. MAZYCK, COMPANY B, 74TH ENGINEER COMBAT BATTALION: Sgt. Mazyck, a cook, had breakfast on the stove about 0530, 24 April. He was somewhat nervous by the sound of firing which sounded very close. The mess sergeant then instructed the mess personnel to load up because the enemy was "just over the hill." Mazyck looked out and saw the British Brigade backing up, coming back down the road and across the fields, firing as they went. Mazyck ran across the river and up a hill to the road. He got on a jeep and rode about a mile to an area behind the brigade.[36]

CPL. OTHO C. BRAGG, COMPANY B, 74TH ENGINEER COMBAT BATTALION: Cpl. Bragg was on guard duty from 0400 to 0800, 24 April. He could see a firefight taking place and hear the firing. At daylight Chinese troops were coming toward the company position, across the field from the river. Bragg was armed with an M1 rifle and grenades. Together with Pvt. Jordan, he manned a .50 caliber machine gun. Warrant Officer Hanna ordered the company to withdraw. Bragg tried to get his machine gun out of the hole but could not. Lt. Crosby ordered him to leave his machine gun. The Chinese were coming too fast. Bragg departed on foot.[37]

CPL. MASON F. SCOTT, COMPANY B, 74TH ENGINEER COMBAT BATTALION: At 2400 everyone in the company was alerted. Artillery and small arms fire in the distance was heard. The fire seemed to come closer and closer. Scott saw trucks going down the road, and ROK soldiers running. He thought everything would be quiet at daybreak. About 0400 Scott was preparing breakfast for the company. At 0500 the mess sergeant told the men there would be no breakfast that morning. Everything was to be broken down and evacuated. Scott cut off the stoves, helped strike the tent. Then he went after his duffle bag. He saw everyone leaving. Men were yelling, "Never mind the stuff; take off." So Scott dropped his bag, got his rifle and some ammunition, and started running across the fields to the river. When he reached the road, he got on a company truck.[38]

PFC ARTHUR LEE GAYLES, COMPANY B, 74TH ENGINEER COMBAT BATTALION: As it was getting light, Gayles got up and saw that the company was already taking down tents in the motor pool area. A mechanic told Gayles that the company had to move out in a rush. Gayles got dressed and got into his truck. He heard firing and saw some flares about one to three miles away. The lieutenant, platoon leader, 3d Platoon, instructed everyone to get out in a hurry. So Gayles drove his vehicle in a column of seven to ten company trucks out to the road and south several miles. He picked up several men of Company C who were coming across the riverbed on foot. British, American, and ROK soldiers were on the road on foot and in vehicles. Many vehicles were wrecked in the ditches.[39]

At dawn the CCF faded back into the hills to seek cover from expected UN air and artillery attacks. Lt. Koch and his men began the process of reorganizing so that they would be prepared for a renewed enemy assault when darkness returned. They quickly became involved in helping the Australians and other American units recover from the night's fighting. Koch, his tankers, and engineers from the 74th Engineer Combat Battalion described the events of the day.

LT. KOCH, COMMANDER, COMPANY A: About 0830 the RAR Battalion ordered Koch to evacuate Australian wounded and vehicles to the rear. Koch instructed Lt. Miller, the 1st Platoon leader, to move south through the 2d Platoon. The 2d Platoon then moved out, followed by the two 4th Platoon tanks. Koch and one tank of the 2d Platoon trailed the column. Australian vehicles interspersed among the tanks were evacuated.

As the column moved toward the rear, Koch noticed approximately 35 jeeps and ¾-ton vehicles and trailers abandoned by Company B, 2d Chemical Mortar Battalion. He also noticed a camp site with water point abandoned by a company of the 74th Engineer Combat Battalion.

At the company bivouac area, the tankers dismounted their wounded, refueled, and took on a resupply of ammunition. Orders were then received from the British 27th Commonwealth Brigade for the company to return to the RAR area in order to evacuate Australian wounded and in order to cover the RAR withdrawal. The 4th Platoon, reorganized into a four-tank platoon, and the 1st Platoon, loaded with ammunition and litters, proceeded to return. The platoons moved to the Middlesex Battalion area in the vicinity of Norukogae. There Koch instructed Miller to take his 1st Platoon to the RAR area in order to carry forward the RAR battalion commander and ammunition and evacuate the wounded. Koch organized thirty-five drivers of the 74th Engineer Combat Battalion, carried them to the abandoned vehicles of the company of the 2d Chemical Mortar Battalion, and covered them as they drove out the vehicles under the supervision of Maj. Briggs, the commanding officer of the 2d Chemical Mortar Battalion. The 4th Platoon then screened while the engineer personnel retrieved their own equipment.

The 1st Platoon brought out a number of wounded, about 1,500. At 1530 the 1st and 4th Platoons moved back to cover the RAR withdrawal. As the tanks on the road covered the high ground to the northwest, the Australians withdrew along the ridgeline on the right from their original positions. When the Australians cleared the ford, the tanks moved south and screened until 2100. The tanks moved again to Tungmudae. There, bugles were heard. Koch expected a night attack. But the tanks waited until the Australians closed in the rear of the Middlesex area. The tanks then moved to the company bivouac.[40]

CPL. SUITER, MEDIC, COMPANY A: Suiter returned to the tanks just before daylight. He pulled in beside Sgt. Baylor's tank, 4th Platoon, and found Sgt. Green, the other company aid man. Suiter and Green waited for the firing to cease so they could pick up the 2d Platoon casualties. Shortly after dawn, Suiter bandaged a wounded

Australian and put another Australian on a litter. He started to take these two casualties back, but the enemy had set up a roadblock to the rear. Sgt. Rutherford and Sgt. Ridinger in two tanks knocked out the roadblock. Rutherford was wounded, and Suiter took him into his jeep. Ridinger then led the litter jeep to the rear. About eleven Australian jeeps followed. Enemy fire came from a house on the way down. Ridinger put fire on the house, and three enemy soldiers ran out. Green and Suiter fired at them with carbines. Suiter noticed abandoned vehicles along the route. Ten or fifteen were on the road, some Australian, some belonging to the 2d Chemical Mortar Battalion, and some to the engineers.

Suiter brought his patients to brigade headquarters, where the aid station was located. This station had only one litter jeep, which had departed to the rear. After leaving the Australian wounded at the aid station, Suiter drove to the Indian hospital and informed them that there were casualties at the aid station to be evacuated. Suiter returned to the company to find the tanks withdrawing. The 2d Platoon casualties had already been evacuated by Indian litter jeeps. Suiter remained at the company rear area while the tanks carried out the wounded Australians and evacuated the abandoned vehicles.[41]

SGT. BURROS, COMPANY B, 74TH ENGINEER COMBAT BATTALION: Sometime later in the morning, the platoon sergeant, 2d Platoon, asked for volunteers to retrieve abandoned vehicles. The volunteers waited for the tank column. A major of the 2d Chemical Mortar Battalion (Maj. Briggs) took charge of the drivers. Burros drove out a jeep; there were thirty-some. Then the engineers returned to their company area and retrieved tent poles, duffle bags, stoves, and one truck. The covering tanks fired against the empty houses along the road.[42]

PFC JOHNNIE L. LEWIS, COMPANY B, 74TH ENGINEER COMBAT BATTALION: When Lt. Esparza asked for volunteers to drive out some thirty jeeps belonging to the mortar company, just about everyone who could drive volunteered to go. The men loaded on trucks and tanks and were taken to the mortar company. The jeeps were driven out. Later that morning the volunteers returned to their own company area and retrieved one truck, several tents, orderly room equipment, and some mess equipment.[43]

LT. MILLER, LEADER, 1ST PLATOON: When orders were received for Company B, RAR, to move east across the valley to the Company A, RAR, positions, Lt. Miller's platoon covered the company on its movement. Then the RAR Battalion commander ordered Miller to escort the Australian vehicles to the rear area. This was done. The tank company then returned to the Middlesex Battalion area between 0930 and 1000 and continued to the company bivouac area for gas and ammunition.

Instructed to report to the RAR Battalion commander at the Middlesex Battalion area, Miller picked up ammunition and stretchers, an Australian doctor, and Colonel Ferguson, the RAR Battalion commander. He received the mission of returning to his original position. There, he was to deliver ammunition to the Australians and evacuate wounded. Drawing some enemy small arms fire as it proceeded north on the road, the 1st Platoon returned to the vicinity of Company A, RAR. Miller drove the tanks to the right of the road and to the base of the hill.

Since there were many wounded to evacuate, Miller asked for volunteers to hold stretchers on the rear deck of the tanks. Three tankers and one Australian soldier volunteered. The seriously wounded were placed inside the tanks. The Australian on the back deck was wounded on the trip out. After delivering the wounded (about fifteen) to the Middlesex Battalion aid station, the 1st Platoon made a second trip, picked up more wounded, and delivered them to the aid station.

On the third trip, Miller placed two tanks on the high ground to the left of the road and three tanks at the base of the hill to cover the withdrawal of the Australians. Miller's loader was wounded by a sniper bullet at this time. A tank commander was struck by a friendly artillery shell fragment.

When the Australians had cleared, Lt. Koch ordered Miller to withdraw to a second position to the south, and there the platoons covered the second phase of the RAR withdrawal until after dark. The company then returned to its company area.

Miller stated that if infantry remained with the tanks, friendly forces could be overrun, surrounded, attacked without having to give way. He felt that because his tanks were camouflaged, the Chinese were not aware of the presence of his tanks until they attacked.

Miller noticed a great many vehicles, equipment, and tents abandoned by the 2d Chemical Mortar Battalion, the 74th Engineer Combat Battalion, and Australian units along the valley. He counted twenty-five jeeps with trailers. At first he thought that these items were ready to be evacuated; not until later did he realize that the equipment had been abandoned.[44]

SFC MYLES P. MOORE, TANK COMMANDER, 1ST PLATOON: About 0700 the platoon received orders to move to the rear. Australian vehicles were evacuated with the tanks. After this movement was made, Lt. Miller, Moore, and two additional tanks returned to the Australians and evacuated Australian wounded. Moore had three wounded men on the outside of his tank. The casualties were picked up between 1000 and 1030 and brought to the British aid station. Moore then returned for more wounded Australians, but found that all had been evacuated. As Moore's tank moved south, he fired two rounds of 76mm against a squad of Chinese who were dug in along the road and were harassing the Australians. Moore eliminated this group about 1130. He then drove to the company bivouac area. Later that afternoon he helped cover the Australian withdrawal. Moore noticed some abandoned vehicles along the road.[45]

SFC TRISCIK, TANK COMMANDER, 1ST PLATOON: The 1st Platoon then covered Company B, RAR Battalion, as it crossed the road and joined Companies A and C about 0800. The 1st Platoon then joined the 2d Platoon, and the tanks moved south to the company bivouac area for gasoline, ammunition, and food. The tanks then returned to their original positions. This time the 1st Platoon took up positions in the riverbed. Australian wounded were carried in the tanks, about four inside, five outside, and brought to the British aid station. Triscik then returned to the company bivouac area about 1600. Triscik saw between thirty and forty wheeled vehicles, including jeeps and engineer and Australian trucks, abandoned about fifty feet southwest of Sokchang-ni.[46]

M. Sgt. Ragen, platoon sergeant, 1st Platoon: Lt. Miller and M. Sgt. Ragen were called to the Australian CP and ordered to evacuate the area. The Australians wanted their vehicles to get into the tank column and be evacuated. With about six Australian jeeps interspersed in the tank column, the platoon proceeded to the rear, met Lt. Koch, and then returned to the company rear area. After refueling, eating, and getting a resupply of ammunition, the tankers went back to the Middlesex area, picked up an Australian doctor, and moved to the original positions to pick up Australian wounded. The tanks also delivered ammunition and radio equipment to the Australians. Three tanks carried litters on the tank deck; one tank carried walking wounded. The tanks brought the wounded to the Indian hospital. A second trip was made for the wounded. Then, while the tanks screened, the Australians withdrew. Artillery smoke also helped cover the withdrawal. No enemy was seen, but some small arms and mortar fire was received. At 1800 the tanks moved two miles south and covered again until 2200, when Lt. Koch instructed the tanks to return to the company rear area.[47]

1st Sgt. Maxwell B. Bowman, first sergeant, Company A: Of the 142 enlisted men authorized personnel, 134 were present for duty on 23 April 1951. Twenty-two men and one officer of the 3d Platoon were at headquarters, IX Corps. Seventy-five officers and men were present at the scene of the engagement. Casualties totaled ten WIA, two KIA [2d Lt. Peter DeMartino and Pvt. Alban Chmielewski], and one non-battle casualty. A member of the medical detachment, 72d Tank Battalion, was missing in action. [Pvt. Paul Albaugh was later reported as killed in action, 24 April 1951.][48]

Four tanks were struck by 3.5 bazooka rounds. One of these four had to be returned to company maintenance because it had received a rocket down through the turret.

Ammunition expended 23 and 24 April was as follows: 162 rounds, 76mm high explosive; 32,000 rounds, .30 caliber machine gun; 11,830 rounds, .50 caliber machine gun; 1,600 rounds, .30 caliber carbine; 350 rounds, .45 caliber pistol.[49]

Following the action, Lt. Koch summarized his thoughts about what had happened for Lt. Blumenson.

Lt. Koch listed the following lessons learned: (1) Deception must be practiced. Tanks must be placed where they are not expected. Camouflage must be employed. The 1st Platoon was in an unorthodox position, on high ground rather than in lowlands, where tanks are usually placed. The enemy had no bazooka teams on the ridges and high ground, where the 1st Platoon was in position. (2) If overrun at night it is better to stay in position and fight than run. Friendly elements must hold at least until daylight. During daylight hours friendly forces have the advantage.

Koch stated that the tankers and the infantrymen fought with extreme bravery. There was never any thought of abandoning the positions. Koch had high praise for the Australian infantrymen who remained in their holes and supported the tanks wherever they could. The success of this action, Koch felt, was due mainly to the mutual confidence the tankers and the infantrymen had in each other. Company A, 72d Tank Battalion, suffered two KIA, one MIA, and eleven WIA. The RAR Battalion suffered approximately 26 KIA and 72 WIA. All wounded and equipment were successfully evacuated.

Koch stated that in his opinion the RAR Battalion would have been overrun and destroyed if the tanks had not been in support.[50]

The IX Corps staff officer, Lt. Col. Pickett, provides a more detailed evaluation of the action.

During the Cheryong-ni–Kap'yong actions on 23–24 April 1951, Company A, 72d Tank Battalion (minus 3d Platoon), killed more than 800 CCF, recovered approximately 50 abandoned UN vehicles, and covered the withdrawal of the surrounded RAR Battalion. No tanks were lost during this period although two received AT [antitank] rocket hits. Personnel casualties were three KIA, eight seriously WIA, and four lightly WIA. The company (minus 3d Platoon) entered the action with 15 operational tanks and finished the action with 13 operational tanks.

Prior to the movement of the tank company from its corps reserve position at Hongch'on to Kap'yong, the company commander made an aerial reconnaissance of the entire sector of anticipated employment. Lt. DiMartino and the IX Corps armor officer made a detailed tactical terrain and trafficability reconnaissance of the area on 16 April 1951. The company commander and IX Corps headquarters were provided with marked maps showing assembly areas, objectives, firing positions, routes, and tank capacities of the valley areas. Prior to the enemy attack, the tank company commander had further reconnaissance conducted by small unit leaders.

During the close-in fighting, it was mandatory that commanders' hatches be kept open in order for the tank commander to have better vision of enemy tank hunters. It was also evident that a tank commander with an open hatch is better able to locate enemy tank hunters during daylight than buttoned up. For this reason, tank losses to enemy tank hunters were negligible. Tanks were employed in close support of the RAR battle position, utilizing tank gun and machine gun fire.

The initial action of the 4th Platoon was that of a combat outpost. Ordinarily tanks on combat outpost are employed to support infantry, but in this engagement the tanks alone were a combat outpost.

Mutual confidence between tanks and infantry is essential in any combined arms action. The teamwork between the tank company and the RAR Battalion was outstanding. As the operations progressed, the RAR platoons looked for "their" tank by the large red numbers on the turret. The individual infantryman was not satisfied with just any tanks but wanted his crew. The resolute defense by the RAR and Middlesex Battalion contributed materially to the effectiveness of the tank action by providing a firm base from which tank attacks could sally and behind which they could withdraw to resupply.

A tank is not a weapon capable of continuous action but must have a protected area in which it can be maintained and serviced when refueling and resupply of ammunition are necessary.

The terrain of the Kap'yong valley system was ideally suited for counterattacks by small tank units to include a company. The prior reconnaissance, terrain estimate, and trafficability study materially contributed to the success of each counterattack since the platoon leaders were familiar with the routes, objectives, and possible enemy concentration areas. This prior information enabled the tanks to advance rapidly to known areas and to avoid adverse terrain and areas of poor trafficability.

The effectiveness of tanks against infantry in the open was demonstrated. The relative ineffectiveness of the rocket launcher in open terrain against a coordinated tank effort was apparent. Although two tanks were hit by rockets and casualties sustained, the rocket launchers available to the enemy were ineffective in protecting his personnel and preventing him from suffering staggering losses. This action clearly indicates that the rocket launcher is merely a supplemental antitank weapon and cannot be regarded as the primary weapon of an antitank defensive system. One enemy tank would have been able to inflict much greater losses on the friendly tanks than all of his rocket launcher teams were able to accomplish.

There is no substitute in battle for good leadership. Much of the success of this operation is directly attributable to the aggressive determination and outstanding leadership of the company commander and his platoon leaders.

Lessons learned: (1) Tanks should normally be included in the combat outpost when terrain permits. They may serve as the entire combat outpost; however, they must be screened by dismounted personnel at night. (2) Fewer tanks are lost to tank hunter teams when tank commanders fight with their hatches open than when buttoned up. This does not apply to the driver. (3) A tank commander is more effective when he fights his crew than when he spends a large part of the action firing the turret mounted caliber .50 machine gun. The .50 caliber turret gun is advantageous when tanks are giving overhead fire support to advancing infantry, not in primarily tank actions. (4) Tank unit leaders command by means of their radio net and movement of their tank. A dismounted tank platoon leader is relatively ineffective in attempting to run over the battlefield to direct his tanks. (5) Mutual confidence between tanks and infantry is essential to success. (6) Tanks employed on the MLR are very effective against enemy personnel in the open. (7) Rocket launchers are relatively ineffective against properly supported tank attacks in open terrain. They are effective against tanks operating in close terrain, defiles, woods, and built-up areas. When operating in such areas, tanks should be adequately supported by infantry. (8)

The CCF attack principally at night. In the early light of morning nautical twilight, those CCF forces in the rear areas during this operation apparently were still in their attack formations or assembly areas. Counterattacks during this period have greater possibility of achieving surprise.[51]

The significance of the successful defense of the Kap'yong by the 27th British Commonwealth Brigade and Company A, 72d Tank Battalion, is explained by a IX Corps staff officer, Maj. Thomas A. Murphy, the assistant G-3.

In this action the RAR was engaged on all flanks. Although the British made no estimate of enemy strength, corps felt, from the tactics employed by the enemy and his number of killed, that the enemy force directed at that point numbered a reinforced regiment.

The stand made by the RAR Battalion and Company A, 72d Tank Battalion, prevented a complete enemy breakthrough in the corps zone. The enemy threatened the I Corps flank, necessitating withdrawal of certain I Corps elements. But the stand made above Kap'yong prevented the enemy from getting on the vital Kap'yong–Seoul road. Had he succeeded in doing so, the enemy might have pinched off I Corps by sweeping into Seoul.

Enemy pressure exerted against Kap'yong was greater than against any other point in the corps sector, although greater enemy pressure was exerted on the Uijongbu Corridor.[52]

For their extraordinary leadership and heroism in action during the critical fighting above Kap'yong, Lts. Kenneth W. Koch and Wilfred D. Miller each received a Distinguished Service Cross (DSC) in addition to other awards. The 1st Battalion, Royal Australian Regiment, 2d Battalion, Princess Patricia's Canadian Light Infantry Regiment, and Company A, 72d Tank Battalion, 2d Infantry Division, received an Army Presidential Unit Citation in recognition of their sacrifices and contributions to blunting the Chinese Communist offensive on this sector of the front.[53]

Chapter 5

ARTILLERY IN PERIMETER DEFENSE

92d Armored Field Artillery Battalion, 22–24 April 1951

The Chinese attack that collapsed the ROK 6th Division exposed the flank of the U.S. 1st Marine Division. Several artillery units had moved forward to support the South Koreans and were caught in the enemy onslaught. The battalion commander of the 92d Armored Field Artillery Battalion, Lt. Col. Leon F. Lavoie, describes the situation in his interview with the combat historian 1st Lieutenant Martin Blumenson.[1]

On 20 April 1951 the 213th Armored Field Artillery Battalion and the 2d Rocket Field Artillery Battery were attached to the 92d Armored Field Artillery Battalion north of Kap'yong. These units moved to positions north of Ch'unch'on and deployed on the east–west road along the unnamed tributary of the Pukhan River.

During the period 20–22 April, the Chinese attacked. Enemy forces partially overran the 987th [Armored] Field Artillery Battalion [105mm howitzers, self-propelled], which lost some of its equipment. Enemy troops completely overran the 2d Rocket Field Artillery Battery, which lost all of its equipment.[2] The 92d Armored Field Artillery Battalion remained in position through 23 April, when Brig. Gen. William N. Gillmore, the commanding general of the IX Corps Artillery, ordered the 92d to displace south to the Chich'on-ni area. It was known that the ROK 6th Division had disintegrated and that a serious enemy penetration of friendly lines had been made.[3]

Capt. Wayne D. Hopkins, battery commander, 2d Rocket Field Artillery Battery, which was equipped with 105mm howitzers as

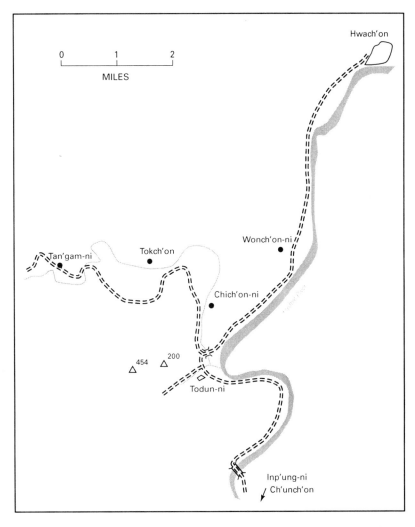

Area of operations, 92d Armored Field Artillery Battalion, 22–24 April 1951. (Original map by author, based on map in Army Map Service series L751.)

well as 4.5-inch rocket launchers, provided additional information about the artillery unit's losses.

On the 22d of April in the morning, we moved up to position [about six miles northwest of Tan'gam-ni]. The 2d Rocket Battery arrived there about 1200 hours and went into position and started firing at about 1300 hours. Large groups of enemy were sighted about 8,000 yards to the front by air OP and taken under fire. We fired continuously until practically all ammo in the battery was expended, except for about 200 rounds. About 1730 hours one of my forward observers was attacked by two platoons of CCF 3,000 yards behind the front lines. The enemy had infiltrated around the right flank of the 2d ROK Regiment, succeeding in disrupting their communications and allowing the enemy to make a penetration in the center of the 6th ROK [Division] sector. A battery of the 27th ROK FA Bn [field artillery battalion] was overrun shortly thereafter, this battery being in position 2,000 yards forward from my own position. A company of the 2d Chemical Mortar Battalion [Company C] was also overrun, and personnel from these two units began to come back through my position on foot. About 2030 hours I gave close station march order and decided to displace to the rear about 3,000 yards to a place roughly in the vicinity of the 987th AFA [Armored Field Artillery] Bn. Just prior to pulling out from our position . . . the enemy was in close proximity, about 600 to 1,000 yards away, and firing small arms and machine guns. Upon displacing to the rear and reaching the position of the 987th AFA Bn, I found that they had closed station, march ordered, and pulled out. I decided to move on and displace to the rear to the vicinity of the 92d AFA Bn. Upon proceeding down the road about one mile farther, I found the road blocked by vehicles of the 987th AFA Bn. The road had caved in, blocking the exit of all vehicles behind it. Higher headquarters (92d AFA) was notified of the situation. I sent about twenty men from my battery to help repair the road and help the 987th get their vehicles out. The effort was unsuccessful.

I pulled my battery off the road into a small clearing about 75 × 75 yards in size. I had four of our howitzers laid on azimuth 5600 for acceptance of fire missions. Two howitzers of the 27th ROK FA Bn that succeeded in getting out were laid for direct fire. About 2330 hours firefights ensued, and the enemy withdrew. About an hour later I was informed by one of my officers that all personnel of the 2d ROK Regiment and the 987th AFA Bn had left. Until approximately 0230 hours on 23 April there were about three more firefights. The battery was still intact at the time. The action at 0230 hours resulted in a penetration of the forward edge of our position. Two enemy succeeded in getting through, reaching the center of the position yelling and throwing hand grenades. They were immediately killed. Up to this time about 400 to 500 enemy had been observed firing from the ridges on the right and on the left. They could be clearly seen in the moonlight. At about 0230 hours I asked for permission to destroy my equipment and withdraw. It was denied by the commanding officer of the 92d AFA Bn, and I was told that absolutely nothing should be destroyed, that we were to try to hold the position, that help was on the way, and should be there by daylight. I "rogered" for the message. We had several more firefights in the next hour or so, the enemy working its way up to within fifteen feet of us on the left flank and throwing hand grenades at us. Point-blank fire by the men with carbines and grease guns discouraged the attempt to penetrate the position on the left flank. At 0500 hours the enemy attacked from all sides and overran the forward half of the area, overran the outpost at the rear of the position, and penetrated the position itself. I was no longer able to remain at my radio. I radioed the CO [commanding officer] of AFA Bn I was closing down the set and withdrawing from the position. At 0510 hours the position was abandoned. I estimate that from about 2400 hours until the position was abandoned that approximately 1,200 CCF troops were engaged in attacking our position.[4]

After removing the firing mechanisms and gun sights from their weapons to render them inoperable, the survivors of the 2d Rocket Field Artillery Battery joined the 92d Armored Field Artillery Battalion and continued to fight. Lt. Col. Lavoie continues describing the situation.

The 92d Armored Field Artillery Battalion, giving the 1st U.S. Marine Division and the 6th ROK Infantry Division reinforcing fire, closed 1700 hours, 23 April, in positions in the vicinity of Chich'on-ni. The men were particularly tired because of the strenuous incidents of the past 36 hours, when they had to man battle stations continually. A great deal of tension existed in the battalion because of the overall military situation. Guards were posted, and the usual battalion perimeter was established for the night.[5]

The commander of Battery C, 92d Armored Field Artillery Battalion, Capt. Bernard G. Raftery, provides additional details.

In the latter part of April 1951, friendly forces were attacking in the area south of Hwach'on. The 92d Armored Field Artillery Battalion was disposed as follows: Battery B was in support of the British on the left. Headquarters Battery and Battery A were in the center. Battery C was on the right with the Marines. Battery A was displaced, passed through Battery C, and took positions northeast of Ma-hyon [just west of Todun-ni]. Battery C displaced north and west along the unnamed tributary of the Pukhan River to a point east of Suyong-dong [two and one-half miles west of Tan'gam-ni]. Headquarters Battery and Battery A joined Battery C, while Battery B moved to the vicinity of Wonch'on-ni to support the Marines. This was the situation on 22 April 1951 as the 92d Armored Field Artillery Battalion reinforced the fires of the 6th ROK and 1st U.S. Marine Divisions.

The enemy then attacked and penetrated friendly positions. He outflanked and routed the 6th ROK Division and pushed south toward Kap'yong. Enemy elements also struck the Marine left flank. Battery C remained in position on 23 April until it was firing Charge 3 at a range of 2,000 yards. Then Headquarters Battery and Batteries A and C were ordered to displace south to the Chich'on-ni area. Battery C took positions just north of the road; Headquarters Battery and Battery A went into positions just south of the road.

Raftery placed the howitzers of his battery in an inverted "W" formation on the reverse slope of an incline. This provided good defilade and excellent protection for the battery. He put his command post forty yards behind the gun line. At dusk a perimeter was set up and wired as usual for the night, with trip flares 75 to 100 yards outside the perimeter. The ten M3A1 personnel carriers (half-tracks), with one .50 caliber and one .30 caliber machine gun, were in the perimeter, tied in with Headquarters Battery in the rear and with Battery A on the left.[6]

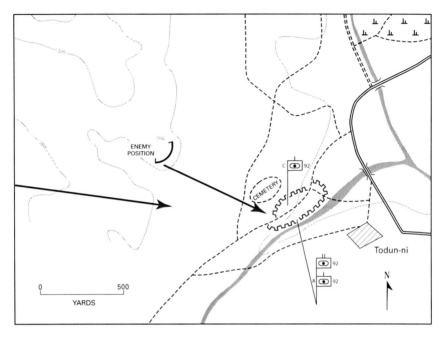

General area, 92d Armored Field Artillery Battalion, 23–24 April 1951. (Based on Russell A. Gugeler, "Artillery in Perimeter Defense," in *Combat Actions in Korea*, p. 157.)

The armored vehicles in an armored field artillery battalion could generate tremendous firepower for local defense, as well as provide protection for its men. Each firing battery was supposed to have ten half-tracks, or M3A1 personnel carriers, while Headquarters Battery had another five. Each of these armored vehicles had one .30 caliber and one .50 caliber machine gun mounted on it. The guns were M41 155mm self-propelled howitzers. Capt. John F. Gerrity, commander, Battery A, describes the position of his battery.

Battery A went into position on the left flank of the battalion position at 1100, 23 April. The battery was on the south side of the road, down in a paddy, four feet below the road level, which provided good defilade for the howitzers. The battery gave cover to Battery C, which moved into position on the north side of the road about 1200, 23 April. Headquarters Battery closed at 1200 on the

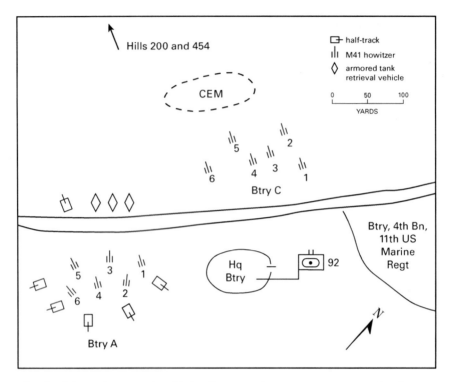

Sketch of the 92d Armored Field Artillery Battalion's position, 23–24 April 1951. (Based on map in CMH manuscript, U.S. Army.)

south side of the road, south of Battery C, to the right of Battery A. The perimeter of Battery A extended from a knoll north of the road and tied in with the other two batteries. Gerrity had four half-tracks on the outer perimeter and six half-tracks on the inner perimeter.[7]

The executive officer of Battery C, 1st Lt. Joseph N. Hearin, provides additional details about the position and recalls their actions after arrival.

Battery C occupied its position during the late afternoon of 23 April. Lt. Hearin laid in the battery and organized the perimeter for the night. Trip flares were set up. The battery was one-half mile from the MSR; the hill mass 1,000 yards to the front of Battery C was supposedly occupied by U.S. Marine elements. The men were instructed to be careful about firing in the direction of the hills to the front.

Battery C did "quite a little artillery firing that night." Lt. Hearin controlled the firing from the Executive Post. He noted that the charges decreased during the night. At 0130, 24 April, he called the gun sections and alerted them to increased machine gun fire on the hill mass in front of their positions. He instructed the men on the perimeter to be on the alert.

Everyone in the battery was tired. Everyone had been up for about 36 hours, with only scattered sleep. The battery was not scheduled to move out early in the morning, but preview or reconnaissance parties were to leave at 0530; the batteries were to be ready to displace shortly thereafter.[8]

Lt. Col. Lavoie describes his actions during the night.

At 0100, 24 April, Lavoie received a call to report at 0130 to Headquarters, 11th Marine Regiment. There he received instructions to have the battalion ready to move at 0530 that morning. Returning to his CP at 0245, Lavoie called the battery commanders and instructed them to have the units ready to move at 0530. He instructed the batteries to feed a hot breakfast to the men.

Lavoie then rested 45 minutes. At 0415 he heard the men get up to strike camp. The battalion was using pyramidal tents because the weather was cool. Lavoie got up at 0430, shaved, went to breakfast around 0500.[9]

As it began to get light, soon after 0500, the battalion was preparing to move, and the men were having breakfast. Unknown to the artillery battalion, the enemy had occupied the high ground to their front and were attempting to infiltrate into the battery positions. A soldier in Battery C first detected the approach of the enemy, and M. Sgt. John D. Elder, a platoon sergeant in the battery, tells what happened.

In the evening, 23 April, word was received that the battery would displace at 0530 the next morning. Guards were posted on the half-tracks during the night. Elder called the men at 0400, and they march ordered their pieces. It was just getting light when a man from the Number 5 gun went to the Korean graveyard to relieve himself. He had no weapon, so when he saw several Chinese, he threw his toilet paper at them and ran back to the battery. At that time, several men of the Number 5 gun were getting warm at a bonfire. The enemy fired at this group; the men broke for cover.[10]

At about the same time that the Chinese were discovered in the cemetery, a trip flare went off. Their hoped-for surprise discovered, the Chinese opened fire on the artillery positions. Men in the area of the Headquarters Battery describe the beginning of the attack.

Lt. Col. Lavoie, battalion commander: As the mess attendant was pouring his coffee, a bullet came through the mess tent, and Lavoie heard machine gun fire. Running outside, Lavoie saw fire coming from the hill. His first reaction was to yell, "Man battle stations," and he did so. He then ran to his CP to contact all the battery commanders. It was only two or three minutes before the battalion machine guns mounted on the half-tracks were returning the enemy fire.

At the battalion radio, Lavoie found the acting battalion executive officer, Maj. Tucker. Contacting the battery commanders, Lavoie asked them to closely control the friendly firing, for the battalion was putting out a terrific amount of fire. Lavoie felt that this enemy attack was only a side issue; he believed that the main attack would come from the west.

Leaving his radio, Lavoie went about Headquarters Battery to several half-tracks and instructed the men to pick targets before firing. He spread out several groups of bunched-up men so that they would be able to spot enemy targets more easily. He saw two enemy machine guns very well dug in among evergreen trees on the crest of the hill to the north. Then he returned to his radio control post.[11]

Maj. Raymond F. Hotopp, battalion S-3: Maj. Hotopp was getting ready to leave on reconnaissance at 0530, 24 April. He placed his belongings in his jeep and walked over to see whether Lavoie was ready. At that moment a machine gun opened fire. He thought someone had accidently tripped a machine gun, but the noise increased in volume, and Maj. Hotopp dropped to the ground and sought cover. He dived under a half-track. Everyone else he saw was taking cover, "but quick." Lavoie ran by, going toward the radio in the CP tent. Hotopp got up. He realized that he had only a .45

caliber pistol. So he moved around to control the firing of the men to keep them from wasting ammunition. It took quite some effort to get their attention to get them to slow down their fire.

Hotopp went to the radio tent and found Lavoie and Maj. Tucker, the Executive Officer, there. Every telephone line (they were strung overhead) to the batteries was out, apparently cut by fire. The only contact with the subordinate elements was by radio. At that time only the CP tent and the mess tent were up in the area. Saying that the tents were too vulnerable to enemy fire, Lavoie sent Hotopp outside. Hotopp got a driver to move a half-track to block the CP tent. When Lavoie came outside to check the area, Hotopp went inside and stayed at the radio.[12]

SFC WILLIS V. RUBLE JR., MOTOR SERGEANT, HEADQUARTERS BATTERY: The battery was going to move very early 24 April, so the men got up at 0300 or 0330 and had early chow. There was some confusion at the chow line because the reconnaissance party was trying to get out, and also because mess kits had to be passed to the 2d Rocket Field Artillery Battery men. All of Ruble's equipment was packed. Only the tent still stood. All of Ruble's crew had eaten except a private and an ROK soldier. Ruble was sitting in his tent waiting for the order to move out when he heard a noise as though someone had thrown a wad of ammunition into a fire. He rushed outside. Another burst of machine gun fire came into the area. Although he realized that some men were being hit, he wasn't yet sure that it was enemy fire because he had been told that the hills in front of the battalion were secured by the Marines. Getting the men out of the tent, Ruble told them to use the armor on the half-track for a shield.[13]

SGT. EDWARD BROWN, BATTALION COMMUNICATIONS SERGEANT: The men started dropping tents at the break of day. A short burst of automatic weapons fire came into the area. Capt. Starrett, the battery commander, and 1st Sgt. Higgins and Brown hit the ground. Brown saw only flashes of fire on the ridge. In a very few minutes friendly machine guns opened up. Starrett ordered a half-track to be turned to face the enemy fire, so Brown crawled about twenty yards to the track. Enemy fire was coming into the area pretty high, tracers from an American .50 caliber gun high on the ridge. Brown figured the gunner was trying to keep the battery pinned down. At the half-track he had a man turn the track around, got another one to man the machine gun. Men started to group up, so Brown sent them down the ditches to take cover along the rear battery boundary.[14]

Sgt. Jessie D. Carter, cook, Headquarters Battery: On 24 April, the cooks got up at 0345 and started chow. Three stoves worked okay, but the fourth stove flooded and set the straw on the ground afire. Carter pulled the stove out of the tent, put out the fire, and pulled it back into the kitchen. Breakfast started about 0445. Everything went fine until 0515, when Carter heard a short burst of machine gun fire. Everyone scattered. The cooks got into their holes in front of the mess tent. Carter saw ten or twelve Chinese coming down the hill 600 yards away toward the battery area. Everyone was firing the machine guns on the half-tracks all through the area, and Carter fired his carbine. Carter soon stopped, however, because he figured the machine guns were doing lots better than he was. Most of the Chinese were in trenches about 1,000 yards distant. The firing lasted approximately one hour and fifteen minutes. Then the march order was given. . . . During the firefight, one cook went into the tent to turn one stove out. He got himself a cup of coffee before coming back to his hole. Twenty-five men were still in the chow line when the firing started. They never did get fed that morning.[15]

Soldiers of Battery A describe the beginning of the attack in their area.

Capt. Gerrity, commander, Battery A: At 0400, 24 April, the battery started feeding. Capt. Gerrity was preparing to meet Lavoie to proceed at 0530 on a reconnaissance preceding the displacement of the battalion. Everything in the battery was march-ordered except the howitzers and the kitchen. Only the kitchen tent was still standing in the area. Gerrity left the kitchen and was getting into his jeep, 0515 or 0520, when he heard firing. It was SOP in the battery that all weapons on the half-tracks be manned against enemy action. Everyone jumped to the weapons. Gerrity was already in the center of his battery.

Enemy fire was coming in from the immediate front, from the south sides of Hill 200, and from Hill 454 on the left front. The battery machine guns concentrated on those two hills, where the Chinese were entrenched. The chiefs of section dispersed the men who were not manning the machine guns to take positions along the bank of the road, which offered cover and firing positions.

Gerrity ordered the half-track on the north side of the road to be pulled back so that the battery weapons could fire without hitting it and to prevent the Chinese from getting to it. The Chinese never were able to cross the road, although several reached the north side of the road in front of the battery. Many Chinese fired from behind piles of rubble and rock in the field between the battery and the hills.[16]

SFC JAMES R. WHITE, CHIEF, NUMBER 6 HOWITZER SECTION, BATTERY A: SFC White's section was on the battery left flank. The bank of the road was twenty-five yards from his gun. Perimeter foxholes were dug in on the bank. The battery was march-ordered, ready to move. White had a man on outpost just south of the road. The man came in, and White sent him to chow. White's half-track was to the left of his gun. Capt. Gerrity came by, and White asked permission to pull the half-track in and hook up the ammunition trailer just to the right of the gun. Permission was granted, and White moved his track. It was just breaking daylight. White told a man to put out a fire in an old powder pit. He walked over to get the men to finish folding up a tarpaulin, the last thing that had to be done before departing the position, when he saw tracers go over his head.

The next thing White remembered was being at the .50 caliber machine gun on his half-track. The enemy fire was so intense that "it looked like you could walk on the tracer fire to the hill." The ammunition belt in the machine gun was crossed. White was shaking so badly that he could not get it straightened out. He was afraid to expose myself above the ring mount. After a bit, he stood up, straightened the belt, and got off a few bursts against the hill. He then noticed that the men in his vicinity had taken cover behind the tank and in holes. The executive officer came to his half-track and cautioned him to have the men pick targets before they fired. White then waited before firing until he saw the location of the enemy machine guns. Following the tracers visually back to the hill, White was able to distinguish the enemy emplacement. White opened up. He saw his own tracers hitting the hill, so he walked in his fire on the enemy position and held it until his belt ran out. He then reloaded his gun (105 rounds are in a belt), but did not fire again. The man on the .30 caliber machine gun on White's track was playing it cool. He was firing in short bursts at the enemy across the road in the field.[17]

SGT. CHARLES R. LINDER, CHIEF, NUMBER 2 HOWITZER SECTION, BATTERY A: Breakfast was served at 0330, 24 April, so that the battery could move at 0530. Sgt. Linder's section was sleeping in squad tents, and all the tents were down. The area was clear. Most of the men had finished breakfast and were washing their gear when the first shots were heard. At 0520 Linder was sitting on a "tank" warming his feet on the motor, which was being warmed up. The first enemy rounds were fired at men either in the chow line or around the fire getting warm. Within a few seconds after the first rounds of enemy fire, every gun in the area was manned. A great volume of fire was put out in a few minutes. The men not manning the half-track weapons took cover in individual holes and fired their individual weapons. The first thing Linder did was jump off and run to the rear of the "tank." Then he controlled the firing of the gun and "tank" both; he was helped by two sergeants.[18]

SGT. AUSTIN E. ROBERTS, ASSISTANT GUNNER IN CHARGE OF MACHINE GUNS, NUMBER 2 HOWITZER SECTION: At 0430, 24 April, everything was march-ordered. All that had to be done before the battery moved was to wind up the spades and pull up the aiming stakes. The majority of the men were washing their mess kits. Roberts was loading equipment on his howitzer when he heard machine gun fire come in over the mess kit line. The gunners of both machine guns on his "tank" took positions immediately. Roberts saw tracers coming from the hills, and practically the entire battery opened up against the enemy trench on the hill.

When the .30 caliber machine gun jammed, Roberts took over and got it started again. He noticed that the man on the .50 caliber gun was firing against the trench where everyone else was firing. He got another man to take over the .30 caliber machine gun, and he took over the .50 caliber gun and fired on the enemy in the field between the battery and the hills. When he ran out of ammunition, he went to the ammunition trailer near the kitchen and secured a load of ammunition.[19]

The focus of the Chinese attack appeared to be on Battery C, which was the closest to the high ground north of the battalion area. Enemy soldiers coming out of the fields and the cemetery just west of the battery attempted to overrun the gun positions. Men of Battery C describe the beginning of the attack in their area.

CAPT. RAFTERY, COMMANDER, BATTERY C: At 0500, 24 April, the men of Battery C, awake and dressed, were preparing to move. Raftery was sitting in his CP tent with Lt. Hearin, the executive officer. At 0520 (he looked at his watch) he heard a Russian automatic pistol fire several bursts. "This is it," he said, getting to his feet, "let's go." Outside he sent Lt. McCord, the assistant executive officer, to establish communications with the battalion commander. He sent Hearin to the gun line. Raftery moved to a central position in the battery to try to determine what the enemy was trying to do. Spontaneously the men of the battery manned the machine guns and took the enemy under fire.

Enemy fire, small arms and automatic weapons, was coming from Hill 200. Raftery estimated six enemy machine gun emplacements on the hill. The Chinese had reached these positions by way of previously dug communications trenches. At the same time that these enemy troops were firing on Battery C, enemy soldiers armed only with hand grenades crawled toward the battery howitzers while enemy snipers took positions of concealment in the Korean cemetery.

Later, Raftery learned that an artilleryman who had gone to the cemetery to defecate saw an enemy soldier crawling on his belly toward the battery. The artilleryman yelled and threw his roll of toilet paper at the enemy soldier who ducked involuntarily. The artilleryman ran to the battery, yelling. At the same time, an enemy grenader set off a trip flare. At that point, the enemy commenced firing.[20]

1st Lt. Robert E. McCord, assistant executive officer: At 0520, 24 April, McCord was in the center of the battery area supervising the loading of equipment when the Chinese opened fire from the hill. His first thought was that it was friendly fire, but he soon realized that the rounds were coming in. McCord heard carbines first, then machine gun fire. The command to man the machine guns went out, and McCord passed it on. The men on the half-tracks started firing at the flashes on the hill. McCord reported to the battery commander in the center of the area. Capt. Raftery instructed him to have the tanks come back off the high ground to prevent them from being overrun and damaged. He passed these instructions on to several howitzer sections. Then he returned to the center of the area and tried to phone battalion. The phone was out. He turned on the radio to the battalion control net and remained at that jeep post during the remainder of the action, in contact with Col. Lavoie.[21]

SFC George T. Powell, chief of detail: The battery was getting ready to move out that morning. Powell was walking to the officers' tent for any last minute details, when he heard automatic weapons fire. He "knew right away that it wasn't U.S. make." It was just breaking day, and Powell began to sweat because he had a great many new men who had never been in combat. He saw two half-tracks not manned, and he ran toward them. By the time he got there, there were men on all the machine guns. Also, several men had gotten a machine gun on a ground mount and were covering the road. Powell stopped sweating. One corporal was at the switchboard in the open, with bullets flying around him. All Powell had to do was go around, check ammunition, keep up morale ("including my own"). No one got excited. They were a "damned good bunch of men."[22]

M. Sgt. Elder, platoon sergeant: Elder was at the Executive post when he heard small arms fire. By the time he got to the gun line, one man in the ring mount on a half-track and one man on the Number 5 gun had been hit by enemy bullets. The commanding officer then had the "tanks" pulled back behind defilade.[23]

SFC Paul T. Roberts, chief, Number 6 Howitzer Section: Roberts was just starting to go into his tent when the automatic weapons fire started. He dropped to the ground and stayed there until he located the direction of the enemy fire. Then he got up and ran to the nearest half-track, about 150 feet away. By the time he got there, the machine guns were already being manned. Enemy fire was coming from the graveyard and from the mountain. The Number 6 gun was on the left flank of the battery, just a little to the rear of the Number 5 piece.[24]

SGT. THERAL J. HATLEY, CHIEF, NUMBER 5 HOWITZER SEC-TION: The battery was getting ready to march. Hatley got the ammunition unfused. He piled some wood on the back of his gun. Sgt. Roberts of the Number 6 gun came over and asked if Hatley was ready to strike the tent. Hatley said yes and ordered some men to strike it. He warmed himself at a bonfire and was moving away when the enemy opened up with automatic weapons. Hatley jumped behind a rock wall. The men near him did not even have their carbines with them. Seeing two Chinese coming toward his "tank," he told the men to move farther down the wall for better cover.[25]

LT. HEARIN, EXECUTIVE OFFICER: Hearin had everyone awakened at 0415, 24 April, and the men began gathering together their things preparatory to moving out. Hearin walked from the Executive post to the [battery] Command Post to get his bag. He was in the tent and was going out when he heard machine gun fire. For a minute he thought someone had accidentally cut loose. Then several machine guns opened up. He and Capt. Raftery got out of the tent at the same time. Hearin ran to the line of half-tracks. From behind the Number 4 gun, he tried to see what the men were shooting at. He observed flashes on the hill from trenches; considerable enemy small arms and machine gun fire was coming into the battery area. The men shouted that the enemy attack was coming from the front.

It seemed unusual to Hearin that the enemy would attack from such a far distance. He looked for enemy elements coming in under the base of fire on the hill mass. At first he saw nothing. Then he noticed much activity at the Number 5 howitzer. Men were running from the Number 5 to the Number 6 gun. Several feet behind them grenades were bursting.[26]

Men in the battery quickly reacted to the threat at the Number 5 gun.

CAPT. RAFTERY, COMMANDER, BATTERY C: It appeared to Raftery that the enemy was concentrating his fire on the Number 5 gun. Enemy fire was so intense in that area that the machine guns on the half-tracks near that gun could not be manned. Enemy grenaders continued to crawl toward that position. Apparently the enemy was attempting to knock out one gun and blow the powder and ammunition for psychological effect.

Having determined the enemy intentions to his satisfaction, Raftery called the chief of the Number 5 gun section and instructed him to pull the gun back into a defilade position. One enemy grenader who got to the Number 5 "tank" . . . was shot off by the executive officer who was manning the .50 caliber machine gun on a half-track. While the machine guns of the Numbers 4 and 6 sections put covering fire on Number 5, Sgt. Hatley, chief of the section, ran up under enemy fire and withdrew the "tank" into defilade and turned it into position for direct fire. This took the initiative away from the enemy. The first sergeant killed an enemy grenader with his .45 caliber pistol at a distance of several feet.[27]

LT. HEARIN, EXECUTIVE OFFICER: Hearin jumped on the Number 4 half-track and swung the .50 caliber machine gun around. He shot a Chinese soldier trying to crawl up on the Number 5 "tank." The enemy soldier was armed only with grenades. At the same time, men on the Number 6 half-track shot at Chinese soldiers coming in from the other side of the Number 5 gun. The Chinese were apparently concentrating on the Number 5 piece, trying to destroy it. About a half dozen Chinese were around the Number 5 section, and Hearin killed two on the howitzer as well as several others lying on the ground near the "tank" and the half-track. Sgt. Hatley then ran forward and pulled the Number 5 gun back. The Number 2 piece was also withdrawn.[28]

SGT. HATLEY, CHIEF, NUMBER 5 HOWITZER SECTION: The battery commander then asked Hatley if he would go up and get his "tank." Green and Hatley ran to the "tank." Two Chinese were lying under the spade. Green went to the half-track thirty yards behind the gun, while Hatley continued to the "tank" and drove it back into defilade.[29]

SGT. POWELL, CHIEF OF DETAIL: During the firefight, Powell fired his M1 rifle and expended about eight clips (64 rounds). He could see the Chinese clearly in trenches on the hill. Some were as close as 100 yards from the battery. Three Chinese were shot off a battery "tank." These Chinese had grenades. Powell thought they were trying to drop grenades down the "tank's" hatch. When the "tanks" were moved back into defilade, one gun ran over and crushed a Chinese soldier who was hiding underneath it.[30]

There was confusion at Marine headquarters. Apparently, orders were issued for a temporary cease-fire until the situation could be clarified. Lt. Col. Lavoie and Maj. Hotopp relate the story.

LT. COL. LAVOIE, BATTALION COMMANDER: At this time the Marine regimental CP ordered Lavoie to cease fire because the battalion was firing on friendly troops. Lavoie answered that those "friendly troops" were inflicting casualties on his battalion.[31]

MAJ. HOTOPP, BATTALION S-3: Because it was difficult to contact by radio the battery of Marine artillery in the near vicinity, Lavoie asked Hotopp to make physical contact. Hotopp secured a jeep and a driver and drove "like hell." One tire was shot out, but they did not stop. At the Marine artillery CP, Hotopp explained what was happening in the 92d Armored Field Artillery Battalion area.[32]

After a brief lull, the men of the 92d Armored Field Artillery Battalion quickly resumed fire. Marine tanks moved into the area to help, and the situation was brought under control. Members of Battery C describe the fighting in their area.

LT. HEARIN, EXECUTIVE OFFICER: In the meantime the battery commander and the assistant executive officer had established contact with battalion headquarters. Instructions were given to cease fire because Marines were supposed to be on the hill. It was amazing, said Hearin; when the officers hollered cease fire, the fire ceased. Several minutes later the battery was directed to take the hill under direct fire of the howitzers. Direct fire was placed on the trenches and on the draw, which was thought to be the enemy avenue of approach.[33]

CAPT. RAFTERY, COMMANDER, BATTERY C: At the same time [that Hatley was relocating Number 5 howitzer], the battery guns began to place direct fire on the enemy on Hill 200. Shortly thereafter, the tracks in the rear of the battery were moved to the front to place fire on the enemy. At the end of the action, the six howitzers and the ten half-tracks of the battery were covering the battery front.[34]

SFC P. ROBERTS, CHIEF, NUMBER 6 HOWITZER SECTION: Men of the Number 5 gun backed their howitzer to their half-track so they could get on the guns of the half-track. During this time the men of the Number 6 gun were firing on Chinese in the cemetery, which had a great many mounds. The howitzers were sitting on a bank or hedgerow. The captain ordered the "tanks" to be pulled back into defilade. The "tanks" then fired on the enemy trenches on the hill. Roberts had his Number 6 gun pointed to the left rear. No enemy troops were in that direction, so Roberts did not fire. The volume of fire was not continuous. It occurred in spurts.[35]

The situation in the Headquarters Battery area is described by the battalion commander and other soldiers in the unit.

LT. COL. LAVOIE, BATTALION COMMANDER: While he was concerned with the Marines [on the radio], Maj. Tucker went outside and moved from track to track, rallying the men. When Tucker returned, both men lay flat on their stomachs in front of the radio. Calling Capt. Gerrity, Commanding Officer, Battery A, on the radio, Lavoie instructed him to deploy his howitzers in a horseshoe toward the west. Lavoie also ordered Gerrity to engage the enemy .50 caliber machine guns with direct 155mm howitzer fire. Lavoie went outside in time to see several rounds of 155mm WP and HE burst at a range of 600 to 700 yards. The concussion was terrific. Parts of human bodies exploded in the air.

As he walked from track to track, Lavoie noticed a great change in his troops. Over their initial scare, they appeared to be having a good time. When two or three enemy soldiers were observed creeping and crawling in a field across the road in an attempt to get into position to use grenades, the artillerymen stood up, thereby exposing themselves to enemy fire, and popped them off. At this time, a great deal of fire was coming in on the battalion, even though the enemy machine gun fire seemed somewhat subdued.

Capt. Bessler, S-2, insisted that according to fire coming in near the Fire Direction Center a sniper with scope must be firing from behind a pile of stones in the field. Bessler climbed on a half-track and pointed out the sniper to one of the sergeants on the machine gun. At that moment the sergeant was killed.[36]

In the Fire Direction Center, Lavoie received a request for one battery to fire a mission. He instructed Battery C to leave one gun on direct fire against the enemy nearby and to engage the distant target with the remainder of the battery.

Lt. Turner in a liaison plane reported into the radio net and asked whether he could be of assistance. Lavoie requested him to cover the valley to the west, feeling still that the current enemy attack was only a diversionary effort. The plane searched the west valley but found no sizeable groups of enemy. The plane, however, did report two groups of twenty-five to thirty men in a draw near the battalion positions. Lavoie thought that these must be part of a reserve force or simply frightened Chinese. He turned this target over to Battery A, which fired. The plane reported the enemy wiped out.

At this moment Lavoie saw a particle of white flash before his eyes, then blood. Tucker, standing near Lavoie in front of the radio, yelled, "Oh, my God." Tucker had been wounded in the arm. Lavoie and a sergeant laid Tucker in a trench. Capt. Arnett, battalion medical officer, came over and administered first aid.[37]

SFC RUBLE, BATTERY MOTOR SERGEANT: [Ruble was then 700 yards from the hill, with a clear field of fire from the left of Battery C to the hill.] Ruble got on the .50 caliber machine gun, unzipped the cover while slugs whistled around him. He looked for a target, discovered four or five persons in the field in front of Battery A positions. Battery A could not see them because the battery was in defilade. Ruble thought at first these individuals were South Korean because they were wearing dirty white civilian clothes. Then he saw one of them carrying a rifle, and he knew they were not Koreans. He let go three short bursts of his machine gun, knocked one down, spun another. He saw flashes on the hill, and figuring that the small arms fire would be able to get the enemy troops close in, Ruble fired at the flashes. When a ruptured cartridge caused his gun to jam, Ruble scooted to the rear of the half-track to the .30 caliber machine gun and ordered another man to insert a spare barrel on the .50. He instructed this man to fire on the flashes on the hill. Because the hill was too far for the .30 caliber gun, Ruble fired into the field across the road from Battery A.

After several minutes, he had the regular machine gunner take over. Ruble turned his radio to the command channel for instructions. He took charge of everyone in his immediate area and dispersed a group of wiremen who were bunched up and got them under cover. He had several ground machine guns set up. Over the radio, he heard instructions to strike tentage and prepare to march order. No equipment was to be left behind.

The fire slackened down, and Lavoie over the radio said everything was under control. The men were to cease fire. The men did so. Then enemy fire came in, so the men fired back. Three Marine tanks came up at this time, and Capt. Bessler, battalion S-2, directed their fire. Then the howitzers were turned, and they fired into the hill. "Everyone relaxed." . . .

During the action, 1st Sgt. Higgins moved through the area making sure everyone was under cover and had enough ammunition and that no one was wasting ammunition. Men of the Rocket Battery outposting the rear of the battery came into the area to help; Sgt. Higgins sent them back to guard the rear. . . . Headquarters Battery was composed of the following sections: Fire Direction Center, switchboard, maintenance (motor section), survey, battery headquarters, battalion command post, kitchen, radio, and wire.[38]

SGT. BROWN, BATTALION COMMUNICATIONS SERGEANT: Twenty minutes after the firefight started, word came to cease fire because there were friendly troops on the hill. When the men got up and moved around, enemy fire came in again. Brown was running to the medical jeep, which had a .50 caliber gun mounted on it, when Lt. Moody was hit in the ear, the bullet passing through his helmet, but wounding him only slightly. Brown got to the jeep just as another cease-fire order was given. As the aid man went to help Maj. Tucker, who was hit in the arm, Capt. Starrett called and told Brown to get off the high ground. Brown moved off the knoll and into a foxhole. Lavoie came around a corner and said they had the thing whipped. He told the men to fire only when they saw something. Then he disappeared. Brown moved to the wire section and found better cover for two men. Then he went to the mess hall area. At that time someone hollered all clear.

The march order was received, and the battery got up on the road when the men were ordered to return. Brown spotted three Chinese soldiers fifteen yards from the road. He went over to Battery A and called Lt. Love's attention to them. Love gave the men permission to fire. Brown's carbine jammed. Two Marine tanks came in and blasted the hill, trying to move the Chinese out of their trenches. The tank machine guns raked the hill. Some Battery A men followed the tanks into the field. One Chinese dead, one Chinese wounded and one Chinese unhurt were brought back.[39]

MAJ. HOTOPP, BATTALION S-3: When Hotopp returned [from the Marine CP], the firefight had become a series of individual actions. Each man was firing against the enemy with confidence. Capt. Bessler, S-2, moved a howitzer to fire directly at an enemy machine gun nest. The howitzer blasted the position with several rounds of 155mm ammunition. Bessler gave the impression he was back in the States on a firing range. His indifference in the face of enemy fire inspired the men to be cool.[40]

Men in Batteries A and C described the end of the action.

CAPT. RAFTERY, COMMANDER, BATTERY C: Collecting and organizing twenty men, Raftery sent ten up the right flank along a rock wall. He took the other ten men in a skirmish line across the battery front to clean out the Korean cemetery. These groups moving in on the graveyard killed seven enemy soldiers, captured one. The enemy soldier captured had to be pulled out of his hole.

At about the same time, Battery C received a fire mission in support of the Marines. The executive officer directed Number 6 gun to continue firing on Hill 200, while the other five howitzers fired an indirect support mission for the Marines between 0600 and 0615. By this time the enemy offered no serious threat to the battery. A few snipers remained on the left of the battery front.[41]

LT. HEARIN, EXECUTIVE OFFICER, BATTERY C. At about this time [when the battery was firing directly on the enemy trenches and draw], several Marine tanks came up and set up north of the road to the left of Headquarters Battery. Capt. Raftery, Hearin, and men of the detail and firing sections checked the graveyard. Several Chinese were flushed out; as they ran across the field, they were cut down by tank fire. While the Chinese were being flushed out of the graveyard, Hearin realized that he had only a pistol. He ran back for a carbine. At the battery area, Lt. McCord, the assistant executive officer, told him that a fire mission had been received. So Hearin directed the howitzers to be relaid, and the battery fired an indirect mission for about ten minutes.[42]

LT. McCORD, ASSISTANT EXECUTIVE OFFICER, BATTERY C.: He supervised the evacuation of some of the wounded by organizing groups of men to go out and carry the wounded to the battalion aid station, and relayed instructions via messengers throughout the battery. One such instruction was to hold fire until the men definitely saw the enemy.

About twenty-five men of the 2d Rocket Field Artillery Battery were integrated into Battery C at that time, for the Rocket Battery had lost all its equipment. McCord used them to assist the battery aid men in the evacuation of the wounded. Toward the close of the firefight, McCord received an indirect fire mission to support the withdrawal of a Marine unit. With the coordination of Lt. Hearin, the howitzers were placed in position for indirect fire, the firing chart was set up, and the mission was successfully fired, one round per minute for ten minutes as requested.[43]

SFC P. ROBERTS, CHIEF, NUMBER 6 HOWITZER SECTION, BATTERY C: Several Marine tanks came in on the left flank. Although the enemy had been firing from the front, as well as from the left flank of the battery, the enemy built up on the left. At this time a fire mission was received. The guns were moved back on the high ground out of defilade and relaid on the compass so that the Marines could be supported. After the mission was fired, the captain took a group of men out to clear the holes. Three Chinese were found in front of the battery. Two were killed, one was wounded. Roberts saw a good many dead Chinese in the cemetery.[44]

CAPT. GERRITY, COMMANDER, BATTERY A: Colonel Lavoie ordered the fire to cease, so that the men could be gotten under control and not be allowed to fire indiscriminately. This was accomplished, and from then on the fire of the battery machine guns was under control.

At 0600 Battery A received the march order. Gerrity moved his battery almost to the main road, when Lavoie halted the battery and instructed him to prepare for direct howitzer fire on the hills at a range of 800 to 1,200 yards. Trails were dropped, and the guns began firing direct fire. Gerrity received permission to place two ammunition trucks in the rear of his area. At about 0630 hours, three Marine tanks rumbled down the road, pulled into position north of the road, and fired into the hills. They also placed close-in machine gun fire on the rubble and rock piles between the road and the hills.

Battery C took an indirect fire mission for the Marines, while Battery A continued firing directly at Hills 200 and 454. A battery bazooka on the battery left front also fired on the Chinese; this crew took one prisoner. Fifteen men crossed the road to act as infantry, with the tanks moving north in the field in support. Gerrity instructed the men to clear to the foothills.[45]

SFC WHITE, CHIEF, NUMBER 6 HOWITZER SECTION, BATTERY A: When orders were received that Battery A would displace, bullets were still ricocheting off the tanks. At first the men were scared to move around, open the hatches, or crank up the spades, because it exposed them to enemy fire. White stood up in the ring mount, exposing himself completely, and yelled at the men. Then every man jumped to his job, and the battery was formed into march order.

As the battery was moving out of position, the battery commander stopped the column and told the men to place their howitzers in firing positions again. White's gun fired one round against the hill and made a direct hit on a bunker. But his gun was too low to fire against the field between the battery and the hill. The executive officer instructed White to send all the men he could spare to the foxholes along the bank of the road. Then, after White did so, the Battalion S-2 had White pull his gun back to a better firing position on a small knoll. Several Marine tanks came in about 0615.

"That eased the tension." The men moved out of their foxholes across the road "looking for Chinks." White saw three Chinese roll off the hill after they were hit by machine gun fire. One prisoner was brought in.[46]

SGT. A. ROBERTS, ASSISTANT GUNNER IN CHARGE OF MACHINE GUNS, NUMBER 2 HOWITZER SECTION, BATTERY A: When the march order came, Roberts pulled the aiming stakes, and the battery column moved toward the road. The executive officer instructed Roberts to keep two half-tracks to cover the battery as it moved out. Roberts got his two half-track crews to check in order to make certain they had sufficient ammunition. When he heard the cease-fire order, he ran from track to track to get the men to stop firing. As the battery ceased firing, the Chinese opened up. The battery then fired. When the battery stopped, the Chinese started again.

The .50 caliber machine gunner climbed down for some unknown reason. A Negro soldier of the Rocket Battery took his place. In a few minutes, he was killed [SFC Oliver Porter].[47] Roberts then got into the ring mount. He saw two Chinese, just over the bank fifty to seventy yards distant in the field. He hollered to the executive officer for permission to fire because it was during a cease-fire, [and] was refused permission. Two Marine tanks then came up. The executive officer ordered the men to take individual firing positions in the foxholes along the bank of the road. Roberts could not see very well from there. He had a Thompson submachine gun, and he fired several bursts, got one Chinese.

Then Roberts took ten men and walked across the road. As they got over on the other side of the road, a Chinese with an American Thompson submachine gun jumped up. Someone fired, hit the enemy weapon. The Chinese dropped it and held up his hands. Roberts hollered not to shoot. He told two men to take the prisoner back. The remaining eight men went across the fields examining each hole. In doing this, the men worked like infantry. Roberts had three years of infantry training; the others had never been in the infantry. Walking real low, the men sneaked up to a hole, then charged fast, ready to fire at any movement. They found no live Chinese. They advanced to the foot of the hills, a distance of 400 yards. No enemy fire was received as they crossed the field. The men returned to the battery.[48]

SGT. LINDER, CHIEF, NUMBER 2 HOWITZER SECTION, BATTERY A: Orders were shortly received to pull the guns out of position and displace. The battery moved out of position to the road. All the men were cool and well-controlled. Then the order was received to place the guns so that direct fire could be given on the hills where the enemy was entrenched. This was done. Direct fire was given. The perimeter was very tight and well closed in. The man handling ammunition for the .50 caliber machine gun on Linder's track was killed. Between 0615 and 0630, three Marine tanks came into the area, took positions north of the road, and did a great deal of firing. One tank round killed seven enemy soldiers forty to fifty yards across the road from the battery, twenty-five yards from the tank. Linder watched an enemy .50 caliber machine gun on the side of the hill firing on Battery A. He saw the enemy machine gunner knocked out of the hole and roll down the hill. After the first few minutes of action, the men felt that this was just another job to be done. The battery officers were all up and down the battery, keeping the men cool and directing the fire of the half-tracks.[49]

Lt. Col. Lavoie describes the end of the action and the displacement of his battalion from the area.

Lavoie went to Battery A, 200 yards away. He found the men standing up and firing away. The bazookas were working. Morale was very high. Capt. Bessler insisted a sniper was working on a hill. He said he'd get him. Calling Miller of Battery C to go with him, Bessler got a half-track, and headed for the trenches on the hill. Bessler brought back two M1 rifles with scopes, said they had gotten two.

By then there was a definite cessation of enemy fire. Firing was sporadic. One wounded prisoner of war brought in by three men was turned over to several ROKs, who bound his hands behind his back and gave him hell.

Lavoie checked Maj. Tucker, he checked his radio. He saw Lt. Moody, who had his ear nicked by a bullet that passed through his helmet. At the radio again, he received a message from the Marines to displace one battery when he felt he could clear. There was very little firing. The area was comparatively quiet. He displaced Battery

C at 0745. Then he received word to displace another battery. He moved Headquarters Battery. Then the Marines said they wanted a Marine Rocket Battery covered as it came out from the west. This unit passed. At 0830 Lavoie received instructions to displace the last unit, Battery A. When this element moved, everything was quiet.[50]

The commanders of Batteries A and C provide additional information about the movement out of the position and an overall assessment of the action.

CAPT. RAFTERY, COMMANDER, BATTERY C: Between 0730 and 0800 Colonel Lavoie ordered Battery C to displace south and across the Pukhan River to positions above Inp'ung-ni to cover the withdrawal of the other batteries. Then Lavoie displaced Headquarters Battery and Battery A to positions near Inp'ung-ni. When Battery C displaced, the enemy on Hill 200 had been completely neutralized. Only a few snipers remained.

Raftery was in radio contact at all times with the battalion commander, who directed the overall friendly defense and firing. Throughout the entire action, the executive officer controlled the firing to such an extent that when the order to cease fire was given, it ceased in a matter of seconds. The chiefs of section were controlling the fire of the tracks.[51]

CAPT. GERRITY, COMMANDER, BATTERY A: Then Colonel Lavoie instructed Battery C to displace. Gerrity asked Lavoie whether Raftery, Battery C, could leave two half-tracks of his battery to secure the right flank of Battery A. Permission was granted, and Gerrity sent ten men of the Number 1 and 2 Sections, who were not needed to fire the guns, over to Battery C to get the half-tracks.

Between 0830 and 0900 everything was quiet. Some enemy sniper fire from the hills was being received without effect. The Rocket Battery, 1st U.S. Marine Division, displaced through the 92d Armored Field Artillery Battalion positions before Battery A displaced. The Marine tanks followed Battery A out of the area.

Battery A had three KIA, one WIA. Enemy [losses] were estimated at 200. Marine troops later reported finding a total of 179 counted enemy dead in that area.

The leadership of the noncommissioned officers was outstanding. They had complete control over the men at all times. There was no morning haze that day, and the men were able to distinguish Chinese on the hill 1,000 yards distant.[52]

Lt. Col. Lavoie summarized the action and provided his personal assessment in his interview with 1st Lieutenant Blumenson.

On the following day, the Marines stated that they counted 179 Chinese dead in that area. The 92d Armored Field Artillery Battalion suffered four KIA (including one man attached from the 2d Rocket Field Artillery Battery) and eleven WIA. No equipment was lost or destroyed. Eight tires on vehicles were punctured by bullets, and wiring on two 2½-ton trucks was damaged.

Several Marine tanks came into the area during the firefight. These were not requested; Colonel Lavoie thought the Marines must have sent them over to aid the battalion. One battery of the 4th Battalion, 11th Marine Regiment, was in position 300 to 400 yards from the 92d Armored Field Artillery Battalion. This battery was not under enemy fire. One bullet hole, however, was found in a vehicle.

An aid man from the Service Battery, 92d Armored Field Artillery Battalion, located one-half mile distant, came cross-country at a run to see if he could assist the battalion. He drove the ambulance that carried out the battalion wounded. During the firefight, Colonel Lavoie had the ammunition trucks taken out to the Service Battery to keep them from being ignited by enemy fire.

Colonel Lavoie cited the gallantry of Captain Arnett, the battalion medical officer, who exposed himself continuously to enemy fire.

"Artillery," Colonel Lavoie said, "if it makes up its mind, will set itself up in a proper perimeter so that it can defend itself from enemy infantry action."[53]

There was more to the success than Lt. Col. Lavoie mentioned. First Lt. Martin Blumenson, an experienced combat historian, interviewed many of the participants and prepared a detailed report of the action, "Artillery in Perimeter Defense." Lt. Blumenson provided this assessment.

In view of the past success of enemy infiltration and penetration of friendly lines in Korea, this action is an illustration of how one unit withstood and repelled such attack. As Colonel Lavoie stated it, "Artillery, if it makes up its mind, will set itself up in proper perimeter so that it can defend itself from enemy infantry action."

The officer personnel of the 92d Armored Field Artillery Battalion impressed the interviewer as being one of the outstanding groups he has encountered in Korea. Morale in this unit was superior. The battalion had had excellent training before its arrival in Korea. The personnel of the unit had been together "for a long time" before its commitment to combat.

Prior to the action on 24 April, described in these interviews, the 92d Armored Field Artillery Battalion had held frequent drills and alerts for action against enemy infantry. The command expected that an enemy attack would be repelled. That fact that each man knew his "battle station" permitted each man to act decisively in time of emergency. Establishment of a defensive perimeter to protect the artillery equipment and personnel and permit them to function was not neglected.

Enemy action in the firefight described above did not prevent the battalion from performing its primary function; while it protected itself from immediate ground attack, the battalion continued to fulfill its mission by delivering supporting fire for the infantry as requested.

Once the initial shock of the attack was overcome, the men gained confidence increasingly in their weapons, their leaders, and their own ability to defeat the enemy. In so doing, they reflected their commander's remark: "We were going to move out, but now we'll wait till we secure this position."[54]

Chapter 6

HILL 628

8th Ranger Infantry Company (Airborne), 23–25 April 1951

West of the ROK 6th Division on the right flank of I Corps, the Chinese 27th Army hit the front of the U.S. 24th Infantry Division while part of the Chinese 20th Army moved into its flank and rear through the ROK 6th Division sector. The 8th Ranger Infantry Company (Airborne), a unit organized and trained in the United States late in 1950 and shipped to Korea early in 1951, was assigned to the 24th Division in March 1951. It was ordered to move to the right flank of the 24th Division and make contact with the left flank regiment of the ROK 6th Division. The distinguished combat historian 1st Lt. (later captain) Martin Blumenson, then with the 4th Historical Detachment, Eighth U.S. Army, Korea, completed a detailed study of the subsequent action on Hills 628 and 1010, which ensued when the Rangers stumbled on an enemy force while moving to the location where they were to meet the ROKs. Blumenson describes the situation.

The Chinese April offensive in 1951 caused the 6th ROK Division to disintegrate. As a result of this, widespread readjustment of friendly positions had to be made. For several days, as friendly units withdrew, the situation was fluid. Communications were not always reliable. Supporting units, in the process of moving to new positions, were sometimes unable to render support. Rumors of organizations encircled and destroyed by the enemy gave rise to feelings of uneasiness, presentiments of disaster, nervousness.

The action on Hill 628 must be considered in the light of these factors.[1]

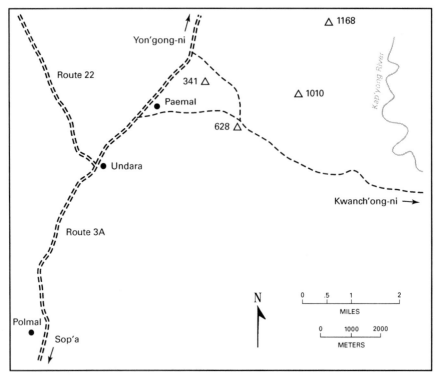

Area of operations, 8th Ranger Infantry Company (Airborne), 23–25 April 1951. (Original map by author, based on map in Army Map Service series L751.)

Lt. Alfred J. Giacherine, executive officer, 8th Ranger Company, recalls the orders received by his unit and their subsequent movements.

The company was . . . [about five miles behind the front line of the 19th Infantry Regiment, 24th Infantry Division] when the Chinese offensive started on 22 April 1951. One patrol was operating in the sector of the 21st Infantry Regiment on the right, and one patrol was out in the sector of the 19th Infantry Regiment on the [left]. The G-3 of the 24th Infantry Division held up these patrols.

On 23 April everyone assembled. The retrograde movement had started in force. The company secured some trucks and moved to . . . near Paemal [about twelve miles south of the company's initial position], opposite the 24th Infantry Division CP. Giacherine reported to the division G-3 at 1600, and Col. Mauz and Maj. Rolland grabbed him. They gave him the mission of taking the company to Hill 1168 [about ten miles northeast of Paemal and nearly two miles north of Hill 1010] to make contact with an ROK unit on the right. The 2d Battalion, 21st Infantry Regiment, was on the left. Giacherine was to get further instructions from the battalion S-3. Giacherine reported this to Capt. James A. Herbert, the [Ranger] company commander, who went to battalion to receive further clarification of the mission.[2] Giacherine alerted the company, saw that the men were fed, and that their gear was packed.

Herbert returned to the company and said that he had been instructed to have the company on Hill 1168 by midnight that night. He instructed Giacherine to take the company to the 2d Battalion CP and have it there by 1900. Giacherine did so. Herbert arrived there at 1930.

The company was carrying two days' rations, bedrolls, and a basic load of ammunition. Giacherine suggested that the load be lightened and that arrangements be made to secure litter bearers. He wanted Koreans to bring the bedrolls and rations up the hill after the company secured it. But this was not done. Arrangements were, however, made for Korean litter bearers and laborers to report to the company on the forward slope of Hill 628 [about one and a quarter miles southwest of Hill 1010 and two and a half miles southwest of Hill 1168] about 0200, 24 April.

The company then proceeded toward its objectives, Hills 628, 1010, and 1168, in that order. Herbert was in the lead with the 1st, 3d, and 2d Platoons, in that order, and Giacherine was at the rear of the column. Nothing occurred until the company was climbing the forward slope of Hill 628 about midnight. Then several shots rang out. The order came back for the 2d Platoon to move to the left up the hill and dig in. The 1st and 3d Platoons withdrew to a small knob and dug in. As the company was digging in, the litter bearers arrived. No reconnaissance was made to determine what was on top of the hill. Herbert and the forward observer with the company tried to call in artillery, but they were informed that no artillery was possible because friendly troops were in the vicinity. Herbert told

Giacherine this when Giacherine went forward to see what was going on. Giacherine had been informed by a sergeant accompanying the litter bearers that there were friendly elements up ahead.

Giarcherine told Herbert this, but Herbert was not convinced. He wanted the 2d Platoon, loaded with equipment, to lead a company assault on the top of the hill. Giacherine asked permission to drop the equipment, but Herbert said no. "Let's march the whole company up there. There's no one there," Giacherine said. Reluctantly, Herbert reassembled the company in its original order and proceeded up the hill. The company discovered one very frightened ROK soldier. It was 0330.

At daybreak, the company was dug in on top of Hill 628, with the 2d and 3d Platoons on top, and the 1st Platoon on a ridge running west. The company bedded down for approximately six hours. At 1000, 24 April, a group of about ten men was noticed about 1,500 meters south of the company position. The group appeared to be a patrol working its way toward the company. Giacherine dispatched four men to go toward the group and make contact. The men returned and reported meeting elements of Company L, 21st Infantry Regiment.

At 1300 the company departed Hill 628 and proceeded to Hill 1010. The men noticed as they advanced that friendly planes were working over an area to the right rear of the company. The company reached Hill 1010 about 1800, and the three platoons established a perimeter on the summit. That evening a patrol was sent to reconnoiter Hill 1168, 3,000 meters away. The patrol reported Chinese to the immediate front of the company, not more than 1,000 meters away.[3]

Members of the patrols sent to investigate the activity to the south and to reconnoiter Hill 1168 to the north describe what happened.

SFC JAMES McNEELY, SQUAD LEADER, 2D SQUAD, 1ST PLATOON, LEADER OF THE PATROL SENT TO THE SOUTH: The company boarded trucks on the evening of 23 April and moved out to the base of Hill 628. Its mission was to occupy Hill 1168. The company reached the top of Hill 628 at 0600, 24 April, after a very steep climb. The weather was very hot. At the top of the hill, the company ate and rested a few hours.

Activity was noticed on Hill 830 to the south, and the platoon leader sent McNeely and one man to investigate. Contact was made with Company L, 21st Infantry Regiment, about 0800, after a twenty-minute walk. The patrol from Company L had been sent out to make contact with the Ranger Company. The men of the patrol said that there was enemy on the right flank of the Ranger Company. McNeely asked about the ROKs who were supposed to be on the right flank. The patrol knew nothing about them.

Approximately 1000, 24 April, the company moved off Hill 628 toward Hill 1010. The company followed a trail. It took four hours of hard walking to reach Hill 1010. The men were very tired. The company then set up defensive positions on the hill. About six men of the 1st Platoon were sent on patrol to Hill 1168. This patrol made contact with the enemy, radioed back the information, then returned to the company.[4]

CPL. HENRY P. SILKA, 2D SQUAD, 1ST PLATOON, A MEMBER OF THE PATROL SENT TO HILL 1168: Silka was an assistant BAR man. Sgt. McNeely, the squad leader, chose Silka to go on patrol from Hill 1010 to Hill 1168. It was Silka's turn to go. M. Sgt. [Philip D.] Moore was in charge of the patrol, a day patrol, which left Hill 1010 about two hours after the company reached the hill. About ten or twelve men from the 1st Platoon covered the patrol by taking positions along a finger leading from Hill 1010 to Hill 1168. The mission of the patrol was to contact the enemy, estimate the number of men, and return immediately.

One thousand yards from Hill 1010, the patrol reached a knoll. Hearing a shot to the right front, the men hit the ground and took cover. Moore sent scouts out to check. Then it was decided that the shot was not intended for the patrol. The men stayed in Chinese positions on the knoll for twenty minutes. Then just as they were about to push off closer to Hill 1168, someone saw movement on it. Moore checked with his glasses and saw about ten Chinese. Moore tried to contact the company commander through his SCR536, but could make no contact.[5]

Moore then sent four scouts one to two hundred yards farther
to a high spot on the ridge where they could observe. They saw that
the hill was unoccupied except for ten Chinese. Moore ordered the
scouts to open fire on Hill 1168 to see if they could draw fire, but
they received none. The patrol then returned to Hill 1010.[6]

*Lt. Giacherine continues his description of the events leading
up to his company's fight with the Chinese.*

At 2400, four men under Cpl. Michael Rosen were sent back to
the saddle where the Company L element had been contacted earlier.
These four men returned at 0330, and reported to Herbert and
Giacherine that they had been unable to make contact. They had
not been able to get around Hill 628 because the hill was full of
Chinese. Herbert laughed at the men and told them that they were
imagining things. The men insisted that the Chinese were there and
that the Chinese had even followed them part way back up the trail.
The men said that they had broken contact with the Chinese so they
could alert the company. Herbert scoffed at them and said they had
heard wind whistling through the trees. Herbert dismissed them.
The men then asked where the drinking water was. Herbert said
that there were five cans outside of the CP dugout in the middle of
the perimeter. The men left.

During the early evening hours, about fifteen ROKs came in
from the direction of Hill 1168. All reported "many, many" Chinese
to the front. The ROKs were stragglers and had lost their units. The
company fed them and placed them in the perimeter.

During the course of the evening, a few rounds were fired.
Giacherine had to contact each platoon physically in order to find
out what was happening, for there was no radio communications in
the company. The only communication that existed was through the
radio of the forward observer, who was in contact with the 2d Battalion, 21st Infantry Regiment. On the retrograde movement, the
company communications sergeant, Sgt. Green, riding with an artillery unit, missed the company CP and went eighteen miles farther
south. Green was supposed to wait for the company four miles to
the south of Amu or Munam-ni. The company departed for Hill
628 in such haste that it borrowed two SCR300 ["walkie-talkie"]

radios from the 2d Battalion, 21st Infantry Regiment.[7] Giacherine had kept one. There were thus a total of three in the company.

Lt. [later Col. Berkeley J.] Strong, a platoon leader [3d Platoon], entered the CP at 2100 and did not move out of there until 0530 the next morning. Herbert was in his dugout at 2100, and did not leave until 0430, to walk a few feet from it. At 0300, a carrying party of fifteen Koreans guided by two NCOs of the 2d Battalion, 21st Infantry Regiment, arrived with a basic load of ammunition, thirty rations, and twenty gallons of water. The carrying party departed at 0315. . . . Contact with the ROKs on the right had not been made. During the night several small enemy groups had probed the company perimeter.[8]

Other members of the 8th Ranger Company add details of the time spent on Hill 1010.

CPL. CHARLES N. LENZ, ASSISTANT SQUAD LEADER, 1ST SQUAD, 1ST PLATOON: Lenz's squad consisted of two ARs [automatic rifles], eight M1 rifles, and one mortar, comprising ten men. On Hill 1010, Lenz's squad faced northwest on the edge of a sharp drop-off. During the night he heard movement. The machine gun on his right fired. Several grenades were thrown. The supply train came up to the company. In the morning, just before the company moved out, some ROK soldiers came in.[9]

SFC MCNEELY, SQUAD LEADER, 2D SQUAD, 1ST PLATOON: That evening about twelve ROK soldiers came up on the hill. The company did not know who they were, and when they were challenged, they could not speak English. Several were wounded before the company recognized them.[10]

SGT. CONNIE M. DRUM, SQUAD LEADER, 1ST SQUAD, 2D PLATOON: Drum's squad consisted of six riflemen, two BARs, the squad leader, and the assistant squad leader.

At noon [24 April] the company moved to Hill 1010 and found dug-in positions already there. During the night someone was moving around the base of the hill. Sgt. Smith threw several hand grenades, and there was no more noise. The 3d Platoon on the left opened up with a machine gun during the night. At 0200, 25 April, laborers came up with water and ammunition. As they left, two men, one from Drum's squad, went with them to contact Company L, 21st Infantry Regiment. The two-man patrol could not locate Company L.[11]

SGT. KEITH W. SMITH, SQUAD LEADER, 3D SQUAD, 2D PLATOON: Smith was a member of the weapons squad, which consisted of a 60mm mortar and a .30 caliber light machine gun. There were eight men in the squad, four men in each section. The squad carried four boxes of mortar ammunition (32 rounds) and six boxes of machine gun ammunition (1,500 rounds).

At 1130 [24 April] the company proceeded to Hill 1010 and arrived there between 1400 and 1500. The company set up a perimeter. Holes were already dug on top of the hill.

Just as it was getting dark, there was movement to the north. It seemed like the rustling of brush fifty or sixty yards away. A patrol sent to Hill 1168 had already come back. Smith asked the platoon leader for permission to burn the area with WP grenades. The platoon leader asked the company commander whether he ought to do so, and he said no. Smith's squad was on the right flank of the platoon, facing north. There was a steep slope in front of his position.

At 2300 the noise in front of Smith increased. The men began to get jumpy. Smith suggested that perhaps the artillery could fire flares in. The company commander thought that might be a good idea, but the artillery would not fire it. Smith thought that the artillery was probably out of range. So he threw three fragmentation grenades at the noise. Each man in the squad threw two or three. There was no more noise.

At 2345 the platoon leader got two men from Smith's squad to go on patrol to Hill 628 to contact the rifle company from the 21st Infantry Regiment that was supposed to be there. The patrol was gone about two hours. When they came back, they reported enemy troops on Hill 628.[12]

CPL. JOSEPH P. MCGREGOR, BAR MAN, 1ST SQUAD, 3D PLATOON: The company reached the top of Hill 628 at daylight and stayed until 1100. Then the company moved to Hill 1010. The three platoons formed a perimeter using holes already dug.

After dark McGregor saw a firefight to the left one mile away. An outpost of three men was twenty-five yards from McGregor's position. Around 2200 the man on guard spotted several Chinese. He shot two at very close range, and the outpost ran back to the perimeter. Later the men went back and got their bedrolls and brought them back into the company perimeter.

McGregor was on the left side of the perimeter facing north. A machine gun was on McGregor's right. About 0200 a grenade went off. He saw nothing. The next morning he saw several dead Chinese about twenty-five yards from the company perimeter. Just before the company moved out in the morning, thirteen ROKs came in.[13]

SFC HARRY ZAGURSKY, SQUAD LEADER, 3D SQUAD, 3D PLATOON: Zagursky's squad had nine men, a section of infantrymen, and one mortar. Each man was carrying at least two rounds of HE for the mortar.

The mission of the company was to go up the hill and act as a delaying force to allow other units to withdraw. The men carried their combat packs, bedrolls, mountain bags, and four to six grenades. The riflemen had three or four bandoliers. Zagursky had an SCR536 radio.

At 1100 the company moved out for Hill 1010. No one knew whether the enemy occupied it or not. The company reached the top of Hill 1010 between 1400 and 1500 and spent the remainder of the afternoon getting into position. The men set the grass on fire with WP so there would be at least fifty or sixty yards of cleared space around them. The positions were wired and booby-trapped. The company was at least two miles from the valley.

At 2100 Zagursky heard firing in the valley. He saw tank silhouettes. He was told that Company L, 21st Infantry Regiment, was supposed to make contact. Shortly thereafter, Zagursky heard movement to the rear of the company, fifty to one hundred yards below the top of the hill. The machine gun fired about twenty-five rounds. Zagursky got his grenades ready. Nothing happened. Around midnight, he saw a man who was not of the company, and the man said he had come up with rations.

At 0200 Zagursky was getting ready to go out on patrol, when the patrol that had been out came in. It reported having been unable to make contact with Company L, 21st Infantry Regiment. . . . Zagursky asked someone in the machine gun section what had happened during the night. The man said they had fired on some ROKs and killed several until they noticed a white flag waving. About fifteen ROK soldiers came into the perimeter.[14]

Lt. Giacherine continues his account of the actions leading up to the engagement with the Chinese.

At 0500, a radio message through the forward observer came from the 2d Battalion, 21st Infantry Regiment. It ordered the company to evacuate Hill 1010 immediately and contact the 3d Battalion, 21st Infantry Regiment, which was 500 meters south of Hill 307 and in positions extending northwest to . . . [about 1,600 yards west of Hill 1010]. Contact with the ROKs on the right had not been made. During the night several small enemy groups had probed the company perimeter. Using the litter bearers as carriers, the ammunition and rations were loaded.

Herbert then asked Giacherine why the patrol that had been sent to Hill 628 had not reported back. Giarcherine said the men had. Herbert denied it. Giacherine sent a runner to get Rosen. "Don't you remember you told them where the water was?" Giacherine asked. Herbert then seemed to remember.

Lt. Strong woke up as the company was ready to move out. The order of march to Hill 628 was 1st Platoon, 3d Platoon, and 2d Platoon. The company departed about 0645. Halfway between Hills 1010 and 628, Giacherine received a radio message that the company was to avoid Hill 628. This came from the 2d Battalion, 21st Infantry Regiment. The reason for this was that a friendly patrol had met stiff enemy resistance in that vicinity. Giacherine delivered the message in person to Herbert. Herbert's reply was, "I know; I received it."

To the left front . . . [about 1,300 yards south of Hill 1010], Giacherine saw a firefight of large intensity, and what appeared to be Navy Corsair planes strafing and napalming the north slope of the ridge.

When the forward elements of the company reached Hill 628, the column halted. At this time Giacherine noticed that the Korean litter bearers were between the tail end of the 3d Platoon and the beginning of the 2d Platoon. Giacherine had them move to the rear of the column.

A radio call from Herbert informed Giacherine that there were "some Chinks in front." "How many?" Giacherine asked. "Fifteen," Herbert replied. After a short interval, Herbert said that he was going to get himself some Chinks.

Giacherine and the platoon sergeant of the 2d Platoon deployed [to] the rear end of the column to protect the company rear. Northeast of Hill 628, a draw on the company east flank looked like an avenue of approach to Hill 628.

The firing started, and Giacherine saw elements of the 1st Platoon deploying on the ridge. Then a radio came from Herbert: "We're going to have to fight our way through; they are coming around the right."[15]

Members of the 1st Platoon describe the beginning of the action.
CPL. LENZ, ASSISTANT SQUAD LEADER, 1ST SQUAD: As the company approached Hill 628 on its way back, some Chinese were spotted. Lenz was in the rear of the 1st Platoon, which was leading the company. The machine guns and the BARs of the platoon were set up, and the platoon opened fire on the Chinese who were in the valley. Then the company received enemy automatic weapons and small arms fire from its left, front, and right.

The 2d Squad was then ordered to lead off while the 1st Squad took positions on the left flank. Lenz moved up on the ridge, and when he was on favorable terrain, the 1st Squad went into a skirmish line on the left flank. There were many Chinese, at least a company, about 200 yards away.[16]

SFC McNEELY, SQUAD LEADER, 2D SQUAD: On the morning of 25 April, the order was given to move back. The company returned by the same trail it had taken. Scouts saw Chinese troops in the vicinity of Hill 628. The company commander said he saw approximately fifteen enemy. He sent two BAR teams to the top of Hill 628 to watch the left flank. He then called up a base of fire squad to fire upon the Chinese who were spotted. McNeely did not see them. Firing continued for about fifteen minutes around 0800.

The order came to move out to the south. Then the company received fire from its right flank, from enemy weapons on a finger ridge running off Hill 628. Enemy small arms and automatic weapons fire halted the company, which returned the enemy fire.

At this time, the 1st Squad of the 1st Platoon was in the lead. McNeely moved from his 2d Squad area up to the head of the column to the platoon sergeant. He saw fifteen or twenty enemy on a finger ridge. Orders then were passed up to continue moving south off Hill 628. The platoon sergeant ordered McNeely to move his squad up into the lead. It was impossible to get into formation at this time because of the terrain, so the company moved forward in single file.

As McNeely's squad moved forward down the hill, it received fire from its front and right. At the base of a small knoll, McNeely formed his squad into a line of skirmishers and continued moving. The squad moved forward with marching fire. McNeely saw the enemy and estimated that there was "damn near a company in front of us." When the squad, with the company following, advanced to about 100 yards from the enemy positions, the enemy withdrew to higher ground. At that time McNeely received machine gun fire from his left flank. He was able to move about twenty-five yards farther, and then he had to stop. The men lay prone out in the open on rolling ground. There were no holes, no trees. The men returned the enemy fire. McNeely saw someone knock out an enemy machine gun at the base of the hill with a grenade.[17]

CPL. EDWARD D. SMITH, 3D SQUAD: Smith was an assistant machine gunner. The company departed Hill 1010 after daybreak and started down toward Hill 628. Smith thought he saw some people on a ridge to his right. The company reached Hill 628, and the platoon leader said that someone was digging in at the bottom of the hill. Smith saw about fifteen Chinese.

The 3d Squad moved up into position, and Smith opened fire on the Chinese. After firing about 200 rounds, the firing pin on his gun broke. Smith was then told to pull back from position, move around to the right. The company was then receiving fire from all directions except the rear, and was almost pinned down.[18]

Soldiers in the 1st Platoon describe their attempt to break through the enemy positions to their front.

SFC McNEELY, SQUAD LEADER, 2D SQUAD: As the company lay on the ground and returned the enemy fire, enemy fire came in from three sides. McNeely and another man crawled forward and knocked out a machine gun approximately 150 yards to the direct front with grenades. Each man fired one grenade from his rifle grenade-launcher. Then enemy mortars started coming in around the company.[19]

CPL. E. SMITH, 3D SQUAD: Several enemy machine gun positions were knocked out with grenades and covering fire. Smith moved to the left into a trench. An ROK soldier was with him, along with the lieutenant who was forward observer and two men with him. The lieutenant was shot in the leg. The ROK soldier and Smith helped him down the ridge.[20]

CPL. LENZ, ASSISTANT SQUAD LEADER, 1ST SQUAD: Half of Lenz's squad got separated from the other half. Lenz made contact with McNeely's 2d Squad. Everyone was then pinned down for about half an hour. Sgt. [Paul O.] Chagnon, the platoon sergeant, more or less jokingly told Sgt. Hall of the 2d Squad to get the enemy machine gun position in a bunker. Hall crawled up to it, and knocked it out with one grenade, which he threw into the position. Then the platoon was not pinned down so much. Lenz saw Chinese pulling back on the right.[21]

Meanwhile, Lt. Giacherine moved forward to assess the situation. He describes what he saw.

The company inched forward, skirting the northwest slope of Hill 628, "every man for himself." There was no base of fire, and every man fired as he pleased.

Giacherine left his position at the tail of the column and reached the machine gun of the 1st Platoon. As he passed through the platoon, he instructed Sgt. Ellis, the platoon sergeant, 2d Platoon, to keep his men moving forward. Giacherine passed through the 3d Platoon to the 1st Platoon, and contacted Cpl. Fiore of the 1st Platoon. Giacherine asked Fiore whether he knew where Herbert was.

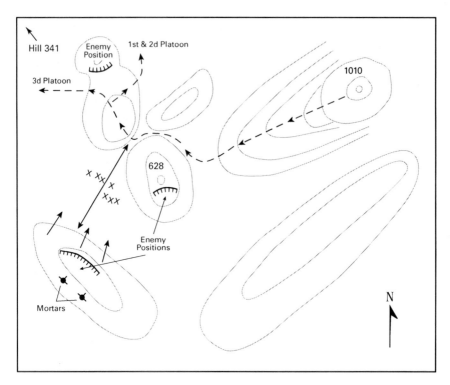

Sketch of action of Cpl. Robert W. Black and 8th Ranger Infantry Company (Airborne), 25 April 1951. (Based on map in CMH manuscript, U.S. Army. Not to scale.)

Fiore didn't know. Giacherine couldn't use his radio because his radio man had broken the antenna on the brush.

Giacherine, as he was moving forward, slipped and fell down the north slope of the ridge. He noticed, when he stopped sliding, that the company was drawing fire from the right. . . . He did not know where Herbert and Strong were. Strong had the 3d Platoon.

Fiore notified Giacherine that there was no one to his front on the ridge. He told Giacherine that his machine gun was out of action because of a broken firing pin. The ridgeline was very narrow and provided no cover.[22]

The 3d Platoon was in the center of the Ranger Company's march column. Members of the unit describe their view of the action.

M. SGT. WILLIAM R. COX, PLATOON SERGEANT: About 0600, 25 April, the company departed Hill 1010 with the 1st, 3d, and 2d Platoons in that order. A message came for Capt. Herbert as the company was moving, which instructed him to avoid Hill 628. The company was going around the right side slope of the hill when Cox saw men of the 3d Platoon moving up the left to the ridgeline. He then learned that fifteen Chinese had been spotted on the other side of the hill.

Cox did not know who opened fire. He moved forward from his position at the rear of the 3d Platoon and found the lead elements of his platoon in a trench and firing. The 1st Platoon was moving toward the Chinese, while the 3d Platoon acted as a base of fire. When a lull came in the firing, Lt. Strong moved the men out to the right, then up on a slope to the left.[23]

CPL. EUGENE C. RIVERA, PLATOON RADIO OPERATOR: The company moved off Hill 1010 about 0500, 25 April, and returned to Hill 628 without incident. Going around the base of Hill 628, the platoon leader of the 1st Platoon spotted fifteen Chinese. It was 0630 or 0700. He sent word of them to the company commander, who said, "Shoot them down." The platoon opened fire for five or ten minutes. It turned out that there were more than fifteen Chinese.

Rivera worked his way down into a saddle and to the other hill to the north. Then he took the ridge. He turned around and discovered that the company commander had disappeared. Rivera went back and found him, started to go forward again. Then Capt. Herbert was hit by enemy fire. Lt. Strong, the platoon leader, also got hit.[24]

SGT. HAROLD J. HOOKS, ASSISTANT SQUAD LEADER, 2D SQUAD: Hooks was acting as an assistant machine gunner. When the company departed Hill 1010, Hooks was in the middle of the column. Word was passed back that there was a "handful" of enemy out in front. The 1st Platoon was to go down and get the Chinese, while the other platoons were to cover with fire.

Hooks and his machine gun and several BAR men moved to the ridge to give support. He saw thirty or forty Chinese on the hill and in the valley. He pointed them out to the machine gunner. When the company opened fire, it received enemy fire from all directions.

Then enemy mortars started coming in. Hooks moved down the ridge to get instructions, and as he was moving forward, he was hit by mortar [fire]. He was bandaged by a BAR man, and he walked out with other wounded men to the tanks.[25]

CPL. ROBERT W. BLACK, 3D SQUAD: Black was a BAR man. Moving from Hill 1010 to Hill 628, Sgt. Moore, in the lead of the company, yelled back to the company commander that he saw approximately sixteen Chinese in the valley. A company machine gun was set up and fired on the enemy. Black and several others (some from the 1st Platoon) were sent to the top of Hill 628. But Chinese were there.

At first the enemy fire did not seem to be very heavy. But as the BARs moved into position, the enemy fire increased in intensity. It came from three sides. The enemy had the company pinned down. Black's BAR failed to function, so he took it apart. While he was busy with it, he lost his squad. Then the company began to take quite a few casualties.[26]

CPL. JESSE CISNEROS, ASSISTANT BAR MAN, 3D SQUAD: He was with the last group of his platoon to leave Hill 1010. The leading elements spotted Chinese in the valley. Cisneros' squad was placed on the ridge to the left to cover the company left flank and rear. The company opened fire and received enemy fire. Cisneros saw no targets to fire on from the ridge. The company commander sent one platoon ahead. The other platoons moved around the ridge to the right. Enemy mortar fire started coming in, and Cisneros came off the ridge. Part of the 3d Platoon moved ahead. Cisneros' squad was split in two.[27]

CPL. McGREGOR, BAR MAN, 1ST SQUAD: The company moved out with the 1st, 3d, and 2d Platoons in that order. The 1st Platoon reported about fifteen Chinese up ahead. The company commander said to go get them. But there were more than fifteen, and the 1st Platoon was pinned down. Sgt. Moore, the platoon leader of the 1st Platoon, was hit. Lt. Strong, the platoon leader of the 3d Platoon, went forward, and he was hit. Strong came back looking for Capt. Herbert. By then the captain was hit.[28]

CPL. WILLIAM A. VARNELL, ASSISTANT BAR MAN, 2D SQUAD: The company moved out from Hill 1010 close to 0600 and reached an intermediate hill. Sgt. Moore of the 1st Platoon spotted the enemy and yelled for the company commander. Moore said that there were only fifteen or sixteen Chinese, but there were many more. The company commander ordered a squad to deploy in a base of fire with a machine gun and fire on the enemy. Sgt. Cox of the 3d Platoon pulled the BAR men and assistants up on the ridge, while the 1st Platoon moved down toward the enemy. There was much firing.

Twenty minutes later, the company pulled off the hill, the men moving across the 1st Platoon area in threes and fours, covering each other as they moved. Varnell moved down the ridge with Zagursky. A burst of machine gun fire came close to Varnell. Then some mortar fire landed in the area. Varnell got into a trench where a wounded man was lying. The company commander then moved into the trench. He was wounded. He rose up several times to locate an enemy machine gun and was hit by fire a third time. The right rear enemy machine gun opened up and hit the FO party. Capt. Herbert told Lt. Strong to take over the company. Then Varnell and several others moved down the ridge to the tanks.[29]

As the enemy fire continued to come in and a number of leaders went down with wounds, the leading elements of the 8th Ranger Company broke into fragments and withdrew. Members of the company describe the scene.

SFC MCNEELY, SQUAD LEADER, 2D SQUAD, 1ST PLATOON: McNeely and the man with him crawled back toward the company, saw no one. They got back to the cover of the ridge and met a squad leader going down the slope of the hill to the valley. This man said that the company was ordered to "bug out" through the valley. So McNeely took off.

On the road, he saw four tanks and some friendly troops. These tanks and a litter jeep carried out the wounded. One tank came up the trail as far as possible and picked up several men who were coming down the hill. Then McNeely rode a tank back to the assembly area of the 21st Infantry Regiment and a truck to the company CP.

He estimated that at least two enemy companies had engaged the Ranger Company. The company fired generally at a range of 250 yards. McNeely fired three bandoliers and used seven of the twelve grenades he carried.[30]

CPL. LENZ, ASSISTANT SQUAD LEADER, 1ST SQUAD, 1ST PLA-TOON: McNeely went back to make contact with the company, then yelled that everyone was bugging out. Lenz ran down into the valley. He used more than one bandolier of M1 rifle ammunition at aimed targets and in supporting fire.[31]

M. SGT. COX, PLATOON SERGEANT, 3D PLATOON: Cox then moved forward to pick up the men of the 1st Platoon going toward the Chinese. He moved seventy-five yards to the front and found a state of confusion. He then checked to see if the 3d Platoon was organized. He could not see Lt. Strong, and he never saw him again. Confusion increased. Five Chinese approached as in a banzai charge, and friendly fire dispersed them. Cox then realized that the company was split.[32]

CPL. RIVERA, RADIO OPERATOR, 3D PLATOON: There was much confusion on the hill. When the Chinese opened up, they were 150 yards from the company on the right front, 400 yards on the left front, and on Hill 628 on the company's left rear.[33]

SGT. K. SMITH, 3D SQUAD LEADER, 2D PLATOON: Smith was at the base of Hill 1010 and the rest of the company was strung out in single file toward Hill 628 when the firefight started. It lasted 45 minutes. Shortly after it started, the mortar section destroyed its mortars by dropping thermite grenades down the tubes and smashing the traversing and elevating mechanism threads. They kept the sights, dumped the mortar ammunition there.[34]

CPL. MCGREGOR, BAR MAN, 1ST SQUAD, 3D PLATOON: Lt. Strong told the captain that they had to bug out. He yelled, "Let's bug." He took off, taking with him half of the 1st Platoon and half of the 3d Platoon, leaving half of the 1st Platoon pinned down. Because of lack of leadership up front, the 1st and 3d Platoons did not know what to do. There was no one there to direct fire or deploy the men. At this time, McGregor was firing against the ridges, but he could not see any enemy and he was not sure there were any there. When people started to leave, McGregor and three others moved out in a group.[35]

SFC Zagursky, squad leader, 3d Platoon: The company departed Hill 1010 at 0630. When it got to Hill 628, word was passed back that fifteen Chinese were on the hill. Zagursky lay down, crawled forward as fire came in "from all over." [Lieutenant Blumenson concluded: "Zagursky's story from here is incoherent. My impression is that Zagursky, with others, panicked and ran down the hill to the valley. He told of falling down the side of mountains, wading creeks, jumping over ditches. Zagursky sprained his leg. When he approached the tanks, he did not know whether they were friendly or enemy, and by then he did not care."][36]

Lt. Giacherine describes his actions to reestablish control of the company and move it out of the enemy area.

Giacherine instructed Ellis [platoon sergeant, 2d Platoon] to pull his men off the ridge. Then he met Cox, the platoon sergeant, 3d Platoon. Huddled among the rocks on the side of the ridge, Giacherine asked if anyone knew where Herbert was. No one knew.

Giacherine decided to take the 2d and 3d Platoons off the ridge and make his way around the right side of the hill to get out of accurate enemy machine gun fire. He instructed a few men to remain on the ridge to cover this move. As the men started to get off the ridge, Giacherine saw Rivera, Herbert's radioman, carrying an SCR300 radio on his back. He yelled at Rivera, who came over to Giacherine. Wounded men began to appear. Corporal Hardground, the 2d Platoon medical aid man, administered first aid in the immediate locality and then had the men moved to the shelter of an overhanging ledge.

Giacherine established contact with the 2d Battalion, 21st Infantry Regiment, by means of Rivera's radio. He asked whether it was possible to get artillery on . . . [the enemy position]. The answer was yes. Fire was adjusted by Giacherine, and a "damned good barrage" on the point arrived. Enemy harassing fire from this direction ceased. Giacherine requested the artillery to continue harassing firing until further notice on this point.

Someone then brought word that Herbert was wounded. This was about an hour and a half after Giacherine had assumed command of the 2d and 3d Platoons. He instructed Ellis to maintain some men on the ridge and move others into a perimeter. He went to the ridge and directly westward to observe suspected enemy elements . . . which were holding up the front of the company column. He left Rivera because Rivera was exhausted.

On the trail he found several wounded men, and he met Herbert, who was lying in the path all bloodied up. His first words were, "Jack, I'm sorry I got you in this mess." "Hell, you should be," Giacherine said. Herbert asked whether he could do anything. "You've done enough," Giacherine said.

With Sgt. Cox, Giacherine proceeded to a position from where he could overlook the valley to the south (the company front). Leaving Cox there with instructions that Giacherine would call artillery and Cox would adjust, Giacherine returned to his radio. He instructed Ellis to move to a vantage point to insure adjustment. He verified with the artillery, and Ellis acted as forward observer. Enemy mortar fire began to fall into the hollow where the company was. Friendly artillery fire was adjusted to strike the forward slope . . . [where the enemy was located].

Then Giacherine was notified by the 2d Battalion, 21st Infantry Regiment, that a rescue party had been sent out to get the Ranger Company back in. Tanks believed to be from the 5th RCT [Regimental Combat Team] were seen. . . . Enemy mortar fire increased. Then Giacherine received word that the company would have to come out the best way it could. Feeling that the enemy position first neutralized by artillery fire was no longer any danger to the company, Giacherine decided to withdraw along the trail to the northwest. He called the 2d Battalion, 21st Infantry Regiment, and asked them to have tanks meet the company. . . . The answer came, "OK."

Giacherine instructed Ellis to have the company withdraw in an orderly manner to insure the fact that every man got off the ridge. He stopped the artillery harassing fire. Then he sent Ellis to lead off with six men as point. His intention was to follow the path to the left of the stream to the main road. The wounded came next after the point, and then the remainder of the company. As the last element of the company was leaving, Chinese came up to occupy the position. Fifteen men, acting as a cover force for the company, blasted the enemy with small arms fire. By then, the forward elements were out of sight. Keeping four BARs as a rear guard, Giacherine sent the rest of the men to catch up with the company.

Giacherine remained to contact the 2d Battalion. He had to put up a long antenna to reach them. Friendly planes raked the area . . . [the enemy position, just south of Hill 628]. Giacherine contacted battalion and learned that the battalion was moving out. He attempted to call artillery on the ridge vacated, but he was unable to contact the artillery. Tanks then came in on the company channel and . . . [gave their current location], but [said] that they could remain there only a limited time. How long, asked the tanks, would it take the company to reach . . . [the meeting point]. Giacherine said one hour, he hoped.

As he passed Hill 341, Giacherine noticed movement on the hill, what appeared to be ten or twelve Chinese. But no fire came from there, and the Ranger Company did not fire. Prior to reaching the road, Giacherine gathered the wounded together and deployed a perimeter around them. He then frantically called the tanks, which arrived in fifteen minutes. There were five tanks of Company C, 6th Medium Tank Battalion. These tanks had drawn fire from high ground. All the men were loaded on the tanks and were taken back to friendly lines without incident. Ambulances were waiting there to evacuate the wounded. Giacherine counted the men present and realized that only forty-four men had come out with him. He inquired and learned that other rangers had been pulled out by tanks several hours before. The tanks of Company C, 6th Medium Tank Battalion, took Giacherine's group down the MSR to the CP of the 21st Infantry Regiment, where he met the remainder of the company which had come out previously.[37]

Other members of the Ranger Company describe the situation as Lt. Giacherine organized and conducted the withdrawal of their unit.

CPL. RIVERA, RADIO OPERATOR, 3D PLATOON: Lt. Giacherine, who had come forward, assumed command and called for the radio. Rivera worked his way back to him. Giacherine called artillery in on the hills to the company right. Several enemy machine guns were firing on the company. Then enemy mortar fire came in. The company consolidated. Giacherine radioed the 2d Battalion, 21st Infantry Regiment, and learned that they were "bugging out." The lieutenant said that the Rangers needed help to get out. Battalion then said that tanks would come forward to meet the Ranger Company. Rivera got down to the tanks about 1300.[38]

M. Sgt. Cox, platoon sergeant, 3d Platoon: He met Lt. Giacherine. Rivera and Sgt. Ellis, the platoon leader of the 2d Platoon, were with him. Giacherine called in artillery on the right of the company on an enemy machine gun position. Enemy fire came in from three sides. Giacherine was wondering what was in front of the company. He also wondered where the lead elements of the company were. He sent Cox over a knoll about 100 yards to observe the enemy fire. Cox ran into Herbert and with a medic helped him move to Giacherine.

Giacherine figured a route to the valley. He set out flank protection and got the wounded off. When the Chinese came over the ridge to the rear, a burst of fire dispersed them. Cox saw no more enemy after that, and he reached the tanks. "If it hadn't been for Lt. Giacherine," Cox said, "we'd probably still be lying up on that hill."[39]

Sgt. K. Smith, 3d Squad leader, 2d Platoon [in the rear of the company column moving from Hill 1010]: When Smith arrived on Hill 628, the 2d Platoon was spread out on the ridgeline protecting the left flank. Smith set up the machine gun to cover the rear. He had two BARs from another squad of the 2d Platoon covering the company front. This was about 0900. Smith sat there three hours before getting the order to move down into the valley.

The Chinese on Hill 1010 fired down on the company. Chinese were also on the company left flank and left front and firing. Smith fired at a 300-yard range. He could see the enemy running around in trenches. Enemy mortar fire came in on the company. . . . Smith thought that one of his BARs knocked out an enemy machine gun on the left front, for it ceased firing after his BARs concentrated their fire on it.

At 1200, the platoon leader told Smith to have his squad help the wounded down off the hill. Smith left two men with the 1st Squad, 2d Platoon, as part of the rear guard.[40]

SGT. CHARLES B. TAUNTON, ASSISTANT SQUAD LEADER, 3D SQUAD, 2D PLATOON: The company moved toward Hill 628 in the morning. Taunton heard some fire, but he saw nothing. His platoon was in a trench moving across the ridge, and even though fire was coming in, he saw nothing to fire at. Then enemy machine gun fire came in from the left front. He moved around the right of a knoll to escape the fire, then located the enemy machine gun. He started firing at it and got a BAR to flush out the machine gun position. Several enemy ran up the trail, and the BAR man and Taunton picked them off. Taunton got three BAR men, several riflemen, and one light machine gun set up, and this group fired on the ridge and the point of the hill. The men fired at 300 or 400 yards. After the squad to his rear came down the hill, Taunton came off the ridge. He went down into the valley and with three BARs acted a rear guard for the company in case the Chinese followed the company out. The wounded were carried off the hill. As Taunton was going forward to contact the tanks, an air strike hit the mountain.[41]

The first sergeant of the 8th Ranger Company, M. Sgt. Charles R. Craig Jr., summarizes the casualties from the fighting at Hill 628 and what was achieved.

According to the division commander, the action of the company saved the 21st Infantry Regiment from being entirely surrounded, and saved the entire right flank of the division. The 6th ROK Division had completely collapsed. When the company reported back, it brought the first real knowledge of what the situation up front was.

The company sustained 2 KIA [Cpl. Paul E. Snavely Jr. and Cpl. Henry C. Trout Jr.] and 21 WIA.[42] A total of 87 enlisted men and 3 officers participated in this action. Eight enlisted men comprised the company CP in the rear. Each rifleman had four bandoliers (48 rounds per bandolier), two grenades, and one mortar round. Each BAR man carried one belt of ammunition (12 magazines per belt; 20 rounds per magazine). Each machine gun had four boxes of ammunition (250 rounds per box). The company had two 60mm mortar and a total of 56 HE rounds of ammunition. This was the basic load carried by the company on the night of 23 April.[43]

In an interview with Lt. Martin Blumenson on 7 June, some weeks after the Ranger Company's withdrawal, Lt. Giacherine reflected on the experience of the fight at Hill 628 and the insights he gained from being in a Ranger Company.

The final count of casualties was: 2 KIA, 21 WIA (including 2 officers). The FO party of 3 had 2 WIA, one of whom died later [Cpl. Otto T. Perkins, 52d Field Artillery Battalion, 24th Infantry Division].[44]

Not until a month later did Giacherine find out from Maj. Smith, the S-3 of the 21st Infantry Regiment, that Herbert had received a message from the division G-3 relayed by the regimental S-3 as the company was moving from Hill 1010 to Hill 628. The message instructed Herbert to proceed along the ridge across Hill 628 to aid the 5th RCT that was in a firefight and to keep them from being cut off by the enemy.

"This entire mission," Giacherine said, "was not clear to me or my men. General Bryan [Maj. Gen. Blackshear M. Bryan], the 24th Division commander, repeatedly commended the 8th Ranger Company for this action. The third time that he did so, I asked the pointed question, 'Exactly what good did we do?' He looked at me in surprise, and in all earnestness replied that by our action he was definitely able to determine that his entire right flank was exposed. He had had such an idea, but he was not sure. We undoubtedly prevented the 21st Infantry from being cut off, if not the entire 24th Division. I was then satisfied to learn this because men had died and been hurt without knowing why."

Recommendations:

There is no substitute for control over the men. The confusion that came about in the company was due to the lack of plan, as exemplified by the fact that there was not even a base of fire set up when the company moved forward to make contact with the enemy on Hill 628.

Men should not be loaded with equipment to the point where combat efficiency is impaired.

Men who have to perform special missions in the Ranger Company, i.e., communications, scouts, squad leaders, medics, platoon leaders, should be equipped with that in mind. They have a primary mission to perform. To load them with equipment equally with that of the others is incorrect.

The 8th Ranger Company in past operations in Korea has not performed in any other way except as a straight infantry company. Hardships are created as a result of operating as a separate company, which is independent administratively and tactically. For instance, one 2½-ton truck is authorized the company. When the company came overseas, it had five 2½-ton truck loads of equipment.

Adequate support is always a problem. Attachments and detachments occur in the midst of firefights. For example, on 22 May the company was attached to Task Force Plumley for several days. At 2000, 22 May, a plane flew over the company and dropped a note stating that Task Force Plumley was then attached to the 1st Battalion, 21st Infantry Regiment. At 2400 the company commander was instructed to be at a meeting at the CP of the 21st Infantry Regiment. Upon his arrival he was informed of a tentative plan whereby the 8th Ranger Company would be attached to the 21st Infantry Regiment. At 0800, 23 May, he was notified that the plan was cancelled, and that the company was reverting back to attachment to Task Force Plumley. From 0300, 22 May, to 1000, 23 May, the company had no rations, no ammunition, no bedrolls because of the confusion of logistical support.

The Ranger Company is both too small and too large. It is too small to make a concerted attack five or six miles behind enemy lines by aerial drop. It is too large to infiltrate and penetrate lines as a company.[45]

As for the action near Hill 628, the combat historian Lt. Blumenson summarizes his conclusions.

The fluid situation, the lack of exact knowledge of the enemy territory, when combined with individual nervousness, caused part of the 8th Ranger Infantry Company to panic when contact with the enemy was made. The destruction of friendly mortars by American personnel in the first minutes of the engagement, the split of the company into two parts with one half running down the mountain, the failure of the company to maneuver are instances of the difficulty of control in such a situation. This was complicated by the terrain, which forced the company to be strung out in single file over a long distance and by the fact that the company commander and a platoon leader, two of the three officers in the company, were wounded early in the action.

The natural confusion of the action was further obscured by the reluctance of the men to speak of this engagement except in terms of generality. Some individuals of the company, notably Lt. Giacherine, SFC McNeely, and M. Sgt. Cox, among others, were outstanding in their efforts to reestablish control.[46]

Chapter 7

GLOSTER HILL

1st Battalion, Gloucestershire Regiment (the Glosters), 22–25 April 1951

To the west in the U.S. I Corps, the Chinese main attack in the spring offensive fell on the ROK 1st Division and the U.S. 3d Infantry Division, blocking the main routes to Seoul. The 3d Division's front generally followed the Imjin River, which in this area flowed south and then west. The 65th Infantry Regiment, with its attached Philippine 10th Battalion Combat Team (BCT), held the right flank, facing west behind the Imjin. The British 29th Independent Infantry Brigade Group held the left portion of the 3d Division's front line, with the 1st Battalion, the Gloucestershire Regiment (known as "the Glosters"), next to the ROK division, whose nearest unit was a mile to the southwest. Two miles to the northeast of the Glosters was the 1st Battalion, Royal Northumberland Fusiliers (NF). Another mile beyond and across the Imjin lay the Belgian UN Battalion (BUNBN) and the right flank unit of the 29th Brigade abutting the 3d Division's 65th Infantry Regiment. Although all units except the Belgian Battalion were behind the Imjin, the 29th Brigade was vulnerable to attack along a lengthy front line that had many gaps and only two units in reserve, the 1st Battalion, Royal Ulster Rifles (RUR), and C Squadron, 8th King's Royal Irish Hussars.

When the Chinese blow fell, the 29th Brigade fought heroically but was gradually overwhelmed and pushed back. The Glosters were particularly hard hit and surrounded. Only a few soldiers managed to fight their way out. An investigation was conducted following the Chinese Spring Offensive to determine the reasons

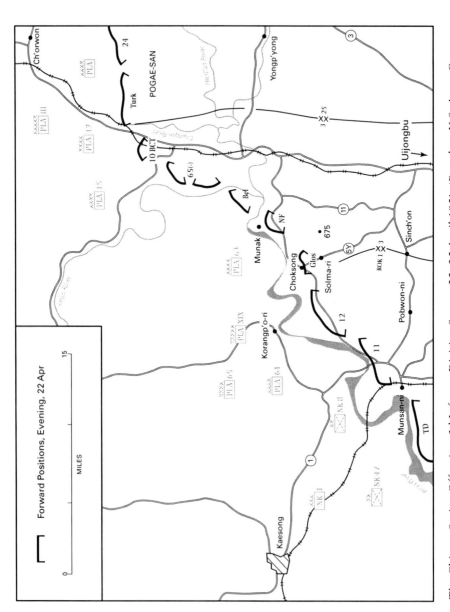

The Chinese Spring Offensive, 3d Infantry Division Sector, 22–25 April 1951. (Based on U.S. Army Center of Military History map.)

*for the disaster with the Glosters and why they could not be res-
cued. Staff officers and commanders of the British 29th Independent Infantry Brigade Group, the U.S. 3d Infantry Division, and
the U.S. I Corps prepared reports of their findings for the Eighth
U.S. Army commander, General James A. Van Fleet. These documents are used to tell the story of the Glosters' fight along the Imjin
River, an action for which they were awarded a U.S. Presidential
Unit Citation.*[1]

The Situation and the Opening of the Chinese Communist Forces' Spring Offensive

*Various headquarters described the situation before the Chinese
attack.*

*British 29th Independent Infantry Brigade Group, Review of
the Battle of the Imjin Fought by 29 Bde [Brigade] on 22–25 April
1951.*

GENERAL: This review does NOT pretend to be a history of the
battle but rather it is an endeavor to describe the deployment of the
enemy and to give an indication of the manner in which he fought
and the tactics which he employed. Though an offensive had been
expected from the 15th Apr, there were no real indications on the
29 Bde front, a front extending over 13,000 yards, that an offensive
of any size was impending. In fact there was a gap of some ten to
fifteen miles between the opposing armies. As a result the posn [po-
sition] was neither wired nor mined. Into this vacuum, task forces
and Jock columns strenuously probed, but with little or no enemy
contact.[2] One PW was eventually taken, identifying the 187th Div,
63d Army, on the 29 Bde front, but from both air and ground little
movement was seen. In fact on the afternoon of 22 Apr, three Bel-
gium officers in AOP [aerial observation post] flew to a depth of
some fifteen miles behind the enemy lines without observing anything that would indicate that in twelve hrs time the whole Bde
would be fighting a pitched battle. All intelligence sources that were
available to the 29 Bde were fully deployed in an effort to discover
what was going on on the "other side of the hill." Task forces penetrated by day to depths ranging between 10,000 and 15,000 yards,

by night fighting and recce [reconnaissance] patrols crossed the R[River] Imjin in effort to catch the enemy moving fwd [forward] and capture PW, of which there was an embarrassing scarcity. Low-level air photographic cover was asked for and flown by the 3 U.S. Div air section. Recce flights with observers from units in 29 Bde were flown by 3 U.S. Div air section. The net result of this effort was still a complete fog. It was known that something was afoot, but where and when the blow would fall was still a complete mystery. In an effort to acquire some concrete indication of the enemy intentions, it was decided on 19 Apr that two long-range patrols from 29 Bde would penetrate to the area south of Sibyon-ni, one patrol from the Belgian Bn would set out on 24 Apr and the second patrol from the 1 NF would set off on 26 Apr; the planning for both these projected penetrations was in progress when the storm broke. Thus it can be seen that it was known that the enemy intended some mischief on a considerable scale. When, with what, and where the enemy intended to do it was largely an unknown quantity.

SITUATION ON 22 APR.: The Bde was deployed on the morning of 22 Apr . . . astride one of the classic routes of entry into Seoul from the north, it was also the pivot from which the line ran north. It can therefore be seen that an enemy intending to capture Uijongbu and encircle the remainder of I Corps would probably strike in some str [strength] against the sector held by 29 Bde. 29 Bde had three patrols across the R Imjin on the morning of 22 Apr, on the left a patrol from the 1 Glosters . . . ; in the centre a patrol from the 1 NF to the general area of Songhyon, and on the right a patrol from the Belgian Bn to the area of Nodong. The first contact with the enemy was made by the 1 NF patrol at 0945 hrs. . . . This was unusual as the enemy had not been recently contacted as far south as this. Throughout the day reports came in of the enemy moving south in small gps [groups] along the whole front. Yet air until late evening did not see any really large body of men moving south, when air recce reported the roads leading south from Ch'orwon crowded with vehicles and men. Nevertheless the real indication that something big was afoot did not come until 1500 hrs, when the Turks in the 25 Div sector captured a Chinese Arty [Artillery] survey officer who stated the big offensive was to be launched that night.

Even though by late afternoon it was apparent that the enemy had surged forward along the whole I Corps front, previous experience of Chinese tactics indicated that though a big battle was imminent, strong patrolling on the part of the enemy in an endeavor to discover and find out our positions would be the order of the day prior to launching an all-out attack. This, however, was NOT to be so, as the enemy attack began in earnest at 2200 hrs that night.

By 1600 hours all three patrols had been in contact with the enemy. The patrol from the 1 Glosters on the left had their first contact at 1240 hrs and thereafter were followed back south down the valley by the enemy to what was generally known as the Gloster crossing. On the right, the Belgian Capitol Bn had contact with the enemy at 1600 hrs, and civilians reported that the enemy were in str [strength]. . . . Thus it can be seen the fog of war was lifting a little, but it was still unsure whether the enemy was just regaining contact prior to launching the expected offensive or that this general fwd movement was the herald of an all-out attack that night. As darkness fell, all the patrols had returned and contact had been broken. 45 Fd Regt RA [Field Regiment, Royal Artillery] shelled small gps of enemy that were observed in the area north of the Gloster crossing. Thus the situation remained until 2000 hrs. At 1900 hrs, 29 Bde was ordered to carry out strong recce patrols across the river the following day, 23 Apr, to maintain contact with the enemy. As it will be seen, this very soon became impossible and unnecessary.[3]

U.S. 3D INFANTRY DIVISION, G-2, SUMMARY OF ENEMY OPERATIONS: During the period immediately preceding the CCF offensive, the 29th BIB [British Independent Brigade] was opposed in their sector by elements of three regiments (559th, 560th, and 561st) of the 187th Division of the 63d Army (Corps). These regiments apparently constituted the screening force for the 63d Army of the XIX CCF Army Group, then reportedly massing in the Sibyon-ni area for attack.

Prior to the actual attack, the three CCF regiments opposing the 29th BIB were not aggressive and offered only delaying action to repeated armored thrusts by the 29th BIB up to 10,000 meters forward of their positions generally along the Imjin River.

Beginning at daylight on 22 April, all observation and recon
agencies of the division reported constantly increasing numbers of
enemy moving south across the entire division sector. Several enemy
units of bn size were observed moving south in the 29th BIB sector,
reaching a line generally 3,000 to 5,000 meters north of the Imjin
by dusk the 22d. These reports included information from the 25th
Infantry Division on our right that Ch'orwon and vicinity was
swarming with enemy vehicles, artillery, and infantry moving
openly in daylight, [leaving] little doubt as to the intentions of the
enemy. By 1500 hours on 22 April, all units of the division had been
informed that the Turk Brigade had captured a Chinese artillery
officer engaged in making a survey for his battery and that this officer stated unequivocally that a general offensive would be launched
shortly after dark that night.[4]

U.S. 3D INFANTRY DIVISION, G-3 SUMMARY: The original mission given to the 29th British Independent Brigade Group was to
relieve the 65th Inf in its sector (the left (W) part of the division
sector); organize, occupy, and defend Line Kansas and Line Utah in
sector. At time this relief was completed the 15th Inf reverted to
control of X Corps in an area NW of Seoul. Aggressive patrolling
fwd of the Imjin R was directed in the original order and repeated
in subsequent instructions. These orders were carried out in letter
and spirit. . . .

Commencing about 220900 Apr, air observation reports,
ground observation reports, and patrols reported an increasing
number of enemy sightings along the division front, particularly in
front of the sector occupied by the 29th BIB. . . . The enemy was
reported moving S and SE, with the largest sightings moving SE, a
course which would lead them into the BIB positions. . . .

The 7th Inf was in reserve positions with the 2d Bn . . . with two
platoons of tanks attached prepared to support the BUNBN or reinforce the left flank of the 65th Inf. The other two battalions had
been preparing Line Kansas and were in assembly areas. . . .[5]

U.S. I CORPS REPORT: On 22 April the Gloucestershire Battalion was charged with defending the left sector of the 29th British
Independent Brigade Sector on the left of the 3d U.S. Infantry Division. To accomplish their mission the Glosters occupied positions on

Hill 314, Hill 182, and Hill 148 astride the primary avenue into the sector. The 12th Regiment of the 1st ROK Infantry Division occupied positions on the left flank in the vicinity of Hill 150 [about two miles west of Hill 148]. To the right the Northumberland Fusiliers occupied positions on Hill 152, Hill 217, and vicinity [near Munak]. The Belgian United Nations Command was committed north of the Imjin River, and the Royal Ulster Rifles were in reserve.[6]

The opening of the Chinese offensive the night of 22–23 April is described by various headquarters.

BRITISH 29TH BRIGADE REVIEW: In retrospect it appears that 2000 hrs was the time set for H hr by the CCF because between 2000 hrs and 2100 hrs all three forward battalions were in contact with the enemy. On the left a patrol of the Glosters were engaging the enemy crossing the river at the Glosters crossing at 2230 hrs; in the centre X Coy [company], 1 NF, were engaged at 2240 hrs with a gp of CCF who had crossed the river, and on the right C Company of the Belgians were engaging a group of enemy who were endeavoring to infiltrate between them and the river. The patrol of the 1 Glosters were forced to withdraw at about 2300 hrs, and by midnight it had become apparent that this was no probing patrol action, but rather it was a case of "cry havoc and let slip the dogs of war."

At 0030 hrs on 23 Apr, A Coy of the 1 Glosters was under extremely heavy attack until by 0400 hrs all companies of the 1 Glosters were heavily engaged. A similar situation was developing on the right. The enemy ambushed the battle patrol of the 1 RUR, who had been sent up to secure the bridges across the Imjin to the rear of the Belgians. This patrol was ambushed at 0200 hrs, and it transpired that the enemy had infiltrated in some strength. Meanwhile, C Coy of the Belgians was heavily engaged with a large number of enemy. In the centre of the position, X Coy, 1 NF, was being very heavily pressed on the left of the bn sector, and on the right Z Coy were under heavy pressure from a force of enemy who had infiltrated between the Belgians and the Imjin. By 0300 hrs X Coy, 1 NF, had had to withdraw. At the same time it became apparent that enemy were infiltrating south through the middle between 1 NF and 1 Glosters, and to the east between the Belgian Bn and 1 NF.

The pattern of the enemy attack was by this time beginning to take shape. The enemy had made two crossings of the river and was advancing in the SE direction one force against each of the three fwd bns. Although it was impossible to estimate the strength of the enemy attack, NOT less than one enemy bn was engaging each of the 29 Bde's fwd bns. At the same time, gps in some numbers were infiltrating around and between the fwd elements. In retrospect it seems that the enemy attacked with three regts fwd with a regt committed to each of the three prongs. An identification was forthcoming later in the day from a PW who was found sitting quietly near HQ 45 Fd Regt RA and the leading fmn [formation] was found to be the 187 Div, 63 Army, 19 Army Gp. It was also becoming clear that the main CCF assault on the 3 Div front was being directed against the 29 Bde.

As the night wore on, the fighting waxed fiercer between 0400 and 0500 hrs. A, B, and D Coys of 1 Glosters were still under attack. W Coy 1 NF was being attacked from the north. B and C Coys of the Belgian Bn were under attack, and in addition there was some sniping going on in the 45 Fd Regt gun lines.[7]

3D INFANTRY DIVISION, G-2, SUMMARY OF ENEMY OPERATIONS: Commencing with a massive artillery preparation in the TAFC [Turkish Armed Forces Command or Turkish Brigade, attached to U.S. 25th Infantry Division] sector on our right at about 2000 hours 22 April, the CCF offensive got under way. By 2130 hours, CCF in small numbers were attempting to infiltrate into the forward positions of the 29th BIB and attached Belgian Bn.

After midnight of the 22d, the attack developed rapidly. The PEFTOK Bn [Philippine Expeditionary Force to Korea, the 10th Battalion Combat Team (BCT)] attached to the 65th Inf Regt north and east of the 29th BIB was in difficulty by 0100, adjacent elements of the 65th Regt rapidly becoming involved. By 0330 the Belgian Bn in the angle of the Imjin where it is joined by the Hant'an was heavily engaged. The Northumberland Fusiliers on their left also became involved with a reported two enemy battalions. The enemy apparently chose to exploit his initial gains in the sector of the Belgian Bn and by dawn had taken this bn under attack from all sides, trying to overrun their positions and gain the pontoon bridge linking the

Belgians with the south bank of the Imjin. Elements of the NF Bn and the Royal Ulster Rifles Bn moved to protect the bridge, but an estimated enemy company infiltrated across the Imjin in this area and gained the high ground overlooking the south end of the bridge. At 0600 hours, D Company of the Gloucester Bn on the left of the 29th BIB sector was under attack by an unknown number of enemy.

The best identification that could be made of the troops attacking along the 29th BIB front and into the angle of the Imjin indicated that they were elements of the 189th Div, 63d CCF Army (Corps), which passed through the 187th Division in the attack.[8]

23 April

During the daylight hours of 23 April the enemy attacks somewhat lessened as UN firepower was brought to bear and the Chinese moved fresh units forward for a renewed effort. Higher headquarters focused on identifying the areas of greatest threat and best locations for commitment of the limited reserves of the 29th Brigade and 3d Division. The situation is described as seen at various levels.

GLOSTER BATTALION SURVIVORS: During the early morning the enemy appeared to have withdrawn toward the river, but at 0645 the enemy attacked again. A Company started pulling back at 0715. D Company pulled off of Hill 182 at 0830. Both A and D Companies withdrew to Hill 235. A Company had 70 men, and D Company had 81 men plus 14 WIA. The enemy had infiltrated to Hill 314, and B Company, in pulling back, had to fight over that hill. B Company secured Hill 314 during the day. C Company remained in the same location that day. During the day the enemy was observed moving south of the Bn positions. During the night the enemy attacked between Hills 182 and 314, then turned east and attacked Hill 314. That night the commanding officer [Lieutenant Colonel James P. Carne] and fifteen men from B Company withdrew from Hill 314 and joined D Company on Hill 235.[9] The enemy attacked the battalion positions throughout the night.[10]

BRITISH 29TH BRIGADE REVIEW: As daylight came the enemy redoubled his efforts. Pressure was stepped up on both the right and left flanks. It was becoming clear the 1 Glosters were being attacked by a regt plus; the attack was being supported by mortar and MMG [medium machine gun] fire. By 0700 hrs the position in front of A and D Coys was becoming serious, and CO 1 Glosters asked for an airstrike. At the same time as these three main efforts were in progress, small groups of Chinese were infiltrating through between the 1 NF and 1 Glosters. Also at this time the occupation of line Kansas had been ordered, so the main Bde HQ moved back to rear at 0845 hrs, leaving a Tac [tactical CP] fwd at the old loc [location]. 1 RUR, less two Coys, was ordered up and took up a posn to east of 1 NF to meet a possible enemy threat to the right flank. In this area, at least one enemy bn was reported astride the rd [road] to the Belgians in addition to those groups of enemy that were moving SE down the valley whence X Coy had recently withdrawn.

By 1400 hrs the action was generally diminishing except on Belgian Bn, and it seemed that the first enemy wave was beginning to exhaust itself; but though their attacks diminished in frequency and intensity, the enemy's reaction to any offensive action on our part was sharp and stubborn. An attempt by the 1 Bn 7 RCT sp by tks [supported by tanks] to open the rd to the Belgians bogged down just in front of the 1 NF FDLS [forward defended localities].

At 1700 hrs the action on 1 Glosters front flamed up again with the enemy attacking from the north and west sp by 60mm mortars and five to six MMGs; in addition, the first indication that the enemy had infiltrated round the 1 Glosters was a report of between fifty and eighty enemy behind them. The Belgians, with the aid of the tks from the 65th RCT, managed to fight their way out eastwards across the river and back to our own lines with very few cas [casualties]. Apart from this the early hrs of the night were fairly quiet, until midnight when the battle was rejoined in full fury, particularly on the left.

Throughout the day, the weight of the enemy attack instead of being evenly distributed across the whole front was now tending to shift to the west; increasing pressure and signs of a greater buildup in front of the 1 Glosters was apparent. A surprising factor was the inability on the part of the enemy to exploit the gap that developed between the 1 NF and the 1 Glosters. This area—mountainous, well covered with trees, sharp ridges, and steep valleys—was admirably suited to the enemy's well-known tactic of infiltration. To compute the cas suffered by the enemy would be impossible. Suffice it to say that the adjt [adjutant] of 1 Glosters, normally reasonably reticent in his statements, said that the enemy had visibly suffered heavily. This pause, which lasted some six hrs, is explained by the fact that the leading enemy div, the 187 Div, [had] been disorganized. It is reasonably safe to say that the enemy expected to penetrate deeper than he in actual point of fact did. The 64 Army was reputed to be a frm [formation] of shock troops, and since it is known that the 64 Army attacked in a column of divisions, it is not unreasonable to suppose that this pause was the occasion for the second div, the 188 Div, to pass through.[11]

3D INFANTRY DIVISION, G-2, SUMMARY OF ENEMY OPERATIONS: During the daylight hours of the 23d, the enemy attack slackened in intensity all along the line except in the Belgian Bn sector. In front of the 29th BIB on its left flank there was a continued buildup even during the day, but no heavy attack. However, it became apparent that the enemy had infiltrated in the BIB sector in the afternoon when at least two ambushes in the brigade trains areas were reported. The Belgians held their positions although surrounded until late in the day, when they came out under heavy enemy pressure across the Imjin above the confluence of the Hant'an. Their stand throughout the day prevented the enemy from gaining the vital river junction and the MSR where it crossed the Hant'an, and thus permitted the 65th and 10th BCT [Philippine Battalion Combat Team] to make an orderly withdrawal across the Hant'an.

Again late in the afternoon of the 23d, the enemy began moving forces in up to Bn strength across the Imjin, probing for a gap between the Glos [Gloster] Bn on the left and the NF and RUR Bns echeloned on the right. The enemy force that had been building up all day on the boundary between the 29th BIB and the 1st ROK attacked after dark, passing to the west of the Glos Bn and exerting greatest pressure on the ROKs. Throughout the day, the enemy continued to filter down along the Changjin River, feeling for the positions of the 7th Regt, which had relieved the 65th along the Hant'an line.

During the night of the 23d the enemy finally found his gap. Locating a thinly held sector between the Glos on the left and the two other battalions of the 29th BIB still echeloned behind the threatened river junction, the CCF poured through. Infiltration groups headed south and east apparently in an attempt to cut the MSR near Uijongbu, but the bulk of the force hung up on the Glos Bn. Withdrawing into a tight perimeter on Hill 235, the Glos Bn withstood all attempts to overrun or displace them. . . . The exact arrangement of the enemy troops in this phase is not known due to scarcity of PWs; however, an estimate of the 29th BIB that they were under attack by one division is considered conservative. Whatever force piled up against the Belgians on the 23d undoubtedly slid westward into the gap on the night of the 23d, since pressure on the river angle decreased after the infiltrated company was cleaned up by elements of the 7th Inf Regt, also backing up the angle late on the 23d.[12]

U.S. I Corps Report: During the day of 23 April A and D Companies retired to Hill 235. B Company attempted to join A and D, but was so heavily engaged that it was unable to effect a linkup during daylight hours. C Company maintained positions.

During this same day (23 April), major attention was devoted to withdrawing the right flank elements of the 3d Infantry Division and extricating the Belgian Battalion from its position north of the Imjin River. . . . It was essential that right flank elements be withdrawn first in order that the integrity of the Kansas line might be maintained. At the time the Belgian Battalion was to be withdrawn, it was necessary to commit two companies of the Royal Ulster Rifles to maintain the position of the Northumberland Fusiliers and to cover bridges over which the Belgian Battalion was to be withdrawn. It was the 3d Division Commander's intention to restore the line between the Fusiliers and the Glosters with the 1st Battalion, 7th Infantry (part of his reserve), but the situation of the Fusiliers and the Belgian Battalion was so precarious that it was necessary to strengthen the right flank of the Fusiliers. The remainder of the division reserve (2d and 3d Battalions, 7th Infantry) was committed to previously prepared positions to provide a base for defense of Line Kansas. The 10th BCT, first elements of the 65th Infantry to withdraw, was moved to the 29th British Independent Brigade area to be used in relieving the Glosters. The Belgian Battalion was withdrawn to the east and south during the evening of 23 April to move to the 29th British Independent Brigade area, but did not close until the afternoon of the 24th. It will be noted that the Belgians could not be extricated over the planned withdrawal route because bridges were denied to them by enemy action. The reserve available to the brigade was committed to hold the position of the Fusiliers.[13]

On 23 April the 3d Division maintained close contacts with the 29th Brigade and carefully husbanded its small number of reserves. The situation is described by Col. O. P. Newman, chief of staff, 3d Infantry Division, in extracts from the 3d Division, G-3 Journal, and later reports on the usage of brigade and division reserves.

COL. NEWMAN: On the morning of 23 April, I was directed by the division commander to make a staff visit to the British CP to ascertain their situation and arrange for coordination between their units and the 1st Battalion, 7th Infantry, that was being ordered to move into that area with the mission of clearing out enemy in the vicinity of Hill 675. I arrived at the 29th BIB CP about 0950 and talked to Brig [Brigadier, later Maj. Gen., Thomas] Brodie at some length. He was particularly concerned with his right flank, where he had committed all of his reserve except one company, attacking along the ridge north of Hill 292. He was also concerned about only having one company left in reserve. I telephoned the division commander, recommending that an infantry battalion be sent to the BIB sector as soon as possible. The division commander stated that he would send the Philippine Battalion to that area as soon as they had completed their withdrawal. Brig Brodie at that time stated that the Gloster Battalion had withdrawn to Hill 235, that they were in a secure position, and he apparently felt no particular concern about them. After meeting Lt. Col. Wyand [Lt. Col. Frederick C. Weyand], CO of the 1st Battalion, 7th Infantry, and explaining to him his mission, I returned to the division CP.

About 1400 on 23 April, the division commander desired to change the mission of the 1st Battalion, 7th Infantry, to attack Hill 257 in order to relieve the pressure on the Belgian Battalion and permit its withdrawal. I again went to the CP of the 29th BIB, and Brig Brodie accompanied me to Lt Col Wyand's CP, where we coordinated his attack plans. I then proceeded with Brig Brodie to his new CP area. Brig Brodie expressed considerable concern at that time over the enemy infiltration in his center around Hill 675 and asked if I could speed up the arrival of the Philippine Battalion. I arranged for trucks to meet this unit at the Imjin River crossing. I returned to the division CP about 1700.[14]

3D DIVISION, G-3 JOURNAL: During this period the highlights were:

(1) Directive to CO 7th Inf (Div Res) at 230730 April 1951 to move one (1) Co [company] plus two platoons Tks from 2d Bn to the support of BUNBN. One platoon tanks crossed the Imjin and took up positions . . . supporting C Co BUNBN. Other platoon took up positions . . . and engaged the enemy located south of the river in effort to regain possession of the bridge over the Hant'an and retain possession of the bridge over the Imjin River. The infantry company, due to heavy S/A [small arms] and mortar fire coming from the hills south of the Hant'an River, remained . . . [about 500 yards north of the Hant'an] awaiting the withdrawal plan of CO, BUNBN.

(2) 1st Bn, 7th Inf, moved during the day to clear out and destroy the enemy reported in an assembly area on Hill 675, but they could not locate the enemy. The bn was then instructed to proceed north and attack and seize Hill 257 to open up a withdrawal route for BUNBN. The attack met fanatical resistance and, although air and artillery were used in copious quantities, did not succeed in dislodging the enemy. Bn disengaged at 2300 hours and started to its Kansas Line positions.

(3) . . . the 29th BIB was instructed to continue efforts to extricate the BUNBN and save their equipment. At 1600 it became apparent that the BUNBN felt it was impossible to bring their vehicles out with them and planned to burn the vehicles (three 2½-T trks, fourteen ¾-T trks, forty-two ¼-T trks) and withdraw by foot. CG, 3d Div, sent a staff officer by helicopter to CO, BUNBN, with instructions to work out a plan, using the available tanks, to extricate the vehicles via the Imjin River

bridge, thence northeast to the road running west from Chongong-ni. The withdrawal plan was coordinated to start with the attack of the 1/7 [1st Battalion, 7th Infantry] against Hill 257 set for 1930 hrs. The BUNBN and vehicles safely reached the south bank of the Hant'an River at 2230 hrs. Seven vehicles were lost during the entire action of BUNBN north of the Imjin River. The BUNBN was moved during the night to an area in . . . [about six miles south of the Hant'an] for further movement after daylight to . . . [an area about three miles south of Hill 675] closer to BIB CP.

(4) The 65th Inf withdrew S of the Hant'an during the day and, minus the 3d Bn, which took up the positions on Line Kansas of 1/7, went into division reserve.

(5) 10th BCT (PEFTOK) was disengaged and moved to an assembly area . . . [about three miles southeast of Hill 675] where it came under operational control CG 29th BIB. Closed at 2000 hrs.

(6) Enemy pressure against entire front of 29th BIB was heavy and intense during this period.[15]

Reserve Units Available to the 29th Brigade and 3d Division:
29TH BRIGADE RESERVES: Battalion, Royal Ulster Rifles, C Squadron, 8th Hussars (20 tanks)

(1) One (1) patrol guarded Imjin R Br [bridge] and one (1) patrol operated in sector of BUNBN during the period.

(2) Two (2) Cos [RUR] standing by to move at daylight 23d to aid NF or the BUNBNs to be accompanied by 1/2 sqdn [squadron] (10 Tks) of the 8th Hussars. This unit moved about 230830 to take over positions of NFs . . . [about 500 yards south of Hill 398] while NFs consolidated . . . [near Hill 217]. This left 2 Cos RURs still in reserve as of 231500. At this time the 29th BIB was informed they would have the 10th BCT attached when it closed their area (ETA [estimated time of arrival] 232000 Hrs).

(3) As of 231500 an additional company of the RUR Bn had been committed in the same area as the first two companies. The remaining company (B) was still in . . . [position about three and a half miles south of Hill 398].

(4) Brig Brodie did not feel he could commit the remaining RUR Co prior to the arrival of the 10th BCT (PEFTOK). The 10th BCT (PEFTOK) did not close the 29th BIB area until 232000 Hrs. Hence no reinforcements were sent to the Glosters nor was the gap between the right flank of the Glosters and the left flank of the NFs filled.

3D INFANTRY DIVISION RESERVES, PRIOR TO CHINESE ATTACK, 22 APRIL: 7th Infantry Regiment, 64th Medium Tank Battalion, 3d Recon Company, and 3d Ranger Company.

(1) 2d Bn, 7th Inf, located north of the Hant'an River . . . for backup of the BUNBN and protection of the left (SW flank) 65th Inf.
(2) 1st Bn 7th Inf and 3d Bn 7th Infantry located along the MSR vicinity Line Kansas, preparing regimental portion of Kansas and prepared to move either to the north or west to block or counterattack in zone of either 65th Inf or 29th BIB.
(3) 64th Med Tk Bn (M46 Tks) had been running daily patrols north and west of the 65th Inf positions and did so this date.
(4) 3d Recon and 3d Ranger Companies had been performing daily patrol missions, either singly or in combined force, into enemy territory and did so this date.
(5) There was no reason to commit or reposition any portion of the division reserve this date.

3d Infantry Division Reserves, 23 April:

(1) 1st Bn, 7th Inf, committed to clean out Hill 675 and later in the day launched a counterattack against strong enemy forces on Hill 257 to assist the evacuation of the BUNBN north of the Hant'an River and relieve pressure on the NF Bn, which had been driven off Hill 257 and was then in vicinity . . . [a mile and a quarter southeast, near Hill 398]. . . .
(3) 3d Bn 7th Inf assumed its position on Line Kansas.
(4) The 64th Med Tk Bn and 3d Recon Co screened the withdrawal of 65th Inf and BUNBN from Line Utah to south of the Hant'an River. . . .
(6) During this period no concern over the Gloster Bn was expressed by CO 29th BIB, and it was not felt that any reserve commitment was called for in regard to their position.[16]

24 April

The Chinese renewed their assault in full fury about midnight, and it continued through the daylight hours of 24 April.

GLOSTER BATTALION SURVIVORS: Early that morning [24 April], C Company and the Bn Headquarters withdrew south of the road. All the Bn was now on Hill 235. Only one section of mortars had gotten out of the draw and with only six rounds of mortar ammunition. Capt Harvey [D Company commander, a survivor and interviewee] estimated that the strength of the Bn was now around 350. On the night of the 24th the Bn drew into a very tight perimeter. A and B Companies had been combined. D Company was in the best shape and held the forward or north slope of Hill 235. At 0900 that morning the Bn had been told to fight its way out, but the Bn commander didn't believe he could do it due to the shortage of ammunition and the condition of the men. The Bn was very short on ammunition, rations, and water. The enemy appeared to be swarming around the positions all during the day. That night the enemy heavily attacked the Bn positions, except for D Company. D Company had radio communications with Bn Headquarters at all times during the battle. . . .

Three officers and six enlisted men made their way out on 24 April. These men were from the Support Company, which, except for MGs, was located generally in the draw behind C Company. These men had been cut off by infiltration and had made their way east and came in through the 29th British Independent Brigade lines.[17]

BRITISH 29TH BRIGADE REVIEW: The enemy attack started again on 1 Glosters at 0045 hrs with the right-hand coy under hy [heavy] attack, which attack was contained by 0235 hrs. But the hardest fighting of the night had yet to begin. What exactly happened is at present unknown, due to bad reception, but it transpired that by 0530 hrs 1 Glosters had had to give up control of the road and withdraw from their posns, and consolidate the whole bn on Hill 235 as a result of an extremely heavy attack. In the morning 1 Glosters reported they thought at least a regt had marched down the road after they had been driven off it. Heavy attacks were going in on the ROK formation on their left, and the enemy had penetrated to the SW of their position. Meanwhile on the right, Y Coy 1 NF and the two fwd coys of 1 RUR were being fairly heavily engaged by the enemy at 0340 hrs.

As dawn came, it became obvious that the enemy had succeeded in infiltrating through the middle between 1 NF and 1 Glosters and had managed to get at least a company onto Hill 675. This was obviously being reinforced as groups were seen moving south along trails immediately to the north. At 0700 hrs CO 1 Glosters sent a msg [message] through to the effect that the enemy buildup in the Glosters' area was such that it would preclude the possibility of a relieving force getting through. It was apparent that the enemy buildup on the left flank was becoming considerable. 1 Glosters were completely surrounded.

Again at 0745 hrs 1 Glosters were attacked from the SE by an enemy bn, and at 0800 hrs reported that they were hard pressed. On the right flank, 1 NF were being heavily pressed. Enemy mov [movement] could be seen on three sides of W Coy, and the enemy could be seen moving down the trails towards Hill 675. 1 RUR reported that the enemy were feeling round their right flank between them and 7 RCT. In the centre five Glosters, who had been captured and taken to Hill 675, escaped after dawn during an air strike and reported that an enemy coy had established itself there during the night, and there had been much mov in a southerly direction by another coy's worth. It was becoming increasingly obvious by mid morning that a large number of enemy were infiltrating south down the centre.

To return to the left, a relief column, consisting of the 10 PEFTOK (Phillipinos) with a half sqn of the 8 H [8th Hussars], moved up the rd to the relief of 1 Glosters. However, as they enter[ed] the valley they were engaged by the enemy in some numbers. Progress thereafter became increasingly slow. At 1015 hrs on the right, 1 NF reported a dug-in enemy battalion . . . and one of 1 NF patrols engaged a body of fifteen enemy moving south. A little farther over, 1 RUR reported that A Coy had been attacked off and on throughout the morning and that the enemy were massing for what looked like a big attack, but the real worry was the possibility of the enemy infiltrating round the right flank of the bn.

To return to the left flank, the relief column, comprising the 10 PEFTOK with a half sqn of the 8 H, was halted by the leading lt tk [light tank] of 10 PEFTOK being knocked out and blocking the narrow rd that ran up the narrow valley between steep-sided hills towards 1 Glosters posn. In the afternoon, the Belgian Bn took up posns with the object of stopping any further enemy penetrations down the centre of the Bde posns. But by this time, a number of enemy gps had penetrated through and were harassing the area south and west of Bde HQ. The afternoon on 1 Glosters' front was generally quiet, and this calm extended to the right flank.

Nevertheless, by 2000 hrs it was apparent that the enemy was preparing again to increase his pressure on the Bde. Z Coy of 1 NF was under attack from the west. 1 Glosters were again being heavily attacked in str. By 2130 hrs those attacks had died down, both being repulsed. No sooner had these enemy efforts been repulsed, but A Coy 1 RUR was heavily attacked at 2140 hrs. This attack was followed very shortly after by a further attack on Z Coy, 1 NF. This enemy effort on the right flank continued until midnight.

As darkness fell, the enemy who had rested and regrouped during the afternoon continued his attacks. It is interesting to note that on this occasion the enemy pressed heavily on both flanks of the brigade simultaneously. At the same time the enemy was reported to be infiltrating in some numbers down the centre.

Again during the day it was impossible to estimate the enemy cas, but in retrospect, it is clear that the enemy had suffered heavily during the night and the morning, and had consequently to reorganize and rest during the afternoon, and as a result, with possibly a fresh fmn, 189 Div, the enemy renewed the attack during the early evening.[18]

3D DIVISION, G-2, SUMMARY OF ENEMY OPERATIONS: By dawn of the 24th the 29th BIB reported that they were under attack by at least one enemy division. Order of battle estimates located the 187th and 189th Divisions of the 63d Army (CCF) attacking abreast from the north fork of the Imjin, striking down the boundary between the 29th BIB and the 1st ROK. . . .

Against steadily mounting pressure, the 10th BCT, PEFTOK, attempted during the daylight hours of 24 April to push north and west to the Glos[ter] perimeter. Spearheaded by tanks, the PEFTOK Bn drove to within 2,000 yards of the Glos before the lead tank was knocked out, blocking the road, and the Bn ordered to fall back. However, the presence of the 10th BCT in the center of the enemy's hard-won gap obviously discouraged rapid exploitation by the CCF. The shoulders of the gap had been held firmly by the Glos on the left and the Belgians initially on the right. The NF and RUR Bns, south of the Imjin on the right, continued to hold their positions throughout this period, and the enemy, attempting to come down the middle, ran into a series of small units, each of which delayed and confused him. At one time or another, a company of the 7th Regt, patrols from the 3d Recon and 3d Ranger Companies, the 10th BCT, elements of the 64th Tank Bn, and of the 65th Inf Regt pushed west up this corridor and engaged the enemy.[19]

3D DIVISION, G-3 SUMMARY: During this period (24 April) the highlights were:

(1) 29th British Brigade was instructed to move an infantry-tank force NW to relieve the Gloster Psn. . . . The 10th BCT, with its own M24 tanks (four), plus half of C Squadron, 8th Hussars (ten Tks) embarked on this mission and encountered heavy resistance in pushing to a point 2,000 yards from the Gloster position on Hill 235.[20] The lead tank (M24) hit a mine (or was hit by a mortar round) at this point and blocked the road. Brigadier Brodie considered it unwise to go farther that night, and 10th BCT was withdrawn initially to positions [500 yards north of Kwangsuwon on Route 57] (then later to positions [1,600 yards north of Ibam-ni on Route 11]) and 8th Hussars returned to Vic BIB CP. At this time the BUNBN was in a blocking position . . . [two and a half miles south of Hill 675]. Contrary to air observation reports, there was no link-up on this date.

(2) 1/7 relieved 3/65 [3d Battalion, 65th Infantry] on Line Kansas and 3/65 moved to join the balance of the regiment in Div Res Assy (division reserve assembly) area . . . [three and a half miles southeast of Hill 675]. (closed 1530).

(3) To regain lost positions in the left sector of the division front, the 1st and 3d Bn of 65th Inf moved from the Div Res Assy area . . . to an attack assembly area . . . (closed 1830), prepared to C/Atk [counterattack] to the NW on the morning of the 25th to regain the Gloster positions and destroy the enemy concentration reported to be on Hill 675. In addition the 64th Med Tk Bn (less one company) was to be prepared to move N . . . to cut off the enemy as the attacking 65th drove him back. Upon restoring the Gloster position, the 65th would take over the Gloster sector, and the Glosters would revert to the 29th BIB.

(4) Enemy pressure against RUR and NF during the entire period was too heavy to permit these units to disengage or to be used elsewhere.[21]

U.S. I CORPS REPORT: It was intended to employ the Belgian Battalion on the morning of 24 April to restore the battle position between the Gloster and Northumberland Fusilier Battalions, but the conditions under which the Belgians were forced to withdraw from their forward positions resulted in a limited disorganization that precluded their employment prior to the afternoon of 24 April.

During the night of 23–24 April remnants of Company B of the Glosters succeeded in reaching Hill 235. During the early morning of the 24th, Company C and the battalion headquarters withdrew to Hill 235, which placed the entire unit on this position. No member of battalion headquarters is included among survivors of the Glosters. However, Capt. Harvey of Company D estimated that the battalion strength on the morning of 24 April was about 350 officers and men. A tight perimeter was established during the evening of the 24th.

On the morning of 24 April, the 10th BCT with ½ squadron of the 8th Hussars (10 tanks) was committed to the relief of the Glosters. The 10th BCT advanced to within about 2,000 yards of the Gloster position when the lead tank was immobilized due to enemy action, blocking the defile through which the column was forced to pass. At this time the brigade commander felt that any further advance was unwise due to the lateness of the hour (1735). Some confusion exists as to the instructions issued to the 10th BCT. The division commander directed that they hold their positions for the night. The brigade commander's orders to the 10th BCT are not clear, but the accompanying tanks were directed to withdraw and since the 10th BCT withdrew as well, it is presumed that they had orders from brigade to do so. No journal entry exists covering this point in the brigade journal and staff members queried have no recollection of the orders issued. The only entry pertains to the Glosters and 10th BCT at 1615, prior to the time the tank was immobilized, which directed both units to hold, which is presumed to mean when the 10th BCT reached the Glosters.

During this same afternoon, the Belgian Battalion was committed to a blocking position to cover withdrawal routes for the Fusiliers and Royal Ulster Rifles. At this time, all forces available to the brigade were committed to the ground, as well as forces available to the division, with the exception of two battalions of the 65th Infantry, which were en route to positions in the brigade area from which they could be committed on the morning of 25 April. The 15th Infantry in corps reserve was placed in blocking positions behind the right flank of the 1st ROK Infantry Division on the afternoon of 24 April, less one battalion which was committed to the reduction of a road block between Uijongbu and the Seoul–Munsan-ni road.

At 240900 the Gloster Battalion was granted permission to fight its way out of its perimeter. According to survivors, the battalion commander decided that such a course of action was not feasible and that he would stay in the hope that relief columns could reach him. The decision was based on his short supply of ammunition and the condition of his men, who were short both rations and water. On this same day, arrangements were made for an air drop of essential supplies. However, the drop could not be made until the morning of the 25th and was cancelled when it was decided that the men remaining would be unable to carry the supplies. Limited quantities of medical supplies and communications equipment were dropped from light aircraft.[22]

25 April

By 25 April efforts of higher headquarters were focused on the rescue of the Gloster Battalion. It quickly became obvious, how-

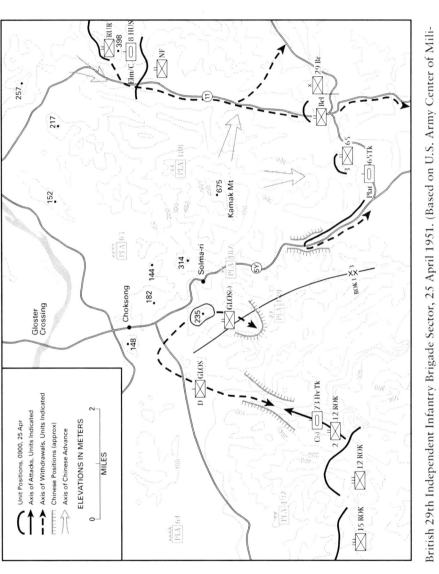

Legend:
- Unit Positions, 0900, 25 Apr
- Axis of Attacks, Units Indicated
- Axis of Withdrawals, Units Indicated
- Chinese Positions (approx)
- Axis of Chinese Advance

ELEVATIONS IN METERS

MILES
0   2

British 29th Independent Infantry Brigade Sector, 25 April 1951. (Based on U.S. Army Center of Military History map.)

ever, that the situation was too desperate and that scarce reserves had to be committed to other areas. The Glosters were left to their own resources as the rest of the 3d Division and I Corps conducted a fighting withdrawal and sought to reconstruct a cohesive defense line farther south.

GLOSTER BATTALION SURVIVORS: At 0900 [25 April] the Bn commander stated that he didn't believe any relief column could make it, so at 1030 the Bn would start out. Bn would move south from Hill 235. Capt. Harvey [D Company commander] decided against that direction because of the enemy seen there and also D Company would be the last out and the enemy would be lying for them even if the others made it. At 1030 the Bn moved out to the south. D Company headed northwest and then turned south and came in through the 12th ROK Regiment. D Company started out with approximately 90 men (including a few more from other units). Forty men (4 officers and 36 men) made it. D Company had contact going out and when they reached the 12th Regt lines (the 12th Regiment and the 73d Hvy Tk Bn were heavily engaged at that time), but met only 2 CCF en route. Capt. Harvey had told D Company that they could surrender or go with him, but once they started everybody kept moving. If a man went down, he would have to be left behind. When they were recognized by the 73d Hvy Tank Bn, the tanks went after them and brought them out. . . .

D Company made its way back in about two hours. Except for the people that returned on 24 April, no one else made it through. . . . The Bn commander and medical officer did not try to get out, but stayed on Hill 235, with litter cases (50–60).[23]

BRITISH 29TH BRIGADE REVIEW: Throughout the early morning of 25 Apr enemy pressure was heavy, 1 Glosters were hard pressed during the night. Z Coy 1 NF were also under heavy pressure as the enemy tried to get behind both 1 NF and 1 RUR. A Coy 1 RUR was under attack intermittently throughout this period. Similarly the Belgians were engaging the enemy who were in considerable str and were debouching from the valley that ran up to 1 Glosters' posn and enemy who were moving south from Hill 675. Elements of the 65 RCT were also engaged throughout the night. When dawn came it was apparent that the enemy had penetrated

through the 29 Bde posn in considerable str. At 0750 hrs an enemy
coy was reported est [established] at . . . [eight miles south of the
Glosters' crossing of the Imjin], and many were the reports of small
groups moving south.

By this time the enemy intention was obvious. His main thrust
down the left flank of the Bde was swinging SE with the obvious
intention of getting behind the 29 Bde and cutting the MSR in the
vicinity of Uijongbu. The thrust from, the number of enemy reported, was estimated to be between two and three regts strong.
The second and parallel thrust was directed to cutting the escape
route behind 1 NF and 1 RUR with the enemy pouring down the
sides of Hill 675 ESE. This thrust is considered to have been approx
regt str plus.

At 0600 hrs orders were received. 29 Bde was to withdraw
through posns to a posn in the Seoul area. This was put into effect
at 0800 hrs. From now on the battle became increasingly confusing.
Against extremely heavy pressure, 1 Glosters found it impossible to
withdraw, and split up in an effort to break out. 1 NF and 1 RUR
withdrew under heavy enemy pressure. B Coy 1 RUR were hard put
in keeping the pass open. Half of C Sqn, 8 H, with one troop of the
55 Fd Sqn, RE [Royal Engineers], acting in an inf role, had a hard
task of keeping the valley open. The majority of 1 NF managed to
clear the pass before the route was cut, but the 1st RUR had to fight
its way southeast over the hills towards Tongduchon-ni. The Belgian
Bn engaged enemy throughout the morning before withdrawing. At
about 0900 hrs 45 Fd Regt RA gun lines were under SA fire. By
noon the number of enemy observed and the multiplicity of enemy
reports became impossible to collate. Units and aircraft were reporting enemy units ranging in size from secs [sections] to bns moving over every possible route, an amorphous mass with only one
intent, to get south. At 1800 hrs on 25 [April] the part of 29 Bde in
the battle of the Imjin may fairly be said to have been over.[24]

3D DIVISION, G-2, SUMMARY OF ENEMY OPERATIONS: During
the night of the 24th and early morning hours of the 25th, the CCF
finally reached the Hant'an line held by the 7th Regt and launched
an attack across the river in estimated strength of two regiments.
These are believed to have been a part of the 29th Div, then consid-

ered part of the 10th CCF Army. There is no reason to doubt the strength or identification of the division in this attack, but later reports indicate that the 29th Div was a part of the 15th rather than the 10th CCF Army.

Daylight of 25 April found the division right flank under heavy pressure, the enemy having infiltrated and surrounded the positions of a battalion of the 7th Regt. Armored patrols relieved this situation, but general pressure forced the entire division front back toward Uijongbu. During the morning of the 25th, elements of the 65th Inf Regt reported they had contacted the Glos Bn and were bringing out the remnants of the Bn on tanks. In the center, the RUR and NF Bns pulled out slowly, fighting their way south through a continuous ambush as they left their positions. All elements of the 29th BIB continued south toward Uijongbu, passing from division control late in the afternoon.[25]

3D DIVISION, G-3 SUMMARY: During this period (25 April) the highlights were:

(1) During the night of 24–25 April the enemy infiltrated through and behind the left and center of the 29th BIB positions to the extent that, at daylight, the 1/65 and 3/65, BUNBN, 10th BCT, and the Brigade CP found themselves subjected to S/A and mortar fire. The MSR forward of the 29th BIB CP to the RURs and NFs was interdicted but not cut by enemy fire. . . .

(3) The last communication from the Gloster Bn was received at 250925 hrs. By this time all units of the division were heavily engaged and experiencing difficulty in disengaging to withdraw.

(4) Enemy pressure prohibited the 1/65 and 3/65 from starting their attack to reach the Gloster Bn. Enemy forces to the southeast of the 1/65 and 3/65 made it imperative that these units change direction and attack the enemy and take up blocking positions . . . to prevent the enemy from cutting in behind withdrawing troops on the MSR. In addition the 3d Rcn Co and 2/65 were dispatched at 1000 hrs via the MSR to take up positions along a line . . . , block the enemy, and drive him back into the path of the 10th BCT, 1/65 and 3/65, who were now advancing SE.

(5) The BUNBN was engaged in withdrawing into blocking positions W and SW of the 29th BIB CP to hold the enemy until the RURs and NFs could fall back thru them and continue SE to line Delta (Elgin) next defensive position.

(6) While the above actions were taking place, a tank column of the 65th Inf (ten Tks) was attempting to break through to the Glosters. This column was not successful. An erroneous air report indicated at one time that it was nearing the Gloster position, whereas in reality, the column never progressed farther [than] the 98 EW grid line [more than 3,000 yards from the Glosters]. A second attempt was made about 1200 hrs to send another tank column (this column included five Centurian tanks) through, but this was also unsuccessful. The Glosters were ordered by Brig Brodie to fight their way out (order was given about 1100 hours . . .).

(7) The delaying actions fought by the BUNBN to assist the RURs and NFs to withdraw resulted in the BUNBN becoming scattered, as were the NFs and RURs after fighting their way out of their Kansas Line positions. For this reason the 29th BIB arrived on Line Delta (Elgin) depleted in strength and with their tactical unity somewhat tangled. It was felt that they would not be able to man their portion of this line properly, so I Corps released the 15th Inf to control of the division, and this unit was given the task of relieving the 29th BIB on Line Delta (Elgin) and assuming responsibility for the sector. The 15th Inf was in the process of moving from positions in the 1st ROK Div sector when released to the 3d Div (1715 hrs). It continued its movement and relieved the 29th BIB by 2330 hrs and the 29th BIB (less 45th Fld Regt) reverted to control I Corps and started move S of the Han River.[26]

The 3d Infantry Division's assistant division commander, Brig. Gen. A. D. Mead, and the division chief of staff, Col. O. P. Newman, recall the situation as it was viewed at their command post on 24 and 25 April as concern for the Glosters grew.

BRIG. GEN. MEAD: Brig. Brodie arrived at the div CP in the forenoon [24 April] for conference with CG. CG told him to push the attack of 10th BCT to link up with the Gloster Bn. CG stated further that he was planning counterattack with 65th Infantry early

morning of 25th to restore the MLR in BIB sector. He asked Brig
Brodie if he felt that this timing was satisfactory in view of the Gloster situation. Brig Brodie answered in the affirmative.

[1515] Departed for the 29th BIB from the div air strip where
the CG was still in conference w/CG 8th Army [Van Fleet] and
CINC FECOM [Commander-in-Chief, Far East Command (Ridgway)]. Talked w/Brig Brodie for ten minutes (1535 to 1545 approx).
Pointed out to him the lack of contact between his right and the left
of the 7th Inf with the resultant danger of enemy penetration there,
which might cut in behind his right. Suggested that he push out
along the nose to the front of his right bn to counter this threat and
assist in tie-in with the 3d Bn, 7th Inf. He stated he could not do it
at this time because of enemy pressure but would attempt it early
next morning. (I subsequently informed the 7th Inf of this in order
that they might pay particular attention to their left flank in accor-
dance w/discussion I had previously had w/Col Boswell [James Boswell, commanding officer, 7th Infantry Regiment] at 1330.)

I then asked Brig Brodie about progress of the 10th BCT toward
the Glosters. He said the 10th BCT was still advancing. I reminded
him that we had plenty of artillery to reinforce his fires and advised
him to call for it. He stated he was doing so.[27]

COL. NEWMAN: About 1730, 24 April, Brig Brodie called me
asking for permission to withdraw the Philippine Battalion, which
had made an attempt to reach the Gloster position, and to order the
withdrawal of the Gloster Battalion that night. During the conversation, the division commander walked into my office, and he talked
to Brig Brodie on the subject. I heard him direct Brig Brodie to leave
the Philippine and Gloster Battalions in their present positions. He
stated that he was certain that the Glosters would suffer severe
losses if they attempted to break out at night, that he was ordering
an attack by two battalions of the 65th Infantry the following
morning to relieve pressure on the Glosters. About 1900, I received
word that the Philippine Battalion had withdrawn about 5,000
yards from their most forward position. I do not know who directed
this withdrawal.[28]

BRIG. GEN. MEAD: [0730, 25 April]. Departed div CP for CP
29th BIB. Arrived CP 29th BIB at 0800. Went to mess tent where

Brig Brodie, Col Harris [commander of the 65th Infantry], Lt Col Hawkins [commander of the 64th Medium Tank Battalion], and others were conferring. Learned that the composition of the task force to relieve the Gloster Battalion was still under discussion, that a British tank comdr [commander] recommended that it should be a smaller number of tanks, that one platoon of the 65th Inf Tk company was being considered. Interrupted to express concern that tanks were not already en route and to emphasize necessity for speed. Col Harris spoke up and stated that he understood his mission perfectly, that he and Brig Brodie were together on it, and if left alone he could assure me they would handle it. Brig Brodie nodded agreement. I repeated the injunction as to the necessity for speed in getting under way and stepped outside in order to allow them to finish.

I then spoke to Lt Col St Clair who stated that his battalion was under pressure and that CCF forces were sliding off his front towards the south, where they would pose a threat to the BIB MSR and the 3d Div MSR. While I was still engaged with Lt Col St Clair, Col Harris came out and reported that he and Brig Brodie were in agreement, that it was a job for M4 tanks rather than M46s, and that a platoon was all that could be profitably employed. He said that his instructions had been issued and that his platoon was about to move out. He added that he could not have moved earlier because of the arrangements which had to be made for communications and for supporting fires and air. I asked if he was prepared to follow up with greater strength if this should prove necessary, and he replied that he was. He then moved on to continue his supervision, and I had a few more words with St Clair. Informed him that the div Rcn [reconnaissance] Co was moving to operate against the threat to the south.

I next went over to talk with Brig Brodie. He stated that the plan he and Col Harris had agreed upon appeared to be the only practical solution. He expressed some concern as to the timing of the withdrawal of the NF and RUR Bns. I told him that instructions had already been issued on this and that I was sure his brig major must have received them through Captain Ellery, his Ln O [liaison officer]. That withdrawal was to have been initiated at 0800 and that every effort should be made to coordinate with the left elements of the 7th Infantry in order to be mutually supporting. We then discussed briefly the threat developing to the south. He stated that he could do nothing about it since the 10th BCT had passed to the control of Col Harris (it had been so ordered effective upon the 65th passing through the 10th BCT), and that the Belgian Bn was needed to cover his withdrawal. I therefore told him that the 65th Inf would be given responsibility to counter the threat to the south.

Leaving Brig Brodie, I talked with Lt Col Childs about the necessity of blocking to the south. I told him that the div Rcn Co was en route to contact enemy reported there and suggested that the 10th BCT was the most available infantry to move there now. He stated he would look after it.

Lt Col Hawkins then reported to me that since it did not appear practicable to use his M46s to support the relief of the Gloster Bn, he felt he should displace far enough south to get out of the congestion which was developing in his present location. I designated a new assembly area for him, which would enable him to assist in blocking the threat to the MSRs and yet leave him within supporting distance of the remainder of the 65th Inf. Directed him to report to the 65th Inf CO or Exec O at once and to continue to support the 65th with his bn minus the company that was supporting the 7th Inf. Also informed him of the location of the 3d Rcn Co and directed him to establish and maintain contact with that company.

I then returned to the division CP, arrived there at 0910 and reported above to CG.

At about 1300 I went by helicopter to CP 29th BIB. Learned that the Belgian Bn was engaged covering the withdrawal of transport and guns from the vicinity of CP. Brig Brodie advised me that he had no recent word of the Glosters and that the CCF were attempting to block a pass in the rear of the NF and RUR Bns, that he had tanks and some infantry attempting to keep the pass open, and that he had placed both bns under the command of one bn comdr (I do not remember which one) with instructions to withdraw as best he could and assemble in the vicinity of Uijongbu. He asked next mission of brigade. I told him it would be to take up designated blocking positions and as soon as our 15th Inf became available, he would pass to corps reserve.

Then returned to the div CP and reported to CG. Who said he would pay a visit to Brig Brodie's CP very soon. Informed CG that most of CP had displaced and that Brig Brodie would probably leave soon.[29]

The end for the Glosters is summarized in the I Corps report.

On 25 April the brigade commander and the commanding officer, 65th Infantry, agreed that the only force capable of reaching the Gloster positions was a tank force composed of M4A3E8 tanks.[30] This column was unable to reach the Gloster positions. After the failure of the attempt on the morning of 25 April, a second attempt was made during the afternoon without success.

According to survivors, the Gloster Battalion commander directed the remainder of his unit to fight its way out. Company D, ninety strong, was the last to leave the position, and after studying the situation elected to attempt to reach friendly lines by moving north into enemy positions and avoiding known centers of resistance. Forty individuals reached the lines of the 1st ROK Infantry Division on the afternoon of 25 April. . . .

It appears that every effort was made to reach the Gloster Battalion when conditions over the remainder of the front are considered. The right flank of the 1st ROK Infantry Division was hit in strength and a gap materialized that threatened the entire corps position. The right flank of the 3d Infantry Division on Line Kansas was hit hard on the night of 24 April as well as the left flank of the 25th Infantry Division. The left flank of the 24th Infantry Division was hard pressed on the afternoon and night of 24 April, and the right flank of the 24th Infantry Division was completely exposed after the night of 22–23 April. The size of the enemy force surrounding the Gloster Battalion appears to have been in such strength that reserve forces available were unable to overcome the resistance.[31]

The award of the U.S. Presidential Unit Citation as well as a number of individual awards recognized the heroism and sacrifices

*of the officers and men of the Gloster Battalion, known thereafter
as the "Glorious Glosters."*[32]

U.S. PRESIDENTIAL UNIT CITATION: The 1st Battalion, Gloucestershire Regiment, British Army, and Troop C, 170th Independent Mortar Battery, Royal Artillery, attached, are cited for exceptionally outstanding performance of duty and extraordinary heroism in action against the armed enemy near Solma-ri, Korea, on the 23rd, 24th and 25th of April, 1951. The 1st Battalion and Troop C were defending a very critical sector of the battle front during a determined attack by the enemy. The defending units were overwhelmingly outnumbered. The 83rd Chinese Communist Army drove the full force of its savage assault at the positions held by the 1st Battalion, Gloucestershire Regiment and attached unit. The route of supply ran Southeast from the battalion between two hills. The hills dominated the surrounding terrain northwest to the Imjin River. Enemy pressure built up on the battalion front during the day 23 April. On 24 April the weight of the attack had driven the right flank of the battalion back. The pressure grew heavier and heavier and the battalion and attached unit were forced into a perimeter defense on Hill 235. During the night, heavy enemy forces had bypassed the staunch defenders and closed all avenues of escape. The courageous soldiers of the battalion and attached unit were holding the critical route selected by the enemy for one column of the general offensive designed to encircle and destroy 1st Corps. These gallant soldiers would not retreat. As they were compressed tighter and tighter in their perimeter defense, they called for close-in air strikes to assist in holding firm. Completely surrounded by tremendous numbers, these indomitable, resolute, and tenacious soldiers fought back with unsurpassed fortitude and courage. As ammunition ran low and the advancing hordes moved closer and closer, these splendid soldiers fought back viciously to prevent the enemy from overrunning the position and moving rapidly to the south. Their heroic stand provided the critically needed time to regroup other 1st Corps units and block the southern advance of the enemy. Time and again efforts were made to reach the battalion, but the enemy strength blocked each effort. Without thought of defeat or surrender this heroic force demonstrated superb battlefield courage and discipline. Every yard of ground they surrendered was covered with enemy dead until the last gallant soldier of the fighting battalion was over-powered by the final surge of the enemy masses. The 1st Battalion, Gloucestershire Regiment, and Troop C, 170th Independent Mortar Battery, displayed such gallantry, determination, and esprit de corps in accomplishing their mission under extremely difficult and hazardous conditions as to set them apart and above other units participating in the same battle. Their sustained brilliance in battle, their resoluteness, and extraordinary heroism are in keeping with the finest traditions of the renowned military forces of the British Commonwealth, and reflect unsurpassed credit on these courageous soldiers and their homeland.[33]

The citation for the award of the Distinguished Service Cross to Lt. Col. (later Col.) James P. Carne, commanding officer, 1st Glosters, reveals the ordeal of the unit as well as his personal courage and leadership. Carne also received the highest British and Commonwealth decoration for heroism, the Victoria Cross (equivalent to the U.S. Medal of Honor), and the Distinguished Service Order (DSO), equivalent to the U.S. Distinguished Service Cross.

The President of the United States takes pleasure in presenting the Distinguished Service Cross to James Power Carne, Lieutenant Colonel, Royal British Army, for extraordinary heroism in connection with military operations against an armed enemy of the United Nations while serving as Commander of the First Battalion Gloucester Regiment (29th Independent Infantry Brigade) in action against enemy forces from 22 through 25 April 1951, during the Imjin River Engagement. The enemy, in numerically superior numbers, started assaults against his position on 22 April 1951 and continued these fanatical attacks for three days and nights. The situation rapidly became critical as hostile forces were able to surround his battalion because of gaps in the Brigade front. In the face of devastating enemy mortar, machine-gun, and small-arms fire and by his indomitable spirit, great courage, and tactical skill, Colonel Carne truly inspired his exhausted men to repeatedly rally and repulse the seemingly endless hordes of Chinese Communists. Continually exposing himself to intense hostile fire, he moved about his troops,

encouraging them to hold firm against overwhelming odds. When it
became apparent that a continued stand might result in complete
annihilation, Colonel Carne organized small parties and ordered
them to return to the rear, but elected to remain with the wounded
to await whatever the future held. Colonel Carne's heroic conduct,
superb leadership, and steadfast devotion to the troops of his unit
reflect the highest credit on himself and the armed forces of the
British Commonwealth.[34]

*Distinguished Service Crosses were also awarded to the mem-
bers of allied military units involved in the difficult fighting on the
Imjin River line associated with the struggle of the Glosters from
22 to 25 April 1951.*

BELGIAN UN BATTALION: Lt. Col. Albert Crahay, Army of Bel-
gium, commander of the Belgian UN Battalion, was awarded a DSC
for his extraordinary heroism while serving with the British 29th
Independent Infantry Brigade.[35]

PHILIPPINE 10TH BATTALION COMBAT TEAM: 1st Lt. Jose M.
Artiaga Jr. and Capt. Conrado D. Yap, Army of the Philippines, were
both awarded DSCs for their heroism in action while trying to hold
their positions against attacking Chinese Communist Forces on the
night of 22–23 April 1951. Both officers were killed in action.[36]

GLOSTER BATTALION SURVIVORS: When the enemy attacked
they would break into small groups and would infiltrate to all points
of commanding ground. Each group usually had from one to two
automatic weapons. When attacking they would try every spur of
the hill until they hit the most narrow front, then they would attack
en masse. D Company stated that they piled them up, but they kept
coming.

The enemy seemed to have plenty of ammunition. At night the
enemy fired a great amount of tracer. Mortar fire was intensive, but
very little, if any, artillery fire was received. The enemy seemed to
have an abundance of automatic weapons.

One man reported seeing five tanks about one mile south of the
river. These tanks resembled T34s but seemed to have a lower sil-

houette. . . . Some of the men stated that the Chinese seemed to be doped. They moved in a stupor.

The first two days several Chinese were seen changing from civilian clothes into uniforms. None of the survivors knew if anything dropped by the liaison planes was recovered. They didn't think so.[37]

BRITISH 29TH BRIGADE REVIEW: Chinese Methods. The most surprising feature of this Chinese offensive was not so much that it came, but rather the manner of its coming. The Chinese, as has been stated, just surged forward without any previous probing. Yet when the attack developed, it was obvious that they knew in gen [general] the locs of our units. As there was only one instance of a Chinese probing patrol, and that being some ten days before the attack started, it is only reasonable to suppose that their intelligence was acquired from other sources. Presumably among these can be included the use of local civs [civilians] as guides, the op [operation] of low-level agents, and the infiltration of small recce gps, which they are known to possess, through our lines dressed as civs. The only feasible remedy for this is the evac [evacuation] of the entire civ population of the Bde area as far back as and behind Bde HQ and the est [establishment] of a no movement line fwd of which no civs shall be allowed to trespass. Any such area, should it be est, and in order to ensure that there can be no enemy penetration as civs, must be effectively policed by native police, and continuous I(B) [intelligence] cover must op [operate].

The Chinese in their attack used their favorite tactic of the human sea. Once having loc [located] and contacted a posn, envelopment of that posn was carried out. While that posn was under attack by that force, other gps were penetrating round the flanks and infiltrating deeper into our posns. The Chinese attacks were not supported by arty, with the exception of one instance when 40mm AA [antiaircraft] fire was used. However, on every occasion the Chinese attacks were sp [supported] by a reasonably high volume of mortar fire varying in caliber from 60mm to 100mm. Much automatic fire and SA were also used. The Chinese use of MMGs is extremely skillful, and every effort is made to dig the weapons in and cam [camouflage] them if possible. Mov [movement] across country is extremely fast, and when the Chinese stop for any appreciable length of time, digging and cam are the order of the day.[38]

The commanders of U.S. I Corps and Eighth U.S. Army stated their conclusions regarding the action of the Glosters.

LT. GEN. FRANK W. MILBURN, COMMANDING GENERAL, I CORPS: It is my opinion that the stand made by the Gloucestershire Battalion in the face of the suddenness of the enemy onslaught and the massiveness of the attack was responsible in large measure for the successful withdrawal of other elements of the I Corps to previously prepared positions. Without this gallant defense, much heavier losses would have been suffered by other corps elements with the grave danger of impairing materially the tactical integrity of the corps.[39]

LT. GEN. JAMES A. VAN FLEET, COMMANDING GENERAL, EIGHTH U.S. ARMY: I have reviewed the contents of this report, and it is my opinion that all reasonable and possible courses of action open to the responsible commanders concerned were initiated in an effort to extricate the Gloucestershire Battalion. Close and continuous liaison was maintained between commanders concerned during this critical period and, as a result, maximum use was made of available reserves, fire support, and tactical air. The overwhelming strength and determination of the enemy's attacks, together with his initial capability to exploit early penetrations by infiltration and enveloping actions, taxed the Corps, Division, and Brigade Commanders' limited reserve capabilities to the maximum. I believe that all decisions made were tactically sound and that subordinate commanders complied with orders to the maximum limit of their capabilities.

The loss of this gallant fighting unit will continue to be felt with deep regret by myself and members of this command. Its magnificent stand in the face of overwhelming odds contributed immeasurably to the maintenance of the tactical integrity of the entire I U.S. Corps.[40]

Numerous postwar analyses have been made not only of the Glosters' fight and controversial loss on Hill 235 but also of the valiant combat actions of the other units of the British 29th Inde-

pendent Infantry Brigade Group. One of the most recent and thorough accounts has come from the British author Andrew Salmon, in his To the Last Round: The Epic British Stand on the Imjin River, Korea 1951. *Salmon concluded:*

> In my opinion, the Glosters were lost due to a combination of factors. The first is their lack of contact with flanking units— itself a consequence of a brigade holding a divisional front—and the hemmed-in nature of their "back door." Once the Chinese attacked, they were doomed by a failure of their own and/or higher command to take decisive action on the 23rd and/or 24th. Finally, it must be remembered that their position covered an important LOC [line of communications] and tied down major enemy forces. Had the Glosters pulled out on the 23rd or 24th, they would have left a gap some four miles wide in Line Kansas, which would have opened the floodgates, especially as Five Yankee [Route 57] was such a well-covered route, ideal for infiltrating vehicles or heavy equipment south. This is the long answer. The short answer is: the fortunes of war.[41]

On 29 June 1957 the U.S., UN, ROK, and British Commonwealth forces in Korea dedicated a memorial to the British servicemen who sacrificed themselves to hold Hill 235, which is known to all UN personnel who have served in the Republic of Korea as "Gloster Hill."[42]

Chapter 8

ACTION ALONG THE NO NAME LINE

U.S. IX Corps

The hard fighting and sacrifices of such frontline units as the Gloucestershire Battalion allowed UN forces to break contact with the enemy and withdraw in good order to prepared defensive positions, while at the same time inflicting heavy casualties and disrupting the Chinese timetable. To the west, U.S. I Corps began pulling back on 25 April. As the withdrawal continued in I Corps to Line Golden in front of Seoul, Lt. Gen. Van Fleet, Eighth U.S. Army commander, drew a new defensive line extending east and northeast from Line Golden to the coast, but he gave it no name. Running south of Ch'unch'on and Inje, this line became known as the No Name Line, or the general defense line that U.S. IX and X Corps and ROK III and I Corps were to occupy as they withdrew to conform with the pullback of the U.S. I Corps in the west. By 28 April I Corps had reached Line Golden, and soon the UN forces to the east took position along the No Name Line.

As a result of the rapid but orderly withdrawal of UN forces, by 2 May the only contact with the enemy was in the far west in the ROK 1st Division sector of I Corps. Van Fleet ordered regimental-sized bases established in front of the main defensive positions, from which extensive patrolling was to be conducted to locate the enemy and provide early warning of a renewal of the Chinese offensive. Strong artillery forces were to support these advanced patrol bases. Meanwhile, along the general defense or No Name Line extensive field fortifications were being constructed.

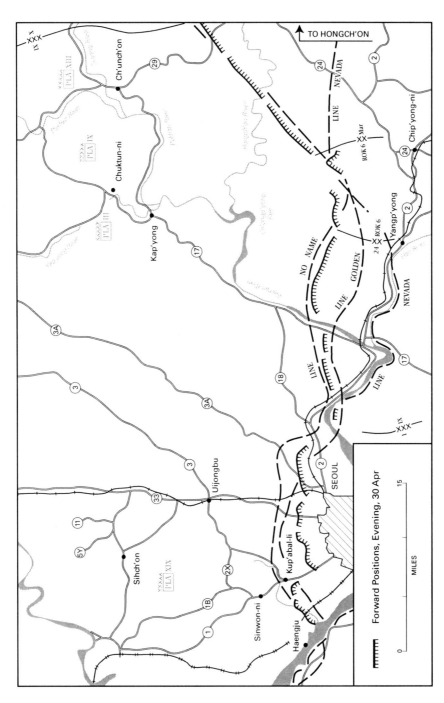

The Chinese Spring Offensive, 1951. (Based on U.S. Army Center of Military History map.)

Forward Artillery Support: Task Force Lindy Lou, 4–21 May 1951

In U.S. IX Corps the 92d Armored Field Artillery Battalion, after supporting the ROK 6th and 1st Marine Divisions during the opening days of the Chinese Spring Offensive, was given the initial mission of providing artillery support to the newly arrived ROK 2d Division, which was inserted into the line between the ROK 6th Division on the east and the U.S. 24th Infantry Division on the west. Because of the unique nature of the artillery grouping, called Task Force Lindy Lou, a combat historian, 1st Lt. Martin Blumenson, prepared a report on its operations. He describes the establishment of the task force.

Task force organizations appear to offer particular opportunities to the interview-historian. Organized for a specific mission and generally comprising elements of several units, the task force upon dissolution does not always record in a formal manner its achievements and its problems as a unit. In order to remedy this situation and because a composite-type organization of artillery elements is rarely encountered, interviews on Task Force Lindy Lou were undertaken.

Task Force Lindy Lou was formed 4 May 1951, under the command of Lt. Col. Leon F. Lavoie, the commanding officer of the 92d Armored Field Artillery Battalion. It consisted of Headquarters Battery and Battery A, 92d Armored Field Artillery Battalion (155mm howitzers, M41, self-propelled), Battery A, 987th [Armored] Field Artillery Battalion (105mm howitzers [M7, self-propelled]), and Battery B, 27th ROK Field Artillery Battalion (105mm howitzers). The 2d Battalion, 21st Infantry Regiment, was attached to render security; Companies A and B, 194th Engineer Combat Battalion, and Company A, 74th Engineer Combat Battalion, were placed in support to improve the task force road net.

At that time, friendly forces were constructing and maintaining a general defense line. In order to maintain contact with the enemy, one regiment of each division operated from a patrol base in advance of the general defense line as a covering or screening force. Task Force Lindy Lou was organized to provide artillery support for the covering regiments of the 2d ROK and 6th ROK Infantry Divisions. The task force was composed so that one artillery unit in entirety would not be withdrawn from positions in support of the general defense line, thereby causing a gap. The small amount of available ROK artillery was considered inadequate to provide the necessary support for the patrol elements. Lack of an adequate road net in the 2d ROK Infantry Division sector further complicated the problem of artillery support.[1]

Lt. Col. Forrest W. Duff, S-3, U.S. IX Corps Artillery, provides more information on the reasons behind the formation of Task Force Lindy Lou.

Task Force Lindy Lou was conceived by IX Corps Artillery and recommended by General [then Brig. Gen. William N.] Gillmore to support the covering forces of the 2d ROK and 6th ROK Divisions. This was done because the terrain in the two division sectors was such that separate artillery support in each division sector was impossible due to the lack of north–south roads in the sectors. At the time the task force was organized, the artillery of the 2d ROK Division had not as yet arrived. The 2d ROK Division had been in line only a short time. The 18th ROK Field Artillery Battalion, in support of one of the ROK corps on the east coast, was to move to the 2d ROK Division and become its organic artillery. Therefore, one-half of the mission of Task Force Lindy Lou was to support the covering force regiment of the 2d ROK Division.

The task force was organized to provide both light and medium artillery for the two covering force regiments. The medium battery of the 92d Armored Field Artillery was made part of the task force to provide additional range into the 6th ROK Division sector. It was necessary to move the task force into position in front of the general defense line through the 24th Infantry Division sector as no other road was available. The task force was moved as road conditions permitted as far into the 2d ROK sector as possible.

It was felt that a composite task force made up of batteries from the 92d [Armored] Field Artillery Battalion, the 987th [Armored] Field Artillery Battalion, and the 27th ROK Field Artillery Battalion (organic to the 6th ROK Division) would least disrupt the preparation of the artillery battalion defensive positions in support of the general defense line.[2]

Lt. Col. Leon F. Lavoie, the task force commander and also the commanding officer of the 92d Armored Field Artillery Battalion, provides more details about the organization and mission of the task force and its preparations for the expected enemy offensive.

Task Force Lindy Lou was instituted on or about 3 May by VOCG [verbal order of the commanding general], IX Corps Artillery. The task force comprised the 2d Battalion, 21st Infantry Regiment; Battery A, 987th [Armored] Field Artillery Battalion; Battery B, 27th ROK Field Artillery Battalion; and Battery A, 92d Armored Field Artillery Battalion. Companies A and B, 194th Engineer Combat Battalion, and Company A, 74th Engineer Combat Battalion, were placed in direct support of the task force effort.

The mission of Task Force Lindy Lou was to operate as a covering force to the front of the general defense line, to detect the enemy, cause him to deploy, harass him, and kill as many as possible. If and when it became necessary, Lindy Lou was to withdraw behind the general defense line. The engineers were to develop interior roads so that the task force could withdraw without having to use the river road, which was exposed to the enemy. The infantry mission was threefold: (1) to secure the artillery in position by outposting; (2) to block the western avenues of enemy approach; and (3) to patrol aggressively to the front and maintain contact with the 5th U.S. RCT on the left and the 2d ROK Infantry Division on the right.

From 3 May to 16 May, the task force developed positions by digging and improving roads, reinforcing bridges, and selecting alternate positions. Several heavy rainfalls caused severe cave-ins on all roads, necessitating concentrated engineer effort to develop the entire road net to a Class 50 system [for heavier all-weather traffic with speeds of up to thirty miles per hour and fifty-ton-capacity bridges]. Roads were improved rearward as well as forward to the Ch'ongp'yong dam.[3]

Other members of Task Force Lindy Lou provide additional information about the formation of the task force and their actions as they prepared for the expected enemy attack.

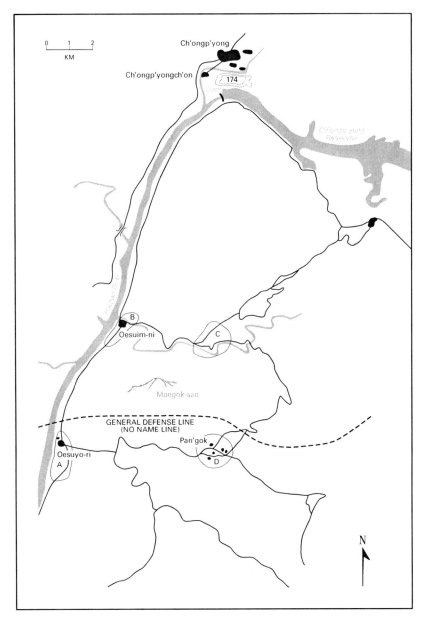

Task Force Lindy Lou. (Based on map in CMH manuscript, U.S. Army.)

1ST LT. LEROY B. MATTINGLY, ASSISTANT S-3, 92D ARMORED
FIELD ARTILLERY BATTALION: On 3 May the battalion was alerted
for Task Force Lindy Lou to comprise Headquarters Battery and
Battery A, 92d Armored Field Artillery Battalion; Battery A, 987th
[Armored] Field Artillery Battalion; and Battery B, 27th ROK Field
Artillery Battalion. The task force assembled in the vicinity of
Chip'yong-ni and moved on 4 May to an assembly area near
Oesuyo-ri. A reconnaissance party went forward to establish com-
mand liaison with the screening regiments of the 6th ROK and 2d
ROK Infantry Divisions which the task force would support. Bat-
tery A, 92d Armored Field Artillery Battalion, took positions in
Area "A" [near Oesuyo-ri]; the two light batteries of the task force
and Headquarters Battery, 92d Armored Field Artillery Battalion,
moved into positions in Area "C." The 2d Battalion, 21st Infantry
Regiment, 24th Infantry Division, contacted the task force and was
assigned the mission of providing a defensive perimeter for the artillery. Two forward observers dispatched to the 2d ROK and 6th
ROK Divisions found themselves at 1800 hours in advance of the
infantry lines; on the following day the infantry moved forward.

The weather was rainy; observation and registration were not
possible initially. The companies of the 74th Engineer Combat Battalion attached to the task force began work on the roads on 5 May
in order to prepare routes from Areas "A" and "C," through "B"
[near Oesuim-ni] and "D" [near Pan'gok], so that the howitzers
would have alternate routes to move forward or displace to the rear.

On 5 May the firing batteries were able to register, and from
then until 16 May, only registration missions were performed. There
were no targets. IX Corps Artillery on 8 May gave permission to the
24th Infantry Division to call on Battery A, 92d Armored Field
Artillery (in Area "A"), for direct support of tank-infantry patrols.

General [William M.] Hoge, IX Corps commander, and General Gillmore, IX Corps Artillery commander, were worried about
the condition of the roads in the Lindy Lou area, and particularly
about moving Battery A, 92d Armored Field Artillery Battalion,
from Area "A" to a forward position. The task force had to clear
with Gillmore personally before making such a move. On 9 May
permission was granted. On 12 May, Battery A, 92d Armored Field

Artillery Battalion, joined the remainder of the task force at Area "C." One M41 vehicle went over the side of the road during this move; it was sixteen hours before the vehicle was recovered. On 14 May the engineers had improved the road forward to the Ch'ongp'yong dam, so that the road could handle heavy equipment to the dam and across it.

On 15 May word was received that the 5th U.S. RCT, 24th Infantry Division, on the left of Lindy Lou was moving back 3,000 yards to new defensive positions slightly northwest of Area "B." Because this exposed Area "B," Task Force Lindy Lou began to concentrate on maintaining the road from Areas "C" to "A" via Area "D" to provide an interior route of withdrawal. That evening Colonel Lavoie decided to move all administrative vehicles and equipment back to Area "A." This was done.[4]

CAPT. JOHN F. GERRITY, COMMANDER, BATTERY A, 92D AR-MORED FIELD ARTILLERY BATTALION: The mission of Task Force Lindy Lou was to support by fire one regiment each of the 2d ROK Infantry Division and the 6th ROK Infantry Division. These regiments were to send patrols in a reconnaissance in force north to the Pukhan River to make contact with the enemy. Artillery on the general defense line was incapable of supporting these patrols which operated from a patrol base line in advance of the general defense line.

The artillery components of Task Force Lindy Lou assembled at a preplanned rendezvous area reconnoitered by Colonel Lavoie by air, then entered positions designated by General Gillmore, commanding general, IX Corps Artillery. These artillery positions formed a rectangle, approximately four by eight miles, and were designated Areas "A," "B," "C," and "D." The road net connecting these positions formed the rectangle. The general defense line ran one-half mile to a mile north of Areas "A" and "D."

Task Force Lindy Lou met its attached infantry security at Area "A," and Lavoie made a reconnaissance by vehicle to check the condition of the roads. Although Battery A, 92d Armored Field Artillery Battalion, was unable to traverse the road net because the roads were in such poor condition, the two light artillery batteries moved into Area "C." Capt. Gerrity set up his battery (155mm howitzers,

M41, self-propelled) just north of Area "A" on the general defense line and on the boundary between the 24th Infantry Division and the 2d ROK Infantry Division. Gillmore visited this position and suggested that Battery A reinforce the fires of the 555th Field Artillery Battalion in the sector to the left as well as the fires of Lindy Lou because Battery A was in a particularly good position to do so.

Battery A remained in this position three or four days until the engineers were able to improve the roads sufficiently to allow the M41 vehicles to travel over the entire road net. This then permitted two alternate routes of movement. Battery A closed into Area "C," physically joining the task force elements. Although the roads had been improved, the shoulders remained flimsy. One Battery A vehicle fell into a ravine when the road shoulder gave way; the vehicle was later recovered.

Battery A remained in Area "C" about one week. The engineers worked on roads forward of the battery positions. Reconnaissance was made for forward area positions. Then the Chinese attacked. . . .

All batteries comprising Task Force Lindy Lou were stripped of administrative equipment such as kitchens, supply trucks, administrative ¼-ton vehicles, and unnecessary wire vehicles. These were assembled in an area south of the general defense line. Food was cooked in the rear and brought forward three times daily, each trip consisting of fifteen miles one way. The weather during the period Lindy Lou functioned was rainy about half of the time.[5]

By 16 May the Eighth Army had identified a shift of enemy forces to the east with a concentration of seven CCF armies of the III, IX, and XIII Army Groups around Ch'unch'on. It was believed that the main enemy attack would drive southwest, down the Pukhan River valley and across the Han River, to isolate Seoul. Attacks on I Corps in front of Seoul and on X Corps down the Ch'unch'on–Hongch'on corridor would support this blow. On the night of 16–17 May, the enemy renewed the offensive. Lt. Col. Lavoie, commander of Task Force Lindy Lou, describes the operations in his area.

On 15 May the 24th U.S. Infantry Division on the left of Task Force Lindy Lou reported no contact with the enemy. During the night of 16 May, the 5th U.S. RCT on the right flank of the 24th Infantry Division was taken under heavy attack by an estimated CCF regiment. Penetration was made into Company I, 5th U.S. RCT, causing the 5th U.S. RCT to drop back 1,500 yards initially, then an additional 4,000 yards. This placed the 5th U.S. RCT on the general defense line, and exposed the left flank of Task Force Lindy Lou. The presence of the Lindy Lou infantry security blocking force proved valuable.

Patrols in the Lindy Lou front contacted only small CCF groups. Prisoners of war reported the same enemy division to the front of the task force as the one attacking the 24th U.S. Infantry Division, with an approximate enemy regiment on the Lindy Lou front.

During the late afternoon of 16 May, contact had been made with the enemy on the north bank of the Pukhan River. Heavy artillery interdictory fires were sustained on the dam and on the trails leading to the dam, recognized as the principal avenue of enemy approach. To the east in the 6th ROK Infantry Division sector, enemy soldiers wore individual camouflage foliage on their helmets, thereby making it possible for them to lean into the brush when friendly planes came overhead. Throughout the night heavy artillery fire was placed on the access to the dam in order to prevent the enemy from reinforcing his troops already across the Pukhan River. Heavy enemy casualties were sustained on Hill 174, just north of the dam.

Lavoie sent two forward observers, Lt. Hertz and Lt. Venable, with the infantry of the 2d ROK and 6th ROK Infantry Divisions, to assist in picking out enemy targets for Lindy Lou artillery fire. Regrettably, although friendly infantry made every effort to advance, the infantry called for artillery fire and fell back. Lack of communications among the infantry elements made it impossible to have accurate knowledge of the locations of friendly units. At 1100, 17 May, Lavoie felt it advisable to displace the artillery to positions 4,000 yards to the rear. Thus, displacement of the artillery was in keeping with instructions, since the enemy had been detected, made to deploy, and was taken under fire.

Task Force Lindy Lou closed in its new positions about 1430. This move was made possible by the fine work of the engineer troops who had transformed the treacherous trails into passable roads.

During the morning of 17 May, a Chinese radio message was intercepted by the 2d ROK Infantry Division. This message directed the CCF to stay away from the high ground because of the high casualty rate received from artillery fire. A short while later, another intercepted enemy message directed the Chinese forces to move to the east. A few hours later, CCF elements were contacted on the task force front.

Task Force Lindy Lou continued to interdict the dam day and night in the hope of denying the only enemy avenue of approach for enemy artillery, vehicles, and heavy equipment. At 1630, 19 May, Task Force Lindy Lou began receiving exceptionally large targets from the 2d ROK Infantry Division. Company- to battalion-size groups were reported. All available artillery was brought to bear on these targets. Assistance was also called for from the 24th U.S. Infantry Division on the left. Regrettably, the infantry in front of Lindy Lou did not seem able to hold the enemy but withdrew to the general defense line. From 1630 through 2100, the two 105mm batteries of the task force fired some 2,300 rounds and the 155mm battery fired some 1,300 rounds.

By 2030, 19 May, reports of enemy progress located the enemy in such positions that the artillery was firing at minimum elevation. Plans to displace the artillery were initiated so that supporting fire could continue to be delivered. When the task force had made its initial withdrawal of 4,000 yards, it was in position on the general defense line; high ground to the front, however, masked the fires of the task force. This high ground, an east–west ridge, was part of the general defense line. For this second displacement, Lavoie could have withdrawn to the south or to the west. He chose to displace the task force to the west so that the artillery could continue to support not only its front but the 24th U.S. Infantry Division on the left also. The displacement of artillery 5,000 yards to the west began about 2045, and was made by echelon to insure continuous artillery support. At this time, the task force was at a critical point; its mission was being challenged. The displacement was completed at 2250. From this position, the artillery could and did effectively support the infantry along the general defense line, and in particular the 31st ROK Infantry Regiment, 2d ROK Division.

About 2030, although the enemy was within 2,000 yards of the general defense line and in range of friendly mortar and light artillery fire, no such friendly fire was placed on the enemy, even though Lavoie could see that the general defense line was being manned. He felt that the fires of Task Force Lindy Lou were responsible in great part for halting the enemy advance. At 0100, 20 May, the command post of the 31st ROK Infantry Regiment [ROK 2d Infantry Division] reported everything quiet and under control. Based upon this report, Task Force Lindy Lou fired a heavy schedule of harassing and interdictory fire missions.[6]

Lt. Mattingly, assistant S-3, 92d Armored Field Artillery Battalion, provides more details about the operations of Task Force Lindy Lou as the enemy advanced.

On 16 May, although there was continued evidence of an enemy buildup on the left of Lindy Lou in front of the 5th U.S. RCT, patrols forward of Lindy Lou made no contact with the enemy. At 0005, 17 May, the 5th U.S. RCT was under heavy attack and was forced to withdraw 4,000 meters. Although this exposed the left flank of Lindy Lou, the Chinese made no effort to penetrate that flank. The route from Area "C" to Area "D" to "A" became the only feasible route of withdrawal for Lindy Lou.

About daylight, 17 May, the first Chinese troops appeared in the task force sector north of the dam. Lindy Lou artillery fired on Hill 174 north of the dam on a reported 400 enemy troops. During the six hours from 0330 to 0930, 17 May, the task force expended 1,100 rounds of 105mm ammunition and 450 rounds of 155mm ammunition in order to neutralize the approaches to the dam and the approaches to the enemy assembly area north [northwest] of the dam in the town of Ch'ongp'yongch'on.

At 1020, 17 May, Task Force Lindy Lou received instructions from IX Corps Artillery to displace by echelon to Area "D," about 2,000 meters behind the general defense line. This was complied with. The enemy continued to build up in the 5th U.S. RCT sector. By 1930, 17 May, the 5th and 19th U.S. RCTs were under heavy attack. But ROK elements continued to hold at the dam in the sector to the front of Lindy Lou.

About 2400, 17 May, Lindy Lou received a report that 300 Chinese had succeeded in crossing the dam. One battery of the 937th (155mm gun) Field Artillery Battalion and one battery of the 17th Field Artillery Battalion (8-inch howitzer) were requested to interdict the dam with supplementary fires, since the light artillery of Task Force Lindy Lou was out of range of the dam from Area "D."

On 18 May there was relative quiet. No enemy attacks were made in the task force front, although the 24th Infantry Division was pressed throughout the day. Task force fires consisted of interdictory fires and were directed by aerial observers rather than from the ground. Forward observers, withdrawn from the regiments early in the morning, 17 May, were sent back on 19 May. These forward observers directed some fire on enemy targets, for the enemy had by then come within range of the task force light artillery.

ROK troops had held very well on the Pukhan River barrier. However, once the Chinese were across, the ROK elements began to fall back. Instead of attempting to halt the enemy advance, instead of using their own mortars, they relied on artillery fire. By 1830, 19 May, the 155mm howitzers of Lindy Lou were firing Charge 3, a range of 4,000 yards. The enemy, continuing to advance, approached minimum artillery range. In order to give effective fire in its sector, Lindy Lou had to withdraw because the hill mass Maegok-san, on which the general defense line was placed, masked its artillery fire.

Having fired a total of 1,200 rounds from 1200 to 1900, 19 May, Task Force Lindy Lou at 1920 displaced by echelon to Area "A" in order to give better support and more close-in fires. The first battery moved at 1930, the last one moved at 2210; ROK infantry elements were supported continuously. While Battery A, 92d Armored Field Artillery Battalion, and Battery B, 27th ROK Field Artillery Battalion, were in the process of displacing, Battery A, 987th [Armored] Field Artillery Battalion, remained in position and fired approximately 700 rounds on one hill in about one hour and thirty minutes. Still there was no concentrated enemy force in front so far as Lindy Lou could determine. By 2400, 19 May, the action had calmed down. During the 24-hour period, 19 May, Lindy Lou fired 3,000 rounds of 105mm ammunition and 1,300 rounds of 155mm ammunition.

It was so quiet by 2400, 19 May, that the task force displaced forward to Area "D," closing there at 1000, 20 May. Lavoie went forward to establish liaison with the 31st ROK Infantry Regiment in an attempt to impress on the unit the necessity for correct utilization of artillery support fires. He stated that unless more accurate reporting of targets and effects was forthcoming, the task force would automatically cut down its ammunition expenditure.

At 1830, 19 May, Task Force Lindy Lou handled six fire missions at once, without knowing either the nature of the target fired upon or the effect of the fire on the target. "Many, many Chinese" were reported continuously as targets; "very good effect, many, many casualties," was the normal report of effect. When ROK observers called for fire, the target was invariably an "enemy company." Battalion-size forces were constantly reported, so that a total of eleven enemy battalions were "located" in the ROK infantry sector during the night of 19 May; only three were actually there. Disorder in the ROK sector was caused by the lack of communication among units. At 2300, 19 May, a ROK regimental command post of the screening force was fired on with small arms and mortar by ROK troops on the general defense line. . . .

In Lieutenant Mattingly's opinion, the bastard organization of Task Force Lindy Lou complicated rather than simplified artillery operations, tactically and administratively. He recognized, however, that it was a good idea to attach light artillery to the task force because the 92d Armored Field Artillery Battalion self-propelled howitzers were initially unable to go forward to the most advanced position. Attaching the ROK personnel meant that the Fire Direction Center had to maintain a staff of interpreters. ROK personnel were difficult to control or locate. Two types of fire direction control had to be maintained, one for 105mm and one for 155mm units, because of the slight differences involved.[7]

Soon after, because of events in other sectors, the enemy began to withdraw before the general defense line in this area was fully tested. Lt. Col. Lavoie provides his reflections on Task Force Lindy Lou and its mission of supporting the ROKs.

Colonel Lavoie commented on the inadequacy of communica-

tions within the Korean divisions and particularly within the 31st
ROK Infantry Regiment. This he based on his repeated inquiries to
the regiment as to the location of its battalions and companies. Sel-
dom if ever did the regiment know the disposition of its subordinate
units because of communications breakdown. In many cases, engagements with the enemy were isolated company actions rather
than coordinated efforts. On two occasions, infantry companies of
the 31st ROK Infantry Regiment engaged friendly troops in fire
because of ignorance of the disposition of friendly elements.

Lavoie felt that there was a general reluctance on the part of the
ROK infantry to engage the enemy and outmaneuver him. Mortar
fire, although available, was not used. The infantry was prone to fall
back and call for artillery fire.

Lavoie believed that the 2d ROK Infantry Division, and particularly the 31st ROK Infantry Regiment, had not regained its self-
confidence since having been overrun by the enemy in January.
Furthermore, a poor relationship existed between the KMAG [Ko-
rean Military Advisory Group] officers and the regimental staff.
During the night when the enemy was 2,000 yards in front of
friendly infantry, the KMAG and Tactical Air parties quitted the
infantry. This, Lavoie felt, was deplorable.

Lavoie added these general remarks. Task forces in order to accomplish their missions efficiently must abide by principles of unity
of command. A makeshift task force organization, such as Lindy
Lou, involving subordinate units of three or four different commands, cannot operate as efficiently as one comprising an integral
command. Specifically, if Lindy Lou's mission was important, then
the complete 92d Armored Field Artillery Battalion might well have
been committed.

Such task forces work undue hardship on staff members, for the
staff designed for one battalion operation was divided between the
efforts of Lindy Lou and the preponderance of the battalion in the
rear of the general defense line [in support of the U.S. 7th Infantry
Division]. The natural staff was divided. The natural desire of the
commander is to employ his own staff. Thus, hardship was created
for Lindy Lou operations and for the remainder of the 92d Armored
Field Artillery Battalion. Lavoie felt that task force organization is

good if unity of command is upheld. The division of a staff makes for inefficiency.

Lavoie further preferred to have his entire battalion because he felt that self-propelled armored artillery is tailor-made for missions such as support for a covering force and advance and rear guard actions. Organizational weapons of the 92d Armored Field Artillery Battalion included 58 .50 caliber and 55 .30 caliber machine guns, 43 bazookas, and 139 "grease guns."

The saving justification for the organization as it was constituted was that the artillery commander of the forward elements supporting the covering force (Lindy Lou) had the prerogative at his discretion to displace behind the general defense line once the enemy was detected, engaged, and harassed. The task force was organized in such a way to prevent the displacement of one entire artillery unit from the general defense line. Displacement of one unit in entirety would have left a gap in this line. Therefore, three artillery units contributed one-third of their forces to form one unit, leaving thereby subordinate parts of those units on the general defense line.

Supplies were complicated by the non-identity of the task force. It was the responsibility of the organic units to supply units comprising the task force as well as the remainder of those units in support of the general defense line. Units are sufficiently flexible to work out these arrangements for a relatively short period of time.[8]

Despite the problems identified by Lt. Col. Lavoie, Task Force Lindy Lou accomplished its mission. Lt. Col. Robert J. Natzel, chief, G-3 operations section, IX Corps headquarters, explains the importance of the work of Task Force Lindy Lou.

The enemy threat developed as anticipated. The enemy attacked, making his major effort against the 24th U.S. Infantry Division. A second attack was later directed against the 2d ROK Infantry Division. The value of Lindy Lou lay in the large number of casualties inflicted on the enemy in the vicinity of the Ch'ongp'yong dam. The task force was composed of every type of corps artillery (one battery, 17th Field Artillery Battalion, 8-inch howitzers, was capable of reinforcing the fires of Lindy Lou). Thus, enemy targets were brought under artillery fire over more diverse ranges than any one field artillery battalion could have done. Targets appeared simultaneously for all types of artillery.

It was realized that the Ch'ongp'yong dam was the only good approach route into the 2d ROK Infantry Division sector. The enemy forced a crossing at the dam, but at a cost in casualties that prevented him from backing up his initial thrust across the river. The enemy attack lost its momentum after the enemy had advanced approximately 4,000 meters south of the dam to a point approximately 5,000 meters north of the general defense line. Much of the success in sapping the enemy strength in that sector must be credited to Task Force Lindy Lou.[9]

Action on the General Defense Line: Company A, 19th Infantry Regiment, 17–18 May 1951

To the west of the ROK 2d and 6th Divisions across the Pukhan River, the U.S. 24th Infantry Division manned the general defense line. It, too, had forces deployed in advance for early warning and to disrupt the expected enemy offensive while work continued on the main positions to the rear. The 19th Infantry Regiment was one of the units on the No Name Line. Capt. Irving C. Hughes, S-3, 1st Battalion, 19th Infantry Regiment, describes his unit's preparations for defense.

The 19th Infantry Regiment was in reserve from 1 to 7 May. On 8 May, the 1st Battalion relieved the 3d Battalion on the left side of the regimental sector. The 3d Battalion had worked on positions with limited equipment for six days. The engineers had laid some mines, but not more than one hundred. Seven fougasses [flame weapons] had been placed in front of Company B.

Soon after the 1st Battalion took over, tools, sandbags, AP [anti-personnel] mines, and barbed wire were sent to the battalion; the battalion got plenty. At least 10,000 sandbags per company were secured. Each company laid a double apron of barbed wire fence. Concertina wire was strung mainly for the crew-served weapons [weapons such as bazookas and mortars whose operation requires more than one person]. The battalion started receiving shipments of these supplies on 13 May.

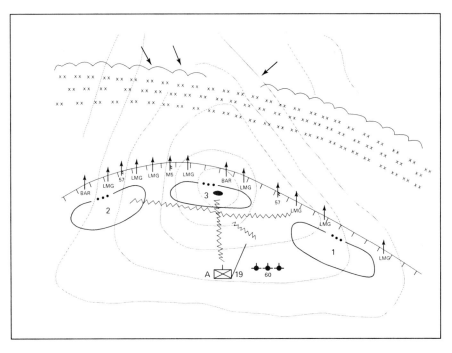

Company A, 19th Infantry Regiment: the situation on 17–18 May 1951. (Based on map in CMH manuscript, U.S. Army. Not to scale.)

Battalion established a priority of work as follows: (1) dig holes as deep as possible; (2) clear fields of fire; (3) construct overhead covers for all personnel; (4) construct barbed wire obstacles; and (5) place booby traps on approaches. Company D, 3d Engineer Combat Battalion, laid antipersonnel mines and the fougasses and supervised the laying of the barbed wire. By 15 May the defense line looked damn good. Only the barbed wire had to be completed. But the key terrain features were already wired in.

The 5th RCT maintaining an OPLR withdrew on 17 May to the MLR. Division established a "no fire" line because of the withdrawal. Gaps in the minefields and the wire had been left for the 5th RCT withdrawal. Those groups which came through the 1st Battalion, 19th Infantry Regiment, positions under officer control were orderly; some groups withdrew in disorderly fashion.

Enemy groups were observed moving toward the battalion defense line. Enemy columns 5,000 to 6,000 meters distant marched toward the battalion. When the "no fire" line was lifted, artillery took the enemy under fire. The enemy attacked all three rifle companies the night of 17–18 May. The attack was repelled by extremely effective artillery and mortar fire and by the infantry remaining in position.[10]

1st Lt. Warren E. Clark, commander, Company A, 19th Infantry, describes the work on his position.

Company A relieved Company L on the unnumbered hill between Hills 251 and 241 on 8 May. Company A dug in on the high ground in two-man bunkers reinforced with logs, dirt, and sandbags. Approximately 10,000 sandbags were used in the positions. Most of the work was done by the men themselves; a few Korean laborers aided. Trenches two feet wide and four feet deep were dug along the top of the hill connecting the bunkers. One hundred and fifty yards in front of the trenches, men of the 3d Engineer Combat Battalion laid one double-apron barbed wire fence. Thirty yards in front of this fence, close to 300 mines were placed along the Company A front on all avenues of approach. Company A laid two double-apron fences, one 75 yards in front of the company positions and one 25 or 30 yards (hand grenade distance). Company A held a 1,200 meter front, which formed an inverted "U" shape.

In each connecting valley the engineers placed 55-gallon drums of fougasse (napalm). The drum was set on an 81mm shell. On each side of the shell was a pound of TNT wired electrically and controlled by a BA70 battery. There were fifteen of these fougasses in the Company A area. Each fougasse had a dispersing radius of 75 yards. They were to be used primarily for illuminating purposes. But after the action started, artillery and mortar shells cut the electrical wires, and the fougasses were not able to be used.[11]

The enemy attacked the night of 16–17 May and pushed back the outposts of the 24th Infantry Division. The enemy struck the general defense line the following night. Lt. Clark describes the beginning of the action.

Company A relieved Company L on 8 May. On 17 May enemy elements were sighted, but there was no contact. Clark and his forward observer, Lt. Yates, saw the enemy in estimated company size moving from Hill 342 [about one and a quarter miles north of Company A's position] into the valley. Artillery fire was placed on this enemy force.

At 1930, an enemy mortar round came into the company CP area. Twenty to thirty rounds of 60mm and 81mm mortar fire came in shortly thereafter, scattered throughout the company area. An enemy machine gun 500 yards distant opened fire immediately after the first mortar round struck. This machine gun had a steel shield and fired on the company until 0300. One man was wounded about 2000.

Knowing that the enemy attack was on, Clark directed artillery (13th Field Artillery Battalion) and the 81mm mortars to fire on the enemy. There was a three-quarter moon that night. The Chinese were camouflaged with brush tied to their heads and backs. The Chinese were very patient as they worked up the slopes toward the Company A position. Later, many Chinese dead were found tied up in the outside [barbed wire] apron. About twenty Chinese bodies were found in one minefield.

The 3d Platoon, Company A, did most of the firing. The 1st Platoon machine gun fired, as did the recoilless rifles and the BARs of the company. Every light machine gun had fifteen boxes of ammunition with ten in reserve. The heavy machine guns had twenty boxes in position and twenty in reserve. Each infantryman had ten grenades; each rifleman had five bandoliers of ammunition plus a full belt. The 60mm mortars had 495 rounds on position. The 81mm mortar must have fired 1,500 rounds that night.

The attack started at 1930. The Chinese worked their way up. The company could not see the enemy, but the men knew the Chinese were coming. At 0300, 18 May, everything had quieted down.[12]

Other members of Company A describe the initial contact with the enemy.

1st Lt. Roy A. Hagen, leader, 2d Platoon: The 2d Platoon on the company left flank tied in with the Australian Battalion.

About 1500, 17 May, Hagen [killed in action, 28 June 1951] observed large groups of enemy, two companies in one sector, two
companies widely dispersed.[13] Hagen called for artillery fire on these
troops. Friendly artillery and mortar fire continued steadily in close
support from dusk throughout the night. Some friendly rounds actually landed in the company positions. . . .

The afternoon before, on 17 May, Hagen spotted an enemy
machine gun about 500 yards in front of the company. Taking three
men with him, Hagen went out to pick up a wounded Chinese near
this enemy machine gun position. Hagen found approximately
twenty Chinese on the reverse slope of the hill where the machine
gun was set up. After firing on the surprised Chinese, Hagen and his
men ran back to the company. The company then knew that the
Chinese would set up their support weapons on this finger. . . . The
enemy approached the right flank of the 2d Platoon, but never actually came through the wire, and so did not come into close contact.[14]

SGT. GEORGE I. CARR AND CPL. RUFUS CLOUD, 2D PLATOON:
On the night of 16–17 May, part of Company E, 5th RCT, came
through the Company A positions from the outpost line they had
been maintaining. Some were stragglers and had lost their weapons.
. . . On 17 May, Carr and Cloud were on a finger ridge on the left
flank of the company. That evening they saw 200 enemy moving
toward the positions in the vicinity of the company CP. The 57mm
recoilless rifle fired at a range of 1,800 yards. Some enemy went into
a house. The recoilless rifle demolished the house. At the same time,
we yelled up to the CP, and artillery was delivered on the enemy.[15]

PFC WILLIE C. HALES, BAR MAN, AND PFC JOHN W. COX,
ASSISTANT BAR MAN, BOTH 3D PLATOON: The first thing that happened that night was a mortar round that hit about seven feet to the
right of Hales's and Cox's bunker. A second mortar round fell three
feet in front of the bunker. A third one struck several feet behind.
When the enemy machine guns opened up (Hales and Cox estimate
there were three), Hales and Cox returned the fire. But the enemy
machine gun put fire too close to the bunker, so they stopped firing
the BAR. Between 0100 and 0300, Hales and Cox threw thirty-four
grenades at noises in front of their position. They had three grenades
left, so Hales crawled along the trench to another position and bor-

rowed three grenades. He made another trip to another position and secured six grenades.[16]

CPL. FRED C. BERRY, 2D SQUAD, 3D PLATOON: Berry [killed in action, 27 June 1951], who was in the 2d Squad, which was on the left flank of the 3d Platoon position, occupied a foxhole on the left flank of his squad.[17] Before the attack, some foxholes partway down the forward slope of the hill, which the Chinese would be able to use when they attacked, were booby-trapped with grenades. The grenades were tied down to roots or to a stake with a wire stretched across the bottom of the hole. Anyone hitting the hole would pull the wire, which would pull the grenade pin. When the enemy attacked, the trip flares that had been set up worked fine. Berry did not do much firing because it was quiet in his sector.[18]

SGT. JOHN A. TIPTON, 4TH PLATOON: Tipton was in charge of a 57mm recoilless rifle section that was on the high ground near the CP. One 57mm rifle on the left flank of the 2d Platoon did not do much firing. Tipton's position was a good one, logged overhead and sandbagged. The 57mm rifle was laid on the sandbags, and a slot was made in the bags. The rifle could be fired in all directions to the front. The weapon fired sixty rounds that night at about 300 or 400 yards' range. The Chinese were firing automatic weapons over the ridge where Company A was emplaced. The Chinese had about three machine guns, which they moved constantly. The recoilless rifles fired at enemy tracers.[19]

SGT. RICHARD A. ROTANZ AND CPL. FRANK BILLEMEYER, MORTARMEN, 4TH PLATOON: Rotanz stated that the three 60mm mortars fired 375 rounds of HE and WP that night. The mortars began firing at 200 yards. During the night the range decreased to 150 yards, then to 100 yards. . . . Billemeyer, who was on a mortar, stated that the mortars at one time were firing at a range of only 65 yards. In order to fire below minimum range, the mortar was elevated and aimed by hand.[20]

CPL. JEROME GOLDBERG, 4TH PLATOON: Goldberg, mortar forward observer for the 1st Platoon, stated that the men were nervous. The bushes were rattling. Many trip flares went off. Friendly troops threw many grenades. One mortar fired 310 rounds that night. Goldberg saw no Chinese at night.[21]

1ST LT. HAROLD L. BENSKIN, LEADER, 1ST PLATOON: Benskin's platoon was on the company right flank and tied in with Company B. Between 1930 and 2000, 17 May, he heard enemy mortar rounds fall on the top of the hill where Lt. Clark and the 3d Platoon were located. He had been expecting an enemy attack, so he told his men to get into their foxholes. Benskin's machine gun fired six boxes of ammunition at the enemy machine guns. The men were jumpy. They threw some hand grenades at noises, but they did not use too much ammunition. Several trip flares went off. Benskin thought they were set off by enemy patrols in front of the 1st Platoon positions. Benskin and his platoon remained on alert until 0330.[22]

Earlier in the evening to the east of Company A, Companies B and C had come under enemy attack. The After-Action Report of the 1st Battalion, 19th Infantry, as recorded in the G-3 telephone journal, IX Corps, describes the action.

Between 1900 and 2000 hours, 17 May 1951, an estimated enemy Bn attacked positions of B/19th. Enemy got within hand-grenade throwing distance of friendly positions, but did not get through the wire obstacles around the friendly positions. Arty, mortar, and HMG [heavy machine gun] fire repulsed the enemy attack, which shifted to the east and attacked C/19th positions. Hand grenades were again exchanged and friendly fire forced the enemy to disengage at 2350. The enemy remained in the vic of friendly positions and were subjected to arty and mortar fire. At 180100 it was reported quiet in the sector.[23]

Following the attack on Companies B and C, the enemy shifted its focus to Company A. Lt. Clark, commander, Company A, continues his description of the fight.

At 0400 hand grenades came into the Company A positions. About fifteen grenades exploded near the bunkers in the 3d Platoon area. Then there were Chinese "all over the place."

Lt. Clark, Lt. Johnson, 3d Platoon leader, and Lt. Yates, forward observer, were in the command bunker at 0400. When the enemy attack started, Johnson left the CP bunker and moved up to keep his platoon in position. Clark went outside the bunker to send anyone back who left his position. Yates remained near the tele-phone and radio. Soon after Clark and Johnson went outside, two Chinese appeared, one on top of the CP bunker and one in front of it. Clark shot the Chinese on top of the bunker with his pistol. The other Chinese opened up on Yates with his burp gun. Yates threw a grenade at him. The Chinese threw a grenade at Yates. The grenade landed on Yates's back at shoulder height. Yates nonchalantly shrugged it off, emptied his pistol of its seven rounds, and killed the Chinese. The Chinese grenade wounded Yates in the back. One fragment went through his helmet. Yates, not seriously wounded, remained at his communications position. "It was odd to see Yates," Clark said, "he reminded me of a horse flicking off a fly."

Johnson and Clark moved around the 3d Platoon area keeping the men in their positions, making sure that ammunition bearers kept the men supplied. Between 0400 and daylight, a duel of hand grenades took place. Two Chinese jumped into a trench between a BAR and a machine gun; one Chinese was shot; the other was beaten to death with a rifle. Then the two men who had killed the Chinese got scared and ran out of their holes, afraid that the Chi-nese had the company surrounded. Company A expended about 1,200 grenades that night. At least fifty Chinese, lying about thirty yards in front of the company positions, just on the other side of the last wire, fired automatic weapons and threw grenades. No one could see the enemy.[24]

Other members of Company A describe the fighting.

1ST LT. DALE N. JOHNSON, LEADER, 3D PLATOON: On the eve-ning of 17 May, Johnson, Clark and the forward observer, Lt. Yates, with several radio operators, were in the company CP bunker. Ene-my overhead machine gun fire came in, then small arms. Johnson left the CP to check his men. As he was returning, two Chinese came in and threw grenades into the BAR position. Hales hit one Chinese over the head.

Friendly troops were throwing grenades at Chinese who were crowding the company positions. The machine gun team started to pull out; they were afraid they would lose their gun if they remained. Johnson kept them in position. Although Johnson tried to keep all of his men in position, some of them left. Enemy machine gun and small arms fire limited maneuver on the knob where the 3d Platoon was located.

Lt. Benskin brought up a squad from his platoon, and Johnson restored his positions by putting them in the abandoned holes. The 75mm rifle section did a good job on the hill by throwing grenades when the enemy got too close for effective 75mm fire. The section also used its individual weapons to repel the attack.[25]

PFCs HALES AND COX, BAR MEN, 3D PLATOON: About 0400 several enemy grenades came close to their bunker and ran Hales and Cox out. They left the BAR and a rifle in the bunker. A Chinese came over the top of the hill and fired into the bunker with a burp gun. Cox threw a grenade and killed him. The Chinese rolled into the bunker. A second Chinese jumped into the trench. Cox tried to fire his carbine, but he had no ammunition, so he dropped his weapon and grabbed the Chinese soldier's burp gun and pulled him over on top of him. Hales picked up Cox's carbine and beat the Chinese over the head. Someone then came up and shot the Chinese with a pistol. Cox and Hales then ran to the rear. Lt. Clark stopped them, sent them back to their position. Cox, instead, crawled into a Company D machine gun emplacement and helped the machine gunner. Hales helped a man who had been wounded in the face back to the aid man, then returned and entered a bunker other than his own. Neither Hales nor Cox wanted to return to the dead man in their bunker. At daylight, Hales and Cox returned to their original bunker and recovered the BAR and rifle. The Chinese was still dead.[26]

LT. BENSKIN, LEADER, 1ST PLATOON: Then Lt. Johnson, 3d Platoon leader, called and said he wanted several men to give him some extra fire power. Benskin took a squad over there, distributed grenades, and got his men into position. Then he returned to his own platoon and reorganized his men to fill the gap in his own lines.[27]

PFCs WILLIAM L. JOHNSON AND JOHN H. ANNACOST, BOTH 1ST PLATOON: Johnson and Annacost were two of the three ammunition bearers from the 1st Platoon who were sent at 0500 to act as riflemen to the 3d Platoon area because an enemy breakthrough was feared. Johnson fired about eight clips, firing at enemy tracers. He actually saw no Chinese. Annacost fired about fifteen rounds in the direction of the enemy, although he saw no Chinese. . . . At 0600 a squad of men from the 1st Platoon was sent to the 3d Platoon area.[28]

SGT. TIPTON, 4TH PLATOON: Two Chinese who got through the wire threw two grenades into the 57mm hole, wounding one gunner. Another man in the hole grabbed the gun and ran out. Tipton, who was outside the hole at that time, stopped the man who was running, brought the gun back to the hole, and sent the wounded man back to the aid man. At daylight Tipton fired about fifteen rounds at 400 yards at groups of Chinese digging in.[29]

Members of the company describe the final gasps of the Chinese attack.

LT. D. JOHNSON, 3D PLATOON: An air strike shortly after daylight seemed to drive the Chinese into the Company A positions. A panicky group of enemy charged the left flank of the 3d Platoon, and the "boys had a field day" as the enemy came through the last barbed wire. This charge ended the attack.[30]

CPL. BERRY, 3D PLATOON: About 0730 friendly planes came over. The Chinese, apparently scared, came running up the slope toward his positions. A BAR man in his squad killed four who were twenty feet in front of his hole. Two men who were cleaning their rifles when the Chinese charged threw grenades. Berry fired several clips. Eleven enemy bodies were counted in front of his squad positions.[31]

SGT. CARR AND CPL. CLOUD, 2D PLATOON: The 2d Platoon did no firing until the morning, 18 May. Then the men saw two Chinese about 400 yards away. A volume of fire from the platoon killed these two enemy soldiers. Three hundred yards away, a Chinese soldier was seen washing his wounded foot in a stream. Several men went out about 0830 and brought him in. These men had to go through friendly wire and mines to get to the Chinese. The enemy soldier was wounded in the foot and the butt. He walked halfway back to friendly positions, and then had to be carried the rest of the way. The company aid man bandaged his wounds.[32]

LT. HAGEN, LEADER, 2D PLATOON: At daylight Hagen saw eight or nine enemy soldiers tangled in the wire in front of his platoon position. These were killed by single-action shots from members of his platoon. At 0600 Hagen went to the company CP to see how things were. Everything was under control. He returned to his platoon. At 0800, as Hagen was inspecting the enemy dead in front of his position, a short artillery round wounded him in the back. Hagen was evacuated. . . .

Hagen, after speaking with various men in the 3d Platoon, felt that the cool work of Clark and Yates had saved the company from being overrun. Yates, who was hit by shrapnel, one fragment of which pierced his helmet, said "Goddammit," and continued calling in fire. Yates remained standing on the knob throughout the attack. Clark was all over the area picking out targets. There was no thought of abandoning the position.[33]

Lt. Clark describes the end of the attack.

At daylight, everything quieted down. At 0730 friendly planes struck an area 1,000 yards in front of the company where there seemed to be a large group of Chinese. The air strike was horizontal to the front. The strike apparently panicked a group of Chinese, for fifty or sixty of them charged toward Company A, tearing themselves on the wire. The entire company opened up. Thirty minutes later, forty dead Chinese were hanging on the barbed wire. Lt. Yates, wounded, remained to direct the artillery on suspected enemy assembly points in the valley. Approximately 500 rounds of VT were expended that night.

That morning between 200 and 250 Chinese dead were counted. Prisoners later said that a regiment had attacked the 19th Infantry Regiment; about an enemy battalion had struck Company A. Company A sustained two WIA.[34]

The G-3 telephone journal, IX Corps, recorded the After-Action Report of the 1st Battalion, 19th Infantry, that summarized the action of Company A.

Between 180300 and 180400 A/19 received long-range sporadic S/A and MG fire. At 0400 A Company was attacked by an estimated two enemy companies. By 0530 the enemy had penetrated the obstacles surrounding the position and engaged Co A in hand-to-hand combat. Til 0600 Co A used S/A, knives, bayonets, and rifle butts to force the enemy from the position. After a lull, an enemy company attacked Co A at 0700 hours and were once again engaged in hand-to-hand combat. This engagement was broken off at 0800 hours. Fifteen enemy were caught between friendly positions and the wire obstacles, six of whom remained same.

The wire mines and trip flares were of great value to the Bn in assisting in repelling the enemy attack. Only A Company's wire was broken. All obstacles are being replaced or repaired in the sector today. The fougasses failed to work because the ignition lines were cut by artillery fire. (Passed to the IX Corps Engr for a possible solution to insure ignition of fougasse even when subjected to arty fire.)[35]

Lt. Martin Blumenson provided an assessment of Company A's actions.

Although Companies B and C were also attacked that night, Company A occupied and held the key terrain in the battalion sector. There was no thought of abandoning the hill. "We couldn't leave those positions," Clark said, "they were too good."

The 3d Platoon had received and repelled the enemy attack. Close and effective artillery and mortar support, the inspiring leadership of Lts. Clark and Johnson, and the coolness of Lt. Yates, forward observer, were responsible for the success of this defensive action. The General Defense Line held.[36]

Task Force Byorum: 6th Medium Tank Battalion, 17–19 May 1951

The IX Corps commander, Maj. Gen. William M. Hoge, was determined not only to hold the general defense line, but also to inflict maximum punishment on the attacking enemy and to destroy as many of the Chinese units as possible. Hoge provided this guidance to his division commanders on the night of 18–19 May.

It is my personal desire that you exploit all fire power and maneuver facilities at your command to destroy the enemy in your sector. You will conduct an active defense, as opposed to a passive defense, making use of counterattacks on each and every occasion and at all echelons to seal off and crush enemy probing attacks and penetrations. The timing of your counterattacks is of extreme importance; they should be employed when the enemy has lost his momentum and is at his weakest, thus preventing his reorganization and withdrawal and enabling you to complete his defeat. So far we can destroy each of his probing forces in turn and thus achieve his defeat in detail. I desire an aggressive and imaginative attitude on the part of your entire command in devising means and methods of making maximum use of all supporting arms and services to disrupt and destroy attacking enemy forces. Utilize armored task forces wherever possible to get behind the enemy and hit him from the rear. Take advantage of your familiarity with the terrain upon which you stand to restore lost positions at the first available opportunity. Keep your major units intact at all times, but do not allow the turning of a flank or a minor penetration to cause a withdrawal of any unit without the express permission of the next higher headquarters.[37]

The 24th Infantry Division had anticipated General Hoge's guidance. On 17 May it formed Task Force Byorum, an armor-infantry task force taking its name from the commanding officer of the 6th Medium Tank Battalion, Lt. Col. Henry M. Byorum. The next day it conducted its first strike into enemy territory. Task Force Byorum's After-Action Report describes its organization, mission, and initial operations.[38]

Orders were received from G-3, 24th Infantry Division, 172200 May 1951 that directed the 6th Medium Tank Battalion [equipped with M46 Patton tanks] to form a task force made up of one tank company and the 8th Ranger [Infantry] Company (ABN) [Airborne] to conduct a patrol forward of the friendly lines. The mission of the force was to gain and maintain contact with the enemy, to inflict maximum casualties, and develop enemy [forces] along the route.[39]

At about 172200 the S-3, 6th Medium Tank Battalion, called G-3, 24th Infantry Division, and requested an engineer detachment complete with a tank dozer. This request was granted, and Company B, 6th Medium Tank Battalion, was then released from attachment to the 29th British Commonwealth [Independent Infantry]

Brigade and put under control of the 6th Medium Tank Battalion for the duration of the task force.

G-3, 24th Infantry Division, called the 6th Medium Tank Battalion at 172330 and stated that other elements had been made available for this task force and requested that the commanding officer and S-3, 6th Medium Tank Battalion, report to the 24th Infantry Division CP immediately to get all the necessary information. Commanding officer and S-3, 6th Medium Tank Battalion, proceeded to the 24th Infantry Division CP and discussed the plans with the G-3, 24th Infantry Division. The additional troops consisted of Company C, King's Shropshire Light Infantry [KSLI], Company C (minus), 6th Medium Tank Battalion, one platoon of the 52d AAA (AW) Battalion, and a forward observer from the 955th Field Artillery.

G-3, 24th Infantry Division, stated that the 24th Reconnaissance Company would furnish five M39 personnel carriers for the infantry and that fifteen more would arrive from IX Corps at 180600 May 1951. An assembly area for the task force was designated vicinity [Mahyon-ni–Nungnae-ri]. G-3, 24th Infantry Division, stated that the task force was to move out of the assembly area as soon as it was formed, and a tentative time of 180730 May 1951 was set to clear that area.

Plans were made, commanders concerned were notified, and a meeting was held at 180412 May 1951 at which time Operation Plan #11 . . . was issued to all commanders. By 180600 May 1951, all elements of the task force were in the assembly area with the exception of Company C, KSLI, which was delayed. Commanding officer, 6th Medium Tank Battalion, notified G-3, 24th Infantry Division, of the delay of the KSLI and received orders to wait for the KSLI and to move out as soon as possible after they arrived.

Company C, KSLI, arrived in the assembly area at 180730 May 1951, and about thirty minutes later Task Force Byorum crossed the IP [initial point]. . . . The task force marched northwest in the 24th Infantry Division zone, crossing the front lines of the Princess Patricia Light Infantry at 180840 May 1951.[40]

1st Lt. Tom S. Groseclose, S-2, 6th Medium Tank Battalion, outlines the organization of Task Force Byorum.

Task Force Byorum on 18 May consisted of the following:

Team A (commanded by Major Evans, King's Shropshire Light Infantry)

    Company C, King's Shropshire Light Infantry

    Company C (minus one platoon), 6th Medium Tank Battalion

    8th Ranger Company (minus one platoon)

    Six tracked vehicles, 52d AAA Battalion (quad-mounted .50 caliber machine guns)

    Detachment (two mine sweeper teams), 3d Engineer Combat Battalion

    Forward observer, 24th Infantry Division Artillery.

Team B (commanded by Captain O'Brien, commanding officer, Company B, 6th Medium Tank Battalion)

    Company B, 6th Medium Tank Battalion

    One platoon, 8th Ranger Infantry Company (Airborne)

    Two tracked vehicles, 52d AAA Battalion (quad-mounted .50 caliber machine guns)

    Detachment (two mine sweeper teams and tank dozer), 3d Engineer Combat Battalion.[41]

Lt. Col. Byorum's plan called for his task force to move behind friendly lines along the road paralleling the Han River, pass through the general defense line, continue northwest until reaching the main road to Seoul, then turn northeast and advance along this road (Route 18), inflicting as much damage as possible on enemy forces. It was believed that Chinese logistical units might be deployed along Route 18, which linked the Pukhan River valley with Seoul and connected with Route 17, the main road north from the Pukhan River valley to Kap'yong and Ch'unch'on. The After-Action Report describes the operations of Task Force Byorum on 18 May.

Team A proceeded northwest along the route that was marked with four bad bypasses for the tanks. Several civilians along the route were questioned, and they reported an unestimated number of enemy troops [southwest of Ilbi-ri]. By 181100 May 1951 Team A had occupied blocking positions on high ground . . . [at the junction

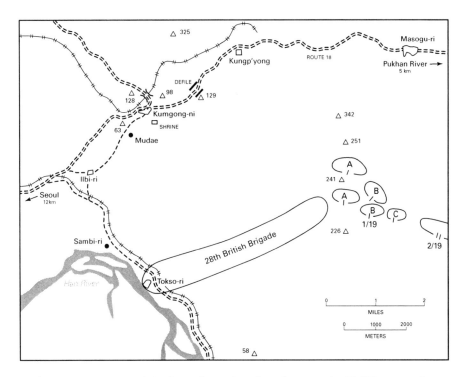

Task Force Byorum. (Original map by author, based on map in CMH manuscript, U.S. Army, and map in Army Map Service series L751.)

of Route 18 and the road that the task force followed out of the Han River valley at Ilbi-ri] and Team B passed through this position to continue northeast. When Team B reached the vicinity of Kumgong-ni, prearranged artillery concentrations Nos. 14, 15, and 16 . . . were fired preparatory to moving [into] that area. Unidentified troops were spotted . . . [about 1,000 yards north of Kumgong-ni] at 181200 May 1951. Friendly artillery fire was lifted at 1235 hours, and Team B continued on mission. Upon reaching Hill 129 [over-looking the main road nearly a mile east of Kumgong-ni], several enemy groups were observed running down the hill towards the column. These groups were fired upon and dispersed.

The lead tank of Team B encountered one seven-foot bangalore torpedo lying across the road vicinity . . . [Hill 129]. Mines were found in the road, and this area was covered by enemy small arms and mortar fire. Artillery fire was placed on the mined area but failed to explode any. At this time, because fuel in the tanks was almost exhausted, the column turned around and withdrew under scattered small arms and mortar fire.

As Team B withdrew, the friendly infantry was also withdrawing southwest from their most advanced blocking position. Through an error in identity, some machine gun fire was placed on these foot troops. This error was corrected immediately, however, and no casualties were suffered by the friendly infantry.

Task Force Byorum returned to friendly lines along the same route used that morning and at 182022 May 1951 closed into an assembly area vicinity [P'oltang-ni, along the Han River]. Upon reaching the assembly area Lt. Col. Byorum was notified that the task force was to refuel and feed in its present position and prepare to patrol the same area the following day, 19 May 1951.[42]

Task Force Byorum's armored foray into the enemy's rear seemed to meet exactly the desires of General Hoge, IX Corps commander. Lt. Col. Robert J. Natzel, chief, G-3 operations section, IX Corps, explains how the situation was perceived in his headquarters.

The mission that IX Corps gave the 24th Infantry Division for Task Force Byorum was to inflict maximum casualties on the enemy. It was felt at corps that an armored task force moving behind known concentrations of enemy troops would inflict great damage. Corps expected Task Force Byorum to proceed a considerable distance along the Kumgong-ni–Kungp'yong–Masogu-ri axis [the latter two being the last two towns east of Kumgong-ni on the road to the Pukhan River]. It was even thought that the task force would drive south of Masogu-ri [three miles west of the Pukhan], make the loop, and establish contact with friendly elements on the right side of the 24th Infantry Division sector.[43]

The After-Action Report describes the preparations for operations planned for 19 May.

The task force was resupplied with fuel and ammunition, and the troops were fed while a critique was held by Lt. Col. Byorum with all commanders of the various units present. Methods of employment were discussed and tentative plans laid to better employ the force on the following day benefitting by the one day's experience gained by working as a team.

Lt. Col. Byorum and Capt. Coady, S-3, 6th Medium Tank Battalion, proceeded to the CP of the 24th Infantry Division to discuss the results of the day's operation and the plans for the following day. G-3, 24th Infantry Division, stated that the mission for 19 May 1951 was to be the same as on 18 May 1951 with one addition; the task force was also to exploit the enemy in the valley extending northwest from Hill 128 vicinity [about 1,000 yards northwest of Kumgong-ni], making a determined effort to reach the head of the valley.

Plans were made at CP, 6th Medium Tank Battalion, and when all commanders concerned were assembled at 190500 May 1951, Operations Plan #12 . . . was issued. The time set for crossing the friendly front lines was first light or as soon as visibility permitted.[44]

Lt. Col. Byorum describes the organization and mission of the task force.

For operations on 19 May 1951, Task Force Byorum was organized into three teams. Team A comprised Company B, 6th Medium Tank Battalion, a detachment of the 3d Engineer Combat Battalion for mine sweeping (including one bulldozer), and a forward observer from the 955th Field Artillery Battalion. Team B consisted of Company C (minus one platoon), 6th Medium Tank Battalion. Team C included the 8th U.S. Ranger Infantry Company (80 men), one company (100 men) from the King's Shropshire Light Infantry, and one platoon (eight tracked vehicles) of quad-mounted .50 caliber machine guns, 52d AAA Battalion.

The mission of this force was to go to Kungp'yong by way of the Tokso-ri–Ilbi-ri–Kumgong-ni axis, destroy the enemy, and secure information on enemy locations.[45]

No one seemed to have any misgivings about sending the task force over the same route it had used the previous day. The After-Action Report describes the beginning of the task force's advance on 19 May.

Task Force Byorum crossed the friendly lines at 190745 May 1951 in the same place as on the preceding day. At 0757 hours the lead tank hit a mine vicinity [northwest of Tokso-ri and southeast of Sambi-ri], but no damage was done to the tank. After the mine sweeping crew from the engineer detachment had swept the area, the column continued. By 1010 hours the head of the column had reached . . . [a point about 500 yards west of Kumgong-ni] and reported 200 enemy on Hill 325 [one and a half miles north of the village]. Radio messages were relayed back to CP, 6th Medium Tank Battalion, and then telephoned to G-3, 24th Infantry Division, to institute action for an air strike on that location. The liaison pilot of the 6th Medium Tank Battalion was over the column, and when the "Mosquito"[46] plane in the area called him, the air strike was laid on, which resulted in an estimated 100 enemy killed.[47]

Lt. Col. Byorum provides a sketch of the movement of his teams as the task force advanced.

The task force moved at 0715 hours across the line of departure [southeast of Tokso-ri]. Almost immediately the lead tank struck a mine at the first road junction [southeast of Sambi-ri], but no damage was incurred. The column continued to Ilbi-ri.

Team A proceeded to Kumgong-ni. Team B moved into the vicinity of Hill 63 to be in position against enemy forces suspected of being emplaced on Hill 128 and Hill 98. Team C placed a small detachment of infantry and AAA quad-fifties on high ground north of the road [nearly a mile north of Ilbi-ri] to prevent the enemy from coming in and mining the road behind Teams A and B. The balance of Team C was held as a mobile force in the vicinity of Ilbi-ri.

The road to Kumgong-ni was a narrow defile between wet and muddy rice paddies. It was difficult for the tanks to maneuver because of the danger of becoming mired in the mud. On the outskirts of Kumgong-ni, a bridge appeared prepared for demolition. The column bypassed the bridge. As the column entered Kumgong-ni, it began to receive enemy small arms and mortar fire. The road junction in town appeared to be heavily mined. Engineers placed a bangalore torpedo through the suspected minefield; the explosion confirmed the suspicion and demolished the mines. The column advanced through town toward Kungp'yong.[48]

After a meeting at I Corps headquarters at Uijongbu on 24 April 1951, Gen. Matthew B. Ridgway (right) confers with his successor, Lt. Gen. James A. Van Fleet, about the critical situation at the front resulting from the Chinese Communist Spring Offensive launched on the night of 22–23 April. SC-365678.

Elements of the North Korean 45th Division attacked the positions of Company B, 32d Infantry Regiment, 7th Infantry Division, north of Ip-tong, from 19 to 22 April and suffered a severe reverse. After the fighting, on 23 April, enemy dead littered the ground. SC-365087.

Back to front: Cpl. Lionel H. Bourgoin, Sgt. Donald H. Boggs holding the handie-talkie SCR536 in his hand, and Cpl. George A. Hill, all of Company B, 32d Infantry, wait for their orders on 23 April 1951, after fighting off the North Korean attack. SC-365082.

Men of Company B, 32d Infantry, rest after several days of combat against the North Korean 45th Division, 23 April 1951. SC-365081.

United Nations aircraft provided timely and deadly air strikes in support of Company B's outpost, which left many of the North Korean attackers dead or seriously wounded. The body of an enemy soldier hit by napalm still smolders on 23 April 1951. SC-365088.

This annotated terrain photograph shows Hill 128, where the forward artillery observation post of the 999th Armored Field Artillery Battalion was located until the beginning of the Chinese Communist Spring Offensive on 22–23 April 1951. CMH, Ms. 8-5.1A BA68, Hill 128.

The 19th Infantry Regiment, 24th Infantry Division, I Corps, withdraws on 23 April 1951 to a new defense line as Ridgway and Van Fleet implement their strategy to absorb the Chinese Communist Forces' Spring Offensive by relocating to better defensive positions. Troops line the sides of the road to clear the way for three tanks—an M46 Patton followed by an M4 Sherman and another M46 in the distance. SC-365190.

An M39 Armored Utility Vehicle (AUV), 724th Ordnance Company, 24th Infantry Division, acts as a personnel carrier as it relocates troops to a new defense line on 23 April 1951. The M39 was used in a variety of roles during the Korean War, and it played a major role in the actions of Battery B, 999th Armored Field Artillery Battalion, at Pobwon-ni on 23–24 April. SC-365196.

Weary infantrymen of the 19th Infantry Regiment, 24th Infantry Division, I Corps, withdraw to new defensive positions farther south after slowing the initial onslaught of the Chinese Communist Spring Offensive, 23 April 1951. SC-365191.

Lt. Gen. William M. Hoge, commanding general, IX Corps, pulls the lanyard on an M41 155mm self-propelled howitzer of the 92d Armored Field Artillery Battalion, sending the unit's 75,000th round into Communist territory during its service in Korea, 24 June 1951. Next to Hoge are Brig. Gen. William N. Gillmore, commanding general, IX Corps Artillery, and Lt. Col. Leon F. Lavoie, commander, who led the 92d as it helped blunt the Spring Offensive at Todun-ni and in Task Force Lindy Lou. SC-372173.

A simple wooden cross marks the grave of Capt. Richard Reeve-Tucker, signals officer, 1st Gloucestershire Battalion, 29th British Brigade, overlooking the Imjin River, where he fell in battle during the fight for Hill 235 (Gloster Hill) on 23 April 1951. SC-371720.

(*Right*) Lt. Gen. Edward M. Almond, commanding general, X Corps, meets with Col. George H. Gerhart, executive officer, 187th Airborne Regimental Combat Team, wearing sunglasses and holding a terrain map, and two unidentified officers at the airstrip at the 187th's headquarters at Chogutan, Korea, on 22 May 1951. Almond made Gerhart commander of the task force that was to clear Route 24 north to Umyang-ni on the Soyang River, for the continuation of the United Nations Command's counteroffensive. SC-367770.

As U.S. Marines move north, following up the advance of Task Force Gerhart, they pass the remains of the 23d Infantry Regiment's vehicles that were destroyed in an ambush by the Chinese along Route 24 south of Chaun-ni on 18 May 1951. Once several of the lead vehicles were disabled, the convoy had little room to maneuver to escape on the narrow road between the steep hill overrun with Chinese and the riverbed below. SC-368656.

Men of the 187th Airborne RCT's intelligence and reconnaissance platoon, part of Task Force Gerhart, hold two Chinese prisoners captured on the push up Route 24 north of Chaun-ni, while another fires the machine gun mounted on their jeep, 24 May 1951. SC-368618.

Lt. Gen. James A. Van Fleet (right), commanding general, Eighth U.S. Army, meets with Col. George H. Gerhart at an advance CP of the 187th Airborne RCT at Umyang-ni, just south of the Soyang River, 25 May 1951. Four M4A3E8 tanks of Company B, 72d Tank Battalion, can be seen in firing position on the high ground in the background. SC-367884.

Upon reaching Umyang-ni, the tanks of Task Force Gerhart were running low on gas and 76mm ammunition for the M4A3E8 tanks of Company B, 72d Tank Battalion. An aerial resupply mission was flown on 25 May to drop needed gas and ammunition. SC-368676.

Its mission completed, Task Force Gerhart was disbanded on 25 May. With Route 24 now open to the Soyang River, the 2d Infantry Division's 72d Tank Battalion and the 23d Infantry Regiment pushed across the Soyang and up its north shore to seize Kwandae-ri and then Inje. Here, on 28 May 1951, tanks of Company C, 72d Tank Battalion, ford the Soyang north of Inje and keep the pressure on the retreating Chinese Communist forces. SC-368681.

Soldiers of the 7th Infantry Division fire on enemy troops near Sinjom-ni on the road to Ch'unch'on during an initial reconnaissance the day before Task Force Hazel began its drive up the road, 23 May 1951. Behind them are PFC Robert Peterson, a Signal Corps photographer, and Bill Burson, a United Press correspondent. SC-367588.

The M4 tank dozer of the 32d Tank Company, 32d Infantry Regiment, 7th Infantry Division, accompanying Task Force Hazel fills in a crater in the road to Ch'unch'on, 24 May 1951. SC-367892.

An M4A3E8 of Capt. Hazel's 7th Reconnaissance Company blasts Chinese positions along the road to Ch'unch'on, 24 May 1951. SC-367595.

Maj. Gen. Claude B. Ferenbaugh (with the binoculars), commanding general, 7th Infantry Division, and his aide, Capt. Malcolm W. Chandler Jr., who were ambushed along the road to Ch'unch'on on 24 May 1951, are pictured here by a photographer observing the 7th Infantry Division in action at Hadaewa on 28 February 1951. SC-359746.

Task Force Hazel's success cleared the way for the Eighth Army's continued counteroffensive against Chinese and North Korean forces. Here the big brass meet at the airstrip in Ch'unch'on to discuss their next moves, 29 May 1951. *Left to right:* Maj. Gen. William M. Hoge (far left, in profile), commanding general, IX Corps; Gen. Matthew B. Ridgway, commander in chief, U.S. Far East Command and United Nations Command; Lt. Gen. James A. Van Fleet, commanding general, Eighth U.S. Army; and Maj. Gen. Claude B. Ferenbaugh, commanding general, 7th Infantry Division. SC-369058.

(*Left*) Task Force Hazel's job was done on 25 May 1951, when its second trip to Ch'unch'on spearheaded the drive of the 7th Infantry Division's 17th Infantry Regiment to continue the IX Corps's push to the north and east. Here convoys carrying the 17th Infantry pass through the heavily damaged Ch'unch'on on the 25th. SC-367605.

After its movement in mid-May from I Corps in western Korea to the X Corps in the east, the 3d Infantry Division was used to strengthen the defensive line against the Second Impulse of the Chinese Spring Offensive (16–23 May 1951) and then to push the Chinese and North Korean forces back. Here the crew of a tracked M19, dual-40mm Bofors antiaircraft gun of the 3d Antiaircraft Artillery Battalion (Automatic Weapons), 3d Infantry Division, and two M4 tanks, which are partly obscured behind the M19, fire on enemy troops in support of the 7th Infantry Regiment near Soksa-ri and Hill 1015, 23 May 1951. SC-367901.

The tracked antiaircraft weapons from the 3d Infantry Division's 3d Antiaircraft Artillery Battalion (Automatic Weapons) supported the infantry in holding the Chinese Second Impulse Offensive and then moved north during the UN counteroffensive. The crew chief of an M19 dual-40mm Bofors talks over the radio, while the crew of one M16 quad 50 scans the hills near Soksa-ri and Hill 1015, and another checks a Korean house, 23 May 1951. SC-367587.

Capt. John A. LaMontia, aviation officer, 6th Medium Tank Battalion, and SFC Russell W. Underhill, an aerial observer, provide more details.

Capt. LaMontia and SFC Underhill learned at 0500, 19 May, that they were to perform reconnaissance for Task Force Byorum. They joined the tank column about 0640 as the task force departed from the assembly area. Flying about 5,000 to 8,000 yards in front of the task force, they saw enemy patrols on the northern slopes of Hill 63 and called artillery on these groups. LaMontia directed harassing fire on the area of the shrine [tomb at Hongnung] south of Kumgong-ni, since enemy had been observed there the day before. As the tanks moved toward Kumgong-ni, they drew enemy small arms fire from Hill 128 and from the wooded area south of the road. LaMontia and Underhill directed harassing artillery fire in front of the tanks.

Colonel Byorum then informed LaMontia that the tanks would advance toward Hill 129. Enemy activity in that area was observed from the air. LaMontia requested a "Mosquito" plane, which was in the area, to check Hill 325. The "Mosquito" reported fifty enemy troops dug in on Hill 325, with the possibility of more, and between 1000 and 1030 hours, the "Mosquito" put an air strike on this area.[49]

As the task force proceeded toward Hill 129, more enemy forces were encountered, as the After-Action Report recounts.

The column encountered an enemy minefield covered by fire . . . [about 1,000 yards east of Kumgong-ni] and artillery was placed on it to attempt to neutralize it. This was not successful, and the column bypassed the minefield and proceeded toward Hill 129. The column paused short of Hill 129 to enable the artillery to adjust fire with VT Fuse, which was to burst over the column as it proceeded through the deep defile in the road at Hill 129. The artillery fire was adjusted, and the lead platoon proceeded toward the defile. The lead tank encountered a tank barrier and a bangalore torpedo in the defile, and HE tank fire was placed on them. At this time the lead platoon was under severe small arms and mortar fire, and at approximately 1330 hours the platoon was attacked by approximately 300 enemy armed with satchel charges, hand grenades tied in clusters and various explosive charges. The platoon had to fire on one another's tanks while they were turning around in the defile to protect themselves. There were three tanks damaged in this action before the platoon could extricate itself from the trap. One of these tanks was disabled but managed to limp back out of danger. The platoon withdrew after inflicting severe casualties on the enemy, and another air strike was called on Hill 129 and the surrounding area.[50]

Lt. Col. Byorum describes the situation and the fight at Hill 129.

Eleven hundred meters east of the road junction in Kumgong-ni, Byorum divided Team A into two forces. Seven tanks and the engineer bulldozer advanced eastward toward Hill 129, while the balance of Team A deployed [about 500 yards west of Hill 129] in support. Byorum did not want to lead his entire team to Hill 129 because the terrain made tank maneuver impossible. It was difficult to move to the left of the road, but impossible to move to the right. The narrow corridor leading through the pass in the vicinity of Hill 129 made it extremely easy for the enemy to drop satchel charges on the tanks from the high ground on the right of the road.

As the tank column advanced to Hill 129, it received a large volume of enemy small arms fire. Friendly artillery covered the tanks with VT fuse 100 yards on both sides of the column with great accuracy and excellent results. Artillery support was so close that shell fragments struck the buttoned-up tanks. The lead tanks blew several enemy bangalore torpedoes by cutting wires with machine gun fire or by exploding the torpedoes with 90mm gun fire.

The lead tank reached the eastern point of the pass at Hill 129 and was able to overlook the valley to the northeast, when it was halted by a tank block consisting of eight-inch logs driven into the ground. The tank block was not effective, but the lead tank commander reported to Byorum that the road beyond appeared heavily mined.

The tanks at this point were spread over a distance of 200 yards. The cut on the right side of the road was 200 yards in height; the cut on the left was 75 yards. Ahead, the road dropped abruptly to the valley floor. Although Byorum could have had artillery placed on the tank barrier and on the minefield, he felt that the terrain itself constituted a perfect tank trap. He ordered the tanks to turn around and return.

As the tanks were turning, the enemy attacked with charges, throwing explosives on the decks of the tanks. The enemy used charges that resembled a woman's stocking, with an explosive charge about the size of a 2½ inch tin, impregnated with grease or oil. Byorum saw one enemy soldier holding a charge against a tank in a suicide attempt to knock it out. A charge thrown on the deck of Byorum's tank fell off when the driver jerked the tank forward. The tank ahead of Byorum carried the artillery forward observer. This tank was partially disabled. A group of about twenty enemy troops descended on this tank with charges and strings of hand grenades. Byorum's gunner fired one round of 90mm high explosive at a distance of about fifty yards and knocked out this group.

Byorum called for two tanks to come forward from Kumgong-ni to cover the withdrawal, as the tanks in the defile returned to Kumgong-ni. Team A then returned to the vicinity of the mobile reserve force and reorganized. From there, Byorum sent the partially disabled tank back to the rear. . . . Enemy troops in the defile (Hill 129) were fanatic in their resistance.[51]

Tank crew members provide more details about the fight in the defile at Hill 129.

SFC CALLEN C. BURRIS, LT. COL. BYORUM'S GUNNER: Although the tank column received enemy fire all along its route, the enemy fire increased in intensity when the tanks reached the defile. There were six tanks and the dozer in the defile, with Colonel Byorum's (Burris's) tank last in the column. Artillery support was perfect. Shells struck both sides of the road. At the beginning of the defile, the lead tank observed a bangalore torpedo. After firing at the torpedo ignition wires, the lead tank turned around and backed over the torpedo.

When the tanks halted, the enemy threw satchel charges and pole charges and bunches of hand grenades on the tank decks. The

2d Platoon was in the rear in support, firing direct fire on the hill slopes.

When Byorum ordered the column to turn back, Burris traversed his turret quickly as the tank turned around. Burris was reloading his .30 caliber machine gun when one Chinese soldier came toward the tank. Burris was unable to get his gun low enough to fire on the Chinese, who threw a charge on the back deck of the tank. The tank jerked, and the charge rolled off the deck. Burris then took the enemy under machine gun fire.

As about 20 Chinese threw grenades and satchel charges on the forward observer's tank, Burris asked for 90mm HE because he knew he couldn't get the group quickly enough with machine gun fire. He was 25 feet from the forward observer's tank when he fired. When the dust and smoke cleared, the loader saw one man get away.[52]

CPL. ALBERT VERGARA, BOW GUNNER IN THE FORWARD OBSERVER'S TANK: He fired on the right side of the road as the tank entered the defile. Although he couldn't actually see enemy troops, he fired into the brush along the side of the road. He ran out of ammunition just as the tank started to turn around. As he was reloading his gun, a big explosion went off just outside the gasoline tanks. The concussion flared inside and shook up everything. The tank lost most of its power, and it took a long time for it to get out. Vergara heard four explosions in the defile. When the tank reached the assembly area, he saw that the side fender was blown off, the gas tank had a hole in it, and the cargo bags were shot up.[53]

Capt. LaMontia describes the air and artillery support for the task force as it attempted to advance beyond Hill 129.

When Capt. LaMontia was asked to check Hill 129, he was unable to do so because of the weather. Since the "Mosquito" plane could fly lower and closer than LaMontia's L19A plane, he requested the "Mosquito" plane to check Hill 129. The "Mosquito" reported enemy troops in bunkers and fortifications. Although the "Mosquito" stated that an air strike would be placed on Hill 129, the strike did not materialize. LaMontia then directed artillery on Hill 129.

A plan had been arranged for artillery to drop VT over the tanks as they went through the defile. This fire was to cover the slopes on both sides, in front of, and to the rear of the tanks.

About 1200 hours LaMontia returned to the rear to refuel his plane. A 24th Division Artillery plane piloted by Capt. Brown remained aloft. Brown related the following to LaMontia. Six or eight tanks proceeded into the defile. After they were well into the defile, enemy infantry came out of the hills, swarmed over the tanks, dropping out of trees on the tanks. The field artillery observer on the ground issued a hurried request for VT fire to be placed over the tanks. Artillery VT plus tank fire drove off the enemy. Enemy troops did not follow the tanks out of the defile.

When LaMontia returned to the area, he had artillery saturate an area 300 yards square on Hill 129. Ten battalion volleys of VT, HE, and WP were placed on this area. LaMontia estimated that 200 enemy were killed by this fire.[54]

The After-Action Report resumes its description of Task Force Byorum's actions after it escaped the trap in the defile near Hill 129.

The task force reorganized and went into position to attack northwest from Hill 128. Team A went into blocking positions . . . , and Team B advanced along the road. After proceeding approximately 1,000 meters along the road under small arms and mortar fire, the column ran into a minefield, and two tanks each had a track broken and suspension system damaged. One tank crewman was injured as a result of this, and he was taken out of the escape hatch of his tank, drug along the ground, and pulled up through the escape hatch of another tank, which evacuated him. After considerable difficulty, due to the fact that adequate recovery equipment is not available for the M46 tank, the two tanks were towed out to the main road. The small arms and mortar fire increased, and in view of the fact that the enemy in large numbers were in the area, the task force was ordered to withdraw. One of the tanks being towed turned off the road and became mired in such a position that even when another tank and a retriever were hooked on it, they could not move it. Lt. Col. Byorum issued orders to strip the tank completely. It was then destroyed to prevent its falling into the hands of the enemy.

Task Force Byorum withdrew to . . . [a position about 500 yards west of Kumgong-ni] at 1905 hours, and at this point, the tank that was being towed became mired hopelessly in a tank bypass. Also at this point, a tank of Company C, 6th Medium Tank Battalion, became inoperative due to failure of the steering apparatus. A retriever was hooked to this tank, and when it started to move it, the last pintle in the task force was broken. These two tanks were stripped, and Lt. Col. Byorum contacted G-3, 24th Infantry Division, as to their disposition as they could not be evacuated. G-3, 24th Infantry Division, said not to destroy those two tanks as the division was attacking the following morning and expected that ground to be in friendly hands.

Task Force Byorum withdrew toward friendly lines, picking up a prisoner on the way. The task force passed through friendly lines and closed in an assembly area vicinity [of Toksim-ni, about half a mile east of Tokso-ri] at 192100 May 1951. The task force was then dissolved by order of the 24th Infantry Division, and the attachments were released to their parent units.[55]

Capt. James F. McIntosh, S-4, 6th Medium Tank Battalion, explains the problems with recovering disabled tanks.

The worst problem of the battalion is that of tank recovery. The M32s [standard U.S. armored tank-recovery vehicles, based on the modified chassis of an M4 Sherman tank] on hand have been deadlined for a long period of time. The battalion has broken all of its tow pintles, and has been forced to use 2½-ton truck pintles. These break very quickly. At the same time, using truck pintles means that trailers cannot be towed [behind trucks]. Informed that sixty-five pintles of all kinds would be airlifted from 8th Army stocks to the 6th Medium Tank Battalion, McIntosh received five on 20 May.

Towing a disabled tank with another tank tears the transmission of the tow tank. Tanks used by the 6th Tank Battalion are M46 (Patton) tanks; they weigh 48 tons combat loaded, with a 90mm gun, two .30 caliber machine guns, and one .50 caliber machine gun. On 18–19 May, Task Force Byorum expended 243 rounds of

90mm ammunition, approximately 36,000 rounds of .30 caliber and 10,000 rounds of .50 caliber ammunition.[56]

Capt. LaMontia recalls the air and artillery support provided to the task force as it attempted to move northwest and then finally withdrew.

The tanks returned to an assembly area [northwest of Ilbi-ri] and regrouped. Then the tanks moved back to Kumgong-ni to take the road north from town. Some tanks remained at the road junction as a blocking force. LaMontia saw one tank strike a mine. Byorum then asked the plane to cover as the tankers attempted to repair the tank or tow it out of the area. As the plane flew over the high ground . . . north of the [railroad] underpass [500 yards north of Kumgong-ni], 20mm fire was received from the ground. LaMontia neutralized this gun with artillery. This was the first time LaMontia saw a 20mm gun since the Pusan Perimeter or received fire from one. When Byorum informed LaMontia that the tanks would withdraw, LaMontia directed fire on the wooded area south of the road. He remained with the tank column until it reached the high ground southwest of Kumgong-ni. Then the weather closed in from the northeast, and LaMontia returned to the rear area.[57]

Lt. Col. Byorum describes the final actions and the withdrawal of the task force.

In the early afternoon, the task force moved out to explore the valley north of Hill 128. Teams A and B advanced to Kumgong-ni while Team C remained in mobile reserve. Team A took positions in support, covering north and south of Kumgong-ni. Team B, instructed to go no farther than the stream [about half a mile northwest of Kumgong-ni], advanced north from Kumgong-ni toward the railroad underpass [about 500 yards north of town].

At the time the lead tank reached the railroad underpass, the third tank in the column struck a mine, which destroyed its track, suspension, and escape hatch on the right side. One man was injured. The following tank, attempting to tow the disabled tank off the road, struck a mine. Enemy small arms fire was being received. As these tanks were towed to the vicinity of the high ground southwest of Kumgong-ni, Byorum ordered Team B to withdraw, covered by Team A. The injured man was evacuated to medical personnel in the rear.

As Team B withdrew, Byorum ordered Team C to move northeast on the Ilbi-ri–Mudae–Kumgong-ni road. Team C was to meet enemy troops moving south from Hill 98 with satchel charges. Team A followed Team B out. Team C was instructed to move back. Byorum and Capt. O'Brien placed thermite grenades on one disabled tank after it had been stripped and set it afire. The other disabled tank was towed toward the rear.

About 600 yards from the front lines, at a difficult bypass, the tank that was towing the inoperative tank became disabled. Byorum received permission from the division G-3, 24th Infantry Division, to leave the tanks and recover them in the morning. The tanks were stripped and abandoned. Byorum took one prisoner shortly before reaching the front lines. The task force returned between 2030 and 2100 hours.

Byorum stated that the tankers performed superbly. There was never any excitement or panic. . . . Byorum stated that the battalion was handicapped by its lack of recovery vehicles. The M32s did not have sufficient power to tow M46 tanks.[58]

Despite the enemy attacks on the general defense line, such as that against Company A, 19th Infantry Regiment, and the strong opposition encountered by Task Force Byorum, by 19 May it was apparent that the main Chinese Communist blow was not aimed at IX Corps and the Pukhan and Han River valleys as expected. Instead, the Chinese directed most of their forces against X Corps and the ROK forces to the east, with the objective of destroying them in the rugged mountainous terrain where UN mobility and firepower would not be dominant.

Chapter 9

ANYTHING BUT PEACEFUL VALLEY

15th Field Artillery Battalion, 16–18 May 1951

Rain and fog limited UN aerial reconnaissance and hid the extent of the Chinese concentration east of Ch'unch'on aimed at U.S. X Corps. The main enemy blow, consisting of two Chinese armies, was to fall on the U.S. 2d Infantry Division manning Van Fleet's designated No Name Line. The 9th Infantry Regiment held the left flank of the 2d Division's line; its 2d and 3d Battalions were dug in on an Outpost Line of Resistance forward of the Main Line of Resistance. The 15th Field Artillery Battalion, organic to the 2d Infantry Division, provided the artillery support for the two battalions on the outpost line. Second Lt. Bevin R. Alexander, a combat historian, studied the 15th Artillery's actions during the Chinese attack and describes the situation.

During a two-day period from 16 May 1951 to 18 May 1951, the 15th FA [Field Artillery] Battalion, the 105mm howitzer outfit that provided direct support for the 9th Infantry Regiment of the 2d Division, participated in a retrograde action down a small valley in the vicinity of Hongch'on before advancing elements of the enemy. During this retreat, the battalion provided defensive covering fire for the 9th Infantry as two battalions of this regiment extricated themselves from a position on the division OPLR that became untenable and retreated to safety behind the MLR, known as the No Name Line.

Here is the physical setting for the action: "Peaceful Valley" is a typical small-stream valley in east central Korea. It is approximately ten miles long and runs southeasterly from where the small stream

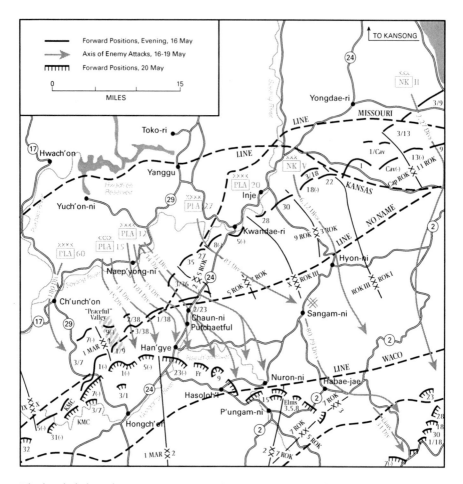

The battle below the Soyang River, 16–20 May 1951. (Based on U.S. Center of Military History map.)

which flows through it rises above Sarangch'on until it turns abruptly southwest a little below Tolmoru, then continues in this direction for approximately three miles before the valley joins the larger Hongch'on River valley [near Sodun-ni]. Peaceful Valley is a narrow, constricted stretch, mountains closely pressing it on both sides and open land at a premium throughout. With the exception of the mouth of the valley, where it widens out into a small plain upon joining the Hongch'on River valley, the hollow proper is never wider than 1,000 yards (at Musumak), and is usually 200 to 500 yards

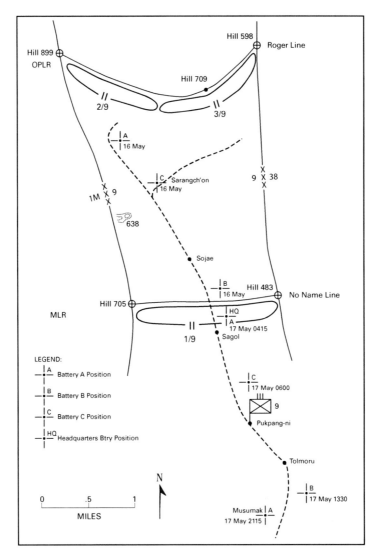

Peaceful Valley, 16–18 May 1951. (Based on map in CMH manuscript, U.S. Army.)

wide. For transportation, Peaceful Valley at the time of the action boasted of only a narrow trail-like road, which pushed determinedly up the valley from the MSR at [Hwadong-ni] until it petered out entirely a short distance above Sarangch'on.

The weather in the vicinity of Peaceful Valley had been bad for air observation for several days prior to 16 May. For three days before that date, it had rained constantly. This had enabled enemy troops and equipment to be moved up without being fully observed by air. On 16 May rain came down in Peaceful Valley intermittently, but by the morning of 17 May skies had cleared, and fair weather prevailed for the remainder of the retrograde.

In this valley on 16 May 1951 the 15th FA Battalion was echeloned in depth in support of the 2d and 3d Battalions of the 9th Infantry, which were holding the left flank of the 2d Division OPLR (the Roger Line) to the north of the valley. The 9th Infantry's portion of the Roger Line was as follows: from Hill 899 through Hill 709 to Hill 598. The 2d [Battalion] held the left side of this line adjoining positions of the 1st Marine Division, while the 3d Battalion held the right side adjacent to the 38th Infantry Regiment, 2d Division.

The 9th Infantry's MLR was held by the remaining battalion of the regiment, the 1st Battalion. The 9th Infantry's portion of this MLR (No Name Line) was some 5,000 to 6,000 yards behind the OPLR and extended from the 1st Marine boundary on the west at Hill 705 east to Hill 483, where the line joined to elements of the 38th Infantry Regiment. This MLR crossed Peaceful Valley at a right angle just over 500 yards north of Sagol.

The battalion's batteries were in the following locations: Battery A was the lead element about 2,500 yards northwest of Sarangch'on. . . . Battery C was next down the valley at Sarangch'on, the battalion command post and Headquarters Battery were established at Sagol, Battery B was about 1,200 yards north of Sagol, and Service Battery was at the mouth of the valley near the Main Supply Route.

The valley concerned in this action came to be named "Peaceful Valley" under unique circumstances. Prior to the commencement of the retrograde down the valley, Battery B, under the command of extroverted and Brooklyn-born Capt. Lawrence R. Daly, had been emplaced at Sagol for several days with little firing to do. So placid had become the battery's existence during this pre-attack period that members of the battery commenced calling the little hollow "Peaceful Valley," a name that ceased to have authenticity shortly thereafter, but which stuck to it.[1]

*Capt. Henry M. M. Starkey, artillery liaison officer with the
9th Infantry, contributes additional information.*

The Roger Line had been established prior to the expected enemy attack as a delaying line for the 2d Division. The line was
strongly held, however, and though called an Outpost Line of Resistance (OPLR) was actually sufficiently prepared with artillery concentration areas, wire and lines, and minefields to be a Main Line of
Resistance (MLR). The designated MLR was the No Name Line,
which was approximately 5,000 to 6,000 yards behind the OPLR in
the sector manned by the 9th Infantry. The regimental plan . . .
called for the two lead battalions on the OPLR (the 2d and 3d) to
withdraw in a delaying action down Peaceful Valley if the OPLR
became untenable and thence take up positions in the No Name
Line.[2]

*Other members of the battalion describe the situation before
the enemy attack.*

1ST LT. DONALD L. KELLEY, COMMANDER, BATTERY A: The
battery had been previously instructed by the battalion commander
. . . to be prepared to move on very short notice—a movement which
subsequently took place—because a retrograde movement was anticipated from the Roger Line to the MLR (No Name Line) by the
infantry following an expected enemy attack. Battery A was a considerable distance north of the MLR on 16 May.

In preparation for the rearward displacement down the valley
where the artillery battalion was emplaced (Peaceful Valley), Battery A's commander had selected alternate battery positions [north-
west of Sagol], which were later occupied. Wire had been laid to this
alternate position, which had formerly been occupied by a battery
of 155mm howitzers, but further preparation had not been made
prior to the enemy attack. . . .

For perimeter defense of the battery . . . Lt. Kelley set up six
outposts: three six-man caliber .30 LMG [light machine gun] teams
placed on the left flank on an adjacent hill (two teams) and one team
on the right flank; one outpost was placed on the stream that passed
near the battery position. The other two outposts were composed of
an M16[3] mount AAA piece which was placed in front of the howit-

zer positions, and an M19[4] AAA piece which was placed along the stream to the rear of the battery position. The AAA pieces were attached to the battery for perimeter and air defense and remained with the battery throughout the entire retrograde movement down the valley.[5]

CAPT. LAWRENCE R. DALY, COMMANDER, BATTERY B: Battery B, like the other elements of the artillery battalion, had expected an enemy attack for several days, and displacement positions had been selected farther down the valley where possible retreat for the battalion had been planned. This valley . . . had been occupied by the battalion for several days prior to the enemy attack, which initially struck the 9th Infantry on the night of 16 May. Before the attack, Battery B had remained at its location near Sojae with very little firing to do, and . . . the battery had found conditions so halcyon that it had dubbed the long, narrow hollow "Peaceful Valley," a name which stuck to it but shortly thereafter became a misnomer, for Peaceful Valley turned into anything but the placid, quiet area its designation implied. . . .

During the day of 16 May, prior to the enemy attack, the Battery B commander, upon directions from the battalion commander, had made a reconnaissance to the rear down Peaceful Valley to pick out alternate positions in the event rearward displacement would prove necessary. This was the first time any plans were made for a retrograde movement. . . . At 1700 16 May the battery CO picked a position southeast of Tolmoru, which was later occupied in the subsequent displacement. The battery did not lay wire to this alternate position, but the battery commander measured azimuths, sites, and minimum elevations from this position and laid stakes out for the "line of metal," the line in which the battery howitzers were to be emplaced. The battery commander also located outpost positions for perimeter defense and selected fields of fire for AAA defense units, which never actually were attached to the battery. The battery CO also picked another alternate position southwest of Tok-kogae [a pass on the MSR to the east of Hwadong-ni at the mouth of Peaceful Valley], which was never occupied.[6]

SFC ALLEN D. KNAPP JR., OPERATIONS SERGEANT, 15TH FA BATTALION: Since the division plan called for a preliminary defense of the OPLR and a withdrawal to the MLR if necessary, and since the 9th Infantry battalions manning the OPLR were to retreat down Peaceful Valley, it was necessary for the 15th FA Battalion to also make plans for a retrograde movement. Prior to the enemy attack the artillery battalion had selected positions farther down the valley for planned leap-frogging of the battalion's batteries when the retreat of the infantry occurred. These positions, which were actually occupied, were selected as follows: Battery A was to move to a position at Sagol for its first displacement rearward; Battery C was to move to a small valley in the vicinity of Pukpang-ni below Sagol; Battery B was to move to a position about 1,000 yards northeast of Musumak, while Headquarters Battery and the battalion FDC [fire direction center] were to occupy a battalion position at Musumak. Also, further positions for all three gun batteries had been planned at Musumak, which was behind the MLR a considerable distance.

This displacement to the rear by the artillery battalion was planned. Batteries were to be pulled out to rear locations one at a time in order that two batteries of the battalion would be firing at any given time. The retrograde positions had been selected by about 10 May, and some preparations had begun thereafter. Battery FDC and battalion FDC positions were dug, wire was laid to all planned positions, and all wires from all positions in the valley were tied into one network. . . . Some of the selected positions had been formerly occupied by other artillery units, while some had not. Positions not previously occupied had not been fully prepared.[7]

1st Lt. Paul G. Gonzales, forward observer, Battery A: 1st Lt. Paul G. Gonzales on 16 May was in a forward observation post with Company G, 2d Battalion, of the 9th Infantry Regiment, at a position approximately 6,000 yards forward of Battery A, 15th FA Battalion, which was then emplaced 2,500 yards northwest of Sarangch'on. . . . Company G was in a defensive position on Hill 899 on the Roger Line in anticipation of an enemy attack. The company was in the center position on the regimental front.

The enemy attack was anticipated for the following reasons: Company G was meeting each day strong enemy probing patrol actions, with new enemy positions observed daily nearer to the company's (and battalion's) lines. Further, reports of enemy buildups in front of the 2d Division had been forthcoming for several days from air observers. In preparation for this expected attack, FO Gonzales had, prior to 16 May, laid in concentrations for artillery fire from the 15th FA Battalion on all possible lines of approach in front of Company G.[8]

Capt. Starkey, liaison officer to the 9th Infantry Regiment, describes the beginning of the enemy attack.

Capt. Starkey was at the 9th Infantry command post at Pukpang-ni on 16 May. That night of 16 May at 2200 the 3d Battalion of the regiment received what he "considered a light attack of company size." The 3d Battalion held the right flank of the OPLR adjacent to the 38th Infantry. Capt. Starkey also that night received reports that the 38th was receiving heavy attacks on its left flank. The light attack on the 9th Infantry sector was accompanied by sporadic artillery and mortar fire, but the attack was repulsed. The next day the enemy attack shifted east and the main impact of the assault hit other elements of the UN line, notably the 5th ROK Division.[9]

Lt. Gonzales, forward observer with Company G, describes the attack on the front line positions and the beginning of the withdrawal.

The enemy attack upon his front commenced at about 0600 on 17 May. "The attack was first reported by air observers . . . and I heard the report over my radio that Chinese forces were coming up the ridgelines. I looked out from my position on Hill 899 and saw a considerable number coming up the valley ahead of me." By the time the FO observed the area closely, the enemy was within about 100 yards of the company positions. "I saw a thousand of them," estimated Lt. Gonzales, but he qualified his statement with the observation that the count was made hurriedly.

"I immediately called for fire missions and began laying in heavy fire on observed targets with very good results." . . . Gonzales also laid in fire on concentration areas where he was certain (from the direction of the enemy attack, and suspected enemy positions) elements of the enemy were located. During this initial assault by the CCF (who were identified by the FO by their uniforms), Gonzales was constantly adjusting fire on two or more targets at once, and was directing fire missions not only for the 15th FA Battalion but also for the 503d FA and the 96th FA Battalions.

The lieutenant fired missions steadily during the morning of 17 May until 1400. He stated that he kept up a continuous volume of artillery fire because observed targets were "all over the place." At 1400 an enemy force of estimated company size reached within fifty yards of Gonzales's observation post. "I told the company to get down in their positions while I placed artillery about fifty yards in front of the lead positions of the company upon the advancing Chinese." . . . The enemy kept coming through the ensuing artillery barrage, which was placed by the 15th FA Battalion immediately . . . despite heavy casualties. At this time (vicinity of 1400) the Company G commander received orders from the 2d Battalion CO to withdraw from the hill. The reason for the withdrawal was given that the 9th Infantry would have to retreat to the MLR due to reverses suffered by the 38th Infantry on the 9th's right and the resulting softening of the flank. [Gonzales] was with the G Company commander and heard the order come over the telephone. "We took off down the rear side of the hill in hot retreat," he said. By the time the company reached the bottom of the hill (Hill 899), the CCF were already in the company's old positions on the crest and were firing down on the retreating infantry.

"Just as we reached the bottom of the hill, the company commander received orders from the battalion commander to emplace the unit as the buffer company to cover the retreat of the 2d and 3d Battalions, which were pulling off the Roger Line at the same time, and to stop the enemy from approaching the artillery positions down the valley (Peaceful Valley) 8,000 to 9,000 yards to the rear. . . . The entire regiment (the two battalions on the Roger Line) were pulling back to the previously determined defensive line to the rear called the No Name Line." . . .

The company pulled back approximately 2,000 yards down the road leading to Peaceful Valley and about 1530 were preparing to dig into Hill 638 for delaying action. But it "never had a chance to finish because the Chinese were coming up too close behind."

The lieutenant observed Chinese coming down the road and

across the ridgelines while the company was emplacing on Hill 638. "As soon as we saw them and I started fire missions on them, we got orders from the company commander to pull out. So I closed the back door on the company by calling two batteries of the 15th to fire on our positions fifteen minutes later." . . . The battalion was to fire three or four rounds every three minutes for fifteen minutes after the initial delay of fifteen minutes had elapsed. This he did several times during the retreat. This allowed the company to pull off the hill and retreat farther down the road, and brought fire down on the hill after the advancing Chinese had occupied it. According to Gonzales, this heavy use of artillery for covering fire kept the enemy from overrunning the buffer company and the other retreating elements of the 2d and 3d Battalions down the valley. The artillery fire placed by the entire battalion upon the seen enemy by FO Gonzales, who was the only forward observer of the 15th FA Battalion directing fire during this back-peddling movement, kept the pursuing CCF pinned down and exacted casualties upon the advancing enemy, thus slowing up his attack. After this action, the 9th Infantry credited the artillery battalion with 500 known enemy KIA and an additional estimated 300 KIA. . . . When the company pulled off Hill 638 and resumed its retreat, Lt. Gonzales actually observed CCF within 100 yards of the hill.

The FO's method of laying covering fire for the retreating company was as follows: He drove his jeep down the retreat road, stopping every few hundred yards and registering on a point ahead of his position. He used this registered fire for destruction of unseen enemy and for shifting to fire on CCF later observed. The lieutenant directed the battalion FDC to place fire on these registrations at specific intervals of a few minutes each. "I had run out of previous concentration areas because of the retreat and had to adjust fire by direct observation," stated the FO concerning his need for new registration fire.

This method of fire continued down the valley until the screening Company G pulled behind the No Name Line and the company reached Battery A of the 15th FA Battalion, which was emplaced just behind the No Name Line at Sagol. When the buffer company reached Battery A at about 2100, 17 May, the battery immediately march ordered and retreated down the valley to a previously selected battery position at Musumak. Company G of the 2d Battalion, along with other elements of the 2d Battalion and with the 3d Battalion, moved into reserve positions behind the No Name Line for the remainder of the night. Company G occupied Hill 483. . . .

It was learned by Gonzales after this action that what infantry observers estimated as an enemy regiment had pursued Company G down Peaceful Valley.[10]

Capt. Starkey, with the 9th Infantry Regiment, explains the overall situation and the beginning of the withdrawal.

During the night of 16–17 May the two battalions of the 9th Infantry on the Roger Line remained in their positions. On 17 May . . . the two battalions were ordered off the OPLR and told to retreat behind the MLR. The 3d Battalion cleared first, followed by the 2d Battalion, with enemy elements close behind. On 17 May the infantry moved down Peaceful Valley occupied by the 15th FA Battalion (Peaceful Valley). . . . All elements of the two battalions had cleared the OPLR by 1200 on 17 May.

Because the 9th Infantry pulled off the OPLR on 17 May and was filing down the valley, only one forward observer was functioning in this area. He was 1st Lt. Paul G. Gonzales, who was with Company G, 2d Battalion, which was the screening company for the regiment's retreat down Peaceful Valley. However, the 15th FA Battalion was far from idle, and fired not only for Gonzales in covering the 9th Infantry's retreat, but also for the 38th Infantry on the right flank. . . .

When the first enemy attack came upon the Roger Line on the night of 16–17 May, the planned retrograde movement of the 15th FA Battalion began. The most forward unit, Battery A, was the first to displace, and it was ordered to move early on 17 May by the 2d Division Artillery. Battery A moved from its position above Sarangch'on during the early hours of 17 May and arrived at its first rear position at Sagol at 0415 on 17 May. Battery C, the next battery in line down the valley, was second to move, leaving its position at

Sarangch'on shortly after Battery A displaced and arriving at its new position in the vicinity of Pukpang-ni at 0600 hours on 17 May. Battery B remained in its same position above Sagol through the night, as did the battalion FDC and Headquarters Battery, also at Sagol.

On 17 May when the 9th Infantry battalions pulled off the OPLR and began their retrograde down Peaceful Valley to reserve behind the No Name Line, the second series of the 15th FA Battalion leap-frog displacements took place. On the morning of 17 May, Battery B pulled up stakes from its position above Sagol and dropped back to its selected rear position just above Musumak . . . closing at that location at 1330, leaving Battery A at Sagol as the lead firing battery of the battalion. Also on the morning of 17 May, the battalion FDC and Headquarters Battery, then at Sagol, displaced to the prepared battalion positions at Musumak, but left a forward FDC under the command of Lt. [Horace D.] Nalle, with PFC Thomas D. Fagg and Cpl. Erman W. Martin, with Battery A. This position was about 1,000 yards behind the lead positions of the No Name Line.

Throughout this entire retrograde movement, the 15th FA Battalion kept up a tremendous volume of fire. On 16 May the battalion shot 2,612 rounds; on 17 May, 3,616 rounds; and on 18 May, 2,670 rounds, when the retrograde down the valley ended.[11]

1st Lt. Horace D. Nalle, assistant S-3, 15th FA Battalion, provides the perspective from his position.

During the night of 16–17 May, the 15th FA Battalion was called upon to fire in support of not only the 9th Infantry but also the 38th Infantry. The battalion fire direction center (FDC) diverted Battery B and Battery C to this mission [supporting the 38th Infantry], and approximately 2,000 rounds were fired. . . . Fire was called down in front of the 38th Infantry's positions, and at one time was called down upon company positions of the 2d Battalion of the 38th, so close were enemy elements. Fire was kept up on this front for the entire night, directed by forward observers attached to the 38th.

Fire by the 15th FA Battalion was in part placed on previously planned concentrations of fire in the 9th Infantry OPLR front in

conjunction with the 503d FA Battalion, a 155mm howitzer outfit
that was also emplaced in Peaceful Valley at this time. . . .

On 17 May Lt. Nalle was operating his forward FDC with Battery A at Sagol, but was getting fire missions in the 9th Infantry
sector only from Lt. Gonzales, then with the rearmost retreating elements (Company G) of the 9th Infantry as they came down the valley
from the OPLR. Nalle reported that Gonzales, who was firing missions via radio as he retreated with Company G, said the CCF troops,
whom he identified by their uniforms, were close on the heels of the
rear elements of the infantry regiment. Nalle said that Gonzales
would come on the air "for about a minute or two with a fire mission," then, after registering on target and calling for "battalion 10
rounds a minute for 10 minutes" or other fire for effect requests,
would report hurriedly, "I'm how-ableing [hauling ass]. I'll be back
on the air shortly." Nalle said, on several other occasions, Gonzales
would suddenly cease a radio communication with, "Closing stations." And Nalle said he could hear the forward observer breathing
quickly and making fast preparations for departure.

Nalle also said that Gonzales called artillery fire down to
within fifty yards of the infantry positions because the enemy was in
that close pursuit. The FO would also request a mission directly
upon his own position with instructions to the FDC to hold fire for
several minutes to enable the retreating 9th Infantry troops and
himself to vacate the premises and to allow the pursuing CCF to
occupy the location. "That's how the enemy was kept from using
the infantry's former positions to bring fire down on the retreating
infantry," observed Nalle concerning Gonzales's method of fire.
This close support of retreating infantry continued for over an hour,
when Gonzales reported all enemy contact had broken off.

Approximately an hour later (exact time was not known), after
all of the leading elements of the 2d and 3d Battalions of the 9th
Infantry had gone past Battery A and forward FDC position, Nalle
suddenly saw Company G coming down the road (with the CCF
presumably behind them), and with Gonzales amongst the infantrymen. "It scared the hell out of me. . . . The next thing we did was
promptly march order A Battery" and displace the unit and the
forward FDC to the planned battalion position near Musumak . . .

closing at the new location behind the No Name Line at 2115 on 17 May.

The other batteries of the battalion remained in their first displaced positions for the remainder of the day and night of 17 May and the morning of 18 May, and, with Battery A, fired for the 38th infantry and for the single battalion (1st Battalion) of the 9th Infantry, which was the only unit of the regiment on line (the 1st Battalion held the MLR, while the 2d and 3d Battalions had gone into reserve behind the MLR following their retreat from the OPLR). Enemy activity on the 1st Battalion front was nil. However, it was learned later that the main enemy assault had shifted east.

Nalle reported that the period of 16–17 May by the 15th FA Battalion was one of a frantic series of displacements by all elements of the battalion in the valley. He said, however, communications were excellent during the retrograde movement and "couldn't have been better."[12]

Men of Battery A describe their actions during the enemy attack and subsequent withdrawal.

LT. KELLEY, COMMANDER, BATTERY A: On the night of 16–17 May, the battery, as ordered by the battalion FDC at Sagol, fired harassing missions (H & Is) for the 2d Battalion of the 9th Infantry, which, with the 3d Battalion, was holding the Roger Line. On 16 May we fired a total of 909 rounds.[13]

1ST LT. ALBERT C. FISCHER, ASSISTANT EXECUTIVE OFFICER, BATTERY A: During the night of 16 May the battery began receiving enemy artillery fire in the vicinity of the battery emplacements. The rounds were identified as enemy because the sound of the shells in the air indicated they were incoming and because 1st Lt. Albert C. Fischer was sent the next day to reconnoiter the area and observed fragments of burst shells, reporting them as around 155mm in caliber (ascertained because of the size of the blast craters) and identifying them as enemy because some fragments had a triple groove band, which . . . is not characteristic of U.S. artillery.[14]

The cannonade on the battery area was erratic and was obviously unobserved area fire, although the enemy guns had the battery fairly well located and were placing bursts close in to the battery positions. According to Lt. Fischer it was evident the enemy was using area fire because the fire was "walking up and down the valley," the normal application of fire on an area. The reasons given for the enemy knowing artillery was emplaced in the vicinity of Battery A's position were these: The battery had been firing constantly for several hours and was close enough to the front that the enemy could ascertain by sound and flash methods that artillery was in that general location; also, CCF elements had recently pulled out of the area and doubtless knew the terrain features of the section well. Because of the smallness and narrowness of the valley and the height of surrounding hills, the enemy knew only a limited number of positions there were suitable for artillery. These possible positions had probably been plotted by the enemy, and when sound and flash devices reported fire coming from Battery A's vicinity, the enemy knew the general location of the firing battery.[15]

LT. KELLEY, COMMANDER, BATTERY A: Kelley observed, however, "I think we confused them a skoch bit because they underestimated our capabilities of getting up the valley road with vehicles, and we got the battery up closer than they expected," probably contributing to the inaccuracy of the enemy counterbattery fire. The road up Peaceful Valley was very poor and ran out entirely a short distance above the battery's position.

Nevertheless, enemy artillery fire was coming in very close to the battery, and one round landed fifteen to twenty-five yards from the battery's mess tent. The enemy fire began getting so close that parts of two gun crews and members of the battery FDC sought sanctuary in an old enemy bunker located in the battery area, which had good overhead cover and was relatively safe from shell bursts. About ten men were clustered in the bunker during the shelling.

When enemy artillery rounds began falling in the vicinity of the battery, Kelley called the 15th FA Battalion headquarters to report the fact to the battalion commander, Lt. Col. Carl Wohlfeil. When the battery commander reported enemy fire, his commander said, "What size is it?" Kelley replied, "Hell, I don't know, but it's coming in mighty close." He added that he "thought it was best to get out because seven or eight rounds had landed right over us, and it looked like they had us pretty well located."

One of the shells knocked out the telephone line from the battery command post to the battery FDC, but no other disruptions occurred. . . . At 0205 hours on 17 May, the battery received the order from the 2d Division Artillery to displace to the rear, which the battery, according to Kelley, "pretty hurriedly did." The battery passed Battery C farther down the valley and Battery B still farther down, and went into the previously selected position at Sagol near the battalion FDC and Headquarters Battery, closing station at 0415.[16]

Lt. Fischer: As Battery A passed by Battery C during this leapfrog maneuver, Fischer saw that Battery C was in march-order, that men and equipment from Battery C were loaded on trucks, and that only the six firing pieces themselves were still in position with their prime movers backed up to the piece trails, ready for instant displacement. Fischer stated that an officer of Battery C told him as he passed by that they were waiting for Battery A to get by before they also pulled up and headed toward the rear. Fischer said Battery C followed Battery A back very shortly.[17]

Lt. Kelley: When Battery A got into position at Sagol, it did not fire again until daylight. "But we started firing again at the crack of dawn," observed Kelley. "When it was light enough to see the Chinks, that's when we started shooting," elaborated Lt. Kenneth M. Head, then acting as a forward observer with Company E of the 9th Infantry. On 17 May, Battery A fired 3,158 rounds, which was . . . roughly five times the normal daily rate of fire for the battery. This fire was in direct support of the 9th Infantry, which during the day retreated down the valley from the OPLR (the Roger Line).

During the day Kelley called Colonel Wohlfeil, who told him to "fire as long as we have observers, and then to displace to the rear around dark." By the afternoon of 17 May, Battery A was again the lead element of the battalion in the valley because Battery C had already displaced behind Battery A to the vicinity of Pukpang-ni. . . . Early in the morning of 17 May, Battery B displaced to a position about 1,000 yards above Musumak . . . arriving at 1330 on 17 May, and Headquarters Battery pulled out of Sagol and moved to Musumak, leaving only a forward FDC with Battery A.

Battery A remained at Sagol, firing constantly, until the night of 17 May, when Company G of the 2d Battalion, 9th Infantry, which had acted as the rear guard force for the 9th Infantry's retreat from the Roger Line, filed through the battery position, accompanied by 1st Lt. Paul G. Gonzales, battalion FO with the infantry company. This ended the 9th Infantry's retreat from the OPLR, and as soon as the company passed the battery's positions, Battery A march ordered and pulled back to the position at Musumak . . . closing there at 2115. The battery was accompanied by the forward FDC that had been left at Sagol that day.[18]

M. Sgt. Glen G. Kimes, chief of firing battery, Battery A: Throughout the retrograde down the valley, the battery "shot from the trucks," according to M. Sgt. Glen G. Kimes, Chief of Firing Battery, during the action. Because it was known that the battery was going to be pulling out of position in a hurry, personnel's gear, unit equipment, and even ammunition were kept on the battery trucks. Only the actual firing howitzers and absolutely essential equipment were taken from the vehicles.

Cpl. Orn G. Brooks, the acting ammunition sergeant during the retrograde, received special praise for the expeditious manner in which his section kept the battery supplied with ammunition during the movement and while such inordinately large lots were fired.[19]

Lts. Kelley and Fischer: Kelley and Fischer stated, however, that all of the ammunition received consisted of mixed lots and mixed weights and all of it was old ammunition; the shell cases had been previously fired and reloaded. "This was a distinct contribution to inaccurate firing," said Fischer, "because we were firing so fast that it was impossible to sort the ammunition received, and we had to use what we had—and fast." He added that during this action "normally out of 25 shells received, there would be twenty-five different lot numbers." Kelley said because of this, "You can't bring in as close fire to friendly infantry positions as you could if you were positive the actual way the ammo would behave."[20]

Several members of Battery B provide their perspectives of the enemy attack and subsequent withdrawal.

Capt. Daly, commander, Battery B: An attack on elements of the 9th Infantry was reported at approximately 2100 hours on the night of 16 May, and for an hour the battery fired in direct support of the two battalions of the 9th Infantry manning the Roger Line. At 2200 hours a call came from the battalion FDC that an estimated two companies of CCF had hit and overrun elements of the 38th Infantry on Hill 775, which were holding the Roger Line to the right of the 9th Infantry, and that the battery was directed to re-lay its guns on Hill 775 to fire on these attacking enemy. Capt. Daly reported the battery fired concentrations on this hill for the remainder of the night, receiving fire directions "probably from one of the forward observers with the 38th Infantry, but corrections of course came through the 15th FA Battalion FDC."[21]

M. SGT. R. G. VIRGIL BAKER, FIRST SERGEANT, BATTERY B: During the night of 16–17 May, M. Sgt. R. G. Virgil Baker said he timed SFC Sam McGhee's gun section (Gun Section No. 1), and "it fired five rounds every twelve seconds" for a considerable period. This . . . was typical of all the gun sections of the battery.[22]

CPL. WILLIAM J. ELLIOTT, DRIVER, BATTERY B: "There was so much noise from the artillery firing in the valley during the early morning hours of 17 May that men not needed for servicing the pieces could not sleep." . . . During these early morning hours of 17 May movement of some sort was noted at the battery from down the Peaceful Valley road. Elliott was sent by Capt. Daly to the road to ascertain what unit was coming. He returned and stated that it was Battery A displacing to the rear.[23]

CAPT. DALY, COMMANDER, BATTERY B: "I waited to see if Charlie Battery was coming on their tails. . . . Nobody knew what the situation up the valley was. It was all confused. The first inkling we had of what was happening was when Elliott brought a man to the CP tent at 0430. He was soaking wet and asked if it was all right to stand by the stove and dry off. He said he was an infantry wireman who was checking some wires far up the valley, and some 120mm shells started coming in on him. He said his buddy went back to their jeep and was knocked off and the jeep destroyed. He said he walked back to our location. That was the first we actually knew of what was going on up front. . . ."

The next morning (17 May) Battery B continued to fire on targets of opportunity and known concentrations called in by forward observers or refired because it was known at battalion FDC (from forward observer's reports) that certain previously fired concentration areas were occupied by the enemy. At this time Battery B was the lead battery of the battalion in Peaceful Valley, as Battery A and Battery C, which had been ahead of Battery B the previous day, had displaced to the rear during the early hours of 17 May.

Early in the afternoon of 17 May, the battalion commander ordered Battery B to pull back to the battery's previously selected position near Tolmoru. The battery march ordered at 1320, 17 May, and arrived at the new position at 1410, a displacement of three miles. Daly said the battery fired until the moment it pulled out of its positions at Sojae. He asserted the howitzer prime movers were loaded and backed into position directly behind the howitzers, and everything else belonging to the battery had already been packed, and when the order came for the battery to displace, the pieces were fired the last time, the trails were hooked to the prime movers, and the battery pulled out.[24]

1ST LT. ALBERT B. GENTRY, ASSISTANT EXECUTIVE OFFICER, BATTERY B: 1st Lt. Albert B. Gentry, battery executive officer, was left to destroy all salvageable containers and wooden boxes that might have been of use to the enemy for constructing bunkers and defensive positions. Gentry destroyed this equipment by dousing it all with gasoline and then striking a match to it. He jumped on the last vehicle of the battery as it pulled out of position.[25]

CAPT. DALY, COMMANDER, BATTERY B: The battery remained in position at Tolmoru throughout the afternoon of 17 May and the night of 17–18 May, firing almost continuously. The battery was firing missions at such a rate, during the entire period from the night of 16 May through 18 May, that everybody, including officers, mess cooks, and anyone else who "wasn't doing something for the war effort," was put to work unloading, passing, and preparing ammunition for firing. . . . Daly, commenting on the use of all available personnel for passing ammunition, said he went by a line of men who were handing ammunition from a truck to the pieces and "somebody handed me a shell and I was there for five minutes passing ammo before I could get away."

On the afternoon of 17 May Daly stated the battery received a load of ammunition from the battalion ammunition train. The battery ammunition recorder, Pvt. Charles Haines, immediately went over to the ammunition truck to record the number of rounds received. But by the time the ammunition sergeant supervising the delivery told him he was leaving 600 rounds, 120 of those shells had already been fired. Daly asserted it all happened in a matter of four or five minutes that the 120 rounds had been "unloaded, unpacked, uncrated, put in the pieces, and fired" in that length of time. "We fired every damn thing but the tubes at them that night (17 May)." . . . During the 24-hour period during 16 and 17 May, the battery fired a total of 2,760 rounds of ammunition. . . .

Daly stated that the Service Battery of the 15th FA Battalion, throughout the action of the battalion in Peaceful Valley, remained at the mouth of the valley near the main supply route near Hongch'on . . . in a big open field. The service personnel of this battery kept ammunition and supplies with the batteries in sufficient amounts during the entire action, he added.[26]

The fighting to their right, where the main enemy blow was delivered, dictated the withdrawal of the 9th Infantry from the OPLR to the MLR. Capt. Starkey, the artillery liaison officer with the 9th Infantry, explains the situation and the plan to shift the 9th Infantry to the east to deal with the threat.

What actually happened was this: the 38th and 23d Infantry Regiments of the 2d Division, located east of the 9th Infantry, received strong enemy attacks on 16 and 17 May, which effected a gap of approximately 4,000 yards in the division front between the two regiments. The 9th Infantry was thereupon shifted laterally across the division front to plug this gap. The 9th Infantry's MLR positions were then occupied by elements of the 1st Marine Division, which itself made eastward shifts to contain the vacated positions of 2d Division elements. Therefore, the 9th Infantry's portion of the No Name Line was occupied in the attack only until 18 May, when the lateral shift began. The retrograde movement of the two lead battalions in the regiment, however, with the subsequent rearward leap-frogging of the 15th FA Battalion, took place according to plan on 16–18 May. . . .

Besides the 15th FA Battalion, the following other artillery units were in general support of the 9th Infantry (and other elements of the 2d Division) on 16–17 May: 503d FA Battalion, firing 155mm howitzers; 300th FA Battalion, less one battery, firing 105mm self-propelled howitzers; 96th FA Battalion, firing 155mm howitzers plus two attached 8-inch howitzers; and Battery A of the 937th FA Battalion, firing 155mm self-propelled guns. With the exception of the 15th FA Battalion and the 503d FA Battalion, moved laterally east on 18 May to plug the gap between the 38th Infantry and the 23d Infantry, only one battery of the 300th FA Battalion and one battery of the 503d FA Battalion also moved with them. The remainder stayed in position behind the No Name Line, although a shift did take place later.[27]

Capt. Daly, commander, Battery B, describes the move from Peaceful Valley.

After remaining in its retrograde position near Tolmoru throughout the afternoon and night of 17 May and the morning of 18 May, the battery at 1000, 18 May, was visited by a reconnaissance force from a 1st Marine Division artillery unit (outfit not known). The leader of this Marine party said that his unit was to emplace in the valley and wanted to occupy Battery B's position, and that the Marine battery would arrive shortly. At approximately this time, the commander of the 15th FA Battalion issued an order to Daly and other battery commanders to "displace all but the necessary sections of the battery to the location of Service Battery and rendezvous there" in preparation for the lateral shift of the entire battalion to the east in support of the 9th Infantry, which was moving eastward to plug the gap in the 2d Division line between the 38th and 23d Infantry Regiments. This ended the action of Battery B in Peaceful Valley.[28]

Chapter 10

THE BATTLE BELOW
THE SOYANG RIVER

Company C, 72d Tank Battalion,
16–18 May 1951

East of Peaceful Valley and the U.S. 9th Infantry Regiment, the Chinese planned to deliver their main attack. This blow was designed to smash the 2d Infantry Division's center and right and to separate the Americans from the ROK divisions to the east. The enemy would then drive down the Hongch'on corridor into the UN rear logistics areas while the South Korean forces on the east were destroyed by follow-up attacks. The key element in the Chinese plan was the rapid destruction of the 38th Infantry Regiment and Task Force Zebra, which held the center and right flank of the 2d Infantry Division, linking the Americans with the South Koreans and blocking the Hongch'on road.
(See the map on page 224.)

The commander of Task Force Zebra, Maj. George R. Von Halban, describes the situation before the Chinese attack.
At the time of the action, 16–18 May 1951, Major George R. Von Halban [executive officer, 72d Tank Battalion; retired as a colonel in April 1962] was in command of Task Force Zebra. Task Force Zebra, which was composed of the French Battalion; 2d Battalion, 23d Infantry Regiment; Ranger Company, 2d U.S. Infantry Division; and the 72d Tank Battalion (minus A Company), had the mission of guarding two approaches into the "No Name Line" . . . One approach was down the MSR (Ch'onggu-ri–Han'gye road) [Kwandae-ri–Ch'onggu-ri–Umyang-ni–Chaun-ni–Han'gye–

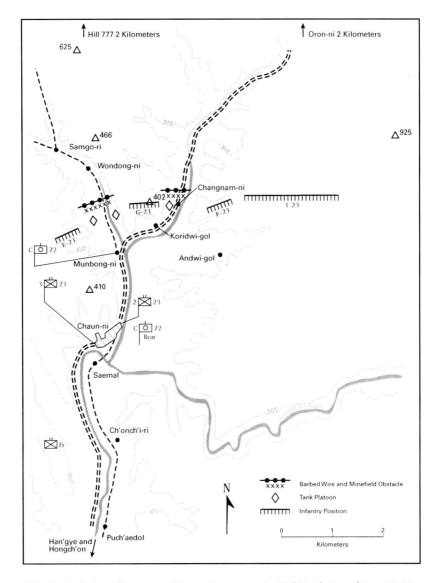

The battle below the Soyang River, Company C, 72d Tank Battalion, 16–18 May 1951. (Original map by author, based on maps in CMH manuscript, U.S. Army, and in Army Map Service series L751).

Hongch'on road, Route 24] from the northeast, and the other was a
natural valley approach from the northwest. . . . All the draws to the
Task Force's front led either into Hill 1051 or into the MSR. On
Task Force Zebra's left flank on Hill 1051 (five kilometers west of
Chaun-ni) was the 38th Infantry, and on the right on Hill 925 was
the 36th Regiment, 5th ROK Division.

Task Force Zebra was in position for three weeks prior to the
Chinese offensive in May, during which time it strengthened its
positions—set out minefields, laid barbed wire, and dug entrench-
ments. The approaches (valleys) into the No Name Line were extensively mined and each had two barbed wire aprons with minefields
in between. The roads were left opened for patrols that were sent as
far north as the Soyang-gang [Soyang River]. Several of the patrols
suffered casualties due to enemy mines in the roads adjacent to the
river. The terrain for infantry was excellent for defense—"cliffy"
and straight. It was never thought the enemy could successfully attack over the cliff.

For one week prior to the enemy offensive, the 5th ROK Division moved diagonally to the northwest across Task Force Zebra's
front, trying to force the enemy's hand. G-2 reports indicated a
heavy enemy buildup to the north. On 16 May, the ROKs were at
Oron-ni [five and a half miles north and east of Chaun-ni], and the
Ivanhoe Security Force [a U.S. 2d Division company-size unit of
ROK soldiers originally organized for rear-area security] was out as
a blocking force from [nearly two miles west-northwest of Chaun-
ni] to Hill 625 [a mile and a quarter north of Samgo-ri]. The Chinese
attacked down the valley from the northwest and down the MSR,
overrunning the Ivanhoe Security Force and the [3d Battalion, 36th
ROK Regiment, 5th ROK Division].[1]

*The 72d Tank Battalion's Company C held a key position on
the No Name Line astride the MSR (Route 24), where the valley
road from the northwest merged into Route 24 coming from
Kwandae-ri and Ch'onggu-ri on the Soyang River in the northeast
at the village of Munbong-ni, a little more than half a mile to the
north of Chaun-ni. Company C's commanding officer, Capt. Orlando Ruggerio, describes the situation facing his unit.*

Company C, 72d Tank Battalion, 2d U.S. Infantry Division [hereafter, 72d Tank Battalion], was an organic part of Task Force Zebra and had the mission of defending two approaches in the vicinity of [Munbong-ni] which led into the "No Name" Line above the village of Chaun-ni. One approach was down the MSR (Ch'onggu-ri—Han'gye road) [Route 24] from the northeast, and the other was a natural valley approach from the northwest. . . . The ground adjacent to the northwest valley was steep (42°–60°) with many draws, and the hills were covered with heavy foliage—pine trees near the top and small maples along the slopes. The lower slopes were under cultivation. The valley to the northwest was approximately 200–300 yards wide and was split by a small meandering stream, but the streambed had many huge boulders making it impassable for tanks. There were rice paddies on each side of the stream, and on the left, the paddies were terraced. Dry irrigation ditches led into the paddies. A secondary road went up the valley to the northwest about 4,000 yards where it joined with another small secondary road that branched to the northeast. The two roads continued approximately 2,000 yards farther until they dwindled down into small trails.

The adjacent ground to the valley to the northeast was comparable to the valley to the northwest, although the valley was wider (600–700 yards). The MSR, which was a dirt road approximately 15–20 feet wide with a good roadbed, extended up the valley to the northeast.

The 1st Platoon, Company C, 72d Tank Battalion, had the mission of defending the MSR from any threat of enemy troops and armor from the northeast. The platoon was in position . . . [on Route 24 about a mile and a quarter northeast of Munbong-ni and near the village of Changnam-ni] behind a double-apron barbed wire entanglement and minefields that stretched across the valley. The platoon had concealed positions during the daytime under trees and foliage, but took positions immediately behind the minefield at night. . . . Two infantry squads from Company F, 23d Infantry, which was on the high ground to the right, furnished protection for the tanks.

The 3d Platoon, Company C, had the mission of defending the valley to the northwest. Two double aprons of barbed wire (approximately 100 yards apart) stretched east and west across the valley to the high ground. Between the two aprons, antipersonnel mines and trip flares were buried. The platoon was camouflaged under trees during the daylight hours, but at night pulled to 50–100 yards behind the minefield. Two infantry squads from Company G, 23d Infantry, with two light machine guns guarded the 3d Platoon's tanks in the valley. Company G had defensive positions on Hill 402 [northeast of the road junction at Munbong-ni]. Company E, 23d Infantry, was on the high ground . . . [west of the road junction].

The 2d Platoon, Company C, 72d Tank Battalion, was in reserve in the vicinity of the Company C CP at the village of Munbong-ni, but had alternate positions selected behind the 3d or 1st Platoons in case of an enemy attack.

The 4th Platoon, Company C, 72d Tank Battalion, occupied prepared positions on the high ground [approximately 800 yards east of Munbong-ni and Route 24] overlooking the valleys to the northeast and northwest. The platoon was set up as an antitank defense and could fire 3,000 yards up the two valleys and on the adjacent high ground.

On 15 May the 3d Battalion, 23d Infantry, took defensive positions to the east of Company F, 23d Infantry; and on 16 May Task Force Zebra was attached to the operational control of the 23d Infantry. . . . Company C, 72d Tank Battalion, was placed in support of the 2d Battalion, 23d Infantry. The 3d Battalion, 36th ROK Regiment, 5th ROK Division, and the Ivanhoe Security Force were screening in front of the "No Name" Line.[2]

Soldiers of Company C provide additional information about their positions before the enemy attack.

For fifteen days prior to the enemy attack, Company C, 72d Tank Battalion, had been occupying and preparing defenses guarding two approaches (one from the northwest and one from the northeast) into the No Name Line. The 3d Platoon, Company C, occupied positions south of a minefield [1,100 yards south Won-dong-ni, across the road coming down the valley from Samgo-ri] with the crew-served weapons, 76mm cannon, co-axial .30 and .50 caliber machine guns, pointed in a northwest direction. The 2d

Platoon was in reserve in the vicinity of the company CP 400 yards to the rear; however, positions had been selected near the 3d Platoon and 1st Platoon in the event of an enemy attack. The 1st Platoon occupied blocking positions behind a minefield guarding the MSR that came down the valley from the northeast. The 4th Platoon was dug in on the high ground . . . [about 800 yards east of the company CP at Munbong-ni] where it could support the 1st or 3d Platoons if necessary and also act as an antitank defense. Revetments had been prepared by the 4th Platoon for its tanks. The 1st, 3d, and 4th Platoons had a full complement of five medium [M4A3E8 Sherman] tanks armed with 76mm cannon, co-axial .30 caliber machine guns, and a .50 caliber machine gun mounted on the turret. The 2d Platoon had only four tanks with the same armament because one had been evacuated to the company rear CP at Chaun-ni for maintenance repairs. Two squads of infantry with two light machine guns from the 2d Battalion, 23d Infantry, were attached to both the 1st and 3d Platoons for security.[3]

Capt. Ruggerio describes the beginning of the enemy attack.
During the afternoon, 16 May 1951, Capt. W. J. Richard, S-2, 72d Tank Battalion, called Ruggerio, commanding officer, Company C, and said the 3d Battalion, 36th ROK Regiment, had had several probing attacks on its right flank, and that a small group had succeeded in breaking through. During the later part of the afternoon, groups ranging from 25 to 75 of ROK soldiers and "Blue Boys" (Civilian Transportation Corps [South Koreans]) were coming down the valley four and five abreast from the northwest and passing through the opening in the minefield and barbed wire aprons and continuing on southward. The road had been left open to permit patrols to pass through to the north. Ruggerio estimated that a thousand came through in three or four hours. However, at 2130–2200, Richard again called and said a KMAG officer reported that the 3d ROK Battalion had regained its former positions.

About 45 minutes later, a large confused group of ROKs (approximately 300) with their wounded battalion commander came through the barbed wire and started intermingling with the tanks. Ruggerio called the 2d Battalion, 23d Infantry, CP for instructions.

Before this, he sent two men (Cpls. Carroll Warren and James W. Randolph) with a South Korean interpreter to the opening in the first barbed wire apron (northernmost) to check the column as they came through. "They were just a disorganized mob," Ruggerio said. As the captain was calling, a group of civilians (about fifteen men, women, and children) came down the road, and about fifty yards behind them was another column of troops. The night was very dark—"jet-black"—and when Randolph and Warren spotted the column, they challenged twice for them to halt. The column failed to do so, and the South Korean interpreter hollered out, "Chinese soldiers!" The enemy group immediately opened up on the three men with burp guns, and at least fifty rushed towards the entrance through the minefields. Warren and Randolph opened fire with their carbines, but three or four approached so close that the men were forced to use their carbine bayonets on them. It was later said that Warren had to shoot one enemy soldier off his bayonet. All during this time, Randolph and Warren were yelling to the tanks to go on the alert; they then ran to the left, jumped into the riverbed, and worked their way south to the tanks.

The tanks in the 3d Platoon opened fire on the enemy column with 76mm, co-axial .30 caliber machine guns, and .50 caliber machine guns mounted on the turrets. The 2d Platoon immediately reinforced the 3d Platoon. As the enemy tried to take cover within the minefield, they exploded several mines and sent up several trip flares. Several enemy soldiers worked to the riverbed and attempted to infiltrate southward to the tanks. However, one tank from the 2d Platoon, commanded by Sgt. William G. Gates, fired its 76mm rifle point-blank at a ten-yard range into the riverbed with its gun depressed as far down as possible. Another tank in the riverbed was hit three times with 2.36 bazooka fire and antitank grenades, which disabled it, causing two casualties.

During the fighting, Ruggerio called for two previously prepared artillery concentrations (the 37th Field Artillery Battalion was in support) at the trail junction [northwest of Samgo-ri] and the valley in front of the minefields. Arrangements had been made to "walk" the artillery fire slowly up the valley to the north (slowly advancing the volleys northward). The artillery gave excellent support, coming in on the target but with undetermined results. On the night of the 16th, one battery of the 96th Field Artillery Battalion was displaced 100 yards south of Company C's CP. After the attack began and the volume of fire was increasing, the battery commander asked if the tanks were going to remain in position, and Ruggerio told him his orders were to stay. About half an hour later, the battery moved out.

During the night, the tank platoons (2d and 3d) received thirty to thirty-five rounds of inaccurate enemy 105mm artillery or 120mm mortar fire and about twenty rounds of 60mm mortar fire. Ruggerio said that he saw flashes of the guns firing in the northwest and estimated that there were three guns firing at an azimuth of 55° (the other men in the company could not recall any artillery fire on their positions—interviewer). The tanks used mostly their .50 caliber and .30 caliber co-axial machine guns on the enemy, and resupplied the infantry machine gun squad with ammunition.

The enemy, which had deployed within the minefield, exploded eight to ten mines, and others deployed to the high ground to the northwest and on the flat ground to the northeast beyond the minefields. The enemy returned fire with small arms and automatic weapons until 0630 hours in the morning, 17 May, but they had no established base of fire. When the tanks eased up firing, the enemy would return fire, and then the tankers would fire at the flashes.

At daylight, 17 May, sixteen or seventeen enemy dead were counted within the 3d Platoon's perimeter, and bodies were seen lying in the minefield and on the road. Seventeen of the enemy caught in the minefield surrendered during the morning. Ruggerio estimated approximately 450 enemy dead were in front of Company C's positions. From the inside of the northernmost wire apron to the village of Wondong-ni [about 1,000 yards up the northwest valley], 125 enemy dead were counted on the road and in the riverbed. Dead bodies were seen on the high ground adjacent to the valley and in the rice paddies. Intelligence reports, based on documents found on the enemy dead, proved that the initial force of fifty or sixty that rushed through the opening to the minefield was an assault team. All the enemy soldiers carried grenades, mines, bangalore torpedoes, and either an automatic weapon, such as a burp gun, or a light machine gun of .31 caliber. Their uniforms were light brown and blended perfectly with the rocks and boulders in the area.

During the night, the 1st Platoon had no enemy contact; however, around 0415 hours, the 1st Platoon started pulling back to their daylight positions. . . . Approximately fifteen minutes later, twenty to thirty ROKs came running down the road from the northeast firing their small arms to the north. The five tanks in the platoon pulled out on the road and went forward approximately 200 yards, and deployed with three tanks going to the right and two to the left. A small enemy group of ten to fifteen soldiers was spotted 1,800 yards to the front on the ridgeline. The tanks fired on the enemy group with .30 caliber co-axial, .50 caliber machine guns, and 76mm guns for approximately 45 minutes, and during this time, the tanks received approximately ten to twelve rounds of inaccurate 60mm mortar fire and some scattered ineffective small arms fire. About 0515 the 1st Platoon withdrew to its daylight positions.[4]

Other members of Company C provide additional details about the fighting during the night of 16–17 May.

1st Lt. Fred W. Rodgers, executive officer, Company C: During most of the action of the period 16–18 May 1951, Lt. Fred W. Rodgers was at Company C's rear CP at Chaun-ni. The company trains were located across the road (right side looking north) from the 2d Battalion CP, 23d Infantry.

About 1800, 16 May, Rodgers received word from Task Force Zebra that the Ivanhoe Security Force, which was forward on Hill 1051, near the Choygang-gang [Choygang River], was under a heavy enemy attack. At 2200, Rodgers called Capt. Ruggerio, Company C commander, at the Company's forward CP and was told by the captain that the ROK soldiers were withdrawing through Company C's positions. This had already been reported to the 2d Battalion, 23d Infantry, by Ruggerio. Upon being told of the ROKs' withdrawal, Rodgers immediately went by jeep to Company C's forward CP, a distance of one and a half miles. On the road, the lieutenant passed several hundred ROK soldiers; some had equipment, but the majority appeared to have thrown their weapons away. At 2230, after going approximately one-quarter mile, Rodgers came to the French Battalion CP where he was informed that the French had the mission of reorganizing the ROK troops. Some of the ROK soldiers stated that the Chinese (CCF) were attacking from a northward direction.

The lieutenant proceeded on to the company CP and arrived there at 2300, where he found that Ruggerio had already deployed the company behind a double-apron barbed wire entanglement with the tank weapons (76mm and .50 caliber machine guns) pointed north. All the men were awake and at their assigned posts in the various tanks. ROK soldiers in large disorganized groups (200–300) were coming on the road through the barbed wire from the northwest. Ruggerio and Rodgers tried to reorganize the ROKs, but efforts to contact some ROK officers in the groups failed; the ROKs continued on southward.

Sometime after midnight, someone from the 3d Platoon, which was approximately 400 yards north of the command tank, came to the CP and stated that an extremely large group—"about 1,200 the man said"—had stopped at the 2d Platoon's tanks. (The 2d Platoon was slightly to the rear of the 3d Platoon on the left of the trail.) Ruggerio sent Rodgers to see exactly what the situation was. It was "pitch black" and impossible to determine exactly how many were in the area. After much questioning, Rodgers located an ROK battalion commander who had been wounded, and while assisting him to the command tank, sporadic burp gun fire began within the group; and the ROKs dispersed in all directions with some taking cover behind the tanks. At the same time, a machine gun opened fire in the general direction of the 3d Platoon. Upon reaching the command tank, Rodgers learned via radio that the Chinese were following the ROKs at a distance of approximately 200 yards. 1st Lt. George H. Ensley, 3d Platoon leader, said that a large enemy formation was on the road and that some had gotten through the first barbed wire apron. . . .

When the 3d Platoon opened fire, the enemy deployed to the right and left within the minefield, exploding many mines and sending up trip flares. The flares revealed several large platoon-sized groups within the minefield and to the north of the 2d double apron. The enemy north of the barbed wire scattered to the right and left and placed heavy automatic weapons and small arms fire on the tanks. Succeeding waves of the enemy tried to climb the barbed wire and were shot in the attempt; however, some did manage to reach the high ground to the east where automatic weapons fire was placed on the tanks. (The following day, Rodgers was informed by Ruggerio that 1,500 Chinese composed the initial assault on the 3d Platoon's positions.)

Some of the enemy worked their way to the company CP 400 yards to the south of the minefields, where they were killed by carbine fire at close range. Seven were taken prisoner. These were armed with burp guns and hand grenades. A steady volume of enemy small arms and automatic weapons fire lasted throughout the early morning hours. Some of the tanks in the 3d Platoon received "elephant gun" (57mm AT) fire from the high ground to the right.

About 0630 the enemy fire slackened, and at that time, Rodgers asked permission to move the company trains farther south of Chaun-ni, but Ruggerio refused. At 0700 Rodgers left for the rear CP and saw no enemy on the way. Upon arriving there, he found everyone alerted, but there was no indication of an early evacuation.[5]

OTHER SOLDIERS OF COMPANY C: During the late afternoon and early hours of darkness on 16 May, large groups of ROK soldiers (some as large as 100–200) were coming down the valley from the northwest following the trail through the two barbed wire apron and minefields. . . . Capt. Ruggerio, Company C commander, had sent two men, Cpl. Carroll Warren and Cpl. James W. Randolph, from the tanks together with a Korean interpreter to screen the ROK troops as they came through the northernmost barbed wire apron. A BAR man was set up by the attached infantry to the rear of the 2d barbed wire apron to guard the men. (Four days before, a Chinese doctor had been captured who stated that the Chinese would soon attack the 2d U.S. Division with the mission of annihilating it. Because of this, and the fact that the ROKs were withdrawing through the defensive line, the men were all alert and "on edge." The night was very dark with no moon.)

About 2200, a large group of ROKs had passed through the barbed wire on the road, and a few minutes later Cpl. Robert L. Krimminger saw sparks as bullets from Warren's and Randolph's carbines hit the road north of the southernmost barbed wire apron. Krimminger turned to the tank driver and said, "Well, this is it." When Warren and Randolph opened fire, a large undetermined number of enemy deployed to the right and left within the minefield, exploding many of the antitank mines and sending up trip flares. . . . The enemy could be seen in platoon-sized groups within the minefield and north of it. All the tanks opened up with all weapons to the front. Some of the enemy were observed trying to climb the barbed wire and were shot in the attempt. Krimminger said, "They were hanging all over it." (The interviewer went through the position a month later and saw parts of bodies still hanging on the strands.)

Immediately after the 3d Platoon opened fire, the 2d Platoon took up its previously selected positions and returned fire on the enemy. The enemy was firing small arms and automatic weapons from the direct front and from the high ground to the east and west. The men could not determine the number of enemy, but one man said the volume of fire was "heavy as hell." About 2230, Sgt. Mike Petro's tank was hit by a 2.36 bazooka round near the turret ring. The round broke Petro's wrist and jammed the traversing mechanism. The tank was immediately sent back to the 72d Tank Battalion near Puch'aedol. Sgt. Will G. Gates's tank immediately replaced Petro's tank. Two or three more bazooka rounds landed in the vicinity of Gates's tank, and Gates thought they were coming from the high ground to the right of the valley. Firing was heavy until about 0430 at which time it slackened down to sporadic long-range small arms fire from the high ground to the east and west. During the night, artillery was placed up the valley to the northwest and on the high ground to the northwest. The 4th Platoon fired approximately fifteen rounds of HE over the heads of the 2d and 3d Platoons in close support, but the 1st Platoon had no enemy contact. The two tank platoons under attack used up their basic load of ammunition during the attack; however, each tank carried extra ammunition on the rear deck.

At daybreak on 17 May, ten Chinese on the road between the two barbed wire aprons surrendered, but seven in the minefields resisted and were shot.[6]

By the early hours of 17 May, the Chinese offensive, which had begun the day before, was well under way. Holding attacks sought to pin the U.S. I and IX Corps and the 1st Marine Division and the left flank of the U.S. 2d Infantry Division of X Corps. The enemy main attack hammered the ROK 5th and 7th Divisions of X Corps and the ROK III Corps. By midnight of 16 May, Lt. General Edward M. ("Ned") Almond, X Corps's commander, gave the formal order for his two ROK divisions to withdraw to the No Name Line. The enemy followed rapidly on the heels of the South Koreans as they pulled back, seeking to break through the U.S. 2d Infantry Division units manning the No Name Line defenses. The U.S. 38th Infantry Regiment and Task Force Zebra came under heavy attack during the night. Company A, 38th Infantry, was pushed off one of its positions, which allowed the Chinese to drive into the 2d Division's rear in an attempt to cut their main supply route at Puch'aedol. Elsewhere the American line held. Daylight of 17 May brought a temporary halt to most enemy attacks, and the French and Dutch Battalions moved to close the gap in the 38th Infantry's line and eliminate the Chinese who had broken through. The 23d Infantry Regiment assumed control of Task Force Zebra, and Company C, 72d Tank Battalion, was ordered to use its firepower to break up any enemy forces forming for attack. Capt. Ruggerio describes the actions of his company on 17 May.

About 0900 Ruggerio ordered the 3d Platoon up the trail to the northwest about 300 yards in front of the minefield, and instructed the tanks to fire into the adjacent hills overlooking the trail. Prior to moving out, an approximated enemy regiment was spotted on Hill 777, approximately 3,800 yards north of the 2d and 3d Platoon's positions, and Ruggerio called for artillery. It was not registered on the hill, and no artillery fire was received. There was no artillery forward observer with the company. Ruggerio then called for air support and marked the target with fifteen to twenty rounds of WP. Four U.S. Navy Corsairs [F-4Us] came over but evidently did not see the WP, and no air strike was delivered on the enemy group. The company then fired forty rounds of HE on the hill with undetermined results. The enemy column was about one to one and a half miles long and was moving northward when the planes went over; the column then angled to the northwest over the ridgeline. The 3d Platoon moved out, and Lt. Richard P. Kenney [then platoon sergeant, 3d Platoon] spotted an estimated enemy battalion in a closed-up column of twos about 3,000 yards away on high ground . . . [northwest of Samgo-ri]. The 3d Platoon fired approximately forty rounds of HE into the enemy group, and the rounds could be observed falling among the enemy soldiers, causing them to run in all directions. Four planes later came over and bombed and napalmed the hill. The 3d Platoon returned in about half an hour.

About 1000, the 2d Platoon was ordered out and proceeded up the road about 400 yards firing on the high ground on both sides of the valley. The tanks received sporadic inaccurate sniper fire. The platoon fired on the hills for approximately 45 minutes and then returned. About 1130 the 3d Platoon went up the road again and observed a squad of enemy soldiers and ten or twelve enemy in a tree area . . . making out as if they were dead. Some had bundles of wheat and straw over them; others had mats and branches of trees around them. Carbine, .50 caliber, .30 caliber co-axial machine gun fire was placed on them at a range of about thirty yards. Ruggerio accompanied the 3d Platoon and saw one wounded enemy soldier near the trail. Ruggerio saw that Lieutenant Kenney was going to shoot the soldier and called over the radio, "Don't shoot the b——, I want a prisoner." Just then Kenney killed the enemy soldier with a .50 caliber machine gun. About 1215, the 3d Platoon returned after killing an estimated twenty-five enemy soldiers. When the tanks returned, all firing had ceased and hot chow was brought up to the company. When the mess sergeant was taking the chow from tank to tank, enemy sniper fire was received from the vicinity of Hill 466 [about half a mile east of Samgo-ri], causing the men to take shelter behind the tanks.

About 1400, Maj. Lloyd K. Jensen, 2d Battalion, 23d Infantry commander, ordered Company C to send one platoon of tanks up the trail to the northwest to fire into all the draws and valleys leading into the high ground occupied by the 2d Battalion, 23d Infantry. Ruggerio asked the major for infantry support to accompany the tanks because the tanks would be confined to an area 150–175 yards wide with only one way out. Jensen told the captain that none was available, and Ruggerio was reluctant to let the tanks go. "You've got to do it. We're under terrific pressure here," Jensen said. (Jensen later said that the tank patrol relieved considerable pressure on the 2d Battalion, 23d Infantry.)

The 2d Platoon, commanded by SFC Arthur Zayat, was ordered out, followed by the command tank with Ruggerio. Two U.S. Navy Corsairs covered the approach of the tanks up the valley to the northwest. The tanks had to stay on the road until it reached the trail junction . . . [near Samgo-ri] where the tanks could maneuver a little to the left side of the road. When Zayat's tank reached the trail junction, the sergeant radioed back and said he saw an estimated 250 enemy soldiers along the road in an irrigation ditch and on the high ground overlooking his position. . . . The tanks remained for approximately half an hour and placed .50 caliber and 76mm cannon fire in the draws to the west and southwest leading into the 2d Battalion, 23d Infantry's positions. During this time, the tanks were receiving inaccurate long-range small arms and automatic weapons fire from the high ground on the right side of the trail. The two Navy planes were strafing the high ground during this time.

About 1430 Zayat called back and said that the enemy was trying to mine the road between the 2d Platoon and the command tank. This made Zayat very excited, and he set up a tank perimeter and had the tanks firing in all directions. Ruggerio heard Sgt. Gates telling Zayat, "The old man said we had to stay here and fire in these damn hills, and there's nothing we can do about it." Ruggerio called the platoon and told them to come back only on orders and to use the radio net only when necessary. About 1530 Zayat called the captain and said that a small enemy group was attempting to mine the road behind them. Because of this and the lack of infantry support, Ruggerio ordered the platoon to withdraw at 1600. The platoon withdrew back behind the minefield amidst scattered small arms fire, firing their tank weapons on the high ground to the left and right on the way back.

When the platoon rejoined the company, it moved into its night positions behind the minefield in the open and fired 76mm cannons and .50 caliber machine guns at small enemy groups of ten or fifteen moving on the ridgeline to the right and left. Every time the tankers saw trees moving (the enemy used tops of pine trees on their backs as camouflage), they would fire the 76s using tree bursts.[7] The 2d and 3d Platoons remained in position until dark, receiving sporadic small arms fire. The tanks were resupplied by alternating back to the vicinity of the company CP for supplies. During the day, the 4th Platoon fired approximately 40–45 rounds of HE per gun at a range of 2,000 to 2,500 yards in support of the 2d and 3d Platoons.[8]

Other members of Company C describe the action.

About 0930 [17 May], three tanks from the 3d Platoon pulled about 1,000 yards north of the minefield (a secondary road extended up the valley to the northwest for about 6,000 yards where it dwindled down into a narrow trial) and shot up all likely enemy positions and enemy troops pretending to be dead. The tank commanders could see their heads turning to follow the movement of the tanks. About twenty to thirty were in a group of trees about 300 yards north of the minefield and were eliminated with three rounds of 76mm HE fire. . . . The enemy dead had antitank grenades hanging around [their] waists and shoulder straps. During the movement up the trail to the north and on returning, the tanks received ineffective long-range sniper fire from the high ground to the east and west. One tank had a satchel charge thrown at it but suffered no damage.

In the meantime, one tank in the 2d Platoon broke an oil line and was pulled to the rear CP by the maintenance tank retriever. The tanks in the company resupplied by going to the rear (vicinity of the Company CP) by sections. While some of the tanks were resupplying, a small group of 5 or 6 enemy soldiers was seen in the village of Wondong-ni, and another large group of 200–300 was spotted on Hill 466. Co-axial machine gun fire was placed on the group in the village, and 76mm HE fire was placed on the large group. About 1330, the 3d Platoon was instructed to mark the hill with WP rounds for an air attack, but the four Navy Corsairs that came over evidently didn't see the rounds and flew away.

About 1400–1430, four tanks from the 2d Platoon were ordered to counterattack up the valley to the northwest. The tanks moved out without infantry support and proceeded about 4,000 yards before receiving small arms fire from the hills bordering the road. The first three tanks passed one enemy soldier who was crouched in the ditch to the right of the road, waiting evidently for the last tank. SFC Charles R. Brown, the tank commander of the last tank, could not depress his turret .50 caliber machine gun low enough to place fire on the enemy, so he took a hand grenade, pulled the pin, and rolled it down on the enemy. "It landed in his lap and made a hellava mess," Brown said.

When the lead tank reached the trail junction . . . [near Samgori], Brown spotted a group of forty to fifty enemy soldiers lying on the ground behind a stonewall with straw over them. He fired six rounds of HE at them. The range was about ten yards, and Brown stated that if the rounds didn't kill them, the muzzle blast did. Brown also stated that outside of one hut near the trail junction, he saw an enemy soldier defecating. "That big ass was a perfect target, but my machine gun jammed. So, I fired a round of HE and made a bull's eye," Brown said. The other tanks were firing at small enemy groups in the draws leading to Hill 1051 and on the high ground to the northwest. About 1500 the platoon sergeant ordered the tanks to withdraw back to the positions behind the minefield. "It was about time, for there was no damn sense of being out there without infantry support," Brown said. The tanks returned by 1600, killing several scattered enemy soldiers on the way back. The tanks immediately went into position behind the barbed wire apron and resupplied ammunition.[9]

Lt. Rodgers, executive officer, Company C, describes his actions on 17 May to support the troops in the forward positions.

At 1000, Rodgers moved his command half-track adjacent to the 2d Battalion, 23d Infantry, CP in order to maintain closer communication between the battalion and Company C. Rodgers asked permission from Maj. Jensen, the 2d Battalion commander, to evacuate Company C's trains. He was told to contact the 2d Battalion's motor officer, and when the battalion's trains moved, to move Company C's with them. Jensen stated that he had orders from higher headquarters not to move the trains southward until notified to do so.

About 1400, 17 May, the lieutenant again went forward to Company C's positions and found out that Jensen had ordered a platoon-sized counterattack to relieve enemy pressure on the infantry companies on the high ground. Tanks from the 2d and 3d Platoons had moved up the valley to the northwest in the general direction from which the enemy first attacked the tanks. Ruggerio was with the attacking tanks. Rodgers had taken a truck of HE and small arms ammunition and a truck of gasoline, so he unloaded what he thought was necessary to resupply the tanks and departed for Chaun-ni. There was no firing at the forward CP at this time, and no enemy was observed en route to the rear CP. The weather was clear, and visibility was good. Upon arriving at Chaun-ni at 1500, Rodgers stated that small arms and automatic weapons firing could be heard to the west about 2,000 yards, and some firing could be heard to the north.

About 1800, Rodgers again went to the forward CP with hot rations. Upon arriving, he found that the two platoons had returned from the counterattack and were firing on the hills to the east and west. Small enemy groups of "a dozen or so" were firing small arms and automatic weapons on the tanks' platoons from the high ground on both sides of the valley. The men in the 2d and 3d Platoons left the tanks one crew at a time and returned to the company CP for chow.[10]

Company B, 72d Tank Battalion, was in reserve south of Chaun-ni. First Lt. Thomas W. Fife, leader, 1st Platoon, Company B, describes his platoon's actions on 17 May.

At 1000 hours, 17 May, the 2d Battalion, 23d Infantry, requested two platoon-sized tank patrols to run up the MSR to Oron-ni [a village up the northeast valley about three and a half miles north of Company C's position] to relieve a surrounded ROK company. This move was cancelled when elements of the 36th ROK Regiment started to withdraw through Chaun-ni. However, at 1300 the 1st Platoon, Company B, proceeded north along the MSR through Company C, 72d Tank Battalion, to a point south of the pass . . . [about a mile and a quarter south of Oron-ni] where it received eight to ten rounds of 82mm mortar fire and light small arms fire from the hills to the right and left front. Fife said it was impossible to determine the size of the enemy group. When fired upon, the platoon deployed off the road to the left and right with intervals of 50–100 yards between the tanks. "We shot the hell out of the hillside," Fife said. The platoon fired approximately 50 rounds of 76mm, 2,500 rounds of .50 caliber, and 2,000 rounds of .30 caliber in the space of an hour at the enemy group. The platoon withdrew about 1530, passing through Company C, which was not fighting at the time. About 1830, the 2d Platoon, Company B, was sent southward down the MSR to Task Force Zebra at Puch'aedol, but it had no enemy contact. The 2d Platoon remained that night at Task Force Zebra's headquarters.[11]

Meanwhile, during the daylight hours of 17 May, the Chinese expanded their penetration into the 2d Infantry Division lines. The enemy captured Hills 1051 (three miles west of Chaun-ni) and 914 (1,000 yards northeast of Hill 1051) and held them against the Dutch Battalion's counterattack. The French Battalion located 500 enemy troops northwest of Puch'aedol but were unable to make headway against them. The 2d Infantry Division rapidly shifted unengaged units of the 38th Infantry to plug holes in the line, but more help was needed. General Almond correctly assessed the strength of the Chinese attack and warned General Van Fleet that this was the main attack. Van Fleet reacted by shifting boundaries and units to allow the 9th and part of the 38th Infantry regiments to move east against the enemy penetration. The ROK 8th Division and the U.S. 3d Infantry Division also started moving toward the area as reinforcements. Increased artillery ammunition expenditures were authorized, and heavy B-29 bombing attacks against enemy columns began the night of 17 May. All of these measures would take time to produce an effect on the enemy and stop the attack. For the moment, Company C, 72d Tank Battalion, and the other units of the 2d Division had to hold the line against continued attacks. Capt. Ruggerio describes the fighting during the night of 17–18 May and the next morning.

About 2100–2130, the 2d and 3d Platoons received a small probing attack from the northwest by an estimated reinforced enemy platoon using 82mm mortars (25–30 rounds), small arms, and automatic weapons fire. The enemy came down the valley using the trees and terraced paddies as cover and hit the platoons frontally. The lead enemy soldier would dig a small mound of dirt in front of his position and then would crawl forward. The next man behind him would crawl to the mound of dirt while the lead man prepared another one. In this way, the enemy soldiers advanced. The enemy opened fire on the tanks with burp guns from a range of 75–100 yards. Ruggerio immediately called for artillery fire on the trail junction at Samgo-ri and at a point 100 yards north of the minefield; he had the fire shifted from the left to the right on call (the artillery had been zeroed in prior to the enemy attack). The fire was called in volleys of three to six rounds together with illumination flares. A searchlight was placed in the vicinity of the company CP and illuminated the valley to the northwest for approximately 100–150 yards in front of the tanks.

During the hours of darkness, the tanks would only fire when fired upon. The enemy never succeeded in reaching the southernmost double apron, and the probing attack lasted for approximately one hour. During the night scattered automatic weapons and small arms fire was received from the north and northeast. About 0100 the volume of fire increased considerably from the same area, and Ruggerio called nine or ten artillery concentrations on the enemy positions during the night. After the artillery fire, the enemy fire slackened considerably for the rest of the night.

Between 0700 and 1000, the tankers could see small enemy groups of four to six moving up the draws and on the high ground leading toward Company G, 23d Infantry, on Hill 402. Fifty-caliber machine gun fire was placed on the enemy causing him to withdraw to the opposite side of the ridgeline. About 1000, the 2d and 3d Platoons reported a large number of enemy troops moving in the draw . . . [between the minefield and Hill 402] and about the same time, a machine gun opened up but was destroyed by a 76mm tree burst at a range of 300 yards. The ridge down which the enemy was attacking Company G had heavy foliage near the top. Towards the bottom of the hill were wheat fields with wheat about three feet high. The tanks placed fire on any movement noticed to their front and right flanks. The company supply trains, which included four trucks of ammunition, were at Chaun-ni, and Company C had perfect ammunition supply.[12]

Other members of Company C provide additional details about the fighting.

About dusk an approximated enemy company hit the 2d and 3d Platoons frontally down the road and on the high ground to the left flank, placing small arms and automatic weapons fire on the tank positions. The enemy was taking advantage of all natural cover— rock walls, paddies, and ditches. About 2030, an enemy machine gun was firing from a ditch bordering the road to the northwest. Sgt. William Gates spotted the gun but waited for another burst to be sure of its position. Just then Lt. Richard Kenney (then Sgt.) silenced the gun with a 76mm HE round. Gates yelled over the radio, "You dirty son of a bitch, that was my gun." The enemy attack lasted until about 2230 at which time the volume of fire slackened. The rest of the night, the tanks received sporadic small arms fire and very effective sniper fire. Cpl. Krimminger stuck his helmet out of the turret on his carbine to see how effective it was, and the sniper put a hole through it.

In the meantime, about 2200, a company commander from the 3d Battalion, 23d Infantry (which had moved into a blocking position to the right of the 2d Battalion, 23d Infantry) wanted to move the 4th Platoon up the old gold mine road [to the east] . . . to support the 3d Battalion from a possible enemy attack from the east. Ruggerio protested it because of the risk involved (there was no space for the tanks to maneuver), but he was ordered to do it by Maj. Von Halban, 72d Tank Battalion executive officer. Von Halban stated that the ROKs had given away in the east. The tanks moved up the draw about two miles with no infantry protection, and went into positions about twenty-five feet apart. A mortar squad from the 3d

Battalion and several ROK outposts were to the front. The mortars fired continuously all night, and at about 0500, a machine gun on the high ground to the left fired continuously. After daylight, Chinese patrols were spotted to the east about 1,400 yards away. When asked how many, Sgt. Wilfred J. Jokerst said, "They were in a column from the low ground to the high ground." The tanks opened fire with the 76s and .50 caliber machine guns, and the enemy withdrew to the reverse slope. The tanks continued firing off and on for approximately one and one-half hours, and by 0930 all firing ceased in the 4th Platoon's sector.

In the meantime, the 2d and 3d Platoons saw continuous lines of enemy on the high ground approximately 1,400 yards to the northwest. Machine gun and 76mm fire was placed on the enemy, which seemed to be moving to the northeast. Four Navy Corsairs flew over and radioed that they wanted the target marked with smoke. Two tanks fired six rounds of smoke on the enemy's positions, but again the planes flew off. Company C had no aerial observer or artillery FOs with them. However, all artillery had been zeroed in before the enemy attack on 16 May and was firing on the high ground. The tanks were firing super quick for tree bursts and delayed fused for ricocheted fire. In spite of the fire, the enemy kept coming over the hill. "We never did see the end of them," Gates said.[13]

During the night of 17–18 May, the situation in the rear deteriorated. Lts. Rodgers and Fife of the 72d Tank Battalion describe the situation.

LT. FIFE, LEADER, 1ST PLATOON, COMPANY B: About 2400 the 1st Platoon, Company B, was sent southward to eliminate a reported enemy roadblock between Chaun-ni and Puch'aedol. However, we reached Task Force Zebra's headquarters with no enemy contact, but upon arriving at Puch'aedol, could hear firing up the draw to the east. . . . The 1st Platoon remained until 0300 with no enemy contact and returned to Chaun-ni without incident. When we arrived at Chaun-ni, the remainder of Company B had moved into the village across the road from the 2d and 3d Battalions' CPs, 23d Infantry.

About 0400, 18 May, an enemy burp gun opened up in the vicinity of the 3d Battalion CP, and an ammunition truck exploded in the schoolyard. . . . Several tanks in the company opened fire in the general direction from which the enemy fire came, but later held fire when word was received that friendly troops were in the area. Sporadic small arms fire lasted until daybreak. During the early morning hours, friendly mortars in a nearby draw . . . were firing on the hills to the west.

About 0800, the 4th Platoon was sent southward down the east side of the river [Hongch'on] to . . . [about 500 yards south of Saemal] where it was to fire on an unknown number of enemy reported to be trying to cut the road from the west. The 4th Platoon went approximately 1,000–1,200 yards south of the village and could be observed firing on the high ground to the west.

All during the morning the 1st Platoon received scattered (ten rounds) 82mm mortar fire and sniper and small arms fire from the high ground . . . [west of Chaun-ni]. . . . The platoon fired several hundred rounds of .50 caliber and a few rounds of 76mm at small enemy groups (5–10) as they appeared on the skyline. About 1100 Fife was ordered by Capt. William E. Ross, Company B commander, to send two tanks up the draw where the mortars were firing to evacuate some wounded and to give covering fire while the infantry personnel withdrew. The two tanks went up the draw about 1,000 yards and placed fire on the high ground to the west, knocking out a machine gun. The two tanks returned about 1145.

About 1230, Ross again instructed Fife to send two tanks up the same draw to evacuate more wounded. Two enemy machine guns were harassing the wounded soldiers and were destroyed by 76mm HE fire. The tanks then withdrew about 500 yards, and the enemy came over the hills from the west and northwest "in mass" (an estimated company). The tanks fired about ten rounds of 76mm and five to six boxes of .50 caliber at a range of 800 yards at the enemy troops. In spite of the tank fire, the enemy kept coming over the hills, and the tanks were ordered to withdraw.[14]

Lt. Rodgers, executive officer, Company C: At about 1930 [17 May], Rodgers returned to the rear CP, and the firing on the hills to the west seemed closer. Everyone was tense and wanted to move. The 2d Battalion S-3 informed Rodgers that the Chinese had broken through the 38th Infantry to the west of Chaun-ni. Before midnight, someone told Rodgers that the Chinese had reached the high ground to the southwest of the 2d Battalion, 23d Infantry, and that the French Battalion was trying to stem the enemy's attack. During the early morning, flashes of small arms and machine guns could be seen on the hills to the southwest.

At 0300, 18 May 1951, a platoon-size enemy group infiltrated into the 2d Battalion, 23d Infantry, CP area and blew up an ammunition dump in the schoolyard, and placed small arms and automatic weapons fire on the vehicles in the area. At the time, a small enemy group broke into Company C's rear CP area and an exchange of small arms fire (mostly ineffective) lasted until daylight, at which time the enemy withdrew to the high ground to the west. At daylight, several hundred Chinese could be seen on the high hills to the west and southwest. One medium tank with a 76mm rifle, which had been evacuated to the company maintenance shop at the rear CP several days before, fired sixty rounds of HE and several boxes of .50 caliber ammunition at a range of about 1,000–1,500 yards at the enemy on the high ground. The enemy was placing machine gun and mortar fire (25–30 rounds) into the village, which wounded several people.

During the firefight, which lasted throughout the morning, M. Sgt. John Dougherty, the first sergeant of Company C, asked Maj. Jensen's permission to evacuate the trains. Jensen said that he would be the one to give orders when the trains moved back. When Rodgers also asked the major, he received the same reply.[15]

Because of the deteriorating situation in the rear, plans for withdrawal were prepared, as Capt. Ruggerio recalls.

About 1030 [18 May], Ruggerio was ordered to report to the 2d Battalion CP at Chaun-ni. When he arrived there about twenty minutes later, the CP was under enemy machine gun fire from the high ground to the southwest. . . . Maj. Jensen told Ruggerio that the road to the south had been cut by the enemy and that it was necessary to make plans in the eventuality of a withdrawal. At the same time, Lt. Col. Beverly Richardson, commanding officer, 3d Battalion, 23d Infantry, said that the road was clear and that traffic was moving. However, Jensen stated that if a withdrawal was necessary, it would start at 1500. Jensen then asked Ruggerio what to do with the tanks. "It's the first time an infantry commander ever asked me what to do with the tanks in Korea," Ruggerio said. The captain replied that he thought it best to put all the tanks under his (Ruggerio's) control because it would enable the tanks to fight a better delaying action. "The control is better; they are all under one command; and they can move on order," Ruggerio said. Jensen concurred with the suggestion.

The plan of withdrawal was for Company C to remain in position while the 3d Battalion, 23d Infantry, withdrew down an "Old Gold Mine" road . . . southward to Chaun-ni. The 2d Battalion was then to withdraw, followed by Company C. Company K, 23d Infantry, was to hold the high ground . . . [southeast of Saemal, about 1,500 yards south of Chaun-ni] while Company C's tanks were to assemble at Saemal. Company B, 72d Tank Battalion (minus one platoon), was to deploy to the west side of the riverbed . . . [southwest of Saemal] and place fire on the high ground on the left side of the road while Company C either (1) pulled through them, (2) supported them with fire, or (3) stayed in position on call. Ruggerio told Jensen that he did not want infantry support for the tanks because it was daylight, the terrain was good, and it was still in friendly hands. He also stated at the time that the tanks could move faster without infantry.

Ruggerio returned to his CP at 1330 where the platoon leaders were already assembled. He explained the possibility of the company having to fight a delaying action and also of the roadblock south of Chaun-ni, but he also stated that it had been cleared. He then gave the order that if a withdrawal was necessary, the 1st Platoon would withdraw . . . [to a position about 500 yards north of Chaun-ni] under the covering fire of the 4th Platoon; the 4th and 1st Platoons would remain there and cover the withdrawal of the 2d and 3d Platoons to Saemal. The 1st and 4th Platoons would then rejoin the rest of the company at Saemal. He further stated that the platoons would only move on order.[16]

Other members of Company C recall the situation.

About 1000 the tank platoons were alerted to withdraw. They were told that the ROKs had disintegrated on the right and the 38th Infantry had given away on the left; they were also told that a road-block had been set up between Chaun-ni and Puch'aedol. The tanks were to remain in place until the infantry withdrew.

The plan of withdrawal for Company C was for the 4th Platoon to reoccupy its previously dug-in positions on the high ground over-looking the road junction. The 1st Platoon was then to withdraw to positions approximately 1,000 yards to the southeast of the 4th Platoon . . . , where the two platoons could protect the withdrawal of the 2d and 3d Platoons. The 2d and 3d Platoons were originally to move to a point southeast of Chaun-ni . . . where they were to cover the withdrawal of the other two platoons.[17]

Capt. Ruggerio describes the beginning of the withdrawal.

About 1400, Company G and Company E, 23d Infantry, broke contact with the enemy and moved to the rear. At approximately 1430 Maj. Jensen called and said that the plan was in effect. When Company G, 23d Infantry, withdrew, the tanks sighted an estimated enemy battalion on the high ground previously occupied by Company G. Two or three battalions of artillery placed TOT [time on target] fire on the hill, and four to six planes napalmed and strafed the ridgeline. All during this time, the tanks were firing .50 caliber and 76mms at the enemy.[18]

Other members of Company C provide additional details about the start of the withdrawal.

About 1030, the plan was put into effect, and the 4th Platoon withdrew to the high ground by the road junction with no enemy contact. About 1100, the 1st Platoon moved out and sighted no enemy; moving into position on the right side of the riverbed with three tanks on the high ground and two near the riverbed, the crew members of the various tanks spotted small groups (two to three) on the high ground near some bunkers approximately 900 yards to the west of their positions. 76mm and .50 caliber fire was placed on the enemy who withdrew to the reverse slope.

The 3d Battalion, 23d Infantry, had moved to the rear around 1000; and at 1130 the 2d Battalion, 23d Infantry, moved overland in a southward direction. At about 1200 hours, the 4th Platoon (on the high ground) spotted an enemy column (approximately 100) moving down the MSR towards the 1st Platoon's old positions. The five tanks in the platoon fired twenty-five to thirty rounds apiece at the column, and bodies could be seen flying through the air when the shells landed. At the same time, the 2d and 3d Platoons were covering the withdrawal of Company G, 23d Infantry, firing at platoon-sized enemy groups that were charging Company G as it withdrew. One GI was seen rushing the Chinese with several grenades in his hands. He rushed over the crest of the hill, and in a few minutes returned empty-handed. The tanks in the two platoons were firing at enemy groups ranging from squads to companies on the high ground approximately 600–800 yards to the right, left, and direct front. The 1st Platoon from its positions could see the high ground to the front and both sides of the 2d and 3d Platoons and said "that every bare spot on the ridges for 3,000 to 4,000 yards had Chinese on them." The men in the company were anxious to leave the area—"we knew we were out front like a sore thumb."[19]

Developments in the rear were reaching a critical point. Capt. Ruggerio explains.

About 1500, Maj. Jensen called and said to move the 2d and 3d Platoons (nine tanks) to his CP at Chaun-ni immediately. At the time, Ruggerio did not know that Chaun-ni was under attack and that the road was cut, but his executive officer, 1st Lt. Fred W. Rodgers, called and informed him of the situation and that Maj. Jensen was going to use the tanks to get the wheeled vehicles through an enemy roadblock. A few minutes later, Ruggerio heard over the radio that one of his tanks had hit a mine and was disabled. "I knew then that there was trouble because we had no support on our left flank," Ruggerio said. He then called back to the 2d Battalion for instructions and found out that he had no communications with them. He later found out that all the vehicles in the 2d Battalion had to be abandoned.[20]

Officers in the rear and soldiers from the 2d and 3d Platoons of Company C provide more details about the situation in the rear.

CAPT. W. J. RICHARD, S-2, 72D TANK BATTALION: During the morning of 18 May 1951, Capt. Richard at the 72d Tank Battalion CP [near Puch'aedol] was notified by the French Battalion that the Chinese were mining the road . . . [about 1,500 yards north of the CP]. The French were on the high ground to the left [west] overlooking the road. He asked them at the time to stop the Chinese and was told that the Chinese were going down the draw to the road disregarding the small arms and machine gun fire that was being placed on them. Richard immediately notified the 2d Battalion, 23d Infantry, of the mines in the road. He stated that he talked with an enlisted man who said that no officers were around at the time. The captain told the enlisted man carefully what had happened and had the enlisted man repeat it back. (Capt. Richard stated that he was of the opinion that Maj. Lloyd Jensen, commanding officer, 2d Battalion, 23d Infantry, did not receive the message. "If he had," Richard stated, "he would not have sent his trains down the road knowing the road was mined.")[21]

CAPT. PERRY SAGER, S-3, 2D BATTALION, 23D INFANTRY REGIMENT: "If such a report [that the road south of Chaun-ni was mined] was received, it was never given to any officer at the CP; in fact, this is the first I have ever heard about it. Maj. Jensen would never have sent his trains down the road if he knew it had been mined.

". . . The night of the 17th, Company B, 72d Tank Battalion, ran tank patrols up and down the road. One patrol made it as far north as Chaun-ni without enemy contact; however, a regimental wire team in a jeep was ambushed about 0100 south of Chaun-ni."

[In the early morning hours of the 18th], "the enemy evidently came down from the high ground to the right (looking southward from Chaun-ni) and hit the 3d Battalion, 23d Infantry, CP, which was located approximately 400 yards south of the 2d Battalion CP. The enemy blew up an ammunition truck in the schoolyard and then hit the perimeter guards of the 2d Battalion before they were repulsed. . . . On the morning of the 18th, we could see the enemy on the high ridges on the right (looking southward). Maj. Jensen decided then to run the roadblock with tanks in order to get the vehicles out. He called for a platoon from Company C, which arrived at Chaun-ni shortly after noon."[22]

LT. RODGERS, EXECUTIVE OFFICER, COMPANY C: About 1300–1330 the enemy attacked down the high ground to the rear of the 2d Battalion CP (this CP was in a log hut at the base of a steep [50°] hill), but the men at the CP placed small arms and automatic weapons fire on the enemy and checked his attack. At this time, Maj. Jensen called Capt. Ruggerio for tanks to come to the 2d Battalion CP to assist the wheeled vehicles in running a roadblock that the enemy had set up to the rear [north of Puch'aedol]. . . .

The 2d and 3d Platoons, Company C, arrived at the CP about 1400, at which time the enemy was still attacking down from the high ground immediately to the rear of the 2d Battalion CP. Maj. Jensen ordered the tanks to move south with the wheeled vehicles interspersed between them. Company C's trains fell into the column along with the trains of the 2d and 3d Battalions, 23d Infantry. (The 3d Battalion trains reached the area on the afternoon of 17 May.)

Rodgers mounted the first tank with Lt. George H. Ensley, 3d Platoon leader, and started out in fourth gear as fast as the tank would go and the conditions of the road would permit. The tank crews were firing the co-axial .30s and the .50 caliber turret machine guns at the gulleys and high ground to the right of the road where small enemy groups were seen. The tanks had heard reports over the radio that the enemy had reached the vicinity of . . . [the road just north of Puch'aedol], and the tanks were going at maximum speed so that the wheeled vehicles would receive as little enemy fire as possible.

Prior to moving out, Rodgers told Ensley that the roads were not mined, and that he had been told this by Maj. Jensen. The commanding officer, 3d Battalion, 23d Infantry, Lt. Col. Beverly Richardson, also assured Rodgers in the presence of Ensley that the road was not mined. "Had we known the road was mined, we would have proceeded down the road with caution and exploded the mines with tank (76mm) fire," Rodgers stated.

The lead tank went about 2,000 yards south of the 2d Battalion CP on the road (the road dropped off abruptly on the left and had a sheer cliff on the right) and hit a land mine that blew off the left track. The tank driver of the lead tank later told Rodgers that he saw several mounds of dirt on the road, but not expecting mines, he failed to slow down in time to avoid running over them. None of the personnel in the tank were injured by the mine explosion. The wheeled vehicles (about ten) following behind closed up on the disabled tank, and immediately all the personnel in the tank and wheeled vehicles abandoned the vehicles and took cover behind the embankment on the left (east) [side of the road]. Enemy small arms, machine gun, and automatic weapons fire was coming down the draws and from the high ground to the west of the road. Ensley, however, went to the right of the road and saw four or five Chinese lying in a ditch bordering the road. He then ran to the other side and jumped down the embankment.

Prior to the wheeled vehicles moving out of Chaun-ni, two platoons of tanks from Company B, 72d Tank Battalion, had been deployed along the rice paddies to the east of the small stream bordering the road . . . and were firing all their crew-served weapons (76mm, co-axial .30 caliber machine guns, and .50 caliber machine guns on the turret) on the enemy on the high ground to the west.

After the first tank was disabled, the second tank in the column bypassed the abandoned vehicles, pushing some of them out of the way in order to get by, and reached the disabled tank. It pushed the disabled tank to the left side of the road and then continued on approximately 600 yards farther down the road where it hit an enemy mine. From the 2d Battalion CP in Chaun-ni, the tanks were seen hitting the mines, and the remainder of the vehicles was diverted across the stream to the east. The vehicles attempted to negotiate the rice paddies and stalled; others attempted to drive over the hill; still others were abandoned. "It was a confused mass of vehicles," Rodgers said. "It was impossible for them to negotiate the rice paddies and irrigation ditches."

In the meantime, the men who had abandoned the vehicles behind the lead tank were crouched against the embankment for protection from enemy fire from above. However, the men were afraid
of the fire from the tanks of Company B and the remainder of the
tanks from Company C, which had deployed to the right and joined
with the two platoons from Company B, so, the men waded the
shallow stream in small groups to the east amidst enemy small arms
and automatic weapons fire, which could be seen splashing in the
water around them, and ran over the rice paddies to the tanks.[23]

MEN OF THE 2D AND 3D PLATOONS, COMPANY C, 72D TANK
BATTALION: About 1330, the 2d and 3d Platoons were ordered to
withdraw by Capt. Ruggerio, and after passing the road junction,
they received little enemy fire until they reached Chaun-ni. (The
command tank withdrew with the 4th Platoon.) When the tanks
reached Chaun-ni, wheeled vehicles from the 2d Battalion, 23d Infantry, were coming out of the riverbed to the right of the road. Lt.
Ensley, who was leading the tank column, halted the tanks and instructed the tank commanders to allow eight to ten wheeled vehicles
to intersperse between them. Ensley then took off, followed by the
wheeled vehicles and then another tank commanded by SFC Don
Shields. After going approximately 2,000 yards, Ensley's tank
struck a mine and veered slightly to the left towards an embankment. Enemy troops were on the high ground to the right of the
road, and two platoons from Company B, 72d Tank Battalion, were
across the river to the east firing on the enemy positions. . . . The
road bordered a high (55°) hill on the right and a sheer embankment
of about twenty feet on the left (looking southward). Shield's tank
pushed some of the vehicles following Ensley's tank off the road so
it could bypass the disabled tank. It continued on approximately
700 yards farther and came to a bypass. Shields remarked, "As I
was coming up through the bypass, I thought I had made it through."
Suddenly, Shields saw a grass mat on the road and tried to stop the
driver so he could blow it off the road with the 76mm cannon. The
driver couldn't stop the tank in time, and it struck a mine under the
mat, which blew off a track.

The remaining vehicles and tanks got halfway through the town
and jammed up bumper to bumper. Officers south of the village

turned the column to the east across the river. The vehicles raced to the high ground. SFC Earl K. Pointdexter said, "There was no control of the vehicles; it was just a wild herd." Another man in a tank farther to the rear stated that when his tank came into Chaun-ni, "The vehicles were all over the damn hills."

The tanks did not follow the wheeled vehicles to the high ground, but negotiated the rice paddies until they joined with the two platoons of tanks from Company B. During all this time, enemy small arms, machine gun, and automatic weapons fire was coming down from the high ground to the west on to the vehicles. Some of the wheeled vehicles went up a trail leading over a small hill to the rear of Company B's tanks (approximately twenty-five feet high). The trail led into a draw where fifty to sixty vehicles and trailers were assembled, not knowing which way to go. Lt. [then Sgt.] Kenney's tank came up and told the drivers to follow him southward down the riverbed. He started out, but a heavy enemy mortar barrage set some of the wheeled vehicles on fire, and ammunition trailers started to explode. In the meantime, two tanks from the 2d and 3d Platoons helped evacuate wounded and doughboys and followed the riverbed southward until out of the enemy's fire.[24]

LT. FIFE, LEADER, 1ST PLATOON, COMPANY B, 72D TANK BATTALION: About 1330–1430 the tanks withdrew to Chaun-ni, and Capt. Ross ordered the entire platoon to go to the left of the river and move southward over the rice paddies through the 4th Platoon and to form a skirmish line facing west so that fire could be placed on the high ground to the west. Prior to this, some tanks from Company C, 72d Tank Battalion, had tried to escort the wheeled vehicles south along the road but were disabled by mines. The remainder of the vehicles veered to the left across the river in an effort to skirt the base of the hills southward. Company B had previously selected an alternate withdrawal route southward in case the road was mined, and had marked it with expended brass [shell casings]. Fife, after crossing the river, tried to direct the vehicles southward to the alternate route, but the drivers wouldn't listen. They headed straight up the hills, stopped, and wouldn't return. "The vehicles were in a mass of confusion. It didn't look like anyone was in charge; it was every driver for himself," Fife said. During this time, the vehicles and tanks were receiving scattered small arms fire from the high ground to the west.

Around 1400, the 2d Platoon, Company B, was sent from Task Force Zebra's headquarters and also formed in line with the 1st and 4th Platoons and placed fire on the high hills to the west and up a draw near where the second tank from Company C was destroyed by a mine. Heavy small arms and automatic weapons fire was coming from the draw. Fife personally saw fifteen to twenty small enemy groups (ten to fifteen) on the high ground and in the draw. While in position to the east of the river the 1st Platoon fired approximately 200 rounds of 76mm, sixty boxes of .50 caliber, and sixty boxes of .30 caliber at a range of 500–1,200 yards on enemy groups on the high hills to the west. The tank fire forced the enemy to withdraw to the reverse slope of the hill. All during the day a steady artillery fire was placed on the enemy groups on the high ground.[25]

Meanwhile, the remainder of Company C, still holding its positions north of Chaun-ni, began to withdraw. Capt. Ruggerio describes the action.

The company remained in position for approximately three-fourths of an hour, firing at small enemy groups as they appeared on the high ground to the front and right. About 1600 Ruggerio ordered the 1st Platoon to move to its designated blocking position, and when it did it received small arms fire from an unestimated number of enemy on Hill 410 [about 1,000 yards north of Chaun-ni]. After the 1st Platoon moved out, the 4th Platoon reported enemy in unestimated numbers coming down the MSR from the northeast and another group coming down the "Old Gold Mine" road [running southwest from the 3d Battalion's area to Chaun-ni]. . . . Artillery concentrations were called on these targets, and the 4th Platoon, together with the command tank, withdrew southward down the riverbed. Friendly artillery fire covered the road and the high ground to the right and left, firing fifty yards to the rear of the last tank. "Very heavy artillery concentrations really plastered the road," Ruggerio said. While the 4th Platoon was withdrawing, the 1st Platoon received ten rounds of smoke around its positions.

As the captain, in his command tank, was proceeding south-ward down the riverbed, he saw Company K, 23d Infantry, on the high ground about 1,500 yards south of Chaun-ni. He then moved the 4th Platoon to Saemal where it went on high ground (25–30 feet) overlooking Chaun-ni. Ruggerio stayed with the 1st Platoon. When the 4th Platoon radioed that it was in position (it was then about 1630), Ruggerio called the 72d Tank Battalion and asked for instructions. He was informed that a tank platoon was being sent northward in an effort to reduce the enemy roadblock. About fifteen minutes later, Ruggerio told the 1st Platoon to remain in position while he went to Saemal. "When I got there, I was flabbergasted," stated Ruggerio. "I saw trucks overturned and burning; burned ¾-tons; abandoned trailers loaded with ammunition and guns; and rations and supplies scattered all over the riverbed. Our company supply half-track was completely burned."

About 1715 Ruggerio saw his kitchen truck in the riverbed be-tween Saemal and Chaun-ni and noticed a body in the cab. He or-dered his driver to move his tank parallel with the truck. Just then he started to receive small arms fire from the west side of the road. Disregarding the fire, he pulled alongside the vehicle, and the driver and assistant driver dismounted on the shielded side of the tank and went to investigate the truck. When the men dismounted, the enemy fire ceased, and they said that it was one of the cooks [Cpl. Rudolph W. Soellner] and that he was dead. Ruggerio then said to put the body on the deck of the tank. During this time, the loader was out of the tank, and the captain was sitting on the rear turret with his earphones off. At this time, some of the men in the 4th Platoon were trying to call and tell Ruggerio that the enemy was on the road to the rear of the tank. The road was twenty-five yards to the west overlooking the riverbed and was about seven or eight feet higher. While the men were placing the body on the rear deck, the loader turned around and said, "Who are they, ROKs?" Ruggerio then looked around and saw 300–400 enemy soldiers on the bend of the road behind a high dirt embankment. The embankment looked as though a bulldozer had pushed dirt off the road. (Other men in the 4th Platoon stated that there were 35–40 enemy soldiers and the interviewer personally inspected the embankment and found it more logical to believe it was 35–40 enemy soldiers.) When Ruggerio looked around, the enemy soldiers were all standing with burp guns in their hands and were laughing. He then yelled "Chinese," threw his hands over his head, and fell into the turret. The two drivers ran and dove head-first into their compartments, and the tank moved out in a hurry. The loader had followed the captain into the turret. All during this, the enemy had not fired one round at the tank crew.

The tank moved westward about thirty-five yards, turned around facing the enemy, and pointed the 76mm at them. The Chinese then scattered and opened fire on the tank. The command tank, together with the tanks from the 4th Platoon, placed 76mm and .30 caliber co-axial fire on the enemy. While engaging them with fire, the 1st Platoon radioed and said that a large enemy group was moving down the trail to the southeast, and that enemy activity was increasing on the high ground to the east. . . . At 1745 Ruggerio told the 1st Platoon to move down the road through Chaun-ni with sirens open because he had "a couple of hundred gooks pinned down on the curve." At this time, Ruggerio did not know that fifteen American stragglers had joined with the 1st Platoon and were mounted on the decks of its tanks.

Ruggerio saw that infantry were on the tanks as they came through the village, but it was too late to hold up fire. Several infantrymen were seen to fall off the tanks. The platoon overshot the road leading to Saemal and continued southward down the MSR to the knocked-out tank. Ruggerio then ordered the 4th Platoon to counterattack up to Chaun-ni, then to come back, which they did about fifteen minutes later. Only one Chinese was seen to walk away from the dirt embankment. Ruggerio then instructed the 1st Platoon to back up the tanks 200 yards to the road and rejoin the 4th Platoon. The platoon leader, however, tried to bypass the disabled tank by going down an embankment that led to the riverbed. In trying to do so, the tank broke a propeller shaft. The other tanks got down the twenty-foot embankment to the riverbed; however, another tank broke a propeller shaft. The disabled tanks were destroyed by tank fire. The 1st Platoon then linked with the 4th Platoon at Saemal. During this time, the two platoons received heavy small arms, automatic weapons, and 82mm mortar fire from the high ground to the west of the road.

Ruggerio called the 72d Tank Battalion for instructions as to what to do with the abandoned vehicles, and was told to stand by until higher headquarters was contacted. About ten minutes later, he was instructed to tow them out. Ruggerio stated that there were too many and that the rice paddies and riverbed would prevent him from doing so. Three other times he called for other instructions; finally, he took it upon himself to run over the trailers and to blow up the trucks and jeeps with 76mm fire. While the tanks were doing this, a heavy air strike of six to eight planes napalmed and strafed the high ground to the west of the road and also dropped 500-pound fragmentation bombs.

About 1815 hours, Capt. Ruggerio ordered the 4th Platoon to move over the trail in . . . [the high ground south of Chaun-ni where Company K of the 23d Infantry had been located] to see if they could locate any friendly troops, but ten minutes later, the tanks returned and reported that there were no friendly forces in the area. However, they did spot four to five abandoned vehicles, but before they could destroy them, four planes napalmed the area, nearly hitting the 4th Platoon's tanks. Ruggerio immediately called the 72d Tank Battalion S-3 and told them to call off the air because they were bombing and strafing within 75 to 100 yards of Company C. After fifteen minutes, the planes withdrew. The enemy then started to set up two .50 caliber machine guns at the high ground . . . [just south of Saemal], but these were knocked out by 76mm fire. An enemy company then started coming down the draw behind Chaun-ni, taking cover behind the buildings and any natural concealment. During this time, the tanks were picking up wounded and stragglers in the area, and one tank had eight or ten men in the turret. Twenty-five to thirty rounds of 76mm fire were placed on the enemy in the draw, but with undetermined results.

At 1830 Ruggerio received a call from the 72d Tank Battalion and was told to withdraw immediately. When he asked about the vehicles, he received the answer, "To hell with them, get out." Ruggerio then said, "I'll be out in a short while." He then received the reply, "Short while, hell, I want you out in fifteen minutes." The captain had the 1st Platoon lead out, followed by the 4th Platoon. The command tank with another tank fought the rear action. As the tanks started to withdraw, it rained heavily for about fifteen minutes, making it difficult for the tanks to negotiate the rice paddies. During this time, friendly artillery was bombarding the high ground to the east and west of the riverbed.

On the way southward, Chinese soldiers were driving 6x6s out of the draws near Ch'onch'i-ri and were looting other vehicles. They were surprised to see the tanks and were completely caught off-guard when the tanks opened fire on them with all crew-served weapons. As the tanks were going down the rice paddies paralleling an irrigation ditch, Ruggerio saw approximately 75 to 100 enemy soldiers double-timing down the ditch, throwing grenades at the tanks about thirty-five yards away. When he saw the enemy on both sides of the riverbed and following the tanks out, he called and asked the 72d Tank Battalion to set up some type of roadblock. He was informed that one was in place. Travel southward was slow as the rice paddies adjacent to the riverbed were muddy, and the riverbed had many huge boulders. The rice paddies were diagonal to the tanks' approach, and when the tanks hit them, they would rock to the left and right.

After reaching the road, the tanks passed through the friendly road block near Puch'aedol and continued to Han'gye, where the company reassembled. When the tanks reached the assembly area, several unexploded grenades were found on the tanks' decks. During the whole delaying action, there were no casualties in the tank platoons.[26]

Other members of Company C with Capt. Ruggerio describe the withdrawal.

About 1430–1500, the 4th Platoon, which was still on the high ground at the road junction, saw a company of Chinese crossing the MSR eastward in the vicinity of the 1st Platoon's original positions. It placed small arms and .50 caliber fire on the group (the tanks were running low of 76mm ammunition at the time). Enemy mortar and machine gun fire started coming in around the 4th Platoon from the high ground formerly occupied by Company G, 23d Infantry. The tanks then pulled out and followed the river bottom to the original company assembly area south of Chaun-ni. . . . The tanks pulled into position about 1530 and received no enemy fire. A few minutes later, however, small arms and mortar fire came into the area. This lasted off and on for about two hours.

About 1700, Sgt. Jokerst spotted 75–100 troops coming down the high hill behind the electric power plant in Chaun-ni [on the southwest side of the village]. At first Jokerst thought they were ROKs and called Sgt. Ernest L. Sink in another tank to verify it, but Sink didn't know. Just then, Ruggerio spotted the company supply truck on the river bottom and pulled up alongside of it. A group of thirty to forty Chinese watched him for a minute and then opened fire. Ruggerio pulled his tank over with the others and opened fire, with all weapons, on the enemy group.

[Ruggerio] then called 1st Lt. Wallace H. Nutting, 1st Platoon leader, on the radio and instructed him to come down the road through Chaun-ni with sirens open and guns firing to eliminate the enemy in the village. At the time, approximately fifteen GI stragglers had joined the 1st Platoon, and so Nutting had them mount the decks of the tanks. (The men claimed that Captain Ruggerio knew the infantry was with the tanks at the time.) Nutting took the lead position, followed by Pointdexter, SFC Orville Mann, SFC George Bell, and SFC Franklin King. The turrets were traversed to the right to bring co-axial .30s into action and to prevent firing on the 4th Platoon. The drivers buttoned up, but the tank commanders fired the 50s as the tanks went through the village. Several small groups of about fifteen [enemy troops] were seen and fired upon by the tanks.

As the tanks went through the village, Sgt. Jokerst [4th Platoon] said that he saw infantry on the decks and warned the other tanks by radio not to fire. Evidently, the message was not received in time as Jokerst saw several infantry fall from the tanks (five were wounded and one killed).

Company K, 23d Infantry, was supposed to protect the withdrawal of Company C, 72d Tank Battalion, and was in position . . . [on the high ground about 1,000 yards southeast of Chaun-ni] when the 2d and 3d Platoons came through. However, when the 1st and 4th Platoons reached Chaun-ni, Company K had withdrawn.

The 1st Platoon missed the turn to the east (south of Chaun-ni) which led to the 4th Platoon and continued down the road to where Lt. Ensley's tank was destroyed. Burned vehicles littered the road. There was a twenty-foot bluff on the right side that led down to the riverbed, and Nutting saw that it was impossible to turn around, so he went down a bluff. Pointdexter's tank tried to go down and snapped a propeller shaft. Bell's and Mann's tanks made it down the embankment safely, but the following tank also snapped a propeller shaft. Nutting continued on down the riverbed, but Bell, after crossing the stream, returned and helped evacuate the tank crews. The disabled tanks were destroyed by thermite grenades dropped on the engines. The men, upon leaving the disabled tanks, received heavy automatic weapons fire from a draw to the right of the road. Mann's tank spotted the enemy and silenced him with a 76mm round. The fire eased off, and the men followed the tanks, shielding themselves from the enemy small arms fire, and reached the 4th Platoon by 1700 hours.

The 4th Platoon was then sent up a trail to try to contact Company K, but only the lead tank reached the top of the hill. The others managed to turn around when it [the lead tank] reported that Company K had left. During this time, the 1st Platoon was receiving light enemy fire. The bullets could be heard whining and could be seen as they hit the ground around the tanks. The two platoons then destroyed abandoned vehicles (jeeps, 2½-ton trucks, and trailers) for about fifteen minutes. During this time, small enemy groups were seen on the hills to the east, west, and south. "In other words we were surrounded," [SFC] Brown said.

About 1800 it started to rain very hard and got cloudy and dark. Ruggerio ordered Nutting to lead out the two platoons while he brought up the rear. As the tanks moved southward, the men saw an enemy column—"A column of twos"—crossing the valley from the east to the west. All the tanks, except one, which had some wounded infantrymen on the deck, opened fire with 76s and .50 calibers on the enemy group. When the .50s jammed, the tank commanders fired their carbines at the enemy. Heavy small arms fire was hitting the tanks, and Sgt. Pointdexter said, "It sounded like heavy hail." Ruggerio was firing at the abandoned vehicles as he brought up the rear.

The advance up the rice paddies was slow, and the enemy was running up to the tanks, throwing grenades and satchel charges (one had a pointed stick with a huge ball on the end), and attempting to climb up on the rear decks. The tankers were pulling grenade pins and rolling the grenades out of the turret. "It's the first time I ever threw grenades on the deck of a tank," Sgt. Donald Myers said. The enemy troops that rushed up to the tanks did not fire small arms; they only threw grenades and satchel charges. Each tank had eight to ten men on the inside, and one tank had some wounded on the rear deck.

The tanks continued down the paddies and riverbed southward for about one mile, and the tankers said that they could look up at any hill (the hills now were about 400 feet high) and could see enemy groups of 200 to 300. Sgt. Jokerst said, "They were all over like flies." The enemy kept placing small arms and automatic weapons fire down on the armored column. About 1900, the tanks rejoined the remainder of the company near Han'gye.[27]

Earlier, soon after 1700 hours, Company B's tanks south of Chaun-ni had pulled back because of ammunition and fuel shortages. As a result, Capt. Ruggerio's force from Company C was on its own as it withdrew to Han'gye. He summarizes the fighting since the beginning of the enemy attack.

Capt. Ruggerio thought that there should have been an artillery forward observer with the company while it was occupying blocking positions. Ruggerio stated that during the three days' action, communications were perfect . . . that the company expended over 350,000 rounds of .50 caliber ammunition, 200,000 rounds of .30 caliber ammunition, and 3,000 rounds of 76mm ammunition. On the 16th, one tank from the 3d Platoon was disabled by bazooka fire and was evacuated to the 76th Tank Battalion. On the morning of the 18th, another broke an oil line and was evacuated to the company rear CP where it was later abandoned. Two tanks from the 2d and 3d Platoons were disabled by mines. Two other tanks from the 1st Platoon broke propeller shafts south of Chaun-ni and had to be destroyed.[28]

In this battle below the Soyang River, the 23d Infantry Regiment alone suffered very heavy casualties, losing 72 killed, 158 wounded, and 190 missing, along with more than 150 vehicles of the trains of the 2d and 3d Battalions and Company C, and large quantities of heavy weapons, ammunition, equipment, and supplies. The stubborn defense of the 23d Infantry and Company C, 72d Tank Battalion, along with that of the 38th Infantry Regiment and the French and Dutch Battalions, had slowed the Chinese offensive long enough to allow time for UN commanders to shift reinforcements into the area. For their heroic resistance during the period of 16–22 May, the 2d Infantry Division and their attached units, including Company C, 72d Tank Battalion, were awarded the Presidential Unit Citation.[29]

The cost to the Chinese had been high, some 3,600 casualties having been inflicted in the 23d Infantry Regiment's sector alone. Of greater significance was the momentum lost to the Chinese offensive, something from which the enemy never recovered. By 20 May, UN forces in the U.S. I and IX Corps zones as well as the 1st Marine Division, X Corps, were counterattacking. Soon the 2d Infantry Division itself would launch a counterattack. Never again would the Chinese be able to mount a major offensive operation.

Chapter 11

THE SUPPLY BATTLE OF THE SOYANG RIVER

U.S. X Corps, 10 May–7 June 1951

Logistics was one of the greatest challenges facing the UN forces as they fought to halt the main enemy attack in the X Corps sector. Maintaining the movement of critical supplies to the front lines and ensuring the rapid shift of reinforcements to threatened areas was essential to stopping the Chinese Communist offensive. It was even more difficult because of the rugged terrain. Indeed, the Chinese had selected this region for their main attack because they believed that American firepower would be largely negated owing to the mountainous terrain and limited road net, which would restrict the employment of tanks and artillery and make ammunition resupply difficult.

The U.S. X Corps was able to win the supply battle, and following the battle a combat historian, 1st Lt. John Mewha, studied the reasons for success. Lt. Mewha explains the basic problem that had to be overcome.

During the Battle of the Soyang (10 May–7 June 1951), the ferocity of the battle against the massed Communist hordes and the necessity of moving additional troops to prevent [their] advance and later to afford friendly troops the opportunity of a counterattack presented the technical services of X Corps with an unusual challenge. The basic and most immediate problem was the resupplying [of] the Corps Artillery battalions with ammunition. The tonnages fired were far excessive to any previous battle. During this period, the amount of ammunition fired reached an all-time high [of]

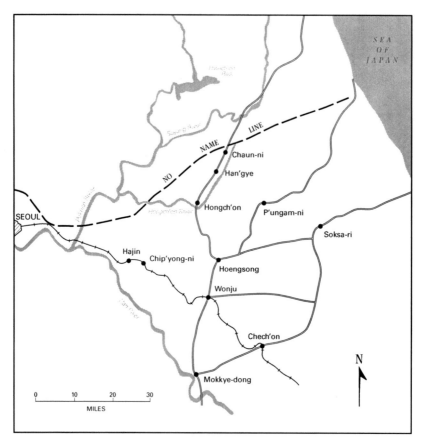

The supply battle of the Soyang River, 10 May–7 June 1951. (Original map by author, based on U.S. Center of Military History maps and maps in Army Map Service series L751.)

24,800 tons—2,380 tons of supplies were required in one day alone, 1,810 tons of which were ammunition.

There were many times when the field artillery battalions had less than their basic loads on hand in the battery positions. The basic load for an artillery battalion is 13,450 rounds of ammunition. One day during the latter part of May, the 15th Field Artillery Battalion had only 2,784 rounds of ammunition on hand; the 37th Field Artillery Battalion, 5,577 rounds; the 38th Field Artillery Battalion, 3,809 rounds; and the 503d (155mm) Field Artillery Battalion, which normally carries a basic load of 2,700 rounds, had only

1,174 rounds on hand. Between the 18th and 22d May, the artillery battalions were firing the "Van Fleet rate of fire"—250 rounds per piece per day. Between the period 12 May to 6 June 1951, the daily ammunition expended ranged anywhere from 7,000 rounds to 49,986 rounds at the peak on 22 May.

Prior to the enemy attack, the ammunition buildup in the forward areas had been accomplished, and each artillery battalion had all authorized loads in position. The ammunition points at Hongch'on and Wonju were at the levels prescribed by the Eighth U.S. Army, but the battle against the tremendous numbers meant a terrific and unanticipated consumption of ammunition. The batteries fired up to five times a normal day's rate of fire. Ammunition Supply Point #50 in Hongch'on could not handle the tremendous demand, and this meant that trucks had to go to Wonju, nearly a day's trip, to pick up supplies. Heavy ammunition and grenades were flown into the K46 airstrip south of Hoengsong, which reduced the turnaround time for the trucks by six hours. On one day, approximately 300 tons of ammunition were flown into the K46 airstrip.[1]

Capt. Davis L. Mathews, commander, 69th Ordnance Ammunition Company, describes the ammunition resupply operations of his unit at Hongch'on.

During the entire Communist Spring Offensive, the 2d Magazine Platoon, 69th Ordnance Ammunition Company, remained in positions at Ammunition Supply Point #50 in Hongch'on, even though all other technical services supply points, and even some division supply units, had pulled farther southward. At one time, the enemy was only eight miles from the ammunition dump, and an infantry company was assigned to guard it. The dump was also well forward of one of the X Corps's artillery battalions, the 96th Field Artillery Battalion, which was approximately two miles farther southward. The magazine platoon carried out its mission of supplying the Corps Artillery without interruption.

During the seven days of the heaviest fighting in May (15–22 May), the platoon loaded out 2,896 rounds of 8-inch howitzer, 4,700 rounds of 155mm howitzer, 4,396 rounds of 155mm gun, and 150,240 rounds of 105mm ammunition—or a total of 8,139.82

tons of artillery ammunition. A magazine platoon is supposed to handle 500 tons of ammunition during a 24-hour period, but during this time the platoon averaged 1,162.83 tons per 24-hour period. On or about 20 May 1951, the magazine platoon, with the help of 125 Korean laborers, loaded or unloaded 540 trucks between the hours of 2000–0400. Each truck carried a load of approximately four tons.

The ammunition resupply for the dump in Hongch'on came from the railhead in Wonju. An inventory was taken of existing stocks three times a day, and reported immediately to the Ordnance Officer, X Corps. As the ammunition trucks came in from Wonju and whenever possible, the trucks from the railhead and the artillery battalions loaded tailgate-to-tailgate without one round touching the ground. Sixty percent of the ammunition was loaded in this fashion. None of the ammunition trucks went directly from Wonju to the gun positions, but reported to the supply point in Hongch'on first. This was done for two reasons. First, it was necessary to keep record of the amount of ammunition issued; and second, X Corps would not allow Eighth U.S. Army transportation to go beyond the ammunition supply point because of the danger involved.

When the artillery battalions moved to the vicinity of Ammunition Supply Point #50, the turnaround time from the guns to the ammunition dump was only fifteen to twenty-five minutes. It took approximately fifteen to twenty minutes to load a truck from the ground, and about ten minutes by tailgating.

Ammunition Supply Point #50 in Hongch'on supplied all the ammunition for the artillery battalions supporting the 2d Infantry Division. Capt. Mathews was of the opinion that the 2d Infantry Division would have [had] to retreat from Hongch'on if the ammunition supply point had not been there at the height of the fighting. "The division used a wall of steel instead of the infantry to stop the Communist drive," Mathews stated.[2]

The X Corps's Ammunition Officer, Maj. Herman C. Hinton, provides more detail about ammunition resupply.

Ammunition Supply Point #50, which was located in Hongch'on, reported three times daily the amount of ammunition on hand. The ammunition officer would then contact the artillery battalions to get the estimated number of rounds they anticipated shooting in the next twelve-hour period. Based on this, ammunition was then ordered through the Eighth U.S. Army supply point at Wonju. The ammunition supply point in Hongch'on was the only service unit that did not move to the rear during the Chinese Offensive and, at one time, the artillery pieces were surrounding the ammunition dump. "It was the short turn around that saved X Corps from being in Hongch'on and not Wonju now," Hinton stated.

During the period from 10 May–7 June 1951, over 24,000 tons of ammunition were expended. After the 7th ROK Division had regrouped, its artillery support was resupplied from Wonju direct to the gun positions on line.[3]

Col. J. K. McCormick, G-4, X Corps, provides more information about the problem and how it was resolved.

Basically, an infantry division has organic transportation for forty-five miles under ideal conditions. However, road conditions were poor during the May attack, and the defiles were all one-way traffic. This, together with the fact that from the ammunition dump in Hongch'on to the farthest point in the "No Name Line" involved a turnaround time of about twelve hours, constituted a tremendous transportation problem to the technical services of X Corps. When the attack broke, the corps's organic transportation (truck companies from Eighth U.S. Army) was insufficient to haul the required tonnage.

The various technical services chiefs were called together and were instructed to canvass all of their units for available trucks to help facilitate the supply problem. These vehicles were placed into a truck pool, which was referred to as the "truck bank." Vehicles of various types—2½-ton trucks, ¾-ton trucks, dump trucks, low boys (equipment trailers)—were drawn from the signal battalion, engineer battalions, MASH [mobile army surgical hospital] hospitals, and other units. Every available truck was utilized to haul one type of supply or another. All in all, it was as near 100 percent utilization of cargo transportation as possible. Various military police checkpoints were set up adjacent to the supply points; every vehicle going northward without a load was commandeered, sent to the supply dumps for a load, and then sent forward. Notes were given to the drivers stating where the trucks had been commandeered and the amount of time they were used.

Many problems were encountered and overcome by the close coordination of the G-4, X Corps. Additional drivers were needed to keep the vehicles rolling twenty-four hours a day; these were furnished mainly by the parent organizations, although others were actually brought to the vehicles. It was attempted to work two twelve-hour shifts; however, some drivers drove as long as physically possible (eighteen to twenty hours) without relief. Service stations were set up to maintain the vehicles, and the mechanics did all the necessary 1st and 2d echelon maintenance work while the drivers slept nearby or in the cabs. Emergency repair crews patrolled the MSRs, and helicopters with radios were used to spot disabled vehicles. Special kitchens were set up at the ammunition points and operated around the clock. All persons that could be spared—military as well as South Korean—were all used as laborers at the supply dumps. Special crews from the X Corps headquarters were sent out to load ammunition. Five to six thousand carriers (Korean Civilian Transportation Corps) were used to carry the supplies [from] the advanced supply points to the forward positions.[4]

Maj. Harry J. Dodd, executive officer, 52d Transportation Truck Battalion, explains in more detail the transportation problem and how it was resolved.

At the height of the May Offensive, the 52d Transportation Truck Battalion had elements of seventeen truck companies, including the X Corps truck company. Each company had an average of thirty-two trucks running. Truck companies were stationed at Wonju, Chech'on, and Hongch'on. Two truck companies, the 715th and 252d Transportation Truck Companies, were hauling from the Class III [fuel] and V [ammunition] dumps at Chip'yong-ni and Hajin.

During the height of the action, X Corps set such a high requirement for Class V (ammunition) that the battalion could not handle it. A provisional group, which consisted of trucks from the 52d

Truck Battalion and TO/E [table of organization and equipment, or unit organic] vehicles from organizations in X Corps, hauled nothing but ammunition. A control point was established at the railhead in Wonju to feed the vehicles into the ammunition dump in order to eliminate any possible confusion. The trucks were sent out in serials of five to ten vehicles, and an average of twenty trucks were dispatched an hour. The 52d Transportation Battalion had to divert some trucking companies from Wonju to the airhead south of Hoengsong when X Corps transportation could not haul away the ammunition flown into it. On one day over 300 tons of artillery ammunition were flown into the airstrip.

In the month of May, the 52d Transportation Truck Battalion hauled over 93,000 tons of Class I [food], III [fuel], and V [ammunition] supplies (60 percent was Class V and 40 percent was Classes I and III). The Eighth Army truck companies hauled thirty tons of ammunition less than was expended by X Corps.

Priorities on supplies were set up at each twenty-four-hour period. Each technical service would give an estimate of tonnage desired for the next day; if the quartermaster battalion could not haul it, it was supplemented with vehicles from X Corps. The vehicles from corps were instructed to report to the operations officer of the 52d Truck Battalion where they were gathered into groups of five to ten and dispatched to the dumps. However, some trucks never reported and went directly to the ammunition points. Over 1,000 tons of Class II [clothing and weapons] and V a day were hauled out of the Chip'yong-ni and Hajin railheads to Hongch'on by the two quartermaster trucking companies. After the action subsided it was necessary to slow the two companies down. The ammunition trucks from the supply points met the artillery battalion trucks at Hongch'on and loaded tailgate-to-tailgate. It was then decided that it was unnecessary, and the trucks hauled the ammunition directly to the gun positions.

The 52d Truck Battalion had its kitchen and maintenance crews on a twenty-four-hour schedule during this period. Maintenance and feeding of X Corps personnel and vehicles [were] handled by the battalion. The trucks were making two 60-mile turnarounds a day when there were not personnel hauls. Ordnance support was excellent, and the battalion had first priority on spare parts and replacement trucks. Some drivers drove eighteen to twenty hours a day, and one driver made four trips in one twenty-four-hour period.[5]

Maj. Hinton, the X Corps ammunition officer, describes the maintenance problem.

During the period of the Chinese Offensive and the UN counterattack, the 328th Medium Maintenance Company operated three to four maintenance road teams (wrecker and jeep) around the clock giving emergency ordnance repair service. Service stations were set up adjacent to the ammunition supply points for second echelon maintenance. However, it was the driver's responsibility to maintain his own vehicle—gas, oil, tires, and the tightening of body bolts. Some repair work on tanks and artillery pieces was done in position on line by emergency ordnance repair teams.

On 20 May, one group of 98 EM [enlisted men] and five officers was flown to Pusan to bring back replacement vehicles. Ordnance personnel from the Eighth U.S. Army and the 2d Logistical Command said it would take at least eight days to bring the vehicles to Hongch'on. However, the group brought the 70 jeeps, 14 2½-tons, 10 ¾-tons, and 10 ¾-ton ambulances, plus 30 trailers, a distance of 332 miles to Hongch'on in 48 hours. The group arrived at Pusan at 1330 and left at 1600 hours, driving night and day and halting only for short intervals while the drivers could rest and do a little maintenance work. The officers and enlisted personnel were furnished from the 1st Medium Maintenance Company, the 19th Medium Maintenance Company, and the 515th M.A.M. [Medium Automotive Maintenance] Company.[6]

Col. McCormick, G-4, X Corps, and Maj. William H. Barker, assistant provost marshal, X Corps, discuss the problems of traffic control.

COL. MCCORMICK: Traffic control played a high role to the success of the operation. The supply convoys were run in block systems so as to have an even rate of trucks coming into the supply points. The trucks were gathered into holding areas adjacent to the ammunition points and dispatched into the dumps evenly, so that no trucks were waiting within the area. Traffic jams and bottlenecks were eliminated by the effective placing of military police at the vital passes and one-way bridges. Helicopters and light aircraft with radios were used to keep traffic moving and to eliminate the bottlenecks. These were also used to fly small amounts of essential parts, radio equipment, and weapons to forward areas.[7]

MAJ. BARKER: During the Chinese Offensive and the United Nations counteroffensive in May 1951, the problem of traffic control was great. On 16 May, the G-4, X Corps, ordered an MP check point set up at Hongch'on opposite the ammunition dump and at Wonju to commandeer any empty vehicles going north, to make sure [they were] loaded, and to insure delivery to the artillery gun positions at P'ungam-ni. The main problem encountered by this office during the period was traffic. Shortly before, the main problem had been rounding up ROK troops that had broken. Only priority vehicles were allowed on the road, and ammunition and troops were given priority.[8]

Capt. Jasper N. Erskine, highway regulating officer, X Corps, discusses the effect of the movement of reinforcements into the X Corps area and provides more information about supply operations.

On 16 May the transportation officer was notified to furnish forty trucks to effect the movement of the 3d U.S. Infantry Division from I Corps to X Corps. Actually the entire 3d Infantry Division moved from south of Seoul to Soksa-ri. Movement came at the rate of one regimental combat team a day, and each corps furnished forty vehicles a day to accomplish this mission.

Since the forty trucks shorted the supply hauls of X Corps, the G-4, X Corps, called all the technical services chiefs together and told them to screen their units for all available trucks. This included all organizations assigned, attached, or in support of X Corps—4th Signal Battalion, 1st and 2d MASH Hospitals, 520th Quartermaster Battalion, 69th Ordnance Battalion, and the 8224th Engineer Construction Group with all its battalions. These vehicles were pooled and were called the "truck bank." During the period from 17 May to 30 May, 550 truckloads of supplies were carried by truck bank vehicles. Four or five transportation truck companies were supporting the corps, and approximately fifty to sixty truck bank trucks were assisting in the hauling.

Movement of the truck bank trucks was coordinated by the 52d Transportation Truck Battalion at Wonju, which was in direct support of X Corps. Miscellaneous vehicles checked in with the 52d Transportation Truck Battalion's operations center and were dispatched to the supply dumps by them. At the height of the battle, X Corps consumed over 2,300 tons of supplies in one day, and each truck hauled approximately three to four tons. From 1500 17 May to 0700 18 May, truck bank trucks hauled 117 truckloads of Class V (ammunition) from Wonju to Hongch'on. These trucks also hauled ammunition from the K46 airstrip in Hoengsong to Hongch'on. During 19–21 May, military police had a roadblock set up outside of the K46 strip and commandeered an average of twenty-five vehicles a day that were going northward empty. These were loaded with ammunition and sent to Hongch'on. Actually, X Corps was performing the Eighth Army job by having to assist them.

Maintenance of the truck bank vehicles was furnished by the parent organizations and from ordnance maintenance teams on the road. The vehicles were making one haul of thirty-five miles from Wonju to Hongch'on and another haul of twenty-five miles from Wonju to Chudong-ni.

On 18 May 1951, ninety-four empty (2½-ton cargo) trucks from various organizations in X Corps were commandeered at Hoengsong to effect the movement of the 15th RCT, 3d U.S. Infantry Division, from Hoengsong to P'ungam-ni. There was not time to notify the units that the vehicles were being commandeered; however, no emergency vehicles were taken. No arrangements were made for gasoline or the feeding of the drivers. "The individual driver fought for his own supply, and they were strictly on their own except when in convoy," Erskine stated. The commandeering was necessary because all organic transportation vehicles were tied up on various missions—ammunition, supplies, and troop movement. The commandeering started at 0900 and was completed by 1800.

The units of the 3d Division did not know where they were going, so between 18–20 May when the troops arrived at Wonju, Erskine (who was at Wonju at the time) advised each serial commander of his destination and the route over which the serial would travel. On 19 May eighty trucks from IX and I Corps took the first regiment [of the] 3d U.S. Infantry Division to Hoengsong and left them there. It was necessary to commandeer vehicles to effect [their] movement to P'ungam-ni.

At 0900, 22 May, Erskine was notified by Lt. Gen. Edward A. Almond, X Corps commanding general, that the 187th [Airborne] RCT was to move from just south of Hoengsong to Han'gye at 1000 the same day. The 187th RCT only had its organic transportation and not enough to move its entire organization. Erskine managed to get twenty trucks from the X Corps transportation companies and had to draw forty others from the truck bank units. All arrangements for these vehicles were made by telephone within one hour. Some engineer dump trucks and ordnance low boys were used in the move. The entire 187th RCT cleared its IP by 1400 hours.[9]

Maj. Dodd, 52d Transportation Truck Battalion, summarizes his unit's actions in moving reinforcements.

During this period, 90,000 troops were hauled. On 18 May, the 52d Truck Battalion was given six hours' notice to furnish 200 trucks to move the 3d U.S. Infantry Division. Later the battalion assisted in moving the 1st Marine Division and the 187th RCT. After the 3d U.S. Infantry Division moved into the X Corps sector, artillery ammunition was hauled directly from Chech'on to the division's gun positions. Three trucking companies supported the 3d Division.[10]

Following the successful defense against the enemy attack, UN forces began a counteroffensive. Maj. Barker, assistant provost marshal, X Corps, explains some of the problems encountered in this operation.

When the counteroffensive started, military police were located all the way north to the Soyang River along the MSR. Every defile and one-way bridge was manned by military police. The main problem encountered during the counteroffensive was moving the U.S. Marines up to the vicinity of the Soyang River and moving the empty vehicles back to the vicinity of Chaun-ni to pick up another shuttle of Marines. During this movement, a traffic jam developed around the pass north of Chaun-ni. This jam was spotted by a helicopter borrowed for one hour from Lt. Gen. Almond, commanding general, X Corps. "It was all the longer he could spare it, so he said," Barker stated. The helicopter landed at the side of the road, and the vehicles that were not top priority were ordered on to the shoulders to allow priority traffic to pass by. "I would suggest a helicopter be made available to the corps Provost Marshal Section on call so traffic movements can be coordinated," Barker said.[11]

Col. McCormick, G-4, X Corps, summarizes some of the lessons learned from these supply efforts.

In the type of terrain found in Korea, the consumption factors of World War II were exceeded in every category due to the type of terrain and enemy tactics. Consumption of everything is far greater. This means that pipelines have to be larger and farther forward. Combat equipment, both for individuals and organic to units (radios, vehicles, guns, etc.), must be on hand in the forward areas to effect relief replacement. Because of the intensity of fighting against massed hordes, replacement items must be available to keep the troops supplied and in top fighting condition.

Airfields must be constructed well forward and must be large enough to bring in cargo and evacuate wounded. It is also necessary to construct light airfields (C47) as far forward in the corps area near the divisions as possible for emergency replacement supplies. Division and regimental headquarters must develop L19 [liaison aircraft] strips (this is the SOP in X Corps area). In May there were occasions to fly critical needed parts to some regimental headquarters. These strips also served for emergency evacuations and facilitated higher headquarters commands.[12]

The success of the supply effort was noteworthy not only because of the role it played in stopping the enemy offensive, but also because it allowed UN forces to go immediately on the counteroffensive as the Chinese regrouped for another effort.

Chapter 12

TASK FORCE GERHART

Company B, 72d Tank Battalion, 24 May 1951

On 19 May 1951, as the 2d Infantry Division took up positions on a new defensive line in the Han'gye area, enemy pressure lessened. The Chinese commander, General Peng Dehuai, had ordered a rapid withdrawal because of heavy losses to his main attack forces in the X Corps's sector. Sensing that the enemy was off-balance, General Van Fleet ordered counterattacks to begin on 20 May in the U.S. I and IX Corps areas. As it became apparent that enemy forces were withdrawing, the UN counterattacks soon spread to the X Corps area. A combat historian, 1st Lt. John Mewha, completed a detailed study of one of the actions in X Corps, a successful armor exploitation, and describes the situation.

During 16–23 May 1951, the Communist forces had hurled division after division at the United Nations lines in the X Corps sector, forcing the 5th and 7th ROK Divisions to disintegrate. The 2d U.S. Infantry Division, although badly mauled, was able to fight a stubborn withdrawing action, enabling the Eighth U.S. Army to send reinforcements to bolster the retreating ROKs and the 2d Division. The 187th Regimental Combat Team was attached to the 2d U.S. Infantry Division, and the 3d U.S. Infantry Division was moved from I Corps to X Corps to support the 5th and 7th ROK Divisions.

Realizing the Communist forces had expended most of their energy in their forward advance, Lt. Gen. Edward A. Almond, commanding general, U.S. X Corps, ordered the United Nations forces under his command to take the initiative against the enemy.[1]

On 23 May, the 187th Airborne Regimental Combat Team (ARCT) attacked north and gained four miles. Seeking to achieve a breakthrough and seize critical crossings of the Soyang River, Almond ordered an armored-infantry task force to attack up the main Hongch'on–Han'gye–Puch'aedol–Chuan-ni–Umyang-ni–Kwandae-ri –Inje road (Route 24) the next day. The task force was to retake the same road over which Company C, 72d Tank Battalion, had battled the renewed Chinese offensive little more than a week before (see chapter 10). Lt. Mewha describes the mission of the task force.

On 24 May, at 0900, the 2d U.S. Infantry Division was ordered to organize and form a task force consisting of not less than two tank companies, one infantry battalion, and engineer elements. This task force was to form in the vicinity of Han'gye, [and] at 1200 the same day (24 May 1951) was to advance up the Han'gye–Umyang-ni axis to seize the high ground overlooking the Soyang River. The 1st U.S. Marine Division, utilizing one regiment, was to be prepared to follow the 2d U.S. Infantry Division task force at 1500 hours, 24 May 1951, with the mission of seizing the high ground . . . [Hill 452, west of the Soyang River] and exploiting to the north and northwest thereof. The 23d Infantry was to assemble in the vicinity of Han'gye and was to be prepared to exploit along the Umyang-ni–Inje [Route 24] or Umyang-ni–Yanggu [Route 92] axis.[2]

The 72d Tank Battalion was to play a key role. Officers of the unit describe the initial alert and the formation of the task force.

MAJ. (THEN CAPTAIN) WILLIAM E. ROSS, COMMANDER, COMPANY B: On the morning of 23 May 1951, Company B, 72d Tank Battalion, was south of the pass below Han'gye after transferring the 3d Battalion, 23d Infantry Regiment, to Hongch'on. At 1000, a runner from G-3, 2d Infantry Division, gave Capt. (now Maj.) William E. Ross a message stating that the company was to attack with Company A, 187th Airborne Regimental Combat Team, at 1300 hours on the same day. The runner said that he had been trying to contact Company B since 0800 hours.

Ross immediately reported to Col. William Gerhardt [Col. George H. Gerhart],[3] the executive officer, 187th Abn RCT, at

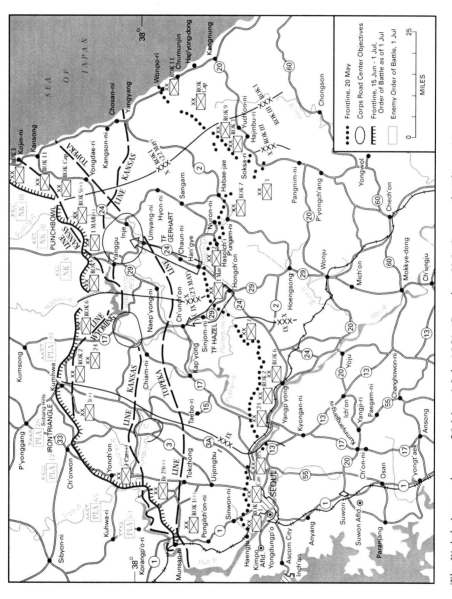

The Eighth Army advance, 20 May–1 July 1951. (Based on U.S. Center of Military History map.)

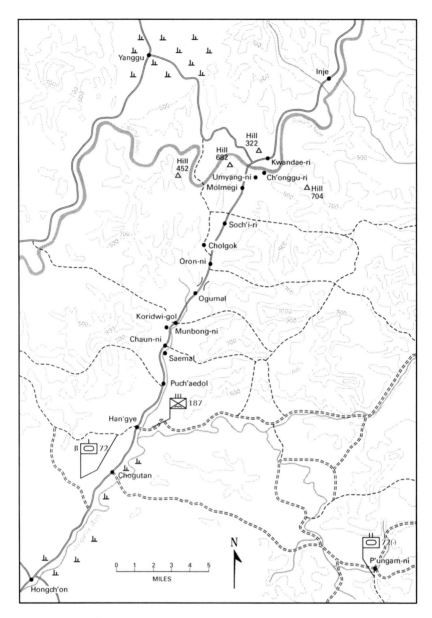

Task Force Gerhart. (Original map by author, based on maps in CMH manuscript, U.S. Army, and in Russell A. Gugeler, "Task Force Gerhardt," in *Combat Actions in Korea*, p. 184.)

Chogutan, arriving there at 1020 hours. However, Gerhardt said that because Company B had just come out of the line, it would remain at Chogutan and not be used until the next day. Ross was ordered to report to Han'gye for instructions.

At the midnight briefing, Company B, 72d Tank Battalion, was instructed to move to Han'gye by 0730 hours, 24 May, and to take up indirect firing positions in support of the 187th Abn RCT. By 0700 hours, Company B had moved into the indirect firing positions and had tied in with the artillery. . . .[4]

MAJ. JAMES H. SPANN, S-3, 72D TANK BATTALION: At 0600, 24 May 1951, Lt. Col. Elbridge Brubaker, commanding officer, 72d Tank Battalion, received a telephone call from the G-3, 2d Infantry Division, warning the 72d Tank Battalion that it might be part of a new task force being formed. At 0940, a telephone call from the 2d Division G-3 confirmed the alert—the 72d Tank Battalion (minus Company A) was to be attached to a task force from the 187th Airborne Regimental Combat Team. Maj. Spann remarked that he didn't know whether Brubaker or the commanding officer of the 187th RCT was in charge at the time. "It was such a 'hurry-hurry' detail that Colonel Brubaker and I flew to the 187th CP to meet the division G-3 and a representative from the 187th," Spann said.

The two men left the 72d Tank Battalion airstrip about 0945 hours and landed in the vicinity of Han'gye about 1030 hours. From there they went by jeep to the headquarters of the 187th RCT. When the two men arrived at 1100 hours, they met Col. George H. Gerhart, executive officer, 187th RCT; the S-3, 187th Abn RCT; and the G-3, 2d Infantry Division, Lt. Col. Hutchin [Claire E. Hutchin Jr., later Lt. Gen.]. The division G-3 stated that a task force was to be formed consisting of one battalion of infantry, at least two tank companies, an engineer company, and an intelligence and reconnaissance (I&R) platoon. At the time Hutchins did not state, in Spann's presence, who would be in charge of the task force. He did say that the task force was to move northward as soon as possible along the Han'gye–Inje axis to seize a bridgehead at the Soyang River. A force consisting of a platoon of tanks, an engineer platoon, and an I&R platoon was to act as a covering force for the task force.

After the meeting, Spann, Gerhart, and Brubaker got into a jeep with the idea of going to a forward OP to talk with the commanding general of the 187th Abn RCT, Brig. Gen. Frank Bowen. The men went to the general vicinity of Puch'aedol, but were unable to find the general or the forward OP. The men then returned to the 187th's CP at Han'gye.[5]

Upon return to the CP of the 187th RCT, Brubaker informed Capt. Ross, of Company B, which was positioned nearby, of the mission. Ross explains.

The company remained in position until 1100 hours [24 May] without firing a round. At that time, Lt. Col. Elbridge Brubaker, commanding officer, 72d Tank Battalion, came to the company and told Ross to prepare to move forward, that a task force was being organized. He further stated that Col. Gerhart would be in command, and that the task force would move northward at 1200 hours. Ross immediately reported to the 187th RCT CP and stayed there until noon. The company remained in position.[6]

Meanwhile, the remainder of the 72d Tank Battalion, except for Company A, which was unavailable and operating in another corps sector, began to move forward from its position some twenty miles southeast of Han'gye and on the far side of a difficult pass. Capt. W. J. Richard, S-2, 72d Tank Battalion, provides more information about the movement of the rest of the 72d Tank Battalion to Han'gye.

Around 0900–1000 hours, 24 May 1951, Lt. Col. Elbridge Brubaker, commanding officer, 72d Tank Battalion, informed the battalion staff that the battalion was going on another task force. The destination and composition were unknown at the time. Brubaker said that he was going to fly to Han'gye to the CP of the 187th Airborne Regimental Combat Team, and for the rest of the battalion to join him there as soon as possible. The column moved out at approximately 1030 hours from P'ungam-ni and arrived at Han'gye at 1350 hours. Brubaker met the column and said it was moving out in thirty minutes and that the S-2, S-3, and battalion executive officer were to accompany him. The remainder of the battalion was to stay at Han'gye. Even then, Brubaker did not know the exact composition of Task Force Gerhart. He said that as far as he knew, it was supposed to be elements of the 187th Abn RCT and a company of tanks. The destination was the Soyang River.[7]

Soon after 1200 hours, Col. Gerhart assembled his commanders and issued orders. Capt. Ross describes the situation.

Shortly after noon, Ross was ordered to send one platoon forward to Puch'aedol—the task force's IP [initial point from which it would start]. The 3d Platoon, which was to be the lead element of the task force, moved forward and assembled in the riverbed to the west of the village. The weather was clear and warm, and the rice paddies were wet but firm. After the 3d Platoon moved forward, Ross ordered the other three firing platoons out of their indirect firing positions into the riverbed behind the 3d Platoon—the platoons lined up in the order 3d, 1st, 2d, and 4th. Orders evidently had been given at the 187th Abn RCT for the other units of the task force to assemble at the IP, because vehicles from the engineers, medics, infantry, and artillery began to assemble off the road in the sandy and rocky portions of the riverbed.

About 1215, Col. Gerhart assembled the unit commanders together in the riverbed and gave the following orders:

(1) The mission of the task force was to secure crossings of the Soyang River and to cover by fire the enemy escape routes through Inje.
(2) Air support could be had simply by firing WP at any target.
(3) Enemy positions south of Cholgok had to be cleared to enable the 1st U.S. Marine Division to go up the draw to the northeast and then angle north to seize the high ground.
(4) A Marine regiment was to move to the left of the task force, but no support would be on the right.
(5) The advance guard was to consist of a rifle company, an engineer company, a machine gun platoon, a section of 81mm mortars, and a platoon of tanks.
(6) The task force was to move out as rapidly as possible.

Immediately after the briefing, Ross went over to his jeep and briefed his platoon leaders. Company B had the 3d Platoon with the point. The main body was to be the 1st Platoon, Company B, 72d Tank Battalion; Company E, 187th Abn RCT; command group; a battery of artillery; 2d Platoon, Company B, 72d Tank Battalion; Company B, 64th Tank Battalion; flak wagons; engineer company; Company G, 187th Abn RCT; and the 4th Platoon, Company B, 72d Tank Battalion. The platoon leaders, after the briefing, immediately contacted the other unit commanders to coordinate movement.[8]

Maj. Spann, S-3, 72d Tank Battalion, had remained at the CP of the 187th Airborne RCT to help coordinate the operation. He explains some of the problems in getting the task force organized.

About 1330, Brubaker told Maj. Spann to remain at the 187th's CP as a liaison and to pick up the 72d Tank Battalion's column as it came by. Company B, 72d Tank Battalion, and Company B, 64th Tank Battalion, were already in the general vicinity of Han'gye and had been attached to the 187th Abn RCT. Brubaker and Spann had no transportation and no means of communication with the tank column. The 72d Tank Battalion headquarters never arrived until 1400 hours, and were supposed to jump off at 1200 hours. The 72d Tank Battalion headquarters was on the other side of the pass at P'ungam-ni, and it took five hours to get to Han'gye. The telephone call at 0940 told the battalion to move.

Just then, Maj. Charles A. Newman, executive officer, 72d Tank Battalion, came forward with two recon jeeps. Newman had been surveying the damage done in the CCF attack of 18 May. Spann kept one jeep with him, and Brubaker and Newman went forward with the other. Before leaving, Brubaker told Newman, "Newman, you come with me. I'll want you to organize the covering force, and you'll probably have to go with it."

It appeared to Spann at the time that the 187th Abn RCT took no initiative to organize the task force or covering force, and Brubaker had to take it upon himself to do it.[9]

Maj. Charles A. Newman, executive officer, 72d Tank Battalion, finally arrived on the scene. He describes his actions on the morning of 24 May and provides information on the formation of the task force and his personal task of leading the point of Task Force Gerhart.

At 0530, 24 May 1951, Maj. Charles A. Newman went to the vicinity of Saemal to inspect the wreckage of tanks and wheeled vehicles of the 72d Tank Battalion destroyed on 18 May. While he was in the vicinity, Task Force Gerhart was formed. The task force was composed of the 2d Battalion, 187th Airborne Regimental Combat Team; Reconnaissance Platoon, 187th Abn RCT; Company B, 72d Tank Battalion; Company B, 64th Tank Battalion; one company 187th Airborne RCT Engineers (minus); four sections of flak wagons, 82d AAA Battalion; and one battery, 674th Abn Field Artillery Battalion. . . .

About 1300, 24 May, Newman was informed that he was to be in command of the point of Task Force Gerhart in the absence of Maj. George Von Halban, 72d Tank Battalion. The point was to consist of the 3d Platoon, Company B, 72d Tank Battalion; Recon Platoon, 187th Abn RCT; and an engineer platoon, 187th Abn RCT. The advance guard of Task Force Gerhart was composed of Company I, 187th Abn RCT, and Company B (minus), 72d Tank Battalion. The point was to be followed as quickly as possible by the remainder of the task force at a five-minute interval. The weather was warm and clear, affording good visibility. The mission of Task Force Gerhart was twofold: first, to reach the Soyang River as quickly as possible; and second, to destroy as many enemy as possible.

Newman accompanied Lt. Col. Elbridge L. Brubaker, commanding officer, 72d Tank Battalion, to the briefing of Col. George H. Gerhart, executive officer, 187th Airborne Regimental Combat Team. At the meeting Gerhart wanted to know where Maj. Von Halban was, and when told he would be late in arriving, asked if someone else could take the point. Brubaker was granted permission to use Newman. Gerhart then instructed Newman to move northward up the road slowly, with the engineer platoon in front probing for mines. He also instructed him to stop every 2,000 yards and report the situation.

The 3d Platoon consisted of four M4A3E8 medium tanks, each with a 76mm cannon, a .30 caliber co-axial machine gun, and a turret .50 caliber machine gun. The tanks carried the equivalent of two basic loads of ammunition. The Recon Platoon, 187th Abn RCT, consisted of twelve men mounted in two jeeps, each having a mounted .30 caliber machine gun. The order of march for the point was two tanks, two jeeps, two tanks, and two 2½-ton trucks carrying the engineer platoon.

At 1415, the point passed through elements of the U.S. Marines near Koridwi-gol; the Marines had an advance outpost consisting of a BAR and a light machine gun. As the point was passing through Chaun-ni, Newman saw the recon and engineer platoons sitting by the side of the road. "I simply latched on to them," Newman said.

When the point reached the trail junction at Ogumal [north of Koridwi-gol], Newman halted the vehicles to try to coordinate the radio nets of the recon and tank platoons. Just then, a helicopter bearing Lt. Gen. Edward A. Almond, commanding general, X Corps, landed beside the tanks. Newman reported to the general, and when asked why the tanks were halted, he explained that he was trying to establish radio communications. Almond said, "I don't give a god damn about communications. Get those god damn tanks on the road and keep going until you hit a mine. I want you to keep them going at twenty miles per hour." As a result, Newman moved out at the greatest speed possible.[10]

M. Sgt. (later 2d Lt.) Edwell D. Clements, platoon sergeant, 3d Platoon, Company B, 72d Tank Battalion, provides additional information about the movement of the point and the visit of General Almond.

At 1100, 24 May 1951, Capt. (now Maj.) William E. Ross, commander, Company B, 72d Tank Battalion, briefed the 3d Platoon and said that it was to be the point of Task Force Gerhart. The platoon was to move at 1230 with the mission of protecting engineers as they probed for mines northward along the Han'gye–Inje MSR. At the time, Company B was in an assembly area below Puch'aedol. The 187th Airborne Regimental Combat Team was in the vicinity of [Puch'aedol] when Col. Gerhart gave the order to move out. Prior to moving, Gerhart was upset that Maj. Von Halban was not present to take charge of the point for the task force.

At the time of the action, the 3d Platoon had only four M4A6 medium tanks armed with 76mm cannon, co-axial .30 caliber machine guns, and a .50 [caliber] machine gun mounted in the turret. The weather was warm and clear, and Clements remarked, "I was sweating up a storm." The platoon moved out in the order of the platoon leader, 1st Lt. Douglas L. Gardiner, Maj. Charles A. Newman, Clements, and SFC Michael R. Kuhel. As it passed through Chaun-ni, it was joined by an engineer platoon and an I&R (Intelligence and Reconnaissance) Platoon from the 187th Abn RCT. The Reconnaissance Platoon was mounted in three jeeps armed with mounted .30 caliber machine guns. About ten to twelve men were in the jeeps. The engineers were in two 2½-ton trucks at the rear of the column. The column moved out with two tanks, one jeep, two tanks, one jeep, two 2½-ton trucks, and a jeep.

The tanks went northward to the fork in the road [near Koridwi-gol], where the platoon halted while the engineers probed the road for mines. Just then a helicopter descended, and Lt. Gen. Edward A. Almond came over and wanted to know what the slow-down was. Newman said the minesweepers were out and that the column was preparing to move out. "General Almond was cussing like a god damn sailor and shaking his swagger stick," Clements said. "You'll go down the road, and the hell with the mines," Almond said. Newman then ordered the column to move out in 5th gear (22 mph). The column started rolling about 1400.[11]

Back at the CP of the 187th Airborne RCT, Maj. Spann met the leading elements of the 72d Tank Battalion as they began to arrive. He describes the visit of General Almond to the CP.

Maj. Spann remained at the 187th CP until 1430. At that time the Headquarters Company and Recon Platoon came by under the command of Maj. George Von Halban. Spann briefed Von Halban and told him [Lt.] Col. Brubaker had directed that he (Von Halban) take the battalion CP to Puch'aedol and to contact Brubaker in the same vicinity. Spann kept the 72d Tank Battalion's communications officer with him to establish the communications network between the various units of the task force.

While Spann was discussing the communications in front of the

187th's CP, a helicopter descended and out stepped Lt. Gen. Edward A. Almond, commanding general, X Corps. Spann reported to the general, and he asked the major what organization was this. When told he asked, "Why aren't the tanks moving?" Spann replied that they were actually in the process of moving; whereupon Almond said they were all in a field to the north and that none were moving. Maj. Spann told the interviewer, "I had no reply to this." He stated that the general seemed disturbed about something—"He seemed emotionally upset." Almond asked Spann for his commanding officer's name. When told, he replied, "Tell Brubaker to get that god damn tank column moving whether they got infantry support or not." Just then the S-3, 187th RCT, came out, and Spann left to go forward to locate Brubaker to deliver General Almond's message. He went to Puch'aedol and ran into Von Halban and Capt. Richard and told them the general's message; he then tried to locate Brubaker at Munbong-ni, about 5,000 yards farther north. Spann decided to return and check the tanks along the riverbed. He returned to Company G, 187th RCT, and was told by a GI that some tanks had passed. Spann thought the covering force had gone out.

As Spann started north through Chaun-ni again, an enemy mortar barrage (approximately twenty-five rounds of 82mm mortar fire) fell on the road and wounded several men. Spann bore off to the left, followed the creek bed, and saw tanks from the 1st Marine Division. He finally contacted Brubaker on the radio and passed on the message from General Almond. At the same time, Spann saw Company B, 72d Tank Battalion, coming up the creek bed (about 1530 hours) onto the road at Chaun-ni. Brubaker had told Newman that Von Halban would command the covering force, but when Von Halban was slow in coming, Brubaker told Newman that he would have to take it. In the vicinity of Chaun-ni, Lt. Gen. Almond, Maj. Gen. Clark L. Ruffner, commander general, 2d Infantry Division, and Brubaker met. Brubaker was relieved and Von Halban took command.

Von Halban instructed Spann to get the tanks moving—the tanks had been waiting for the infantry to come up. Company B, 72d Tank Battalion, moved out, but Company B, 64th Tank Bat-

talion, was lagging, so Spann rode with its tanks. The main part of
Task Force Gerhart left Chaun-ni at 1530–1600.[12]

*Capt. Ross, commander, Company B, 72d Tank Battalion, and
Capt. Richard, S-2, 72d Tank Battalion, provide more information
about the attempts to get the task force moving and the relief of Lt.
Col. Brubaker.*

CAPT. ROSS: Lt. Fife came up to Ross's tank and informed him
that General Almond was in the area. Ross immediately informed
Brig. Gen. Frank Bowen, commanding general, 187th Abn RCT,
and he went to find General Almond. During this time the entire
column was moving out on the road. Col. Gerhart came rushing up
to Ross and told him to disregard the organization of Task Force
Gerhart and to get the tanks on the road and to the Soyang River as
fast as possible. This was impossible to do immediately because the
tank platoons had occupied their relative positions in the column
and were jammed in the riverbed or on the road. The lead tank
platoon was well on its way to the river.

After much jockeying around and getting the wheeled vehicles
out of the way, the 1st Platoon was sent alone to join up with the
lead (3d) platoon. As the 1st Platoon moved out, Ross received a
message from the 3d Platoon stating that they had cleared Oron-ni
and were still moving forward. Fifteen minutes later, the 2d and 4th
Platoons were also dispatched.

As Ross went forward with the 2d Platoon through Chaun-ni,
Maj. Von Halban stopped Ross's jeep to question him about the
disposition of Company B, 72d Tank Battalion. When Ross stopped,
the two tank platoons passed by. General Almond came up in a jeep
and asked Ross where his tanks were. When told they were on the
way to the river, the General wanted to know whose tanks were in
the flats to the west (Saemal). He was referring to Company B, 64th
Tank Battalion. Ross told him who they were, and Almond then
instructed Ross to bring [Lt.] Col. Brubaker and General Ruffner,
who were in the area, to his jeep. After doing this, Ross then asked
permission of Von Halban to go forward with his company. Von
Halban told him to remain until he saw the results of the conference

between Ruffner, Brubaker, and Almond. The remainder of the wheeled column was passing by. Von Halban came over to Ross and told him that he (Von Halban) was now in command of the 72d Tank Battalion, and General Almond had ordered them to rejoin the head of the column.[13]

CAPT. RICHARD: The column moved out, and Richard was in a jeep behind [Lt.] Col. Brubaker. After going approximately 300 yards the column halted, and Richard was told by Brubaker it was waiting for Company B, 64th Tank Battalion. Brubaker then sent Richard to contact the commanding officer, Company B, 64th Tank Battalion, and to have the company move out. The commanding officer was to report to Maj. James H. Spann at the head of the column.

In the meanwhile, the column moved out, and Richard returned to the old CP area where he met Brubaker. Brubaker informed him that General Almond or General Ruffner had relieved him, and that Richard was to go help Von Halban and Spann.[14]

SFC Glen M. Poppler, tank commander, 2d Platoon, Company B, 72d Tank Battalion, was nearby when Lt. Col. Brubaker was relieved. He provides additional details of the situation.

About 1100, Lt. Col. Elbridge Brubaker, commanding officer, 72d Tank Battalion, and Maj. Von Halban, executive officer, came up to Company B and ordered us to spearhead for the 187th Abn RCT. At the time, Brubaker did not know where they were going, nor how they were going. He did say that they were to go to the Soyang River at the 38th parallel to seize a crossing.

The company remained in position until the 3d Platoon moved out as a spearhead to be followed by the 2d Platoon at an interval of thirty minutes. The men knew they were hitting behind the enemy's front lines because air and Marine reports indicated several thousand enemy to the north. The weather was clear and fairly warm.

When the 3d Platoon moved out, four to five friendly vehicles from other units were in the area. The remainder of the company ate chow and checked the ammunition supply. Each tank carried a basic load of twenty-four boxes of .30 caliber machine gun, six boxes of .50 caliber machine gun, and seventy-one rounds of 76mm cannon ammunition. In addition to this, each tank had twenty-five boxes of extra .50 caliber and twenty-five boxes of .30 caliber ammunition.

Thirty minutes later, the 2d Platoon moved to an assembly area three to five hundred yards south of Saemal. An infantry company from the 187th Abn RCT was in the area at the time. As the platoon was sitting there in a column, Lt. Gen. Edward A. Almond, commanding general, X Corps, came over in a helicopter, landed, and instructed the tanks to move out. [Lt.] Col. Brubaker came up, and Sgt. Poppler heard General Almond relieve him and place Maj. George Von Halban in command of the 72d Tank Battalion. The officers in the area had been given orders, but time did not permit the tank commanders to be informed. About 1330, the tanks pulled out and soon went to 5th gear.[15]

Maj. Newman, with the 3d Platoon at the point of Task Force Gerhart, radioed back to Capt. Ross to coordinate the advance. Newman describes the conversation and the actions of the 3d Platoon after General Almond left them.

When Newman crossed the IP he radioed back to Capt. William E. Ross (now major) and told him to move the rest of Company B, 72d Tank Battalion, on the road and to move northward immediately. "Forget the five-minute interval," Newman said. Ross replied, "I will get it on the road as soon as I can; I've got to clear the vehicles off the road." The road leading to the line of departure (LD) was clogged with supply vehicles, Brockway [tactical bridge] Engineer trucks, and other miscellaneous vehicles. When Ross said this, Newman told him that he was going on and for him to follow as quickly as possible.

The vehicles went approximately one mile [north of Koridwigol] and reached a blown bridge. . . . As the lead tank approached within fifty yards of the bridge, they spotted two men with a 3.5 bazooka at the left-hand corner of the structure. When the tanks rolled forward, the men dropped the weapon and ran to the northwest up the riverbed. The lead tank, commanded by 1st Lt. Douglas L. Gardiner, opened fire on them with the .50 caliber machine gun and killed both. As soon as the tank opened fire, ineffective small arms fire came from an estimated enemy platoon in the valley north of the bridge. Eight or ten were on the high ground (fifty feet) to the right. Newman said, "The fire was steady but not heavy." Newman was in the second tank; and his tank, together with the one following, returned fire with .50 caliber and .30 caliber machine guns on the enemy to the right. The result of the fire fight was undetermined, but all firing from the right ceased; however, sporadic small arms fire still came down from the valley from the left. All the tanks in the platoon started firing with all crew-served weapons at a range of 300–500 yards, whereupon eight to ten enemy soldiers jumped out of foxholes (which had been dug along the riverbank) and started running up the valley to the northwest. Five or six were killed, but there were three or four that managed to escape up a draw. The entire action lasted about five to six minutes.[16]

M. Sgt. Clements adds additional details about the fight at the blown bridge.

The 3d Platoon first contacted the enemy at a blown bridge. . . . Prior to coming to the bridge, the platoon reconnoitered four or five suspected enemy positions (these were places suitable for bazooka teams or ground that appeared to have been tampered with) by fire. Lt. Gardiner crossed a bypass to the right of the bridge and continued on approximately fifty to sixty yards. "We took a chance by taking the bypass, for they are usually mined," said Clements. SFC Roy Goff, who was in the second tank with Maj. Newman, started to cross the bypass, and an enemy light machine gun (a ground type with a round clip on the top) opened fire from a concealed position beside a lone tree 700 yards to the left front. The machine gun was firing short bursts at the tank. A bullet passed through Goff's mechanic's cap, knocking it to the ground, but he was not injured. Goff immediately returned fire with his turret .50 caliber, and the enemy soldier with the machine gun crossed in front of the tree in the open in an attempt to change positions. All the tanks in the platoon opened fire with .50 calibers and cut him down. This short action lasted about two and a half minutes.[17]

Maj. Newman describes the 3d Platoon's advance north from the blown bridge toward the Soyang River.

When the enemy fire ceased, Newman ordered Lt. Gardiner to move out. As the tanks moved northward, they reconnoitered with .30 and .50 caliber machine guns every bunker, cave, or foxhole that could be seen. (Later a soldier hunting for souvenirs the morning of 25 May found seven dead CCF in a cave that had been fired upon.) Prior to moving out, Newman reported the action to the 72d Tank Battalion and told them the bridge was out but a good bypass was nearby. About 1445, the 3d Platoon continued . . . [about 800 yards north of Ogumal], where Gardiner stopped and reported two houses on a bend commanding the road. Before stopping, the platoon had received occasional ineffective sniper fire from about a dozen scattered CCF on the high ground to the left and right of the road. These would duck into foxholes when .50 caliber fire was placed on them. Newman told Gardiner to fire into the houses. He proceeded to set the houses on fire with .50 caliber machine gun fire, but no one came out of the houses.

The platoon continued on the road to another blown bridge over a small (four-foot) stream . . . [about 500 yards south of Oronni]. Just before reaching the bridge, a culvert was under the road. Gardiner's tank crossed the culvert and went to the bridge, where he started firing all his crew-served weapons to the front, left, and right flanks. He radioed back to Newman, "You'd better watch the draw on the right; there's a lot of stuff in it." Newman then pulled ahead of the culvert where he could see the draw to the right. Before stopping, he saw an estimated CCF platoon run into the culvert from the right of the road. Just then the recon platoon leader, a Lt. Carroll, came up to the Major's tank, and the Major told him to take a section of his platoon up the draw about 100 yards and fire on any enemy contacted. The recon section moved out. During this time, the tanks were getting heavy small arms fire from the draw to the east and from enemy bunkers on the high ground to the right of the road.

Newman had M. Sgt. (now Lt.) Edwell D. Clements cover him and the tank bow gunner, while the two went to investigate the enemy in the culvert. Newman stated that he went down the bank to the mouth of the culvert and motioned the enemy soldiers out, calling "Ittywa" to them. While he was doing this, small arms fire was heard whistling around his head and hitting the ground in the general area. "Three or four kicked dust on us," Newman said. After Newman called to the enemy, they laid their weapons (twenty rifles, burp guns, concussion grenades, and twelve magnetic grenades) in the culvert and came out with hands over their heads. Most of the enemy soldiers wore tan cotton uniforms, and one carried a satchel charge made up of four blocks of dynamite wrapped in a cotton sack with a rope loop and a foot-long fuse attached to it.

Thirty-seven enemy came out of the culvert, and when they did, all firing from the right ceased. In the meantime, the recon section that had gone up the draw to the east was firing violently with its BAR, LMG [light machine gun], and rifles. Carroll ran back out of the draw to the Major's tank and said about a thousand enemy soldiers were escaping eastward out of the draw. Gardiner's tank was too far in front to support the recon section, so Newman turned his tank and the one following and fired approximately ten to fifteen rounds of 76mm HE at a range of 600–800 yards. It was impossible to determine the results. However, all firing from the draw ceased. The PWs were loaded on the engineers' trucks and accompanied the tank platoon northward. The entire fire fight lasted about twenty minutes.

Gardiner then moved to the bridge at Oron-ni but found the bridge unable to support the tank, so he bypassed it to the right. Two enemy soldiers were by the bridge and fired at the tank with burp guns; these were killed with .50 caliber machine gun fire. The tanks did not stop but continued on to Soch'i-ri, where approximately 200 CCF (on the high ground on both sides of the road and back of the village) opened fire with small arms and automatic weapons. The tanks stopped outside of the village and fired at the enemy with .50 and .30 caliber machine guns. The enemy volume of fire was sporadic and ineffective. Thirty prisoners . . . had been taken out of the houses in the village by the recon platoon armed with rifles, burp guns, and grenades. At this point Newman had to make the decision to mount the PWs on the tanks or leave them on the road under guard. He decided on the latter. Seventy PWs were left at Soch'i-ri under four guards from the engineer platoon. The entire action took approximately thirty minutes.

The tanks moved northward and saw several large enemy groups (100–200 each) moving up the draws to the east and west. Pack animals and supply trains were with the troops. The tanks halted and placed .50 caliber and about thirty rounds 76mm HE fire on them at ranges from 500–1,000 yards.

No further resistance was encountered until the tanks approached a slight rise . . . [about two miles north of Soch'i-ri]. There a liaison plane appeared overhead and dropped a message stating that approximately 4,000 enemy soldiers were on the road about one mile to the north [at Molmegi]. The message also stated that two flights of jets were on the way to the target area. The tanks were not receiving fire at this time. The plane cautioned the tanks not to move in until the jets had made their napalm run. The tanks halted, and Gardiner came back to Newman's tank. "What in the hell are we going to do now?" he asked. Newman replied, "We're going to attack the Chinks; we'll run into General Almond if we turn back."

The jets arrived about 1600 and made the napalm drops. The tankers could see the drops; and when the planes came back from strafing runs, the tanks moved on up the road. When the tanks reached [a bridge, about 500 yards north of Molmegi], they caught up with the tail of the retreating enemy column. In the column were pack mules, horses, and captured vehicles (jeeps and 2½-tons) from the 23d Infantry. The tanks opened up with all weapons, and the jets were strafing about 100 yards in front of the tanks. "We could see the jet's fire impact 100 yards in front," Newman stated.

From the bridge . . . to Ch'onggu-ri, approximately a dozen dead mules and horses and 100 enemy soldiers could be seen as a result of the napalming. A jeep and a 2½-ton truck were seen moving to the northwest of Ch'onggu-ri and were destroyed by Gardiner's tank. In the excitement, the gunner fired a round of WP instead of HE, but it served its purpose. About thirty to forty mules containing ammunition and rice were recovered in the area.

Prior to moving up and firing on the tail of the enemy column, the tanks reached a bridge. . . . Newman had one man reconnoiter the bridge to see if it was mined with primer cord. It was not, and the first tank was led across safely. The rest of the vehicles followed. A well-worn bypass to the right of the bridge showed evidence of being mined. (The ground was freshly dug in some places.) New-man relayed a message back to Col. Gerhart that the bypass was probably mined, and that he did not have time to probe it. Later in the evening, after the position was consolidated, a 2½-ton supply truck used the bypass, struck a mine, and was destroyed.[18]

Other members of the 3d Platoon provide additional informa-tion about the advance north toward the Soyang River.

M. SGT. CLEMENTS: Groups from squad to platoon were seen at various places on the high ground on the left and right of the road all the way to the Soyang River. The tanks continued northward along the road approximately one mile [from the blown bridge north of Koridwi-gol], and an enemy group (fifteen to twenty) on the road waved their hands at the tanks in a friendly manner. The lead tank opened fire on them with its co-axial .30 caliber. Just then, other groups (four to five) were seen on the high ground to the left of the road. As the enemy groups dispersed on the road, the groups on the hill appeared in a state of confusion. "They didn't seem to know what way to go. They would scamper one way and another," Cle-ments said. The enemy soldiers were dressed in light brown uni-forms and were wearing new tennis shoes. They were carrying new rifles and burp guns.

The platoon had anticipated trouble at the pass south of Oron-ni, but none developed. However, when the tanks were coming out of the pass, two enemy machine guns opened fire on the column from a knoll fifty to seventy-five feet high on the right overlooking the road. . . . Clements placed .50 caliber fire (approximately two boxes) and three rounds of 76mm HE on each gun; Kuhel's tank also opened fire. The other two tanks had reached Oron-ni and were not in a position to fire on the enemy machine guns. When the machine guns opened fire, the machine gunners on recon jeeps re-turned fire with the riflemen deployed to the flanks of the tanks.

Just then a liaison plane came over and dropped a message stat-ing a large number of enemy troops were on the hill to the right, and [asking] if the tanks wanted an air strike to fire several rounds of WP. The tanks silenced the two machine guns, but did not wait for the air strike and moved on northward.

As Clements's tank and Kuhel's tank started into the village [Oron-ni], they received automatic weapons fire from a draw to the west. "It was a constant pinging hitting the tanks," Clements said. The tanks fired their .50 calibers and six to eight rounds of 76mm HE up the draw. The fire either silenced or neutralized the fire as the enemy fire on the tanks ceased. Four CCF soldiers surrendered by the road and were motioned to the rear. This action took about ten minutes.

The platoon moved northward and saw three or four enemy groups (five to fifteen) on a high ridge to the west of the road. The tanks did not stop, but the tanks' commanders placed bursts of .50 caliber fire on them. When the tank column reached Araedamu-ri [a small village about 1,000 yards north of Oron-ni], it spotted several enemy emplacements on the sides of a small draw to the east. The emplacements were dugouts with covered roofs. . . . Gardiner fired one round of 76mm HE at the emplacements nearest the road, and one CCF came out with his hands over his head. Newman, who had moved to Clements's tank to utilize his radio, instructed Clements to send the men in the next jeep up the high ground to the east to work to the northeast to the emplacements and to neutralize them. Three men armed with BARs and carbines went up the slope under the covering fire of the two rear tanks. The other two tanks had moved on up the road. The three men managed to get to the emplacements and neutralized them with hand grenades.

As the men were working towards the emplacements, Newman got out of the tank to investigate a culvert fifty yards to the front. He took Clements's tommy gun and went down the embankment. As he was doing so, scattered small arms fire was hitting around the tank from the high ground to the left. Clements then told Kuhel to cover the hills to the left while he covered the major. Newman went to the mouth of the culvert and yelled, "Come out," and forty to fifty CCF came out with hands over their heads. Newman then ordered two men from the engineer platoon to guard the prisoners, and he told Clements to radio back for another platoon of tanks. He said the 3d Platoon could not be delayed by taking care of prisoners. This action took about fifteen minutes.

The other two tanks saw the prisoners coming out of the culvert and stopped. When the two remaining tanks rejoined the column, the column moved out. The tankers saw several enemy pack trains of nine to fifteen mules, with two men to a mule, in three or four draws. . . . The pack trains appeared to be moving away from the road. The tanks stopped and fired approximately thirty rounds of 76mm HE and sprayed the enemy with .50 and .30 caliber machine gun fire at ranges of 800 to 1,500 yards.

The tank column continued on to [the] south of Molmegi where four jets came over. The tanks stopped while the planes strafed, napalmed, and rocketed an estimated enemy company on the road to the north. The tanks did not fire for fear of endangering the aircraft. "The planes were so low I could feel the heat of them," Clements said. When the planes stopped, the tanks moved out with all weapons firing.[19]

SFC MICHAEL R. KUHEL, TANK COMMANDER, 3D PLATOON, COMPANY B: About a mile farther, the platoon came upon a group of approximately 100 enemy foot soldiers armed with rifles and burp guns and about twenty pack animals. The enemy group was marching on the left side of the road towards the foothills. When the enemy spotted the tanks, he attempted to climb the hills while others tried to hide behind bushes and trees. The tanks stopped and fired all crew-served weapons at a range of 200 yards. The tank commanders threw hand grenades at enemy bunkers and foxholes about five to ten yards away from the road. The enemy returned light scattered small arms fire from the valley to the left of the MSR. He [the enemy] wore ragged dirty brown uniforms with small peaked caps, and was carrying rifles and grenades. Before the tanks opened fire, the enemy just stood and stared at the tanks as if they didn't know whether they were enemy or friendly. The tanks fired from sixteen to thirty-two rounds of 76mm HE, six boxes of .50 caliber, and about four boxes of .30 caliber. The personnel in the jeeps took cover next to the tanks and threw grenades. A war correspondent accompanying the tanks went up to the front of the column and took pictures.

After ten minutes the tanks moved out again and went about one mile and halted. Seventy-six-mm cannon fire was placed on enemy dugouts on a hill to the northeast although no enemy was seen. A liaison plane flew over and dropped a green smoke bomb and a hand grenade container with a message. One of the men from the recon platoon got the message, which stated if the tanks wanted air support, to fire WP at any suspected targets. The tanks then continued on about another mile and ran into about 200 more enemy foot soldiers with twenty pack animals coming down the road from the northwest. Some of the enemy column was halfway up the hills on the left of the road. The tanks stopped and fired about five to ten rounds of 76mm and eight boxes of .50 caliber per tank at a range of 300–500 yards. When the tanks opened fire, the enemy scattered in all directions and returned ineffective small arms fire. After firing at the enemy column with excellent results (the men estimated over half were killed or wounded) for about ten to fifteen minutes, the tanks moved on again.

The tanks went about one to two miles to the north to a sharp turn in the road where an estimated 300–400 enemy foot soldiers with 30–40 pack animals were marching southward down the MSR and a creek bed to the left. When he [the enemy] saw the tanks, he turned about and ran northward up the road and creek bed. An L5 [liaison] plane came over and marked the road and creek bed with smoke rockets. The tanks stopped, deployed off the road in a skirmish line, and fired five to fifteen rounds of 76mm HE at a range of 300 yards. Four jets came down and strafed 50 yards to the front and left of the tanks. About 600 yards in front, they dropped napalm bombs.

After firing for ten to fifteen minutes, the tanks moved forward again through a small village. The houses were on fire and the planes were still strafing. "We thought the lieutenant was crazy because the planes were strafing right next to the road," the men said. The tanks received scattered small arms and automatic weapons fire from the retreating enemy column. As the tanks passed through the napalmed area, several enemy bodies and pack animals (eight to ten) were seen burning.[20]

Members of the 3d Platoon describe the scene as they arrived at the Soyang River.

M. SGT. CLEMENTS: The tanks continued on to a point over-

looking the Soyang River where fire was placed on an enemy OP on
Hill 322 [about 500 yards north of the river]. Maj. Newman radioed
back to the task force that the tank column had reached the river
and were engaging the enemy by fire. The enemy was attempting to
flee to the northeast and northwest along the road. An enemy group
(fifty to sixty-five) was also moving down the road towards Yanggu.
. . . Three vehicles were also seen moving in the same direction;
these were destroyed by 76mm fire. As the tanks fired across the
river, scattered small arms, automatic weapons, and light machine
gun fire was hitting around the tanks. Enemy troops were on Hill
322 and on the high ground to the southwest—Hill 682. The tanks
also fired up the draws leading to the MSR and on the high ground.[21]

SFC KUHEL: About 1600 to 1700 hours, the tanks took positions on a hill overlooking the Soyang River and saw about 100
scattered enemy soldiers running northward along the road north of
the river. The tanks fired only a few rounds of 76mm fire (1,200-
yard range) because of the shortage of ammunition.[22]

*Meanwhile, Task Force Gerhart advanced north behind the 3d
Platoon. In some sections of the route, the men also had to contend
with scattered Chinese resistance. The 2d Platoon, Company B, 72d
Tank Battalion, was the leading element of the task force. A tank
commander of the 2d Platoon, SFC Poppler, describes the action.*

About 1330 the tanks pulled out and soon went to 5th gear. As
we moved through Chaun-ni, infantrymen could be seen attacking
a hill to the west. Artillery was landing around the hill at the time.
About 300 yards north of Chaun-ni, the 2d Platoon hit about a
company of enemy troops on a small hill 200 yards to the left of the
road. They were in three groups of fifteen walking southward along
the top of the ridgeline. When the enemy soldiers saw the tanks, he
stopped and acted as if he didn't know what was going on. "My
only thought at the time was to wait until they got into a bunch so I
could shoot the hell out of them," Poppler said. The tanks stopped,
and the first three fired on the enemy with three rounds of 76mm
HE per tanks at a 200–300 yard point-blank range.

The other two tanks had traversed their turrets to the right and
were firing .50 calibers into a clump of trees that could conceal an

enemy group. The men in the tanks were laughing and joking at the perplexity of the enemy, and Sgt. Charles Dunnway said, "I wonder what they think we're doing down here?" The tanks fired approximately five minutes and then moved out.

At 1415, after going about 300–400 yards farther, another enemy column (approximately eighty) was observed coming down the valley from the northwest, two abreast. The leader of the enemy group looked up, waved his arms at the tanks, and kept approaching towards them. Poppler was going to open fire, but Sgt. Dunnway in the tank to the front yelled back, "Let's wait until they get real close so none of them will get away." Lt. Fife had been letting the tanks fire as they spotted a target. The enemy approached to within 100–150 yards of the tanks, and the tanks opened fire with all their crew-served weapons. Approximately three to four boxes of .50 caliber, three to four boxes of .30 caliber, and ten rounds of 76mm HE were fired at the enemy. When the first shot landed in the center of the enemy group, pieces of arms and legs were seen flying through the air. The enemy stood and looked dumbfounded; the leader took several steps forward, several backward, and several forward again, as if in a daze. The tanks continued firing for about five minutes, and the entire enemy group was killed or wounded.

About 1430 the tanks continued northward about five to six miles, bypassing small scattered groups (one to three) of enemy soldiers on the high ground on both sides of the road. The tanks did not fire at them. About 1445 to 1500 the tanks passed a group of forty to fifty enemy PWs with a squad of infantry guarding them at Oron-ni. On the way to Oron-ni, the tanks received a few scattered rounds of small arms sniper fire.

About 1505 the tanks moved northward about 15 miles an hour and saw two companies of CCF with ten to fifteen pack mules, moving down the center of a valley northwest of Cholgok [northwest of Oron-ni]. The enemy was in a column two and three abreast and were moving towards the MSR. The tanks halted and fired fifteen rounds of 76mm HE at a range of 900 yards. The tanks remained a few minutes, but could not determine the results. The tankers could hear the 3d Platoon firing to the north, and they thought the 3d Platoon had hit something big. When the 2d Platoon opened fire, the enemy scattered to the hills on both sides of the valley. Poppler thought that by the way the shells were landing, over half the enemy force must have been killed.

As the tanks moved northward again, the men started to worry about how far they had to go before stopping. They knew a column of friendly troops was following them, but they could not be seen.

About 1530–1545, the platoon went through Tari-gol and Nu-rupchong [about a mile north of Soch'i-ri] and saw two or three enemy groups (ten to fifteen) standing in the doorways of the houses or sitting beside them. As the tanks rolled by, the enemy waved the tanks northward, laughing and smiling. The tanks continued by, thinking they were friendly troops, but as they passed them, they knew by the uniforms (blanket-lined brown uniforms with small peaked caps) that they were enemy troops The tanks didn't open fire because they knew infantry was behind and would pick them up.

The tanks moved through the village of Molmegi to the edge of a valley and stopped. The 3d Platoon, Company B, 72d Tank Battalion, was scattered out in the valley to the front and were firing at approximately 200–300 enemy, with pack mules, as they fled in all directions up the valley to the platoon's front. The enemy was firing .51 caliber machine guns, rifles, and automatic weapons at the 3d Platoon.

About fifteen to twenty CCF were up a draw to the northeast, and others were on the skyline on the hills to the east. Three enemy machine gun nests were set up at the base of a hill by the draw covering the road. The enemy started firing at the 2d Platoon in steady bursts, and would rake the armor of the tanks, stop, and begin again. It took about five minutes to destroy the machine gun nests, which were expertly camouflaged between rocks. Poppler's tank knocked out one with two rounds of 76mm HE at a 500-yard range. SFC Richard Kelly, in the fourth tank, knocked out the other two with one round of 76mm HE on each position. The other three tanks fired at other scattered enemy groups with .50s and .30s. The fifth tank fired at four to five enemy on the high ground to the right of the road. The enemy attempted to climb the hills, would stop to fire on the tanks, and then would attempt to climb again. The groups were so scattered that Sgt. Poppler would not attempt to estimate the number. There were no casualties in the 2d Platoon, but a .50 caliber machine gun blew up in the 3d Platoon, wounding one man.

After the three machine guns were knocked out, a Chinese soldier stood up in the draw and started waving a white flag. The tanks stopped firing and motioned him over to their positions. At first the man hesitated, picked up his gun, but then came over. He laid his gun beside the tank, and in perfect English asked what the tankers wanted him to do. Poppler told him to mount the deck of the tank and then asked him if any more enemy were in the draw. He said there were but they were scared to come in. Poppler gave the Chinese soldier some candy and told him to ask the others to surrender. The Chinese yelled over and said that he would go over and bring them in. He went out and came back with eleven others. All of the PWs were then mounted on the rear decks of the tanks.

In the meantime, the 3d Platoon had scattered out on the hills to the left of the road, and the recon platoon came over and took charge of the 2d Platoon's prisoners. As the 2d Platoon started to move northward again, the PW said a squad of CCF with a light machine gun was hiding in a culvert 200–300 yards farther up the road. He accompanied the infantry soldiers to the culvert and persuaded the enemy squad to surrender. They pushed the machine gun out, and seventeen came out of the culvert with hands over their heads.

The 2d Platoon moved off the road into the rice paddies, formed a skirmish line, and moved up the valley about 1,000 yards, where it halted and fired the co-axial .30 caliber machine guns at the hills and valley to the north and west. Small enemy groups (three to four) were running along the slopes of the high ground, and others jumped out of the grass in the valley and tried to run. About 1730–1800 approximately ten rounds of enemy 82mm mortar fire came in on the left of the road near the 64th Tank Battalion. The fire was scattered and ineffective. The tanks remained in position and fired until about 1930 to 2000 hours. In the meanwhile, the remainder of Task Force Gerhart came into the area about 1730 to 1800 hours.[23]

Officers of the 72d Tank Battalion describe the progress of Task Force Gerhart moving up behind the 2d Platoon.

CAPT. ROSS, COMMANDER, COMPANY B: Ross moved into the column and followed along until it stopped . . . [near Koridwi-gol]. The captain dismounted, went forward, and found someone at the head of the column had been hit by sniper fire and that the drivers of the lead vehicles had gotten out and were lying in the ditches bordering the road. No fire was coming in on the column at the time, and Ross ordered the men back into the vehicles. The column moved out immediately.

Ross remained where he was waiting for his jeep to come up, but General Ruffner came by and ordered Ross to ride with him. The column moved to the northeast about two miles and stopped again. Ross dismounted and found that one man had been killed and another wounded by small arms fire coming from the high ground to the northeast. Some of the riflemen in the lead vehicles were returning rifle fire, but Ross was unable to determine the number of enemy. The captain found Lt. Col. Conner, 2d Battalion, 187th Abn RCT, and a company commander lying in a culvert beside the road. Ross told them that General Ruffner wanted the column to move out as rapidly as possible.

The M46 tanks from Company B, 64th Tank Battalion, had moved on and were moving through the pass south of Oron-ni very slowly; consequently, the wheeled vehicles had to set the same pace. The column again stopped at Oron-ni. Upon investigating, Ross found a tank had broken through a culvert, necessitating the other tanks to bypass to the left about fifteen to twenty yards. Small arms fire was coming into the column from a hill to the left, and riflemen were in the ditches returning fire. Ross could not see the enemy. A group of seventy PWs guarded by two Americans were near a house by the side of the road. Scattered groups of three to four CCF came into the village with hands over their heads.

General Ruffner came up in his jeep and ordered the men to mount up and move out. By this time, the tanks from the 64th Tank Battalion were returning the enemy fire. Ross mounted the lead vehicle—¼-ton jeep of the mortar platoon, 2d Battalion, 187th Abn RCT—and rode the rest of the way to Umyang-ni, arriving about 1730 hours. Ross then dispatched the wheeled vehicles to the left and right off the road and asked Conner for infantry protection for the tanks. From Oron-ni to Tari-gol, the column received sporadic small arms fire. Ross saw ten to fifteen horses and mules running loose around the foothills in several places.[24]

MAJ. SPANN, S-3, 72D TANK BATTALION: Spann saw several small enemy groups (ten to fifteen), but .50 and .30 caliber machine guns and 90mm fire neutralized the enemy fire and kept the column moving. When the column would run on a pocket of enemy, it stopped three to four minutes. One tank commander said he knocked out an enemy self-propelled weapon, but Spann never saw it. The tankers wanted to stop and fire at the enemy, but Spann would dismount, get the infantry back on the trucks and tanks, and would get the column moving. Spann overheard General Bowen say it was not his policy to have the infantry ride the tanks; however, some rode the tanks. "If the fire had been intense, I wouldn't have gotten out of the tank," Spann said. He saw several (ten) infantry casualties fall from the tanks.

The column passed by the prisoners left by Maj. Newman, and Col. Gerhart ordered them to stay there until he sent back two trucks. Spann believed that the trucks were sent back but couldn't locate the CCF prisoners.

The column arrived at the Soyang River about 1700 hours and was greeted by the covering force. The tanks were placed in a perimeter with the infantry, and an arrangement was made to mutually support the other by fire. That night there was a little small arms fire, but Maj. Spann "thought some people were trigger happy."[25]

Maj. Newman and other members of 72d Tank Battalion describe the events after the arrival at the Soyang River and during the unsettled night.

MAJ. NEWMAN, EXECUTIVE OFFICER: About 1715, the remainder of Company B, 72d Tank Battalion, and Task Force Gerhart joined the 3d Platoon. A gap of six to eight miles had existed between the point and the main body due to the inability of getting the tanks on the road at the line of departure (LD).

Newman dismounted north of the bridge and sent the 3d Platoon, Company B, to a small cut and on towards the Soyang River following the retreating enemy column. The 2d Platoon, Company

B, commanded by 1st Lt. Thomas W. Fife, was sent to the high ground on the right to fire at any enemy on the north and south banks of the river. The enemy column succeeded in fording the river . . . [north of Ch'onggu-ri] and had taken his dead with him. These were buried [and later found] in mass graves . . . [just north of the river]. Fife's platoon fired at the retreating enemy soldiers moving northward towards Inje. The tanks had been ordered to halt at the river and therefore did not attempt to cross it. Gardiner's platoon took blocking positions across the valley . . . and Fife's platoon remained on the high ground where the river was under complete observation.

At about 1800, approximately thirty rounds each of 81mm mortar and 75mm or 105mm howitzer came into the area. The fire was ineffective and scattered and caused no tank casualties. All firing ceased about 1815.[26]

M. SGT. CLEMENTS, 3D PLATOON, COMPANY B: During this time [soon after arrival], an American PW from the 38th Infantry with a young Chinese came up to the tanks and said he had escaped from a large Chinese force. At this time, a few rounds of enemy mortar fire came into the area.[27]

SFC KUHEL, 3D PLATOON, COMPANY B: About 1715 hours the remainder of Company B joined the 3d Platoon on the hill and fired on the high ground to the left. The 3d Platoon was then ordered around the road to the north to fire on any enemy that could be seen. An escaped American prisoner and a Chinese walked up to SFC Kuhel's tank and wanted in. The American said that he had hid out in the hills for eight days and had been aided by the Chinese. Just then Maj. Newman came over and took charge of the two men.

Sgt. Kenderish spotted a jeep going up the road to the northwest on the other side of the river (the tanks were stopped at this time), and he asked Sgt. Goff if any friendly jeeps were in the area. Goff had to ask Clements before he found out they were enemy vehicles. All the tanks then opened up with their .50 caliber machine guns with undetermined results. Three more jeeps went up the road in the same direction and the tanks placed fire on them, but the jeeps got away.

Sgt. Clements saw a dust cloud about 800 yards to 1,000 yards to the west and south of the river, and the platoon fired five rounds of 76mm HE, with undetermined results. Small scattered groups (three to four) of enemy soldiers were seen on the high ground to the west. Fifty-caliber and .30 caliber fire was placed on them with undetermined results. About 1730 the 3d Platoon pulled to the rear and set up a perimeter on the left side of the road. About 1830–1900, the 2d Platoon, Company B, was sent to get a group of about seventy PWs that were under guard at Oron-ni; the platoon ran into enemy .51 caliber fire and had to return. There was no contact in the 3d Platoon sector the rest of the night. However, approximately fifty rounds of 120mm mortar fire came in on the right side of the road, but none hit in Company B's area.[28]

SFC POPPLER, 2D PLATOON, COMPANY B: About 2000 the 2d Platoon moved southward about 1,500 yards and went into a perimeter guarding to the south and west. Sgt. Poppler scanned the hills to the right of the road with his binoculars and saw two radios with antennas mounted on top of pillboxes on Hill 704 [2,200 yards east of the road and about 2,000 yards south of the Soyang River]. About twenty-five to thirty enemy soldiers were observed walking around the pillboxes. Sgt. Poppler asked M. Sgt. John Sushinko, Platoon Sergeant, 2d Platoon, whether to fire on them or not. At the time Lt. Fife [leader, 2d Platoon] was at an officers' meeting 100 yards away from the tanks. Sushinko told Poppler to go over and ask Fife what to do. As Poppler went over, a colonel asked him what he wanted; he told him about the radio stations, and after the colonel observed them through binoculars, he ordered Poppler to go over to the 64th Tank Battalion and direct fire on the enemy.

Poppler went over and showed the tankers the target. He had them fire one round of 90mm at 2,000 yards, which was over; the next one was fired at 1,600 yards and was short; the next one at 1,800 yards hit the center of the pillbox. Three direct hits were made on the other two pillboxes.

Later that evening, the tanks resupplied with ammunition and gas from the trucks in the column. About 2300 an estimated enemy squad attempted to steal some trip flares that had been rigged about fifty yards in front of the tanks. However, one was set off, revealing seven enemy soldiers. An infantry outpost with a .50 caliber machine gun that was located twenty yards in front of the tanks opened fire. The fire could be seen hitting among the enemy soldiers, which were lying prone upon the ground. The infantry outpost went out and captured the seven men. The rest of the night was quiet.

Sgt. Poppler stated that on this operation, the tankers were glad to get to go without infantry on the decks. "The enemy doesn't have anything to hurt a tank at long range, but they can play hell with the infantry."[29]

Capt. Ross, commander, Company B: During the night of 24 May, two jeeps were sent to the rear, and both were ambushed with one man being killed [PFC Irvin A. Rackley].[30] The 1st Platoon, 23d Infantry Tank Company, tried to reach them from the south and lost two tanks to bazooka fire.[31]

Officers of the 72d Tank Battalion describe the actions on the following day, 25 May, and provide an assessment of the operations of Task Force Gerhart.

Maj. Spann, S-3, 72d Tank Battalion: On the morning of 25 May, the tanks were sent across the river and went northeast two or three miles where they ran into some mortar fire and small arms fire. The tanks returned to Umyang-ni. At noon 25 May Task Force Gerhart was dissolved, and all units in it joined Task Force Baker.[32]

Spann said if a more complete order had been given at the beginning of the operation, and the job had been given to a specific commander, there would have been less confusion. As it was, no one was sure who was in command. . . . If the task force had been told the situation to the north and that this was an exploitation phase, the task force could have gone farther and accomplished more.[33]

Maj. Newman, executive officer, 72d Tank Battalion: On 25 May Task Force Gerhart remained in the vicinity of Umyang-ni unable to move for lack of supplies. Lt. Gardiner's platoon expended all of its .50 caliber ammunition and had six rounds of HE and two boxes of .30 caliber left. About dusk, 25 May, twenty-four planes dropped twenty-four drums of gasoline for two tank companies (it takes that much for one tank company) and 90mm ammunition instead of 76mm ammunition. (Company B, 64th Tank Battalion, had M46 tanks with 90mm cannons, but fired very little.)

Newman [attributes] the success of this operation to the fact that the tanks and wheeled vehicles kept constantly on the move. The speed with which the tanks moved up the road is worthy of note because it threw the CCF into a total state of confusion. "They went to pieces after we had gone the first three or four miles," Newman said. Newman was positive that the sudden tank march disrupted the enemy's communications. This was apparent because of the lack of control exercised by the enemy over his men.[34]

In his 1954 book, Combat Actions in Korea, *the military historian Capt. Russell A. Gugeler studied the advance of Task Force Gerhart to the Soyang River on 24 May. He assessed the operation as successful, but for reasons other than those cited by Maj. Newman. Gugeler explains.*

Like a boxer who tries to hit his opponent when he has him off balance, the military commander times his counterpunches. When the enemy staggers, careful planning of time and space factors to insure coordination may be discarded in favor of rapid action. This narrative [the story of Task Force Gerhart] shows that a weak but timely jab at a faltering enemy is often effective, perhaps more so than a later, more powerful blow at a prepared opponent. "Strike while the iron is hot" refers to the blacksmith's work, but it applies equally well to the battlefield.

Strict observance of the rules of tactics in all cases is neither recommended nor advised. However, anyone who knowingly violates the rules must be ready to accept responsibility for his actions. If a deliberate violation brings about a victory, he will be a hero. If such violation results in a fiasco, he must be prepared to be the goat.

When General Almond, through the 2d Division, gave the 187th RCT a task force mission, he gave it the responsibility for carrying out a job. When he ordered the point of the task force to move without the main body, he took upon himself the responsibility of the task force commander for the execution of his mission. Such an action is justified only when a superior commander has knowledge of the situation unknown to his task force commander and/or when time will not permit the use of regular channels—apparently true in this case. The personal intercession of General Almond is an example of positive leadership at a critical point by a senior commander.

The very existence of armored units can be justified only because of their superior cross-country mobility and their greater shock effect. When an armored unit is assigned a role that takes advantage of both these characteristics, it is being properly employed. When an armored advance guard is bold and aggressive, it is working as an advance guard should.[35]

On 24 May, the same day as Task Force Gerhart moved north, the U.S. IX Corps to the west also launched an armored counterattack to seize key terrain to disrupt the Chinese withdrawal.

Chapter 13

TASK FORCE HAZEL

7th Reconnaissance Company, 24–25 May 1951

To the west in the U.S. I and IX Corps sectors, the Chinese had sought to hold UN forces in place with limited attacks. This effort failed, and Gen. Van Fleet shifted reinforcements east to reinforce X Corps. With resources in place to stabilize the line in X Corps, Van Fleet next ordered the U.S. I and IX Corps and the 1st Marine Division of X Corps to attack north on 20 May toward Line Topeka, which ran east from Munsan-ni on the Han River to Ch'unch'on (see the map on page 299). Additional thrusts to secure key road centers to prevent an orderly withdrawal and to trap as many Chinese troops as possible were to follow this attack. By 23 May UN commanders had determined that enemy forces were rapidly pulling back. On the same day Van Fleet shifted the IX and X Corps boundary to the east to give the IX Corps responsibility for capturing Ch'unch'on and the road network west of the Hwach'on Reservoir. In IX Corps, the mission of securing Ch'unch'on fell to the U.S. 7th Infantry Division. The IX Corps commander, Lt. Gen. William M. Hoge, urged his division commanders to push aggressively forward, but the results were disappointing. Gains were few, and on 23 May Hoge ordered Maj. Gen. Claude B. Ferenbaugh, the 7th Division commander, to attack the next day up the main road to Ch'unch'on with an armored task force. First Lt. Martin Blumenson, a combat historian who studied this operation, describes the situation.

On 23 May 1951, as the enemy fought delaying actions, IX U.S. Corps forces advanced. The Ch'unch'on basin, with its tactically important road network, was considered by IX Corps the most important geographical area. Seizure of this objective would deny the enemy the use of primary roads from the Hwach'on area south to Ch'unch'on and thence east, thus cutting off one of his important escape routes north from X Corps and causing him to utilize mountainous terrain and secondary roads for withdrawal. A rapid advance in the IX Corps zone would prevent the enemy from regrouping and reorganizing. It would hamper resupply and withdrawal of enemy units in the eastern portion of the EUSAK [Eighth U.S. Army Korea] front. It might cut off certain groups and lead to their annihilation.

Desirous always of driving armor along an axis that would permit disruption and demoralization of the enemy rear, Lt. Gen. William M. Hoge, commanding general, IX U.S. Corps, directed the 7th U.S. Infantry Division to send an armored spearhead to Ch'unch'on via the Hongch'on–Ch'unch'on axis in order to facilitate the division attack. U.S. Marine patrols had reached Ch'unch'on several days before and encountered no enemy. Mines and the possibility that the enemy would block the defiles constituted the only dangers to an armored force.

Headquarters, 7th U.S. Infantry Division, attached the 7th Reconnaissance Company to the 32d Infantry Regiment and instructed the latter unit to send a force to Ch'unch'on to locate enemy troop dispositions, to harass and destroy them, to reconnoiter for river crossing sites, and to assist if possible the liberation of American prisoners of war in the Ch'unch'on area.

On the evening of 23 May 1951, at headquarters of the 32d Infantry Regiment, Capt. Charles E. Hazel, commanding officer, 7th Reconnaissance Company, was instructed to lead a reconnaissance patrol to Ch'unch'on along the Hongch'on–Ch'unch'on axis. Strength, disposition, and tactical use of the patrol were left to Capt. Hazel, but he was given one platoon (six tanks, including a tank dozer) commanded by 1st Lt. Richard C. Ames of the Heavy Tank Company, 32d Infantry Regiment. A squad of Company B, 13th Engineer Combat Battalion, was attached for mine detection. Task Force Hazel was to cross friendly lines at 0700, 24 May, simultaneously with a planned infantry jump-off and proceed to Ch'unch'on.

It was expected that the task force would return to friendly lines before dark. There was no enemy information.[1]

Capt. Chester C. Myers, assistant S-3, 32d Infantry Regiment, provides more information about the situation and the mission of Task Force Hazel.

Shortly after the 7th Reconnaissance Company was attached to the 32d Infantry Regiment, division ordered a strong armored task force to be sent to Ch'unch'on. The 32d was driving toward Ch'unch'on on both sides of the MSR [main road from Hongch'on to Ch'unch'on]. Troops on the western side were heavily engaged; the enemy resisted with mortars, artillery, and small arms. . . . Capt. Myers checked records at regimental headquarters for the following information. At 1500, 23 May, the 32d Infantry Regiment ordered the 7th Reconnaissance Company to (1) prepare to screen the regimental left flank on order, (2) prepare to support the attacking battalions, and (3) send a strong reconnaissance patrol north on the Hongch'on–Ch'unch'on road to the pass [Wonch'ang-kogae]. . . . At 1800, 23 May, the 7th Infantry Division ordered the 32d Infantry Regiment to (1) attack north, destroy the enemy in zone, . . . (2) send a strong tank-infantry patrol into Ch'unch'on on 24 May to develop the enemy situation and make a reconnaissance for river crossing sites, (3) prepare to continue the attack to Line Topeka [Munsan-ni—Ch'unch'on—Inje—Sea of Japan] (see the map on page 299) on order, and (4) maintain contact with the 31st Infantry Regiment on the left and elements of the 1st Marine Division on the right.[2]

1st Lt. Henry H. Parr, executive officer, 7th Reconnaissance Company, describes the activities of his company before moving out on the mission.

The 7th Reconnaissance Company was attached to the 32d Infantry Regiment effective 23 May. The company received the mission from the regimental S-3, Maj. Lash, to screen the left flank of the regiment above Hongch'on. The company CP in the vicinity of Paeng-ni [about two miles northwest of Hongch'on] moved to a point across the road from Won-gol [about one and one-half miles

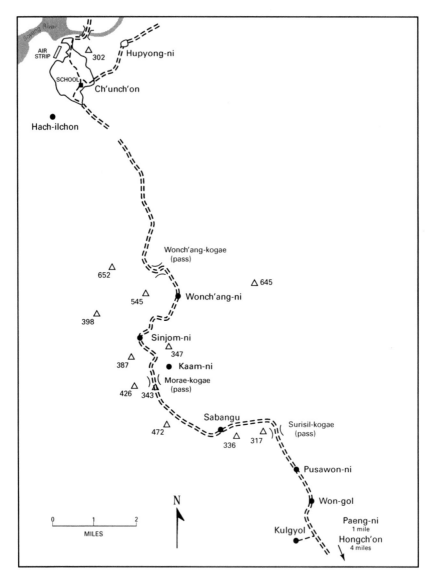

Spring River
AIR
STRIP
△ 302
SCHOOL
Ch'unch'on
Hupyong-ni
• Hach-ilchon
Wonch'ang-kogae
(pass)
△ 652
△ 645
△ 545
• Wonch'ang-ni
△ 398
• Sinjom-ni
△ 347
△ 387
• Kaam-ni
△ 426
Morae-kogae
(pass)
343 △
Sabangu
△ 472
Surisil-kogae
(pass)
△ 336
△ 317
• Pusawon-ni
Won-gol
Paeng-ni
1 mile
Kulgyol
Hongch'on
4 miles
N
0   1   2
MILES

Task Force Hazel. (Original map by author, based on maps in the Army Map
Service series L751.)

north of Paeng-ni] on 23 May. Regimental CP was in the vicinity of
Pusawon-ni [about one mile north of Won-gol]. The 31st Infantry
Regiment was attacking northwest on the left of the 32d Infantry
Regiment, which was attacking north toward Ch'unch'on. . . .

The company [was] authorized two tanks in each line platoon and one tank in the headquarters platoon, for a total of seven, actually had but six tanks, M4A3E8 tanks. Each platoon had one personnel carrier (half-track), which carried an eight- or nine-man rifle squad.[3]

1st Lt. Clifford C. Nunn, leader, 2d Platoon, 7th Reconnaissance Company, provides more details about the organization and equipment of the reconnaissance company.

The organization of the reconnaissance company is as follows: Company Headquarters, two officers and forty-one men, has one tank, two half-tracks, three jeeps, one ¾-ton vehicle, and three 2½-ton trucks. Three platoons form the company, each with one officer and thirty-eight men. The platoon headquarters has one jeep, one officer, and driver. The scout section consists of two scout squads; each squad has two jeeps (one with machine gun and one with SCR510 radio) and six men. The tank section has two tanks with five men in each tank. The rifle squad has one half-track, M3, with nine men and a driver. The mortar squad has five men, two jeeps, two trailers, and one 81mm mortar.[4]

Capt. N. L. James, commander, Heavy Tank Company, 32d Infantry (32d Tank Company), was concerned because he had received information from Marine sources about unmarked friendly minefields in the Ch'unch'on area.

At 1830, 23 May, Capt. James was called to regimental headquarters. There he found Hazel. Both were briefed on the mission of Task Force Hazel by Maj. Lash, S-3, 32d Infantry. Hazel was given the mission to try to go to Ch'unch'on, look things over, then come back, so as to be within friendly lines by dark. James was instructed to attach one platoon of his company with bulldozer to the task force.

That morning, 23 May, James had received a report that the approaches to Ch'unch'on were mined in the north, east, and west. This had been done by the Marines. James did not know where the mines were placed, and the Marines did not know either. They knew where the mines were generally placed, but not exactly. One statement James received was, "If I were you, I wouldn't go through there; in fact, we don't send our own troops through there because we don't know the exact location of our mines." This James received at a Marine company level. He passed this information on to Hazel. Practically every unit had so many mines out that it was impossible to plot their locations accurately. Every unit, however, had left a safe lane for passage of friendly troops.[5]

Lt. Parr, executive officer, 7th Reconnaissance Company, summarized his company's operations on 23 May and the initial plans for operations on the 24th.

On 23 May the 1st Platoon took positions in the pass vicinity of Morae-kogae [about one mile south of Sinjom-ni]. The 2d Platoon was in the valley west of Sabangu [about two miles southeast of the 1st Platoon], in a holding and blocking position. The 3d Platoon was at the pass Surisil-kogae in a blocking position [about one and one-half miles east of the 2d Platoon]. . . . The company went out from 0900 to 1700 hours, 23 May without observing any activity except several enemy troops in the vicinity of Hill 387 [about 1,000 yards south of Sinjom-ni]. The company did not fire, nor did the enemy.

The mission for 24 May, as Parr understood it at the time, was rather vague. The company, with an attached platoon of the 32d Tank Company, was to go out and do the same thing it had done the previous day, except that it was to go farther. The platoon from the 32d Tank Company had five tanks plus a tank dozer.[6]

Capt. Charles E. Hazel, commander, 7th Reconnaissance Company, describes his actions upon receipt of the mission and the subsequent move to Ch'unch'on.

On the evening of 23 May, Capt. Hazel at headquarters, 32d Infantry Regiment, received the mission of taking a patrol to Ch'unch'on. The strength, disposition, and tactical use of the patrol was left to the commander of the force. The 4th Platoon, 32d Tank Company, and one squad, Company B, 13th Engineer Combat Battalion, were attached. The force, named Task Force Hazel, was to cross friendly lines at 0700, 24 May, simultaneously with the jump-off of the infantry. There was no enemy information.

Because the 7th Reconnaissance Company had had no enemy opposition on 23 May, Hazel decided to take his entire reconnaissance company. If there was no enemy resistance, there would there-fore be a strong force at Ch'unch'on. Hazel disposed his elements as follows for the march: 1st Platoon, 7th Reconnaissance Company; 4th Platoon, 32d Tank Company (plus a dozer added because of reported road craters); 2d and 3d Platoons, 7th Reconnaissance Company. Hazel placed two tanks at the head of the column be-cause of the possibility of mines in the road.

Task Force Hazel crossed the line of departure at 0700, 24 May. Proceeding at a speed of ten to fifteen miles per hour, the force crossed the pass at Hill 343 [just south of Morae-kogae and about a mile south of Sinjom-ni] firing at suspected enemy positions such as houses and emplacements. When the lead tank reached a point . . . [about 500 yards southeast of Sinjom-ni], Lt. Miller reported a large crater in the road. Engineers were sent forward to check for mines, and when none were found, the dozer moved ahead and filled the crater. Twenty minutes later, the task force continued its movement forward. Lead elements reached Sinjom-ni when intense small arms and automatic weapons fire was received by the column. This fire was coming from Hill 545 [high ground about one mile north of Sinjom-ni that dominated the Ch'unch'on road], and the column took this point under fire with machine guns. Hazel attempted to have artillery place fire on this enemy position, but the artillery was unable to adjust. Thirty minutes before, however, four Corsair planes had struck Hill 545 with napalm and machine gun fire. This strike was controlled by a "Mosquito"[7] in the air, and Hazel had knowledge of it through Maj. Rumpf, Air Liaison Officer (Fifth Air Force) with the 7th Infantry Division, who was riding in Hazel's tank. Enemy small arms and automatic weapons fire came in on the column from Hill 347 [about 750 yards south of Sinjom-ni] and from Hill 387 [about 1,500 yards east of Sinjom-ni].

Hazel ordered all the light vehicles to withdraw out of range of the enemy fire. All weapons of the task force that could bear on the enemy were engaging him. The tanks were maintained in place until all the unarmored vehicles had withdrawn. The forward observer from the 48th Field Artillery Battalion remained with the light-skinned vehicles. Enemy fire was inaccurate; two men in the column were lightly wounded.

Realizing that the unarmored vehicles would be unable to proceed to Ch'unch'on through the heavy enemy fire, Hazel reorganized his force into an armored column, and at 1315, proceeded forward again in the following order: two tanks, 7th Reconnaissance Company; five tanks and dozer, 4th Platoon, 32d Tank Company; Hazel's tank; two tanks, 7th Reconnaissance Company. Considerable time was necessary for this reorganization since the rugged terrain did not permit easy maneuver of the vehicles. Hazel found that his command tank was too far back in the column for the best control, but the road was too narrow to permit his tank to move forward in the column.

In the Wonch'ang-ni valley, the flat terrain permitted the tanks to fan off the road. The force shot up houses and the hills; no enemy fire was received. Hazel saw no enemy troops until he arrived in Ch'unch'on.

The task force proceeded to Ch'unch'on, moving through the pass Wonch'ang-kogae [at the southern end of the valley and about six miles southeast of Ch'unch'on], and received considerable small arms and automatic weapons fire from the high ground to the southwest. Returning this fire, the force descended into the Ch'unch'on valley. It was obvious by then that the enemy was not employing antitank fire, so the task force barrelled down to Ch'unch'on as fast as possible. The tanks arrived in Ch'unch'on at 1715 and proceeded to the center of town, checking the houses very carefully.[8]

The Reconnaissance Company executive officer, Lt. Parr, had remained behind to man a communications relay station for Capt. Hazel. Parr provides his perspective on the advance on Ch'unch'on from monitoring radio traffic.

The task force departed at 0700, 24 May, with the 3d Platoon, Capt. Hazel, the 32d Tank Company platoon, the 2d Platoon, and the 1st Platoon, in that order. The task force left Kulgyol [about three miles northwest of Hongch'on]. The 32d Tank platoon came up the valley and joined the task force at Sabangu [where the 2d Platoon had been the day before]. The 1st Battalion, 32d Infantry, was deployed along the ridge of Hill 336 [southeast of Sabangu] and was to jump off in attack after the task force passed that place, go to Hill 472, then to Hill 426, then cross the road and advance to Hill 347.

Parr set up a radio relay station in the Surisil-kogae [about one and one-half miles east of Sabangu] while the 32d Infantry was in the vicinity of Hill 343. Air liaison reported the crater in the road south of Morae-kogae. Parr was reading all the chatter on the radio from Hazel, the light aircraft, the regiment, and division.

At 1000 the lead elements of the task force reached the vicinity of the roadblock and drew small arms fire from Hills 426, 343, and the ridge south of Hill 426. Hazel reported a heavy volume of small arms and automatic weapons fire and asked Parr to contact the 32d Infantry. He said that he thought he could move his armor through the enemy fire, but he would not attempt to take his unarmored vehicles. He then ordered his jeeps and half-tracks to withdraw behind cover. Parr talked with Col. Mount [Charles McN. Mount Jr., later major general], commanding officer, 32d Infantry, who was at an OP on the high ground between Hills 336 and 317 [about halfway between Surisil-kogae and Sabangu]. Col. Mount instructed Parr to inform Hazel that if Hazel was receiving nothing but small arms and automatic weapons fire, he was to continue. He was, however, not to overextend himself, and he was not to get cut off completely.

As the task force proceeded it drew continuous small arms and automatic weapons fire from Hill 426 to Hill 387. Light aviation reported large numbers of enemy moving to the north from Hills 398 to 652, west of the MSR. An air strike and artillery were placed on Hill 652. Although there was sporadic small arms fire on the task force all the way to Ch'unch'on, the armored column received little fire from Hill 652 to town.[9]

Other members of the armored column describe the advance to Ch'unch'on.

1st Lt. Israel J. Miller, leader, 1st Platoon, 7th Reconnaissance Company: On 24 May the 1st Platoon led Task Force Hazel. The disposition was two tanks, the scout jeep, the platoon leader jeep, the scout section, the mortar section, the rifle squad. The task force left the vicinity of Paeng-ni at 0600. Reconnaissance by fire was made to the right toward Kaam-ni [about 500 yards east of the road]. The column drew small arms and automatic weapons fire from the hill at Sinjom-ni about 1100. On the first burst of enemy fire, the driver of the lead scout jeep was hit in the leg. As the column returned the enemy fire, fire came in on the rear of the column from Hill 387. Then fire was received from Kuam-ni [a small village about 750 yards northwest of Sinjom-ni]. The lead scout jeep fired his .30 caliber machine gun from the middle of the road, while the others took cover. The fire of the company got four enemy automatic weapons, observed, and also seven individual enemy. The company blasted suspected positions and silenced the enemy fire.

Hazel instructed Miller to pull his jeeps back behind the tanks of the column. The jeeps pulled back to the vicinity of Morae-kogae, while the tank column proceeded to Ch'unch'on. Infantry forces advancing toward Morae-kogae caused the enemy to withdraw and some enemy fire was placed on the vehicles of the 7th Reconnaissance Company. The vehicles remained in that vicinity until about midnight when the task force returned from Ch'unch'on.[10]

SFC George N. Dorn, 1st Platoon, 7th Reconnaissance Company: The 7th Reconnaissance Company left the company area about 0700, 24 May, with the mission of going to Ch'unch'on. Sgt. Dorn was lead tank of the column. After three miles, he encountered a tank trap or ditch across the road, five feet wide and two and a half feet deep. Dorn called the engineers up to check for mines. Twelve engineers checked the ditch with mine sweepers and probing sticks about 0730, found no mines. The tanks had no trouble getting across the ditch; the jeeps went around it.

After proceeding another mile, the column at 0800 struck another ditch, this one three feet deep and seven yards wide. After the engineers checked the ditch, the tank from the 32d Tank Company with its dozer attachment filled the hole, and the entire company crossed. One half mile up the road, enemy small arms fire was received on the tanks. Dorn knew that the jeeps would not be able to get through, so he halted and began to return the enemy fire, which by now consisted also of machine gun fire. Suspected enemy positions in houses and on the sides of the hills were fired on with machine guns and 76mm ammunition at a range between 300 and 1,000 yards.

During the first firefight, the enemy seemed interested more in the jeeps than in the tanks. It is difficult to estimate how much fire was coming in and how many enemy troops were in the hills because of the tank motors and the sound of the returning fire. Dorn was not buttoned up. He fired about 300 rounds with his .50 caliber machine gun and directed about ten rounds of 76mm fire. The firefight lasted till about noon, with enemy fire coming in mostly from the left front. The column was ordered to pull back.

At 1230, Dorn was told that only the tanks would go on to Ch'unch'on, so he "barreled in" to the high ground overlooking the Ch'unch'on valley. "If there was any enemy fire, I paid no attention to it." Hazel then ordered the tanks to move down into town, and the task force did so.[11]

SGT. GEORGE D. REEVES, TANK COMMANDER, 1ST PLATOON, 7TH RECONNAISSANCE COMPANY: At 0600, 24 May, the company moved out about three miles from the company area to a crater that was half dug on top of a mountain pass. Dorn called the engineers up, and they checked for mines. There were none, so the company moved across the ditch and down the mountain about one and a half miles to another crater. Because the tanks could cross but not the jeeps, Dorn and Reeves moved across, after the engineers checked for mines, and outposted while the tank dozer filled up the ditch. Then the company moved across. Three hundred yards farther, the company received small arms fire. Two men in jeeps were hit. About fifteen minutes later, the jeeps were ordered back.

Dorn and Reeves pulled back to cover the withdrawal of the jeeps, then the tanks followed the jeeps back about 500 yards. Hazel told Sgt. Dorn the tanks would go to Ch'unch'on. Reeves saw no enemy during the firefight, which lasted fifteen to thirty minutes. He fired all his tank weapons at suspected positions. The tanks moved to Ch'unch'on, receiving small arms fire all the way in.[12]

SFC HENRY A. CAMPBELL, TANK COMMANDER, 32D TANK COMPANY: On 24 May the task force started out with jeeps and half-tracks and tanks. The engineers were in the lead. A few miles after the task force was under way, sniper fire came in on the column. The jeeps and half-tracks were turned around and sent back with the engineers and mine detectors. Campbell was in the tank dozer, the last tank in the 2d Platoon, 32d Tank Company. The 7th Reconnaissance Company was behind him. He filled a crater before the first sniper fire. Then all of the wheeled vehicles went back. On its way to Ch'unch'on, the column would stop every so often to fire at snipers.[13]

SFC James E. Jubert, platoon sergeant, 4th Platoon, 32d Tank Company: On 24 May, Task Force Hazel started out with part of the 7th Reconnaissance Company leading the column. Sgt. Jubert's tank was directly behind Capt. Hazel. The first enemy fire was encountered in the vicinity of Sinjom-ni. The column turned back, reorganized, and went forward again simply as an armored column. Jubert was then the fourth tank in the column. Although enemy fire was encountered at several places, the tanks got through the passes okay and got to Ch'unch'on "easy."[14]

Sgt. Joseph J. Blaskiewicz, tank commander and leader, 1st Section, 4th Platoon, 32d Tank Company: On 24 May the 4th Platoon departed its company area at 0615. Blaskiewicz was the second tank in the column. At the area of the 7th Reconnaissance Company, one reconnaissance platoon was placed in front of the column. Hazel was behind Blaskiewicz and Campbell. The order of march was: two reconnaissance tanks, the reconnaissance scout section in ¼-ton jeeps, half-tracks, engineer truck, Lt. Ames, Sgt. Blaskiewicz, Sgt. Campbell, Hazel. Three miles up the road, sniper fire came into the column from both sides of the road. Two reconnaissance jeep drivers were hit. The wheeled vehicles were pulled off the road. The tanks moved forward and joined the two reconnaissance tanks. Then the tanks fired at all suspected positions: houses, rock piles, brush. The wheeled vehicles were withdrawn one-half mile. The tanks backed out of the valley, turned around, and joined them. Then the tanks turned around and took off through the fire and went to Ch'unch'on.[15]

1st Lt. Clifford C. Nunn, leader, 2d Platoon, 7th Reconnaissance Company: On 24 May the platoon of the 32d Tank

Company joined us at an assembly area in the vicinity of Won-gol. A squad of the 13th Engineer Combat Battalion was attached for mine detection. Task Force Hazel departed at 0645, with the 1st Platoon, tank dozer, company commander, 32d Tank Company platoon, 3d Platoon, and 2d Platoon, in that order, and passed through Sabangu. The 2d Platoon at the end of the column heard the 1st Platoon in a firefight at Sinjom-ni. It seemed like "quite a firefight." Hazel then instructed Nunn to go to Phase Line 1, which was at Morae-kogae [Hill 343], and hold the pass open. Nunn closed there and waited. He watched an air strike on Hill 645.

At 1000 Lt. Nunn got word that the task force would be reorganized. The half-tracks and jeeps, which had been interspersed among the tanks, were sent just behind Nunn's platoon, and the armored vehicles continued toward Ch'unch'on. Nunn saw four Chinese, "one at a time," on Hill 426, and he ordered machine gun and small arms fire at 700 yards placed on foxholes in that area. The enemy did not return the fire. Then an enemy machine gun "heckled" the group "for a long time." Although the group searched the entire valley trying to locate the gun, the enemy could not be located. Nunn remained at Phase Line 1 with one tank, seven jeeps, and a half-track while the task force went to Ch'unch'on and the remainder of the company vehicles remained behind Nunn's 2d Platoon.[16]

PFC RICHARD I. WINSLOW, TANK GUNNER, 3D PLATOON, 7TH RECONNAISSANCE COMPANY: On 24 May, the company started out pretty early and got over the first mountain pass. The smaller vehicles with the column turned back when the first small arms fire was received. The tanks withdrew and covered the jeeps as they retired to safety. Winslow's tank was near the middle of the column. He could not fire until the vehicles drew back. The .50 caliber machine guns especially were returning the enemy fire. The tanks alone moved forward slowly. Several halts were made to return enemy fire, but then the column hurried on to make it to Ch'unch'on.[17]

Capt. Hazel describes the situation upon arrival of the task force in Ch'unch'on.

Somewhere en route, Hazel received a message from a light aircraft giving an additional mission to the task force, that of checking the fords and the bridge north of Ch'unch'on for possible river crossing sites. In Ch'unch'on, Hazel ordered Lt. Ames, Platoon Leader, 4th Platoon, 32d Tank Company, to proceed to the bridge to block enemy escape from that part of town, and to reconnoiter river crossings. Ames moved his six tanks to the north part of town. Hazel placed two tanks in the vicinity of the school to block enemy escape routes from the east. Hazel and three tanks moved to the western portion of town near the road junction to cover that part.

Civilians came running out of houses in town, waving flags, and shouting at the tankers. In spite of this, however, there was an unearthly quiet in town, and Hazel had a spooky feeling. The task force was seventeen miles from the last known friendly lines.

Prior to disposing the tanks in Ch'unch'on, Hazel warned them to be careful of enemy who might be on Hill 302 [Pongui-san, overlooking Ch'unch'on to the immediate north]. A few days before, he had tried to secure information on mines in the Ch'unch'on area from the 7th Marine Regiment. Hazel had been tipped off several days before that he might have to go to Ch'unch'on. He picked up several map overlays of friendly minefields from the S-3, 7th Marine Regiment, and turned them in to the G-3, 7th Infantry Division, for compilation. Although Hazel continued to try to get mine information, his information remained sketchy. The Marines said they thought that if Hazel stayed on the main roads, he would be OK. Before starting, he warned the tankers to be careful of mines.

Hazel's loader saw some brown uniforms in a house. Hazel halted the tank. Two men jumped from the tank and shouted, "Come out." Three Chinese soldiers came out. One started to run but received four .45 caliber bullets in his butt. The first prisoners of war were taken here, placed on the tank rear deck.

When Hazel and three tanks moved to the western part of town, Hazel's driver called his attention to twelve to fifteen enemy soldiers 400 yards distant running up a ridge of Hill 302 in escape. The tanks took them under .50 caliber machine gun fire and killed about six.

Hazel received a call from a light plane overhead that 500 enemy were running off Hill 302 toward the east then north to Hupyong-ni. Capt. Hazel informed Lt. Ames of this, ordered him to move east along the riverbed, and let the enemy come toward his positions. Although he did not know exactly where Ames was because of communication difficulties, he knew that Ames had a 9,000-yard field of fire and could take care of the Chinese all right. Calling the two tanks he had left at the school, he ordered them to move east, then north along the road to Hupyong-ni to drive the fleeing enemy troops into Ames's platoon. But due to communication difficulties, the tanks at the schoolhouse were unable to understand Capt. Hazel's orders, and therefore they were unable to complete their run. Hazel thought an additional 200 enemy troops would have been caught if they had been able to do so.

Task Force Hazel apparently had gotten into Ch'unch'on before the enemy realized the tanks were there. Then, there was a mad scramble on the part of the enemy to get out of town. Not one shot was fired at the tanks in Ch'unch'on. Overhead the plane providing observation reported the trails the Chinese were using as escape routes and attempted to call in air strikes. Hazel jokingly reported that if he had an infantry battalion in town, he could have cleaned up the whole place.

The plane reported erroneously that Hazel had more prisoners of war than he could handle. Maj. Rumpf informed Hazel that forty sorties were en route. Later, considerable planes were seen overhead. Hazel heard one report of 150 enemy killed as a conservative estimate.

About 1830, Hazel received an order from a plane (Capt. Myers) to form a perimeter and remain in Ch'unch'on overnight. The plane stated that tanks would be reinforced. At first, the plane said, "You might have to stay in town." Twenty minutes later, the plane stated, "You will stay."

Hazel was a bit apprehensive about keeping eleven tanks without infantry protection in a position where he had no knowledge of enemy strength. He ordered all tanks to assemble at the airstrip on the western edge of town, which afforded the best position to establish a tank perimeter because the ground was extremely flat and provided good fields of fire. The tanks formed a tight circular perimeter, placed trip flares, and prepared to remain for the night.[18]

Other members of the task force recall the events after their arrival in Ch'unch'on.

SFC DORN, 1ST PLATOON, 7TH RECONNAISSANCE COMPANY: Dorn and the other 1st Platoon tank commanded by Sgt. Reeves lost communications with the remainder of the column as they moved into town. The radios on both tanks went out. Seeing no tanks behind them, Dorn and Reeves turned around to find the remainder of the column. As they got into the main part of town, a Korean boy yelled at them, so they stopped. The boy told them there were three Chinese soldiers in a house. Putting an old Korean man on his tank to show them where the house was, Dorn with Reeves proceeded to the house. Dorn stopped his bow gunner from firing. He placed one tank in front, the other tank in the rear. Koreans in the vicinity talked three Chinese into surrendering. After placing the prisoners of war on the rear decks of the tanks, Dorn and Reeves followed the tank tracks of the task force into town.

Seeing about seven Chinese 200 yards away on a ridge, Dorn fired his 76mm gun and his machine gun at them, and the Chinese disappeared. Dorn figured he got them. Since he was low on gas, he did not investigate. He then ran out of .50 caliber ammunition, so he borrowed two cases from Reeves. Thirty yards down the road, he picked up two more Chinese who were waiting with safe conduct passes in their hands. Then Dorn found the task force. The radios were still out.

The task force was to the right of the airstrip. The river was directly to the column's front. Sgt. Seebold, 2d Platoon, informed Dorn that 400 Chinese were coming down the forks of the road to the middle of town. Dorn and two other tanks went back to investigate, found nothing. They parked in the school yard. Because they were low on gas, they did not want to travel around. Dorn had the Chinese prisoners on his tank yell for more prisoners to come in. Dorn waited there until 2000, when he was ordered back to the airstrip. There, Hazel received orders to go back to the company.[19]

SGT. REEVES, 1ST PLATOON, 7TH RECONNAISSANCE COMPANY: On the outskirts of town, Dorn and Reeves started to go into town. They lost their communications, lost the other tanks, then returned, and later found the column. Just inside town, a civilian told Dorn that three Chinese were in a house. The tanks fired several rounds of .30 caliber into the house, then yelled. No one would come out. So while Reeves stayed in the rear of the house, Dorn went around to the front. Dorn fired his pistol, and a civilian went in and got three Chinese to come out. Reeves then saw seven Chinese. He fired his 76mm gun at them, did not see them again. Two more prisoners of war were picked up. Dorn, Reeves, and Mullin went back to locate 400 Chinese supposed to be coming into town. They could not find them, so they parked in a school yard. After about two hours, Hazel ordered them to return to the airstrip. This message they received through Mullin's radio. Fifteen minutes after the tanks took positions at the airstrip, just about at dusk, a message was received for the task force to return to the company.[20]

PFC WINSLOW, TANK GUNNER, 3D PLATOON, 7TH RECONNAISSANCE COMPANY: In the center of town [Ch'unch'on], Winslow noticed between twenty-five and seventy-five Chinese running up a hill on the right. He fired one round of 76mm ammunition and 200 to 300 rounds of .30 caliber ammunition at them. Then Winslow took over the .50 caliber because Sgt. Seebold, the tank commander, and Cpl. Fudge, the bow gunner, got out and fired on a house, took four prisoners. When ten or fifteen Chinese refused to come out of the house, the tank behind Winslow demolished the house with a blast of the 76mm gun. Word was received that the tanks would stay in Ch'unch'on all night, so the tanks went to the airstrip and set up a perimeter defense; the tanks were in positions fifteen to twenty yards apart. Then orders came to return. Everyone was worried about the shortage of gasoline.[21]

SFC JUBERT, PLATOON SERGEANT, 4TH PLATOON, 32D TANK COMPANY: The 4th Platoon, 32d Tank Company, in Ch'unch'on split from the reconnaissance company and operated as a unit. There were six tanks (including the dozer), and they split into three sections. The first Chinese were spotted across the river. The platoon turned right before reaching the airstrip, forded the river. Two

Chinese washing their clothes at the river's edge started to run when they saw the tanks and were shot down. Jubert searched them and later turned the papers he took from them over to the 7th Reconnaissance Company. Across the river, one section went east above the sandy riverbed. Lt. Ames's section went north, then east, and crossed the river. Jubert's section went northwest to Karamegi. Investigating the source of some small arms fire, Jubert discovered some gasoline drums. He set them afire with one round of HE. Then he followed Ames's section along the riverbed to the east. He saw Ames's section working on the other side of the river. Then both sections went under the cement bridge, returned to the center of Ch'unch'on, and contacted the 7th Reconnaissance Company. Jubert drove to the airstrip and prepared with the other tanks of the task force to spend the night. A perimeter was established, and trip flares were set out. As soon as this was accomplished, orders were received to return to friendly lines. Jubert had only a quarter of a tank of gas left.[22]

SFC CAMPBELL, COMMANDER, TANK DOZER, 32D TANK COMPANY: Campbell went to the eastern portion of Ch'unch'on. There he saw at least 1,500 Chinese, 2,000 yards away, coming off the hills in full retreat. But Campbell had fired so much coming up from Ch'unch'on that he had to conserve his ammunition for the trip back. So in Ch'unch'on, he fired only on large enemy groups. His gunner, he estimated, got at least 200 Chinese. The Chinese did not return the tank fire. They were throwing away their clothes, their packs, their canteens, and anything else they were carrying. . . . Campbell and Lt. Ames tried to outflank the Chinese. They "burned up" their machine guns firing at them. The task force regrouped and returned to the airstrip after expending as much ammunition as they thought they ought to. The tanks set up a perimeter and prepared to spend the night. Then orders came to move out.[23]

SERGEANT BLASKIEWICZ, TANK COMMANDER, 4TH PLATOON, 32D TANK COMPANY: In Ch'unch'on, some civilians came out of the houses. They seemed happy to see the tanks. One fairly old man, an old woman, and two children pointed out houses where Chinese soldiers were hiding. The Koreans shouted "many, many," and the tanks fired as directed. One enemy soldier ran out of a house and was shot. The platoon under Lt. Ames worked cautiously through town looking for targets. At the river, Blaskiewicz saw two Chinese soldiers washing clothes 150 yards from the tanks. The soldiers started to run. Blaskiewicz got one, Ames's tank got the other. The platoon crossed the river, and Ames told Blaskiewicz to move under the concrete bridge and have a "look-see." He proceeded 400 yards, saw nothing. Then Ames called for Blaskiewicz to rejoin him. Ames said many Chinese were fleeing from Ch'unch'on. Blaskiewicz went 250 yards farther than he previously had. He saw 200–250 Chinese at 1,200 yards running single-file without breaking formation. He opened up with his 76mm gun, saw quite a few fall, and several in the rear of the column hit the ground. The gunner said he saw bodies flying in the air.

Returning to the river crossing, Blaskiewicz joined Sgts. Jubert and McGill. They reentered Ch'unch'on and, trying to find Ames, they ran into Hazel and the reconnaissance company. Hazel contacted Ames by radio, and Ames came into town. Ames then sent Blaskiewicz back to the river to establish a roadblock. Blaskiewicz was later recalled to the airstrip, where a defensive perimeter with trip flares was set up. Word was then received from the recon company that the tanks would "make it back."[24]

After considerable confusion at higher headquarters, Task Force Hazel was finally ordered to return to friendly lines, a potentially hazardous undertaking at night through rugged terrain with enemy forces still roaming the road. Capt. Hazel describes the return journey.

At 2025, Hazel received orders from the G-3, 7th Infantry Division (through a relay station), that Task Force Hazel would return immediately to the 32d Infantry area. Hazel checked the order to make certain it was a legitimate command. Then he asked a light aircraft overhead (Lt. Bristol, Division Light Air Section) how long he could provide cover. Bristol said one hour. He then requested Bristol to fly cover as long as he could as the task force returned. Then, as quickly as possible, the tanks moved out of their perimeter and proceeded back toward friendly lines.

The order of march was as follows: the five tanks of the 7th

Reconnaissance Company with Hazel in the center, the six tanks of the 32d Tank Company platoon. This march order was dictated by the way the perimeter was formed; it was easiest to get out in this order.

The force proceeded to the vicinity of an unnamed village [about two miles southeast of town] without difficulty. Lt. Ames radioed that one of his tanks was out of gas, and he requested instructions. Light was fading fast. Hazel instructed Ames to attempt to tow the tank. If that failed, he was to destroy it. The column moved to the unnamed houses [about one-half mile north of Wonch'ang-kogae], where it came under intense enemy small arms fire from the high ground to the southwest. It was necessary to button up all the hatches. Hazel requested the plane overhead whether he could determine the source of this fire; the plane could not. Ames radioed Hazel that he was towing the tank. Hazel instructed him to button up.

The column moved ahead very slowly. Lights were turned off except for the lead tank, which was instructed to turn them off when the enemy fired. Ames reported that he could tow the tank no longer and was going to destroy it. Hazel said, "Go ahead."

In the Wonch'ang-ni valley, more enemy fire was received. Hazel called Ames and asked him how he was doing. Ames said he was OK and moving rapidly. At a bend in the road [about three-quarters of a mile north of Sinjom-ni], the tanks came under intense small arms fire coming from Hill 545 to the north. At that time, Hazel received orders from the 32d Infantry to halt in place and set up a perimeter for the night. It was impossible to carry out this order because of a steep cliff on the left and a deep gorge on the right. The tanks were canalized and were not able to turn around.

Hazel informed the 32d Infantry that he was halted in place, buttoned up, receiving intense small arms fire, and was low on gasoline and ammunition. The regiment ordered Hazel to hold in place. Hazel again informed the regiment in no uncertain terms of his situation. He gave the coordinates of his location, because it was obvious that the regiment did not know where the task force was. Hazel was then ordered [into] a perimeter . . . [along the railroad about one mile south of Ch'unch'on, nowhere near where he then was] in the vicinity of the bridge and the railroad. Finally, regiment instructed Hazel that if he could not pull off the road in that vicinity, he was to move forward until he found a suitable place to form a perimeter for the night. Hazel assembled his tanks [into] a perimeter in the valley [about one-half mile] above Sinjom-ni. Five minutes later he received orders that the task force would return to the valley west of Sabangu [about three miles south of Sinjom-ni], and that the task force commander was to report to regiment immediately.

Upon reaching the pass Morae-kogae [about a mile south of Sinjom-ni], Hazel physically contacted one of his communications relay stations. There he found gasoline and ammunition trucks. The tanks refueled, and a supply of ammunition was taken on.

While refueling, a sergeant from the 4th Platoon, 32d Tank Company, asked Hazel where Ames was. Hazel informed him that he had had his last radio communication with Ames one and one-half hours before, and that he had tried repeatedly to contact him without luck. This was not unusual, however, because communications had been poor all day long. Further investigation disclosed that Ames had not closed in the last perimeter [north of Sinjom-ni].

The task force took fifteen prisoners of war, one wounded. These rode on the tank decks. All but one were wounded by enemy fire on the trip back.

About 2000 Hazel received a request for information. Was General Ferenbaugh with him? No, Hazel hadn't seen him; nothing but a tank could have gotten through to Ch'unch'on. Sometime later he heard that the general was found and was all right.

On the way back, Hazel saw at the bend of the road the general's jeep on the side of the road, apparently in good order. One hundred yards farther, a military police jeep was found, lying on its right side, its lights burning, and two dead American soldiers in the road.[25]

Other members of Task Force Hazel describe the night move from Ch'unch'on.

SFC DORN, 1ST PLATOON, 7TH RECONNAISSANCE COMPANY: Dorn was the third tank in the column going back. He received small arms fire all the way back from the hills on both sides of the road. He returned the fire, for the most part only when the column halted. The drivers were buttoned up. Dorn remained unbuttoned so he could fire his machine gun. Although it was a dark night, the prisoners did not get off the tanks. The task force returned between midnight and 0100 hours, 25 May.[26]

SERGEANT REEVES, 1ST PLATOON, 7TH RECONNAISSANCE COMPANY: The column started back. Two miles out of town, the tank dozer went off the road. Reeves stopped in case help would be necessary, but the tank behind Reeves pulled the dozer out. Small arms fire came in while the dozer was being towed out. The force reached the company without incident, gassed up, ate, got resupply of ammunition around midnight.[27]

PFC WINSLOW, TANK GUNNER, 3D PLATOON, 7TH RECONNAIS-SANCE COMPANY: About forty-five minutes before darkness, just outside Ch'unch'on, the tanks received enemy small arms fire. They had no time to stop and return the fire. The object was to get back; there was "no time to fool around." Although reinforcements and gasoline were going to be sent up, Hazel said not to do so because it would be impossible for the reinforcing tanks to turn around on the road. Halfway back, Winslow saw two jeeps in the road, one jeep parked, one jeep on its side with the lights on. One dead GI was in the road. The tanks did not stop. They met friendly infantry, then the fuel truck. The prisoners of war were turned over. The tanks gassed up and went to the company CP. There was no moon that night; it was dark. It had been a hot day.[28]

SGT. BLASKIEWICZ, TANK COMMANDER, 32D TANK COMPANY: The tanks started out in this order: 7th Reconnaissance Company, Jubert, Campbell (dozer), McGill, Blaskiewicz, Kammerer, and Lt. Ames in the rear. At the base of the large mountain pass, Blaskie-wicz got word that Sgt. Kammerer's tank behind him had its motor quit. Kammerer said he thought he was out of gas. At this point, the column received its first enemy automatic weapons or machine gun fire. Blaskiewicz looked back and saw Ames's tank pulled up along-side of Kammerer. Blaskiewicz asked whether Kammerer was OK. Kammerer said he was. So Blaskiewicz continued, after instructing his driver to button up because of the enemy fire. The driver soon asked for permission to unbutton. Blaskiewicz told him to unbutton if he couldn't see the road buttoned up. The driver unbuttoned and got over the pass as fast as he could.

As he started down from the pass, he saw McGill stopped ahead. Then he saw Campbell's dozer in the ditch. While Jubert was pulling the dozer out, Blaskiewicz saw a figure coming down from the hill. He told the driver to start his motor up, since the driver had stopped his motor to conserve gasoline. The figure stopped behind a bush five yards away from Blaskiewicz's tank. Blaskiewicz pulled out his .45 caliber pistol. He told the driver to move closer to McGill's tank. The figure stood up. Blaskiewicz fired three shots. The figure fired a burp gun burst straight up into the air and fell. Blaskiewicz saw more figures on the skyline, so he swung his turret and strafed the hill with his co-axial gun.

As the column moved out, Blaskiewicz was the last tank. He kept looking for the other two behind him. The column halted several times, passed General Ferenbaugh's jeep on its side with the headlights on. The column moved off the road into an assembly area and parked, then moved back to the road and proceeded two miles farther back where the tanks refueled. The column moved several miles farther to the rear, where the 3d Platoon was waiting with ammunition resupply and rations and as reinforcements as necessary.[29]

SFC CAMPBELL, COMMANDER, TANK DOZER, 32D TANK COMPANY: On the way back, the 7th Reconnaissance Company took the lead. Campbell was the first tank of the 32d Tank Company vehicles. Approaching the first pass out of Ch'unch'on, the column was fired on, but the tanks didn't halt to fire back. It was dark, and the tanks "kept going to keep up with the reconnaissance company." Campbell was driving blackout at that time. Five minutes later, Campbell went into the ditch. Jubert pulled out the dozer. Some sniper fire was received while the tow cables were being hooked on. On a bend in the road, the column saw a jeep on its side with the lights on. The column proceeded back to friendly lines.[30]

SFC JUBERT, PLATOON SERGEANT, 4TH PLATOON, 32D TANK COMPANY: The 7th Reconnaissance Company led out. Sgt. Campbell's tank followed, then Jubert. Ames brought up the rear. Nothing was encountered until the column reached the foot of the first pass, Wonch'ang-kogae. There barbed wire was strung across the road, and heavy enemy small arms fire was received. It was dusk, and it was difficult to see. Jubert buttoned up his tank. The column proceeded. On the other side of the pass, the dozer ran into the ditch. Jubert pulled him out, and the tanks continued. The tanks operated with their lights on. They turned off their lights when the column halted. It was a pitch-dark night. The drivers were going very cautiously because driving conditions were very difficult.

The column came to two jeeps. One lay on its side with the lights on. Both jeeps still had their transmitters on. Jubert could see the green light. Not far beyond the jeeps, the task force went into a perimeter, "just around the corner from friendly lines." Sgt. Rickard, 3d Platoon, 32d Tank Company, came up and guided the tanks back to the friendly lines. Jubert was out of radio contact all day long. He could transmit but was unable to receive. His radio went out soon after the task force departed in the morning. He received orders by voice alone.[31]

While Task Force Hazel was advancing on Ch'unch'on and making the night move back to friendly lines, other members of the unit had remained to the south in support. These men provide more information about the situation as they monitored the radios and observed the activity in their own area.

LT. PARR, EXECUTIVE OFFICER, 7TH RECONNAISSANCE COMPANY: After the task force had started, Hazel received a further mission of reconnoitering river crossings. Around 1500, Hazel reported being in Ch'unch'on and across the river. By this time, messages from Hazel were being relayed by aircraft to Parr. As the task force entered Ch'unch'on, air reported 500 enemy going from Hill 302 in a northerly direction. Also a large enemy group was reported heading south along the Pukhan [river] in the vicinity of Hill 99. At this time, Hazel had four tanks across the river, two tanks 1,000 yards northwest of the road junction, and two tanks 500 yards north of the road junction. These were "raising much hell." The remainder of the tanks were deployed along the airstrip. Hazel reported getting nineteen prisoners of war. The air force struck in the vicinity of Yulmun-ni [north of the river], and 150 enemy were reported killed.

Maj. Lash, S-3, 32d Infantry, informed Parr that Hazel would remain in Ch'unch'on that night. Reinforcements consisting of another platoon of the 32d Tank Company to be followed by a third platoon of the tank company "were on the way." Hazel organized a defensive position at the airstrip. Parr, at 1800, returned to the 7th Reconnaissance Company CP to secure rations, POL [petroleum, oil, and lubricants], and ammunition that would be carried by the platoon of tanks alerted to reinforce Hazel. While Parr was at the company CP, Lt. Col. Huston, G-3, 7th Infantry Division, radioed Parr that Hazel would return that evening. Parr went to the regimental CP, and regiment acknowledged Huston's message. Soon after, another message came from the G-3, 7th Infantry Division, ordering Hazel to return to the valley [about a mile] south of Ch'unch'on, where he would pick out a defensive area and set up a perimeter for the night. The tank platoon reinforcement advanced to meet Task Force Hazel. Hazel reported being very low on gas. The tanks had been running for thirteen hours. Ammunition was also very low.

It was too late then to be flying relay for communications between 2030 and 2100. Parr finally worked a message through three relay stations to Hazel who was in the vicinity of . . . [Sinjom-ni]. Then it was decided that the task force would return to Sabangu, where it would rearm, reequip, and refuel. Coming back, the tanks received fire from the places fire had come on the way up. All the prisoners of war on the decks of the tanks were wounded by this enemy fire. The task force returned to Sabangu between 2200 and 2300. The command tank of the 32d Tank Company was lost when it went over a bank. The platoon leader was killed. The rest of the crew hid out and were picked up the following morning.

General Ferenbaugh had been ambushed that afternoon. "People stopped worrying about Hazel and started looking for the general." . . .

Parr replaced the basic load of the task force around midnight, 24 May, by distributing 96 rounds (83 of which were borrowed from the 32d Infantry) of 76mm HE ammunition. The task force expended 30 boxes of .50 caliber machine gun ammunition, 29 boxes of .30 caliber machine gun ammunition, and 27 55-gallon drums of gasoline.[32]

LT. NUNN, 2D PLATOON, 7TH RECONNAISSANCE COMPANY: Lt. Nunn watched Company C, 32d Infantry, take Hill 426 after a hand grenade battle on the top of the hill. About 1300, Lt. Stanaway, 32d Tank Company, fired support on Hill 426. Then some quad-fifties came up and gave supporting fire. Later a dual-forty plastered the hill. Some enemy mortar fire came in on the ridge north from Hill 426.

When Nunn received word that the task force was in Ch'unch'on, he was informed that reinforcements and supplies would be sent to Hazel. Later, he learned that the task force was to withdraw to Sinjom-ni. Then, the 2d Platoon moved to Sinjom-ni to await the task force on its return trip. The Rangers were moving north about this time. General Ferenbaugh also passed northward. At Sinjom-ni, the 2d Platoon came under sporadic sniper and machine gun fire from the high ground east of Sinjom-ni. The platoon returned this fire and silenced it.

At dusk Nunn was informed that the task force would withdraw to friendly lines. The general had been lost and found. Nunn was ordered to move back to Phase Line 1 [the pass at Hill 343] with one truckload of POL. Meanwhile, the 2d Ranger Company attacked Hill 545. The task force returned to Phase Line 1 about 2230, bringing fifteen prisoners of war. Lt. Talbert took the prisoners back, and the company assembled [at Sabangu]. The company was fed and bedded down by 0130, 25 May.[33]

SFC J. D. STILES, TANK COMMANDER, 2D PLATOON, 7TH RECONNAISSANCE COMPANY: On 24 May, the 2d Platoon remained on the high ground at a pass, covering it for the infantry which was advancing. The tanks did not support the infantry because of distance. Then, while the tanks proceeded to Ch'unch'on, Stiles remained to hold the pass so that the tanks would not be cut off on their way back. That afternoon, Stiles helped cover the relay station. When a half-track started receiving small arms fire, Stiles put four or five rounds of HE in the hills. There was no more fire until dark. By then, the infantry had advanced to the relay point. When word was received that General Ferenbaugh had been ambushed, Lt. Nunn tried to get permission to take a tank and a half-track to rescue the general, but he was ordered to remain at the radio relay point. The infantry advanced beyond the relay point about 2,000 yards, and word was received that the tanks were returning from Ch'unch'on. Stiles moved forward to a pass and waited for the task force, which got back at 2200.[34]

As already mentioned, while Task Force Hazel was at Ch'unch'on on the afternoon of 24 May, considerable attention was focused on the location and status of Maj. Gen. Claude Ferenbaugh, 7th Infantry Division commander. Members of the division describe what happened.

Capt. Malcolm W. Chandler Jr., General Ferenbaugh's aide-de-camp: This is [an] account of [the] incident from my angle only.

On 24 May, at approximately 1545, General Ferenbaugh, . . . his aide [Capt. Chandler], and driver and accompanying guard jeep, with a mounted machine gun and three MP [military police] guards, left the 32d Infantry CP for the regimental OP. Information as to what the elements of the 7th Recon had found in their drive into Ch'unch'on was sketchy so General Ferenbaugh decided to go on forward where the elements of the 7th Recon were stopped in order to find out what sort of resistance they had run into. At 1610, we reached the elements of the 7th Recon and we inquired whether they had radio contact with Capt. Hazel. They stated they did not have any communications but that the tank relay station would have contact up the road. We passed through elements of the 32d and 2d Ranger and came upon two tanks beside the road and asked where their relay station was. The answer was five miles up the road. This information was a surprise to me because I had no idea they had progressed that far. However, I personally thought it was only a short distance farther to the relay station and the estimated five miles was merely the advance elements of the 7th Recon.

We had progressed only a short distance along the road . . . [in the Wonch'ang-ni valley north of Sinjom-ni], when just as the general's jeep, which was in front, rounded a sharp right-hand turn, there was a heavy burst of machine gun fire behind us, followed by accompanying intermediate blast, which I judged later to be caused by the gunner grasping the trigger when hit by the machine gun fire, but was in error, as the machine gun on the jeep had not been fired. I looked back to see if the jeep was following, but it did not turn the curve so we halted the jeep about thirty or forty yards from the curve, and I jumped from the jeep and ran toward the curve huddling close to the side of the wall as the firing still continued. I was closely followed by General Ferenbaugh. When I reached a point where I could look around the corner, I saw the wrecked jeep and the guards lying in the road. I could tell they were dead [Cpl. Robert M. Handy and Cpl. Oscar D. Martin, both from the 7th Military Police Company, 7th Infantry Division].[35] General Ferenbaugh saw them, too. We turned back just as Sgt. Allan Bralley was turning the jeep around. We ordered him to turn the vehicle around, and then decided on the spur of the moment to continue because the volume of fire on our side of the curve was not too heavy. I jerked the rear star plate out of the insert and threw it aside and gave an order to Sgt. Bralley to proceed. But as we started, the entire ridge opened up, bullets cutting a path across the road in front of the jeep and whining overhead.

We halted the jeep, and all huddled between [the] right side and shoulder of the road. Though the automatic and small arms fire was heavy now, only an occasional whine was noticeable, the accuracy of the fire being poor. Here I ordered Sgt. Bralley to remove the front star plate. He had to make two attempts; the first one almost cost him an arm from an accurate burst of machine gun fire which came through the bumper. I tried the 608 radio, switching to every channel, till I had talked on every channel, but I could not establish contact on any of them. We then took to the hill on the right side of the road, which was very steep and jutted almost perpendicular from the road. Sgt. Bralley first, General Ferenbaugh in the middle, and me in the rear. Luckily, thirty yards up the side of the hill there was thick foliage. Bullets whined overhead as we climbed. Upon reaching the foliage, we alternately dashed for concealment, hugging the ground. The hill we were on was very steep; we huddled closely as possible to the sheer cliff on our right in case there was enemy above us who might throw hand grenades or fire down on us. After reaching the cliff and about fifty to seventy yards above the road, we dispersed twenty feet apart to see what the enemy would do. The enemy was running small groups of men up and down the ridge at a range of 180 to 400 yards from us and along alternate ridges beyond at further ranges.

I secured a fairly safe nook in the wall, being downhill and around a corner from General Ferenbaugh and Sgt. Bralley, so that I could watch fields across the road in case any Chinks wanted to cross to our side. The danger of them coming down [the] ridge on our side or already being there was imminent. I gave Sgt. Bralley orders to keep his eyes on jutting crags above and to our left and not to watch anything else.

This all happened shortly before 1700 hours.

On a low ridge just across the road, the Chinks talked back and forth to each other. Periods of quiet were broken by an occasional burst of machine gun fire and banging of a rifle. No bullets hit around us, until much later when a heavy machine gun (sounded like a .50 caliber) opened up on the ridge across the road, though I couldn't tell which one. About five of these thudded into the cliff above our heads and between me and the road.

About 1930, an armored car cruised by at high speed, slowed down, turned around down the road, and sped back. At about 2000, we heard tank fire around the corner. Shortly after, a quad 50 opened up. Then a tank came up and stopped by our jeep. It killed its motor, and Lt. Stanaway hollered, "General Ferenbaugh." I answered, being closest to the road. He asked if we were all right. I answered in affirmative. He asked me what to do, and I told him that it was too risky coming down the hill in daylight and that we preferred to wait till dark. I asked him if he could wait until dark and would it be too dangerous for him. He said he'd wait. I told him to go down, turn around, come back, and park close to the rock wall (cliff). This they did. All of these vehicles were under intense machine gun and small arms fire and were all buttoned up. The tanks and quad accompanying Lt. Stanaway kept up a continuous fire with the tanks firing point blank into [a] hill (about 150 yards). The quad worked the ridges over in a magnificent manner. So thoroughly that a dust cloud hovered over the first and nearest ridge.

General Ferenbaugh worked his way down to me, and we spent an hour discussing the different angles of the situation. At 2100, all three of us, but not together, moved out. I led off down the hill, breaking a path through the foliage. When I was about fifty feet from and above the tank, I whistled, Lt. Stanaway answered, I asked him how he wanted us to get in. He gave instructions and said to wait five minutes and he'd get ready. We waited, spread out on the hill, until he hollered. Then I crawled on down to the tank and lay by [the] tracks. Lt. Stanaway ordered me around the rear of the tank "fast." I scooted around and found Stanaway under the tank with a .45 in his hand. He ordered me into the tank. I crawled to [the] front and up into [the] escape hatch. The crew inside warned me that they had a wounded man, one of our guards, and not to get on his leg.

General Ferenbaugh was right behind me, and shortly after Bralley. Then I remembered the maps in [the] jeep. Lt. Stanaway, when informed, ordered the tank to back up to [the] jeep, [the] man in [the] turret giving directions. Lt. Stanaway and myself, again under the tank, saw that we were about twelve feet behind [the] jeep. He covered me from any close work with his pistol, firing at random, as I sprinted to the jeep, secured [the] maps, and came back. We entered the tank, moved out to a safe area, transferred to a jeep, and came back to [the] Div CP.[36]

1ST LT. IVAN G. STANAWAY, LEADER, 2D PLATOON, 32D TANK COMPANY: On 24 May, Lt. Stanaway's platoon rescued General Ferenbaugh. The information reported by Capt. Chandler, his aide, was correct, except that there were only armored vehicles in the rescue column; there were no quad 50s. The rescue was made [about 1,000 yards], north of Sinjom-ni, at the same place that Task Force Hazel had encountered its first enemy fire. Stanaway stated that his platoon eliminated two enemy machine gun nests "for sure" while rescuing the general. After picking up the general and his party, Stanaway had a total of ten men in his tank, including the general, his aide, his driver, one wounded MP soldier, and the sergeant who attended the wounded MP. While waiting for the general to come down, he heard someone shout "hello." He thought it was the general, so he opened his hatch and answered. Several feet away stood a Chinese. Stanaway motioned with his .45 pistol for the Chinese to move down the road in front of his tank where he could be covered, but the Chinese started to climb up the front of the tank. The Chinese had his weapon, a rifle. Stanaway shot him six times with his pistol. He thought the Chinese was a diversion for an enemy attack in force. Later a satchel charge was found beside his tank. This consisted of five pounds of picric acid tied to a pole.

A psychological warfare unit in an M8 (light armored car) had come back and informed Stanaway of the general's ambush. Stanaway was at the time organizing his tank column to move ahead of the infantry. Stanaway ordered his platoon to follow him down the road. He picked up the wounded MP and the psychological warfare sergeant, then, as it was getting dark, picked up the general, his aide, and his driver. He backed his tank to the general's jeep while Capt. Chandler got maps from the jeep. Six Chinese appeared up the road 75 yards away, and Stanaway fired at them while Chandler got the maps.[37]

Thirty-second Infantry Regiment's Delayed Activity, Periodic Operations Report No. 49, 232200–242200 May 1951, 26 May 1951.

Delayed rpt of available information covering rescue of Comdg General and party. Approximately 241800 hrs Psychological Warfare Loudspeaker Team Sgt. Lawrence O'Brien in charge was dispatched with an Armored M20 Scout car to join Task Force Hazel, which had already penetrated heavy enemy S/A [small arms] fire to Ch'unch'on. M20 proceeded beyond the 1st Bn area under S/A fire from high ground above the road to vic [about 1,000 yards north of Sinjom-ni] where at approximately 1915 hrs they discovered two jeeps of the Div commander's party ambushed with two friendly KIA and one friendly WIA pinned under the rear vehicle. Sgt. O'Brien dismounted and remained with the wounded man while the armored car returned under heavy S/A fire to the 1st Bn area for assistance. 1st Bn dispatched attached tank plat from RCT 32d Tk Co under command of Lt. Stanaway on rescue mission. Rescue force proceeded thru intense S/A fire to reach ambush scene approximately 2100 hrs where the wounded man and Sgt. O'Brien were taken aboard. Tk proceeded to Div Commanders vehicle where thru skillful use of the tanks covering fire the enemy S/A was subdued sufficiently to effect the rescue of the Div Cmdr, Maj. Gen. Ferenbaugh, and his aide Capt. Chandler. Rescue force returned to 1st Bn area without further incident.[38]

Among the materials in his manuscript, Lt. Blumenson noted a "statement in conversation, 22 June 1951, with an officer who preferred to remain unidentified."

"General Hoge [IX Corps commander] was trying to impress on divisions that this was the time for pursuit of the enemy. No one else seemed to realize the enemy had been damaged so badly. One platoon of the 32d Tank Company was thrown in because no one knew how much enemy was there. When the general [Ferenbaugh] turned up missing, everyone was in a flap, and everyone forgot about Hazel."[39]

Soon after midnight Capt. Hazel was informed that he would pass through friendly lines (Hills 387 and 347) at 0600 hours on 25 May, reinforced with three platoons of the 32d Tank Company, with the mission of returning to Ch'unch'on. The 17th Infantry was to be mounted on trucks and attack through the 32d Infantry, move rapidly to Ch'unch'on, and secure the river crossing sites and the high ground north of town. Capt. Hazel describes the second advance to Ch'unch'on.

At 0130, 25 May, Hazel reported to regimental headquarters near Pusawon-ni [five miles north of Hongch'on]. He received instructions to take the task force back to Ch'unch'on that morning, leaving friendly lines at 0600, with three platoons, 32d Tank Company, attached. Parr, executive officer, 7th Reconnaissance Company, handled preparations for the task force so that Hazel could get some rest.

On 25 May, Hazel picked up the three platoons of the 32d Tank Company . . . south of Sinjom-ni. A forward observer of the 48th Field Artillery Battalion rode in Hazel's tank. The order of march was: 2d Platoon, 32d Tank Company, 7th Recon Company, and 1st and 3d Platoons, 32d Tank Company. Hazel instructed the column to proceed as fast as possible but to be on the alert for mines.

As the force advanced, it fired very little. Just beyond the Wonch'ang-kogae [a pass about two and one-half miles north of Sinjom-ni], three American soldiers of the 32d Tank Company, part of the crew lost the night before, were found. They informed Hazel that Lt. Ames was dead; the tank had gone over the bank. They said everyone else was dead. They crawled into the tanks in the rear of the column. Several hundred yards farther . . . Hazel found Ames's tank lying on its left side, fifty yards down from a steep cliff. There was no movement there, so the task force continued.[40]

One of the survivors of Lt. Ames's group, Sgt. Robert L. Kammerer, describes what happened; his company commander, Capt. N. L. James, provides additional information about the loss of Lt. Ames's tanks.

SGT. KAMMERER, TANK COMMANDER, 4TH PLATOON, HEAVY TANK COMPANY, 32D INFANTRY: The task force left the airstrip a little after 2000, 24 May, with the reconnaissance company leading out. Kammerer was next to the last tank in the column. It was getting dark when his tank "just stopped." Blaskiewicz told Kammerer to hook on to the last tank. It was very dusty, so there was a big interval between the tanks. Lt. Ames pulled around, hooking his cable on Kammerer's tank. After towing Kammerer 300 to 400 yards up the grade to the mountain pass, Ames said he couldn't tow any farther. He ordered Kammerer to drop off his tank and get the guns off. Kammerer's .50 caliber machine gun hadn't worked all day. Kammerer don't know why. But he removed the back plate. His crew removed the .30 caliber machine guns and put them on Ames's tank. He removed the percussion mechanism of the 76mm gun. Someone took the electrical wiring off. Kammerer put a WP grenade on the radio. Everyone got inside Ames's tank; the four prisoners of war climbed on the rear deck. Ames told the driver, "keep going no matter what happens." Kammerer was firing the .50 caliber machine gun, but it wouldn't work too well, so Kammerer got inside the tank. The loader's hatch was open, so Kammerer leaned out to close it. Ames was trying to close his hatch. No lights were on, and the driver was buttoned up. The road turned sharply to the right, and the tank continued straight ahead into a gully forty feet deep, rolling over on its side after a roll of 1½ times. Someone said, "Don't get panicky." Everyone got out of the tank. Three of the four prisoners of war were there when Kammerer got outside. Private Lahr was cut above the eyebrows. They looked for Ames, but he was inside and couldn't be gotten out. . . . Lt. Ames was caught between the gun guard and roof of the tank. He was killed instantly.

Capt. Hazel had said over the radio that he would wait at the top of the pass for Ames, so Kammerer and two men started out to get to Hazel. Nearly at the top of the pass, they heard Chinese talking on the road in front of them. Kammerer dropped over the bank of the road, waiting and listening. Then they heard Chinese to their rear as well as to their front. They just lay and waited. Two hundred yards away the Chinese set up two or three mortars and got off a few rounds. Then friendly artillery started coming into the area. About 0400, Kammerer and the two men crawled fifty yards to the right into a clump of bushes.

When they heard the tanks coming that morning (25 May), Kammerer took off his white T-shirt, crawled to the road, and waved his shirt at the tanks. Each of the three men got into one of the last three tanks. The other men were picked up at Ames's tank, and the column proceeded to Ch'unch'on. All nine men of Ames's tank were placed in the tank that had struck a mine in town, and they waited there until Ch'unch'on was secured later that morning.[41]

CAPT. JAMES, COMMANDER, HEAVY TANK COMPANY, 32D INFANTRY: On 24 May, the 7th Reconnaissance Company and one platoon (five tanks and one bulldozer tank; the latter was added because of reported craters in the road), Heavy Tank Company, 32d Infantry Regiment (hereafter referred to as the 32d Tank Company), formed Task Force Hazel. The task force formed in the vicinity of the pass Surisil-kogae, at Hill 317, and passed through the front lines there. . . .

On the return trip, one tank of the 32d Tank Company ran out of gasoline as the force started out of Ch'unch'on. It was towed. The force had conflicting orders, to stay in Ch'unch'on, to come out. The ambush of General Ferenbaugh, commanding general, 7th Infantry

Division, complicated matters. Finally at 2030, the task force was ordered to pull back and hole up for the night. Arrangements for gasoline replenishment were made so that the task force tanks would not have to return all the way back. The tank being towed was at the rear of the column. James did not know why this was done. He felt that a disabled tank should not have brought up the rear. The last word James heard from the task force was about 2230.

The tanks pulled back within friendly lines between 2330 and 2345, four miles behind the battalion CP, in order to gas up. At that time, James counted the tanks and discovered two missing. It was 0130, 25 May, before James could contact Capt. Hazel and inquire about the missing tanks. Hazel was surprised to learn that two were missing. He said that so far as he knew, all the tanks had come out at the same time. He also said that the tanks must be only one mile out. Communications had been difficult, however, because all the task force radios were not functioning properly throughout the day. James tried to contact his missing tank by radio. There was no answer to his calls; no contact was possible. James got back to his company CP between 0230 and 0300, 25 May, and made plans for the task force that day.

James ran three platoons of his company to the vicinity of Sinjom-ni. This move was made at night. The tanks arrived at 0230. One platoon, which had been posted at Sinjom-ni, had rescued General Ferenbaugh, then established a roadblock so that Task Force Hazel could pass through it on its return to friendly lines.

At daylight, 25 May, the six tanks of the 7th Reconnaissance Company and eleven tanks (three platoons) of the 32d Tank Company formed under Hazel's command to go to Ch'unch'on. The dozer was not included in this organization because it had lost belts on its blade, its clutch was bad, and it was leaking oil. The remaining portion of the 32d Tank Company (five tanks) stayed with the attacking battalion.

Several hundred yards north of the Wonch'ang-kogae, the task force encountered one missing tank. It had missed a turn in the road and turned over. As James recapitulated the story, this is what occurred. The preceding day, after towing the tank without gas a certain way, it was decided that it would be impossible to get it all

the way back. This tank was abandoned at the bend in the road after the radio was destroyed, the wires of the collector ring (the electrical conduits) were pulled out. The men of this tank entered the
tank which had been towing it and proceeded. This tank then carried ten men plus four prisoners of war on the outside deck. When
the driver missed a turn, the tank fell in a gully, turned over. Lt.
Ames was caught under the gun shield and killed. The task force
picked up the nine survivors, plus three of the four prisoners (one
was dead of enemy fire) and took them to Ch'unch'on on 25 May.[42]

*Capt. Hazel continues his description of the return to
Ch'unch'on.*

The tanks arrived at Ch'unch'on at 0830 without opposition
and deployed in the town. Hazel outposted all sides of the town and
awaited further orders. Then he began receiving sniper fire from the
direction of Hill 302 [north of town]. He destroyed two houses and
the schoolhouse, received no further fire.

Lt. Stallcup, 32d Tank Company, came to Hazel, bringing a
small Korean boy with a note from American Marines who had
been prisoners of war requesting that the tanks pick them up. Hazel
was skeptical and hesitated to send tanks into the hills. He instructed Stallcup to hold the Korean boy until he received further instructions. Word then came that the 3d Battalion, 17th Infantry, was en
route to Ch'unch'on and would join Task Force Hazel at 1100. The
task force was to meet the infantry south of town.

Hazel moved three platoons to the northeastern part of town.
He took the 7th Reconnaissance Company tanks to an area west of
the school. In the vicinity of Sinchon [southeast of Ch'unch'on,
while en route], a light plane buzzed the tanks and dropped a message. American prisoners of war had laid out a panel requesting
rescue. Capt. Anderson [7th Infantry Division's Light Army Aviation Section] said he would lead the tanks. Hazel dispatched Lts.
Miller and Nunn and three tanks.[43]

*Other members of the task force and Capt. James, 32d Tank
Company, describe the return to Ch'unch'on and the discovery of
American prisoners of war.*

LT. STANAWAY, LEADER, 2D PLATOON, 32D TANK COMPANY:
On 25 May Lt. Stanaway accompanied Task Force Hazel into
Ch'unch'on. The elements were march ordered as follows: 2d Platoon, 32d Tank Company, 7th Reconnaissance Company, 3d and
1st Platoons, 32d Tank Company. Stanaway rode the lead tank. No
enemy were encountered until Stanaway received sniper fire as he
was crossing the Soyang-gang [Soyang River] 400 yards to the left
of the bridge [north of Ch'unch'on]. He forded the river, which was
about three feet deep. He remained there about an hour. Then he
received orders from Hazel to go northeast to the Wonjin Ferry [on
the Soyang about three miles from Ch'unch'on] to block the northern and eastern approaches to town. On the way there, his platoon
got one antitank gun. The four- or five-man crew of the gun was
sleeping in a house twenty-five yards from the gun. The tankers got
the men first, then the gun, with two rounds of 76mm HE on each.

Going down the road, where the road turned sharply to the
right, Stanaway saw five men in a house. The tanks blew up the
house with WP and HE. Fifty yards from the house in a cave on the
left of the road, two Chinese were sleeping. One Chinese reached
for his rifle. Stanaway shot him with his carbine. The gunner fired
one round of 76mm and got both of them. Stanaway set up a roadblock at the Wonjin Ferry, north of the river. An air OP dropped a
note informing him of thirty to forty enemy in trenches 500 yards
to the tank direct front. He took his platoon on the road, moved
there. The tanks, in skirmish formation, moved across the field toward an unnamed village between Ch'onjon-ni and Tojigori [prob-
ably Hach'onjon-ni, about 500 yards north of the Wonjin Ferry],
firing and running over enemy troops. The infantry on the following
day counted twenty-two enemy dead.

The platoon then pulled back to the Wonjin Ferry. It was thought
that the valley was one of the main enemy escape and supply routes.
The platoon took care of a 57mm recoilless rifle carried by four
Chinese on a ridge. All afternoon, 25 May, the platoon spotted
groups of four to eight trying to escape. The platoon fired at these
enemy groups. Stanaway knew "for certain" that the platoon got
fifteen. The 7th Reconnaissance Company took over his position for
the night. The big valleys around Ch'unch'on comprised some of the

best tank country seen in Korea by Stanaway. Some tank formations were possible, instead of operating as usual, one tank behind
the other.[44]

CAPT. JAMES, COMMANDER, 32D TANK COMPANY: In
Ch'unch'on, the three platoons of the 32d Tank Company were sent
out in a fanning movement. One tank of those sent out to the southeast part of town struck a friendly mine (M5) at a road junction.
The twenty-two pounds of TNT buckled the bottom of the tank
and killed one man [PFC Sherman P. Cruts Jr.].[45] This information
was learned from a map overlay found later. The Marines had mined
all the roads out of Ch'unch'on except the escape route when they
had withdrawn.[46]

LT. NUNN, 2D PLATOON, 7TH RECONNAISSANCE COMPANY: On
25 May a task force consisting of tanks got to Ch'unch'on at 0900.
There was no enemy resistance and no enemy fire. The reconnaissance company tanks went to the dike at the airstrip and lined up.
From there, the tanks placed some fire on Hill 302 [north of town].
About 1100, as Nunn started to move to the southern part of town
on Hazel's order, Capt. Anderson flying overhead dropped a note
and informed the tankers of the presence of released American prisoners of war. Nunn proceeded with three tanks to the vicinity of
Hach-ilchon [about one mile southwest of Ch'unch'on] and found
eighteen U.S. Marines and one soldier. They took the releasees to
the main road about noon, and by then the 17th Infantry was in
Ch'unch'on.[47]

1ST LT. MAX R. STALLCUP, LEADER, 1ST PLATOON, 32D TANK
COMPANY: On 25 May, the seventeen tanks of Task Force Hazel
proceeded to Ch'unch'on without incident. Stallcup's platoon was
last in the column after the reconnaissance company. He picked up
Sgt. Kammerer and others of Lt. Ames's tank. In Ch'unch'on, his
platoon proceeded to the western part of town, 100 yards back of
the railroad dike, west of the airstrip. The platoon blasted a few
possible enemy positions west of the dike. Some of the sniper fire
came in from the high ground in the center of town to the rear of the
1st Platoon and the reconnaissance company. He placed machine
gun and 76mm fire on Hill 302.

A small Korean boy brought him a message written on the back of a Chinese safe conduct pass. This message read as follows:

TO U.S. TROOPS

THERE ARE 19 ESCAPED MARINE POWS AT A POINT NEAR HERE. THIS KOREAN KID WILL GUIDE YOU TO US. WE WERE CAPTURED ON NOVEMBER 30, 1950 NEAR THE CHOSIN RESERVOIR AT HAGARU-RI. YOU ARE OUR FAIRY GOD-MOTHER. FOR CHRIST SAKE GET US OUT OF HERE.

/s/ Charles L. Harrison
S/Sgt, USMC
ex-1st Mar Div M.P. Co

/s/ Saburo S. Limomura
Army Cpl, attached
to 1st Mar Div
163 Mil Intell Svc Det
Hqs Bn.

PLEASE CHECK UP ON THESE 2 SIGNATURES AT HEAD-QUARTERS BATTALION FOR VERIFICATION.

Stallcup gave Hazel the message, and Hazel dispatched several tanks to effect the rescue.[48]

Capt. Edgar N. Anderson, pilot, 7th Division Army Light Aviation Section, provides more information about finding the prisoners, as well as observation of enemy activity in the area.

The Light Aviation Section [L19A aircraft] flew all day long on 24 May for Task Force Hazel. The last plane got in to the strip at darkness, 2130. Ch'unch'on was a key road hub, an escape route for elements on the right of IX Corps. When Task Force Hazel arrived in Ch'unch'on, the enemy bugged out to the north. Division estimated that 20,000 enemy were directly or indirectly affected by Task Force Hazel. Enemy elements north of Ch'unch'on were also affected. The roads north of Ch'unch'on were covered with routed Chinese. The Air Force had a field day on 25 May.

The tanks actually made no contact with 400 to 500 Chinese pulling out of Ch'unch'on on 24 May, although the tanks made an attempt to get within gun range of them. Four planes in one flight and four planes in a second flight hit these 500 enemy troops who were crossing the river north of Ch'unch'on about 1700.

Anderson, on 25 May, saw panels made of wallpaper strips spelling "POW, 19," and underneath the word "RESCUE," spelled out with shell cases. Anderson dropped a message to Hazel informing him of this. He then dropped a message to the prisoners, telling them to get out of the houses and remain in one spot. Because his radio went out, he went back to the airstrip, got another plane, returned, and led three tanks to the American prisoners released by the Chinese. The tanks moved very quickly to effect the rescue.[49]

Capt. Hazel continues his account of his unit's actions in Ch'unch'on.

When they [Lts. Miller and Nunn] reported back with nineteen Americans who had been held by the Chinese, the 17th Infantry Regiment began to arrive in Ch'unch'on. Hazel had been informed that he would be detached from the 32d Infantry and attached to the 17th Infantry upon arrival of the latter troops in town. Hazel informed Col. Carberry, executive officer, 17th Infantry, that he would take the American prisoners of war to the airstrip. Hazel requested air evacuation for them. He received no confirmation. He took the prisoners of war to the air strip, where numerous planes were already landing. The prisoners of war were evacuated by air.

Late that afternoon, the 7th Reconnaissance Company joined the 17th Infantry Regiment on its perimeter. Just before the infantry arrived, one tank of the 32d Tank Company was lost to a friendly mine.[50]

Several officers of the 7th Infantry Division, IX Corps, provide their assessments of Task Force Hazel.

CAPT. HAZEL, COMMANDER, 7TH RECONNAISSANCE COMPANY AND TASK FORCE HAZEL: Capt. Hazel was told that General Ferenbaugh, commanding general, 7th Infantry Division, had stated that

Task Force Hazel on 24 May had broken the back of the enemy defense. After the task force arrived in Ch'unch'on on that date, the enemy fled in all directions. On 25 May, the infantry rode into Ch'unch'on on trucks. Air caught hundreds of fleeing Chinese north of Ch'unch'on in the next 24 hours.[51]

CAPT. JAMES, COMMANDER, 32D TANK COMPANY: On 24 May the task force departed at 0600, returned to friendly lines at 2400. This, James felt, was too long a time interval without refueling, even though the distance involved was only thirty-five miles round trip. In Korea, an armored task force must have air liaison because of the high mountains that throw out all radio communications. Relay stations sometimes are successful, sometimes not. During the operation, it was sometimes necessary to send a communications jeep a distance of 2½ miles for verbal orders.

The armored task force was strong enough, in James's opinion, so that it could have stayed in Ch'unch'on the night of 24 May. Two terrain features, however, militated against permitting the task force to remain. These were the two mountain passes between Ch'unch'on and friendly lines [Wonch'ang-kogae and Morae-kogae] that the enemy could have blown and cut off the task force. After dark, James felt, it would have been better to remain in Ch'unch'on. For, if the Chinese had used any ingenuity at all, the task force would have lost all its tanks on its return trip.

James felt that the task force performed a successful mission. Many enemy probabilities, however, were not fulfilled. The enemy could have blocked the two passes, thereby knocking out most of the armor of the regiment plus the division reconnaissance company. Ch'unch'on had never been defended, either by friendly or enemy forces. Once on the high ground around town, military forces can advance more quickly than the enemy can flee. The enemy could certainly have dug out the road between friendly lines and Ch'unch'on because they were out of artillery range.[52]

MAJ. EDWARD F. DUDLEY, ASSISTANT G-3, 7TH INFANTRY DIVISION: The effect of the task force was to force the enemy to withdraw. At the same time, the task force disrupted the enemy withdrawal. It forced him to abandon considerable supplies and to leave American prisoners behind. It prevented him from further destruction of bridges and roads and from setting up deliberate defenses.[53]

Lt. Col. George B. Pickett, armored officer, IX Corps: The division reconnaissance company exists for the purpose of feeling out and developing the enemy situation within the limitations of its size and materiel. The use of a reinforced armored reconnaissance company developed the enemy situation and made the enemy's plight known to the division staff. The initial successes of TF Hazel on 24 May should have been exploited immediately. If TF Hazel had been reinforced in Ch'unch'on instead of withdrawn, the bag of enemy prisoners would have been greatly increased.

The strength of TF Hazel was inadequate for the mission assigned. A force consisting of two regimental tank companies, one infantry battalion, and the 7th Recon Company, supported by artillery, engineers, and air, would have had the advantage of being self-sufficient after arriving in Ch'unch'on, although some doubt exists if the unarmored infantry could have advanced through the passes into Ch'unch'on with the tank element. In any event, two tank companies and the 7th Recon Company would have been able to get through the passes. In estimating the composition of an armored force, the tank strength should be computed on the basis of the maximum number of tanks, consistent with other tank requirements, that can be employed in the most favorable terrain along the route or on the objective. In order to dominate the Ch'unch'on area, a minimum of two four-platoon companies (regimental type) or three of three-platoon companies (armored division type) are required. This figure is based on no enemy tank opposition. It would be correspondingly higher if enemy armor were present. Communications between the armored task force and the headquarters under which it operates must be continuous and adequate. The numerous relays of messages required during this operation resulted in garbled orders and the resultant confusion of the TF commander.

A fully covered armored personnel carrier that can go anywhere that tanks can go was needed. The lack of overhead protection on the half-tracks required the TF commander to leave his dismounted elements behind since they were unable to run the gauntlet of enemy fire in open half-tracks. Also the need for armored infantry in Korea was once again clearly demonstrated. Deep penetrations and armored operations where organized enemy positions must be bypassed requires tanks, *armored* infantry, *armored* engineer, and *armored* artillery. If any of the components of the team are unarmored, then armored results cannot be fully obtained.

The operation of TF Hazel clearly demonstrates the flexibility of employment of armored reconnaissance units. Here is a situation where an intended routine patrol was quickly converted by the TF commander into an exploitation operation. Although handicapped by inadequate means to perform the mission of blocking the escape of the entire enemy force, the TF broke the back of the enemy resistance in the Ch'unch'on area, completely demoralized the enemy, and "kept the skeer on him."

The operation was hampered by lack of information on the location of friendly minefields, and one tank was disabled by a friendly mine. It is mandatory that accurate information of friendly minefields be disseminated to company level, especially tank and armored reconnaissance companies. Our mine doctrine calls for dissemination of this information; failure to do so is a failure of command. Somewhere information of the friendly minefields in Ch'unch'on existed, but the TF commander did not have it.

This operation also demonstrates the ability of armored forces, roving deep in the rear of established enemy defense lines, to surprise and terrorize forces in the enemy rear. This is even more true against a foe having limited warning (communication) facilities. It also proved that the blanket dismissal of large-scale armored operations in Korea by a wave of the hand and a "Korea's not tank country" attitude is completely erroneous. Every opportunity to employ armor, regardless of the smallness of the scale, should be sought and exploited, for even tank platoon–size employment achieves outstanding results. The CCF, in every engagement where armor has been employed by armored commanders according to armor doctrine, have been demoralized—They have lived up to Forrest's [Confederate cavalry commander Nathan Bedford Forrest] statement, "The best way to lick these Yankees is to put the skeer on 'em and keep it on 'em," by establishing the modern version of "put the skeer on the CCF with tanks and use tanks to keep it on 'em."[54]

Lt. Gen. William M. Hoge, commanding general, IX Corps. Task Force Hazel was a 7th Infantry Division operation; General Hoge directed only that an armored spearhead be sent to Ch'unch'on. The purpose of such a force was to soften up the enemy, disrupt his rear, and facilitate the division attack to capture its objective, Ch'unch'on. General Hoge felt that a company of tanks and a battalion of infantry should have formed the task force.

This operation, General Hoge stated, was a normal use of armor. Corps was constantly examining the situation in order to determine where tanks might be slipped through the enemy lines in order to disrupt his operations. The Hongch'on–Ch'unch'on axis, an avenue that permitted the use of an armor-infantry task force, was one of the few places in Korea where tanks could be used in such a manner. Ch'unch'on was a natural road hub and a center for the concentration of enemy personnel and supplies.

The attack in general was over terrain that was suitable tank country. The Marines had patrolled to Ch'unch'on several days before Task Force Hazel and had encountered no enemy forces. Mines and the possibility that the enemy would block the defiles constituted the only dangers to an armored force.

General Hoge criticized the organization of Task Force Hazel from the point of view of size. At least a tank company should have been used. He would have preferred that a battalion of infantry, a battalion of tanks, [and] a battalion of artillery had been sent to Ch'unch'on, for such a force would have been able to remain there.

Although the infantry was supposed to follow and reinforce Task Force Hazel, the infantry did not take advantage of the opportunity. A force two or three times as large as Task Force Hazel, followed promptly by infantry reinforcements, would have caused much more destruction of the enemy and facilitated the attack of the division. Furthermore, General Hoge believed that a task force could have been in Ch'unch'on twenty-four hours earlier if more aggressive action had been taken.

The purpose of the entire corps's advance at this time was to cut off the enemy who was withdrawing not only to the north, but also from east to west through Ch'unch'on in order to retreat toward Hwach'on. General Hoge had desired that the force remain in Ch'unch'on and be reinforced by infantry that night. He felt that more aggressive action should have been taken to get a larger force there earlier.[55]

CONCLUSION

The United Nations Command and Eighth U.S. Army fully expected both phases of the Fifth Chinese Offensive, and they made several methodical advances to keep the enemy off-balance as well as to position UN forces to receive the enemy counteroffensive on the ground of their choosing. Although forewarned, many UN and Eighth Army units continued to press north to gain a new defensive line rather than wait for the inevitable Chinese attack. In Operation Rugged, at the end of March 1951, Ridgway, then still commanding the Eighth Army, reiterated his three basic principles: coordinating the forces, inflicting maximum punishment on the enemy, and maintaining the Eighth Army's units intact. Attaining Line Kansas would consolidate the line of the UNC and Eighth Army for either attack or defense.[1]

The Eighth Army then continued to move toward Line Wyoming to threaten the enemy buildup in the Ch'orwon–Kumhwa–P'yonggang "Iron Triangle." With Ridgway's concurrence, Van Fleet, the new Eighth Army commander, kept creeping forward in April, refusing to remain static at any time despite the threat of an impending Chinese offensive. When the Chinese Fifth Offensive came on the dark night of 22–23 April, the Eighth Army fell back according to Operation Audacious, a withdrawal plan capitalizing on large-scale artillery traps and terrain withdrawals to maximize enemy casualties. UN forces lost the ground gained in Operations Dauntless and Rugged, the two major UNC offensives before the new Chinese offensive.

Though Ridgway had decided to trade space for inflicting a heavier loss on the enemy, the Spring Offensive bit hard into some unit positions. In the worst UNC loss of the entire Chinese Spring Offensive, the 1st Battalion, Gloucestershire Regiment, known as the Glosters, was annihilated, partially because of the overconfidence of its brigade commander (see chapter 7).

By 23 April Eighth Army intelligence had analyzed the enemy's progress and intentions. Correctly assessing that the Fifth Offensive had begun, the G-2 noted that rapid follow-up movements came immediately after the enemy attacks and that the main effort was in the west, where converging attacks were aimed at Seoul.[2]

Essentially, this was exactly Marshal Peng Dehuai's plan. He had concentrated eleven Chinese People's Volunteer Armies along with two of the NKPA corps for this "First Impulse," a total of forty-two divisions.[3] Only artillery and tanks supported these thrusts because the U.S. Fifth Air Force's cratering of airfields and its forward fighter operations in "MIG Alley," south of the Yalu River, prevented any significant employment of Chinese airpower. Peng skirted the Iron Triangle and the Ch'orwon corridor in his main attacks because they were advantageous to UN armor.[4]

The Ch'orwon approach ran south from the key enemy concentration area of the Iron Triangle. Here, a cut in the northern and southern branches of the Taebaek mountains that ran south via Kumhwa formed the central corridor to the south. In this sector and within the larger approach corridor, the steep hills forming the lower ground of the highlands further limited the usable routes and funneled traffic south on dirt roads toward Seoul along the Uijongbu corridor, Route 3. This began at a Y-shaped road junction that joined at Uijongbu connecting the roads from Wonsan, Kumhwa, and the western coast.[5]

The Uijongbu corridor and the wider "western corridor," from P'yongyang to Seoul, used by the North Koreans in June 1950, were the main axes of advance. While Russian-made tanks and a mix of old Japanese and captured trucks used the roads for night movement, Peng's advancing troops swarmed over every ridgeline and hill mass that bisected the peninsula's trails and unimproved dirt roads, as well as the major roads Routes 1 and 3. This meant that the entire sector was breached, and that roadblocks and holding key terrain were insufficient to halt the Chinese advance.

In meeting the enemy onslaught, Van Fleet ordered a withdrawal behind Line Kansas in the west and center, and he eventually rolled his defense even farther back with the enemy punch to Line Delta, about halfway between the original line and Seoul. With penetrations in both the east and west, Van Fleet modified his "Audacious Plan." He now added Line Waco, north of Seoul, extending from midway on the Kimpo Peninsula and Han River Estuary to the north of Seoul and then on farther east and northeast. The final line became known as the No Name Line.[6] Thus, Van Fleet held Seoul despite Ridgway's permission to abandon it, and the Chinese halted after 29 April to replace and refit for the Second Impulse.[7]

By the end of April Eighth Army intelligence assessed enemy casualties at 70,000. All UN troops now held the designated No Name defense line and patrolled it waiting for the enemy to launch its expected second attack.[8]

Both Chinese and North Korean forces now remained unaggressive, offering little resistance to the Eighth Army's patrols, which ranged as much as five to six miles north of the main line of resistance. The heaviest enemy concentrations remained on the main approaches to Seoul both in the far west (Munsan-ni corridor on Route 1) and in central area (Uijongbu and Route 3 corridors).[9]

No fewer than four full Chinese armies broke contact and moved northward to resupply. An additional four armies now lay north of the UN lines, each with only one division manning a thin outpost line across that army's front. The enemy's capabilities and probable intentions were obvious—Peng was preparing to launch his Second Impulse to the Fifth Offensive; he had the capability of striking individually or in simultaneous locations at any time in the west or west-central sectors. This possibility became more likely following 10 May, after enemy concentrations were located.[10]

Facing the threat of a renewed Chinese offensive, Van Fleet told his troops: "Now [May] is the time to destroy him. I would like to make this our maximum effort and do it north of the Han [River]." The April Chinese offensive had concentrated on the left flank and center of the Eighth Army and was halted. Marshal Peng decided to switch to the right (east) of the line, a scheme of maneuver that fit Van Fleet's offensive plans and which he had already shifted troops to meet. Peng's operational intent still was to destroy UN division-size formations with overwhelming force.[11]

Van Fleet's reconcentration moved the U.S. 7th Infantry Division and 187th Airborne Regimental Combat Team to beef up a widened IX Corps sector and shifted the 1st Marine Division and ROK divisions. These moves put a greater concentration and maneuver force facing the enemy on the direct route from Seoul northward. This part of the line held on rugged ground, though only the westward defense along the Han River Estuary had positions dug in depth. These forces were set by 4 May. On 7 May the ROK I Corps on the east coast was ordered to attack north while U.S. I Corps' ROK 1st Division attacked as a diversion and as a means to strengthen the line. Both flanks met a delaying enemy covering their own preparations to assault.[12]

The enemy resumed major attacks on 16 May with heavy assaults against the right of U.S. X Corps and the ROK III Corps, achieving some penetrations. The previously hot sectors in the west and west-central regions experienced holding attacks. Van Fleet moved the U.S. 3d Infantry Division into the gap that opened when the ROK III Corps withdrew to a main defensive line. The Eighth Army had already absorbed the lessons of the April actions, particularly the destruction of units such as the Glosters. Van Fleet now refined his policy and stressed his new orders on 18 May at the daily command briefing:

> We want maximum casualties on the enemy; minimum on our own troops. Terrain itself doesn't mean much, but certain localities with significance must be held, i.e. SEOUL. . . . We want to hit him here and now. This "roll with the punch" conception is out and I have made this clear to Corps Commanders. We move back only to prevent the loss of a large unit, i.e., a battalion. Units will withdraw only on orders from higher headquarters, Regiment, Division, and Corps Commanders must be alert to critical situations on battalion level and be quick to take needed action. . . . We must fight on this line and put a terrific toll on the enemy; here is our opportunity.[13]

The enemy offensive was waning by 20 May, as Van Fleet launched counterattacks from the Eighth Army's western corps and the U.S. I and IX Corps, causing an enemy withdrawal in the west for several days. Shifting the battle front eastward as he'd foreseen, he stated, "In general, I still believe we should press on all fronts and not give the enemy any chance to regroup." Under the name Operation Piledriver, his final offensive launched on 22 May to clear up the Iron Triangle area. By the end of the month, virtually all enemy elements had begun to defend in the area of the Ch'orwon–Kumhwa–P'yonggang triangle and along the Imjin River in the west, a line almost identical to what they held when the Fifth Offensive began.[14]

The defeat Peng's troops suffered changed the nature of the war, although U.S. troops would continue to grind north, taking limited objectives and destroying the Chinese piecemeal. One Chinese POW gave the Eighth Army the future tactics of the CCF right after the failed Fifth Offensive:

> The objective of the CCF will be to destroy U.S. manpower. . . . Previously the CCF used large units such as three CCF divisions to one U.S. division. In this manner the CCF expected to overcome the U.S. with a sea of men. However, when the CCF concentrated such large numbers of men in a small area, it made them vulnerable to the U.S. "sea of fire" (artillery). . . . The CCF will now concentrate on the destruction of units, attacking one U.S. company with three CCF companies or one U.S. battalion with three CCF battalions. The main emphasis will be on destroying small U.S. infantry units, and to avoid concentrating large numbers of CCF troops where the U.S. can bring its superiority of artillery into effect.[15]

Thus, after May 1951 the Communist forces used massed manpower to destroy individual small United Nations units.[16]

UNC and the Eighth Army would continue limited offensive operations to grind up both North Korean and Chinese Communist Forces. Despite efforts both to limit combat operations and to negotiate an end to the conflict, the summer and fall would see some of the Eighth Army's most concentrated fighting. Van Fleet pressed to prevent the CCF from breaking contact to regroup and renewed fighting in his initial objective area of Ch'orwon and Kumhwa.[17]

The Chinese Fifth Offensive had been costly to both sides, but more so to the enemy. The Eighth Army recorded its April losses as 30,058 for all UN personnel for all causes. U.S. troops suffered 12,309 casualties, including 607 killed in action and 6,487 wounded; the remainder were non-battle or missing.[18] In May, when the entire Fifth Offensive ended and was counterattacked, 33,770 UN losses were reported for all causes. U.S. casualties for the period were 12,293 total; 745 were killed in action and 6,758 were wounded, and the remainder were missing or non-battle casualties.[19]

Van Fleet believed that 50 percent of the April Chinese and North Korean attackers were casualties.[20] In the last two weeks of May alone, the Eighth Army counted over 17,000 Communists dead, captured more than 10,000 POWs, and estimated a total of 105,000 enemy casualties. Chinese sources admit to the loss of 85,000 men during the fifty days of their offensive but do not specify whether they were killed, wounded, captured, or missing.[21] Later Marshal Peng admitted that the Fifth Offensive saw the highest losses the Chinese suffered in the course of the Korean War.[22]

Unknown to Van Fleet or Ridgway at the time, the war would soon have a new aspect at the tactical level, one predicated on the desire to fight while negotiating. Likewise, Marshal Peng would receive new guidance even before the change in UN strategy. Mao Zedong's reading of his Five Offensives required a total shift from major offensives to concentrated attacks designed to annihilate small forces, an approach termed piecemeal warfare.[23] Mao had originally told Peng, the CCF commander: "Win a quick victory if you can; if you can't, win a slow one."[24]

NOTES

1. The War before the Communist
Spring Offensive of 1951

1. Roy E. Appleman, *South to the Naktong, North to the Yalu*. U.S. Army in the Korean War (Washington, D.C.: Office of the Chief of Military History, 1960), passim. Appleman's volume is the beginning of the U.S. Army's official history of the war. It has detailed terrain maps and sketches of the major battles for most of 1950, all of which are necessary for a serious student of the war. For more detail on the events covered in this chapter and the rest of the book, see the bibliographical essay.

2. James F. Schnabel, *Policy and Direction: The First Year* (Washington, D.C.: U.S. Center of Military History, 1972), chaps. 11–14, passim; Anthony Farrar-Hockley, *The British Part in the Korean War*, vol. 1, *A Distant Objective* (London: HMSO, 1990), chaps. 12, 13; Maj. Gen. Charles A. Willoughby and John Chamberlain, *MacArthur, 1941–1951* (New York: McGraw-Hill, 1954), pp. 378–409; Maj. Gen. Courtney Whitney, *MacArthur: His Rendezvous with History* (New York: Alfred A. Knopf, 1955), pp. 396–427. MacArthur's G-2 (intelligence officer), Willoughby, and his primary assistant, Whitney, used excerpts of message traffic and reproduced intelligence reports to make MacArthur's case concerning his pursuit to the Yalu River.

3. Eighth Army War Diary, November 1950, United States National Archives and Records Administration (NARA), Record Group (RG) 407, Records of the U.S. Army Adjutant General's Office (hereafter cited as NARA, RG 407), entry 429, box 1122, sec. 1, pp. 70–114. Appleman, *South to the Naktong*, chap. 39 and passim.

4. Eighth Army War Diary, Section I Summary, November 1950,

NARA, RG 407, pp. 70–114, passim. MacArthur's views are in his *Reminiscences* (New York: McGraw-Hill, 1964). This issue and others were explored extensively in U.S. Senate hearings by the Armed Services and Foreign Relations Committees, 82d Congress, 1st sess., *Military Situation in the Far East. Hearings before the Armed Services and Foreign Relations Committees* (Washington, D.C.: U.S. Government Printing Office, 1951), pt. 1, pp. 1–320, passim.

5. Billy C. Mossman, *Ebb and Flow, November 1950–July 1951* (Washington: U.S. Army Center of Military History, 1990), chaps. 1–5. As Appleman did earlier, Mossman misidentified the CCF commander as Lin Biao. In reality, the Chinese Field Commander was Marshal Peng Dehuai (Peng Te-huai). See Spencer C. Tucker, ed., *Encyclopedia of the Korean War: A Political, Social, and Military History* (New York: Checkmark Books/Facts on File, 2002), s.v. Lin Biao, p. 387, and Peng Dehuai (Peng Te-huai), pp. 516–17. See also Matthew Ridgway's manuscript, "Korea: The First Year," in U.S. Army Center of Military History (USACMH), Special Collections (hereafter Ridgway MS Korea) or its revised commercial version, *The Korean War* (Garden City, N.Y.: Doubleday, 1967), chaps. 3, 4. The manuscript version is superior for its military detail; its final form is more critical of personalities and events, often to Ridgway's advantage. Ridgway ignores Walker's problems and massive contributions, always against great odds. See also Armed Services and Foreign Relations Committees, *Military Situation in the Far East.* For a comprehensive account of Ridgway and his actions from December 1950 to July 1951, see Roy E. Appleman, *Ridgway Duels for Korea* (College Station: Texas A&M University Press, 1990).

6. Charles R. Schrader, *Communist Logistics in the Korean War* (Westport, Conn.: Greenwood Press, 1995), chap. 7. The generally accepted view was that about ten days to two weeks of intense fighting and movement would halt the CCF for lack of supplies.

7. These operations and more combat actions are covered in the first two volumes in this series, William T. Bowers, ed., *The Line: Combat in Korea: January–February 1951* (Lexington: University Press of Kentucky, 2008) and *Striking Back: Combat in Korea, March–April 1951* Lexington: University Press of Kentucky, 2010). During this period the Chinese called their repetitive attacks First Offensive to Fourth Offensive, ending in March.

8. Armed Services and Foreign Relations Committees, *Military Situation in the Far East.*

9. Paul Braim, *The Will to Win: The Life of General James A. Van Fleet* (Annapolis: U.S. Naval Institute Press, 2001), chaps. 10, 11.

10. Ridgway MS Korea, pp. 368, 404–15.

11. Ibid., p. 401.

12. Ibid., p. 405.

13. Ibid., p. 406.

14. Ibid., pp. 409–10.

15. Mossman, *Ebb and Flow*, pp. 441–42. The new use of artillery would give the last two years of the Korean Conflict its reputation as an "artillery war" among some of its veterans.

16. "Terrain Reference Chart," accompanying Eighth Army Command Report, April 1951, NARA, RG 407, entry 429, box 1179.

17. See ibid.; also Far East Command publications, *Terrain Handbook No. 65, Seoul and Vicinity: Korea*; and *Terrain Handbook No. 66, Northern Korea*; Far East Command Geographic Branch, 1950, 1951. Mossman's maps are uniformly disappointing in understanding the ground; see *Ebb and Flow*, p. 363, map 31. Numerous photos, however, demonstrate the character of the battlefield. Map 34, of the Gloster Battlefield, on p. 422 clearly shows the tactical advantages and disadvantages of fighting in Korea.

18. Ridgway MS Korea, pp. 409–10.

19. Ibid.; Eighth Army Report of Operations, April 1951, p. 12. See also Mossman, *Ebb and Flow*, p. 354, map 29.

20. Eighth Army monograph, *Enemy Tactics*, Headquarters, Eighth Army, December 1951, pp. 3–5, USACMH Special Collections, 8-5.1A AL.

21. Ibid., pp. 7–8.

22. S. L. A. Marshall, *The River and the Gauntlet: Defeat of the Eighth Army by the Chinese Communist Forces November, 1950, in the Battle of the Chongchon River, Korea* (1953; repr.: New York: Time Inc., 1962), p. 1.

23. Ibid., p. 9.

24. Eighth Army Periodic Intelligence Report 278, 16 April 1951, NARA, RG 407, entry 429, box 1181, p. 3.

25. Eighth Army Periodic Intelligence Reports 278–83, 16–21 April 1951, NARA, RG 407, entry 429, box 1181, passim.

26. Eighth Army Periodic Intelligence Report 280, 18 April 1951, p. 7. The Eighth Army had adopted the Chinese terminology for the attack, which it had obtained from interrogations of prisoners of war.

27. Eighth Army Periodic Intelligence Report 282, 20 April 1951, p. 7.

28. Eighth Army Periodic Intelligence Report 283, 21 April 1951, p. 7.

29. Appleman, *South to the Naktong*, chap. 3 and p. 78, map 3.

30. Eighth Army Command Report, map to accompany Intelligence Annex, February 1951, NARA, RG 407, entry 429, box 1179. The ground encompassing both minor corridors constituted the Wonsan–Seoul corridor.

31. Mossman, *Ebb and Flow*, chap. 21 and map 32. The naming of corridors follows two practices. The major corridor from Wonsan to Seoul followed the gap of highlands between the North and South Taebaek Mountain ranges. The corridor itself, with the lower hills and its winding roads, was not a wide valley except in very few places until almost reaching Seoul. At the tactical level, corridors were named for major locations within the larger corridor, hence the Uijongbu corridor is the south end of the Wonsan–Seoul corridor. The corridor through the hills and paddies from Kaesong to Seoul is known universally as the western corridor, but these names appear not on maps but on military overlays showing avenues of approach. In Korea any road or trail was often considered an avenue, and wider ones were corridors if they went for great distances. The Chinese referred to the two phases of the offensive as "First Impulse" and "Second Impulse."

32. Eighth Army monograph, *Enemy Tactics*, pp. 1–3.

33. War Department: Field Manual (FM) 100-5, Operations, 1949, chap. 9.

34. S. L. A. Marshall, *Infantry Operations and Weapons Usage in Korea* (London: Greenhill Press, 1988), pp. 120–32. This is a reprint of his 1951 study, *Commentary on Infantry Operations and Weapons Usage in Korea, Winter of 1950–51* (Report ORO-R-13) (Chevy Chase, Md.), completed for the Operations Research Office of Johns Hopkins University on contract to the Department of the Army in Project Doughboy.

35. Shu Guang Zhang, *Mao's Military Romanticism: China and the Korean War, 1950–1953* (Lawrence: University Press of Kansas, 1995), p. 147.

36. Ibid., pp. 146–47.

37. Ibid.

38. Eighth Army Periodic Intelligence Report 284, NARA, RG 407, entry 429, box 1181, p. 7.

2. Battles along the Outpost Line

1. Developed by the U.S. Army Signal Corps, the Signal Corps Radio (SCR) 300 was an FM radio with a range of one to three miles

and weighed about forty pounds. It was carried in a backpack by an enlisted radio man and was used by infantry companies and battalions for communicating and by forward observers as they walked, thus acquiring the nickname "walkie-talkie." For wired field communications, the Army used both telephones powered by batteries (EE-8) and those powered by sound (TP-3) to link outposts, forward artillery observers, company, battalion, and regimental command posts. George Raynor Thompson, Dixie R. Harris, Pauline M. Oaks, and Dulaney Terrett, *The Signal Corps: The Test (December 1941 to July 1943)* (Washington, D.C.: Office of the Chief of Military History, 1957), pp. 69, 73, 75.

2. Interview, Capt. Cecil G. Smith, SFC Lewis E. Spencer, SFC James R. Root, Sgt. Robert E. Workman, and Cpl. Joseph J. Sapuppo by Capt. Pierce W. Briscoe, 13 July 1951, Ms. 8-5.1A BA13, Combat Outpost, U.S. Army Center of Military History, Fort McNair, Washington, D.C. (hereafter cited as CMH).

3. Capt. Pierce W. Briscoe, "Narrative, Hill 902," 3d Battalion, 32d Infantry Regiment, n.d., Ms. 8-5.1A BA14, Hill 902, 3d Battalion, 32d Infantry Regiment, CMH.

4. Interviews, Cpl. Jack A. Fazzino and PFC Billy L. McFadin, and Sgt. William R. Manning and PFC Marvin F. Lottman, both interviews by Capt. Pierce W. Briscoe, 16 July 1951, Ms. 8-5.1A BA14, Hill 902, 3d Battalion, 32d Infantry Regiment, CMH. Capt. Briscoe conducted all the interviews in this chapter, which are contained in Ms. No. 8-5.1A BA14. All cited excerpts are drawn from Briscoe's notes of his interviews as transcribed and reported in this document by him and his assistant, PFC Howard J. Clark.

5. "William R. Lees," National Archives and Records Administration, Access to Archival Databases (AAD), RG 407, Records of the U.S. Army Adjutant General's Office, "Korean War Casualty File, 2/13/1950–12/31/1953" (hereafter "Korean War Casualty File"), at http://aad.archives.gov/aad.

6. Report of the Action of Company I from 21 April to 23 April, in Unit Award Files, 3d Battalion, 32d Infantry Regiment Citation, folder 37, Record Group (RG) 338, Eighth U.S. Army, box 1182, National Archives and Records Administration (NARA). The 3d Battalion was awarded the Presidential Unit Citation for this action.

7. "George H. Allen, Jr.," "Korean War Casualty File," at http://aad.archives.gov/aad.

8. "John H. Beebe," "Korean War Casualty File," at http://aad.archives.gov/aad.

9. Interview, 1st Lt. Harry W. French, 16 July 1951.

10. "Edward D. Strocky," "Korean War Casualty File," at http://aad.archives.gov/aad.

11. "Thomas D. Boyle," "Korean War Casualty File," at http://aad.archives.gov/aad.

12. SFC Guy E. Woodhouse, Report of Action on Hill 902, in Unit Award Files, 3d Battalion, 32d Infantry Regiment Citation, folder 37, RG 338, Eighth U.S. Army, box 1182, NARA.

13. Interview, 1st Lt. Willard B. Rogers, 16 July 1951.

14. Manning and Lottman interview.

15. "Ralph G. Jones," "Korean War Casualty File," at http://aad.archives.gov/aad.

16. Fazzino and McFadin interview.

17. Manning and Lottman interview.

18. "Hiram T. Mabry," "Korean War Casualty File," at http://aad.archives.gov/aad.

19. "Clarence Matthews," "Korean War Casualty File," at http://aad.archives.gov/aad.

20. Fazzino and McFadin interview.

21. Woodhouse, Report of Action on Hill 902.

22. "Daniel F. Benton," "Korean War Casualty File," at http://aad.archives.gov/aad.

23. Report of the Action of Company I from 21 April to 23 April, in Unit Award Files, 3d Battalion, 32d Infantry Regiment Citation.

24. Woodhouse, Report of Action on Hill 902.

25. Report of the Action of Company I from 21 April to 23 April.

26. Rogers interview.

27. Major Lash's observation is drawn from his comment as cited in Briscoe, Narrative, Ms. 8-5.1A BA14, n. 30.

3. Caught in a Chinese Ambush

1. Capt. Edward C. Williamson, Narrative Report, n.d., Ms. 8-5.1A BA68, Hill 128: Forward Observation by Battery B, 999th Armored Field Artillery Battalion (155mm howitzers, self-propelled) during the April Chinese offensive on Seoul, CMH.

2. Interview, 2d Lt. (then warrant officer) David R. Reed by Capt. Edward C. Williamson, 31 July 1951, Ms. 8-5.1A BA68, Hill 128, CMH. Captain Williamson conducted all the interviews used in this chapter. All excerpts are drawn from Williamson's interviews as transcribed and recorded in this document by him and his assistants Cpls. Harold Higgins and Gilbert Perkins for Ms. 8-5.1A BA68, and by him

and his assistants Cpl. Harold Higgins and PFC Glenn A. Dimitt for Ms. 8-5.1A BA67, Pobwon-ni, CMH.

3. Interview, PFC Thomas McCall, 31 July 1951, Ms. 68.

4. Field artillery uses a circle of 6400 mils, where north is 0 or 6400, due west is 4800, south is 3200, and due east is 1600.

5. The M46 medium tank was based on the M26 Pershing heavy tank armed with a 90mm main gun that was introduced into combat in Europe in 1945. The M26 was modified in 1948 with a new engine and transmission and entered production as the M46, the first of a series of three heavy tanks (the M47 and M48 followed in the early 1950s) named in honor of Gen. George S. Patton Jr. The M46 saw extensive action in Korea in both U.S. Army and Marine Corps units. The M46 was armed with a 90mm main gun, a .50 caliber machine gun on the turret, and a bow-mounted .30 caliber machine gun. R. M. Ogorkiewicz, *Design and Development of Fighting Vehicles* (Garden City, N.Y.: Doubleday, 1968), p. 46, and *Armoured Forces: A History of Armoured Forces and Their Vehicles* (New York: ARCO, 1970), pp. 201–2; Robert Jackson, *Tanks and Armored Fighting Vehicles* (Bath, U.K.: Parragon Publishing, 2007), pp. 162–63, 169, 179, 182–83; Tucker, *Encyclopedia of the Korean War,* pp. 46–47.

6. The M39 armored utility vehicle (AUV) was based on the M18 motor gun carriage, a 76mm self-propelled tank destroyer. Developed and produced during World War II, the M39 was the first fully tracked armored personnel carrier to enter service in the U.S. Army when it was fielded in the European Theater of Operations in 1945. The tank destroyer turret and gun were removed and the .50 caliber machine gun added on a ring mount in the front of the open cargo-passenger area with no access doors. The M39 had a crew of three and could carry eight personnel. It was used for hauling personnel, supplies and equipment, ammunition, and the wounded, and it served as a prime mover when necessary. It had little side armor and no overhead armor covering, making it vulnerable to plunging and overhead fire and especially to grenade attacks. Ogorkiewicz, *Design and Development of Fighting Vehicles,* pp. 157–58; and *Armoured Forces,* p. 392.

7. Capt. Edward C. Williamson, Narrative Report, Pobwon-ni: Withdrawal of an armored 155mm Battery, self-propelled, attached to the 1st ROK Division, through an enemy roadblock during the April Chinese Offensive on Seoul, 22–24 April 1951, n.d., in Ms. 8-5.1A BA67, Pobwon-ni, CMH.

8. In the following account, unless otherwise noted, all information is from the group interview, Capt. James W. Welden, 1st Lt. Joseph V.

Spitler, 1st Lt. George A. Buonocore, M. Sgt. Lloyd M. Jenkins, SFC Frank Catalon, SFC George W. Jackson, Sgt. Henry D. Laws, SFC Joseph Word, and SFC Clarence C. Quander, 17 July 1951, Ms. 8-5.1A BA67. This interview is a confusing mixture of direct quotations and third-person narrative text. Excerpts from it will appear as both first- and third-person narrative.

9. Interview, M. Sgt. Enoch Scott, 17 July 1951. During this interview Scott was walking the site with Williamson, describing the ambush.

10. Interview, M. Sgt. Eldrich J. Henley, 17 July 1951.

11. The 20-ton M41 155mm howitzer motor carriage was developed from a M24 Chaffee light-tank chassis fitted with an M1 155mm howitzer. The M41 had a crew of five and carried 21 rounds of 155mm ammunition. Ogorkiewicz, *Armoured Forces,* pp. 377–78. Artillerymen in self-propelled units referred to their howitzers as "tanks." This Army phraseology has been retained in this book.

12. "Timothy Bell," "Korean War Casualty File," at http://aad .archives.gov/aad.

13. "Maurice I. Henry," "Korean War Casualty File," at http://aad .archives.gov/aad. Interview, Cpl. Thomas Meeks, 31 July 1951.

14. Interview, Cpl. Douglas M. Hackey, 17 July 1951.

15. Interview, Cpl. Anthony Jackson, 17 July 1951.

16. Interview, Cpl. Oscar O. Spraglin and Cpl. Amos Green, 17 July 1951.

17. Ibid.

18. Interview, Sgt. Robert J. Thompson, 31 July 1951.

19. Interview, Sgt. Curtis Wilcox and Cpl. Robert L. Howe, 17 July 1951.

20. Ibid.

21. Scott interview.

22. Ibid.

23. Henley interview.

24. For more detailed casualty information, see files "Luther Odums, James C. Harris, Nathan Steele, Jr., Charles Brown, and Clemmett Bennett," "Korean War Casualty File," at http://aad.archives.gov /aad. These files indicate that the 999th also suffered twenty-three wounded-in-action casualties on 23–24 April 1951.

25. Williamson, Narrative Report.

4. Tanks above Kap'yong

1. For a detailed tactical study of the ensuing action from the perspective of the 3d Battalion, Royal Australian Regiment, see Bob Breen,

The Battle of Kapyong: 3rd Battalion, the Royal Australian Regiment, Korea, 23–24 April 1951 (Sydney: Headquarters, Australian Army Training Command, 1992). For general coverage of these operations, see also Mossman, *Ebb and Flow,* pp. 398–409, and Anthony Farrar-Hockley, *The British Part in the Korean War,* vol. 2, *An Honourable Discharge* (London: HMSO, 1995), pp. 138–50.

2. Interview, Lt. A. Argent by 1st Lt. Martin Blumenson, 9 May 1951, Ms. 8-5.1A BA33, Tanks Above Kap'yong, CMH. Blumenson conducted all the following interviews that are contained in Ms. 8-5.1A BA33. All excerpts are drawn from Blumenson's interviews as transcribed and reported by him and SFC Raymond Lapino, his assistant.

3. Interview, 1st Lt. Kenneth W. Koch, 7 May 1951.

4. Lt. Col. George B. Pickett, Study, Company A 72d Tank Battalion (–3d Platoon) at Cheryong-ni–Kap'yong, 23–24 April 1951, n.d., in Ms. 8-5.1A BA33.

5. Interview, Maj. Thomas A. Murphy, 10 May 1951.

6. Interview, Maj. Don W. Black, 11 May 1951.

7. Interview, Capt. Blaine Johnson, 8 May 1951.

8. "Peter P. DiMartino," "Korean War Casualty File," at http://aad.archives.gov/aad.

9. Koch interview.

10. Interview, PFC Leroy W. Ritchotte, 7 May 1951.

11. Interview, PFC Bert Tomlinson, 7 May 1951.

12. Interview, Pvt. Robert B. Brown, 7 May 1951.

13. Interview, M. Sgt. Paul W. Ragen, 7 May 1951.

14. Interview, 1st Lt. Wilfred D. Miller, 7 May 1951.

15. Brown interview.

16. Koch interview.

17. Interview, Cpl. William O. Suiter Jr., 8 May 1951.

18. Tomlinson interview.

19. Ritchotte interview.

20. "Alban Chmielewski," "Korean War Casualty File," at http://aad.archives.gov/aad.

21. Koch interview.

22. Interview, SFC William A. Goad, 7 May 1951.

23. Interview, Sgt. Jerardo Rodriguez, 7 May 1951.

24. Interview, Sgt. Manford Wayson Jr., 7 May 1951.

25. Interview, PFC Wilbert A. Naasz, 7 May 1951.

26. Interview, Cpl. Frederick B. Fowler, 8 May 1951.

27. Miller interview.

28. Interview, SFC Rudolph Triscik, 8 May 1951.

29. Ragen interview.

30. Interview, PFC Louis Berg, 8 May 1951.

31. Koch interview.

32. Pickett, Study.

33. Argent interview.

34. Interview, Maj. Wade H. Padgett, 9 May 1951.

35. Interview, Sgt. Harold Burros, 9 May 1951.

36. Interview, Sgt. John L. Mazyck, 9 May 1951.

37. Interview, Cpl. Otho C. Bragg, 9 May 1951.

38. Interview, Cpl. Mason F. Scott, 9 May 1951.

39. Interview, PFC Arthur Lee Gayles, 9 May 1951.

40. Koch interview.

41. Suiter interview.

42. Burros interview.

43. Interview, PFC Johnnie L. Lewis, 9 May 1951.

44. Miller interview.

45. Interview, SFC Myles P. Moore, 8 May 1951.

46. Triscik interview.

47. Ragen interview.

48. "Paul Albaugh," "Korean War Casualty File," at http://aad
.archives.gov/aad.

49. Interview, 1st Sgt. Maxwell B. Bowman, 7 May 1951.

50. Koch interview.

51. Pickett, Study.

52. Murphy interview.

53. Mossman, *Ebb and Flow*, p. 407n29. For Lt. Koch, see Headquarters, Eighth U.S. Army, Korea, General Orders No. 378 (1 June 1951), and for Lt. Miller, see Headquarters, Eighth U.S. Army, Korea, General Orders No. 642 (14 August 1951). Lt. Miller, a 1950 graduate of the U.S. Military Academy, resigned from the Army in 1954 to pursue a civilian career. He died 28 September 1993. Lt. Koch had first joined the Army in 1943, was commissioned in 1944, and served in the Pacific. He commanded Company A, 72d Tank Battalion, in 1950–1951 and remained in the Army, reaching the rank of colonel. He commanded the 3d Armored Cavalry Regiment and then served as chief of staff, 9th Infantry Division, both at Ft. Lewis, Washington, before retiring in 1975. He died on 15 May 2007 in Tacoma, Washington. See Obituary, "Col. Kenneth W. Koch, USA (Ret.)," *Tacoma News Tribune*, 22 May 2007.

5. Artillery in Perimeter Defense

1. 1st Lt. Martin Blumenson, "Artillery in Perimeter Defense,"

Ms. No. 8-5.1A BA37, CMH. Russell A. Gugeler covered the 92d Armored Field Artillery Battalion's actions, relying heavily on Blumenson's manuscript, in chap. 12, "Artillery in Perimeter Defense," in his *Combat Actions in Korea: Infantry, Artillery, and Armor* (Washington, D.C.: Combat Forces Press, 1954), pp. 154–65.

2. For the sequence of events that led to the losses sustained by these units as well as the Company C, 2d Chemical Mortar Battalion, see Mossman, *Ebb and Flow,* pp. 381–84.

3. Interview, Lt. Col. Leon F. Lavoie by 1st Lt. Martin Blumenson, 8 June 1951, "Artillery in Perimeter Defense." Lt. Blumenson conducted all interviews in this chapter, which are contained in Ms. No. 8-5.1A BA37. All excerpts are drawn from Blumenson's interviews as transcribed and recorded in this document. It is important to note that on 20 February 1951 Lt. Col. Lavoie prepared and distributed to his command a mimeographed set of tactical notes and sketch map, "Paragraphs on Perimeters: The Artillery Perimeter in Korea," which laid out all the responsibilities and actions to be taken should such a situation as this occur. These notes are Part III of his manuscript.

4. Statement of Captain Wayne D. Hopkins, Battery Commander, 2d Rocket Btry, n.d., in Unit Award Files, RG 338, Entry Eighth U.S. Army, box 1180, NARA. Although it was recommended, the 2d Field Artillery (Rocket) Battery was not awarded the Presidential Unit Citation for this action. The unit was awarded the PUC for an action 4–12 October 1952, however; see Headquarters, Department of the Army, General Orders No. 28, 1953.

5. Lavoie interview.

6. Interview, Capt. Bernard G. Raftery, 8 June 1951.

7. Interview, Capt. John F. Gerrity, 8 June 1951.

8. Interview, 1st Lt. Joseph N. Hearin, 8 June 1951.

9. Lavoie interview.

10. Interview, M. Sgt. John D. Elder, 8 June 1951.

11. Lavoie interview.

12. Interview, Maj. Raymond F. Hotopp, 9 June 1951.

13. Interview, SFC Willis V. Ruble Jr., 8 June 1951.

14. Interview, Sgt. Edward Brown, 8 June 1951.

15. Interview, Sgt. Jessie D. Carter, 8 June 1951.

16. Gerrity interview.

17. Interview, SFC James R. White, 8 June 1951.

18. Interview, Sgt. Charles R. Linder, 8 June 1951.

19. Interview, Sgt. Austin E. Roberts, 8 June 1951.

20. Raftery interview.

21. Interview, 1st Lt. Robert E. McCord, 8 June 1951.

22. Interview, SFC George T. Powell, 8 June 1951.

23. Elder interview.

24. Interview, SFC Paul T. Roberts, 8 June 1951.

25. Interview, Sgt. Theral J. Hatley, 8 June 1951.

26. Hearin interview.

27. Raftery interview.

28. Hearin interview.

29. Hatley interview.

30. Powell interview.

31. Lavoie interview.

32. Hotopp interview.

33. Hearin interview.

34. Raftery interview.

35. P. Roberts interview.

36. U.S. Army casualty records for the 92d Armored Field Artillery Battalion reported only PFC Calvin C. Grant and Cpl. Mariano Arredondo killed in action during the fighting on 24 April 1951. "Calvin C. Grant" and "Mariano Arredondo," "Korean War Casualty Files," at http://aad.archives.gov/aad. Although Lavoie states in his interview that four men were killed in action, including Oliver Porter of the 2d Rocket Field Artillery Battery, an extensive search of the "Korean War Casualty Files" produced only the two men identified. The website of the 92d Armored Field Artillery Battalion on its Killed in Action page also lists only Calvin C. Grant and Mariano Arredondo and, erroneously, Oliver Porter. See www.92ndafa.homestead.com/92ndrosterkia.html.

37. Lavoie interview.

38. Ruble interview.

39. Brown interview.

40. Hotopp interview.

41. Raftery interview.

42. Hearin interview.

43. McCord interview.

44. P. Roberts interview.

45. Gerrity interview.

46. White interview.

47. "Oliver Porter," "Korean War Casualty Files," at http://aad.archives.gov/aad.

48. A. Roberts interview.

49. Linder interview.

50. Lavoie interview.

51. Raftery interview.

52. Gerrity interview.

53. Lavoie interview.

54. Blumenson, "Artillery in Perimeter Defense."

6. Hill 628

1. Capt. Martin Blumenson, "Action on Hill 628," n.d., preface, in Ms. 8-5.1A BA99, 8th Ranger Infantry Company (Airborne), CMH. When the interviews for Ms. 99 were conducted in June 1951, Blumenson was a first lieutenant. In April 1952, when Ms. 99 was submitted for review, the typed copy indicated that he was a captain. However, Blumenson did not sign any of the interviews. He was promoted to captain in February 1952 and departed Korea before the manuscript was submitted in April 1952. See File 319.1 (15 Apr 52) in manuscript for details.

2. James A. Herbert (20 July 1924–) graduated from the U.S. Military Academy in 1945 with a commission in the infantry. He served in the Philippines and Japan (1945–1948). While assigned to Airborne Battalion at the Infantry School, Ft. Benning, Georgia, he was given command of the 8th Ranger Infantry Company (Airborne) when it was formed in November 1950 and took it to Korea, where it was assigned to the 24th Infantry Division for combat operations. He was seriously wounded in the fighting described in this chapter. He later served a number of tours in Vietnam, including one as an advisor to the South Vietnamese (1965–1966), one as a battalion commander with the 187th Airborne Infantry Regiment (1966–1967), and one with the U.S. Military Assistance Command Vietnam (1967–1969). He was later promoted to brigadier general and served as assistant division commander, 82d Airborne Division (1972–1973). He retired in 1975 as a brigadier general. Herbert was inducted into the U.S. Army Ranger Hall of Fame in 2005. See Association of Graduates, U.S. Military Academy, *Register of Graduates and Former Cadets of the United States Military Academy, West Point, New York. 2000* (West Point, N.Y.: Association of Graduates, 2000), "James Arthur Herbert," in "Class of 1945," pp. 4–255; "Brigadier General (Retired) James A. Herbert," "Ranger Infantry Companies (Airborne) of the Korean War (RICA)," at www.ricarangers.org/rhof/herbert.htm.

3. Interview, 1st Lt. Alfred J. Giacherine by 1st Lt. Martin Blumenson, 7 June 1951, in Ms. 8-5.1A BA99. Blumenson conducted all of the interviews in Ms. 99 on 7 June 1951. All excerpts used in this chapter are drawn from Blumenson's notes of these interviews as tran-

scribed and reported by him and his assistant, Cpl. Gerald L. L'Heureux, in this document.

4. Interview, SFC James McNeely.

5. The SCR 536 was a short-range (one-mile), five-pound AM radio that could be held in one hand. It was used for communicating between infantry platoons and company headquarters. It was better known from World War II as the "handie-talkie" but was often erroneously referred to as "walkie-talkie" (see Thompson et al., *The Signal Corps*, pp. 73, 75).

6. Interview, Cpl. Henry P. Silka.

7. For information on the SCR 300, see chap. 2, note 1.

8. Giacherine interview.

9. Interview, Cpl. Charles N. Lenz.

10. McNeely interview.

11. Interview, Sgt. Connie M. Drum.

12. Interview, Sgt. Keith W. Smith.

13. Interview, Cpl. Joseph P. McGregor.

14. Interview, SFC Harry Zagursky.

15. Giacherine interview.

16. Lenz interview.

17. McNeely interview.

18. Interview, Cpl. Edward D. Smith.

19. McNeely interview.

20. E. Smith interview.

21. Lenz interview.

22. Giacherine interview.

23. Interview, M. Sgt. William R. Cox.

24. Interview, Cpl. Eugene C. Rivera. For his heroism on Hill 628, Cpl. Rivera was inducted into the Ranger Hall of Fame in 1998. See "Corporal Eugene C. Rivera," "Ranger Infantry Companies (Airborne) of the Korean War (RICA)," at www.ricarangers.org/rhof/rivera.htm.

25. Interview, Sgt. Harold J. Hooks.

26. Interview, Cpl. Robert W. Black. Black was later commissioned in the infantry in 1954 and served in the Army Rangers, reaching the rank of full colonel before retiring. He served in Vietnam and won numerous awards for bravery. He was inducted into the Ranger Hall of Fame in 1995. Col. Black is the leading authority on the history of the Army Rangers and has published numerous books on the subject, including his memoir, *A Ranger Born: A Memoir of Combat and Valor from Korea to Vietnam* (New York: Ballantine Books, 2002), *Rangers in World War II* (New York: Ballantine Books, 1992), and *Rangers in*

Korea (New York: Ballantine Books, 1989). Black provides personal accounts of the 8th Ranger Company's actions in his *A Ranger Born*, pp. 105–14, and *Rangers in Korea*, pp. 137–54. See also "Colonel Robert W. Black," "Ranger Infantry Companies (Airborne) of the Korean War (RICA)," at www.ricarangers.org/rhof/black.htm.

27. Interview, Cpl. Jesse Cisneros.

28. McGregor interview.

29. Interview, Cpl. William A. Varnell.

30. McNeely interview.

31. Lenz interview.

32. Cox interview.

33. Rivera interview.

34. K. Smith interview.

35. McGregor interview.

36. Zagursky interview.

37. Giacherine interview.

38. Rivera interview.

39. Cox interview.

40. K. Smith interview.

41. Interview, Sgt. Charles B. Taunton.

42. See "Paul E. Snavely, Jr.," and "Henry C. Trout, Jr.," and 8th Ranger Infantry Company (Airborne) casualties for 25 April 1951, "Korean War Casualty Files," at http://aad.archives.gov/aad.

43. Interview, M. Sgt. Charles R. Craig Jr.

44. U.S. Army casualty records show that all three of the forward observers from the 52d Field Artillery Battalion were wounded in action and Cpl. Otto T. Perkins died. See "Otto T. Perkins" and 52d Field Artillery Battalion casualties for 25 April 1951, "Korean War Casualty Files," at http://aad.archives.gov/aad.

45. Giacherine interview.

46. Blumenson, "Action on Hill 628," preface.

7. Gloster Hill

1. The documents contained in this chapter are records written as the events unfolded or prepared immediately following the Chinese attack. For more complete coverage of the British 29th Independent Infantry Brigade Group, the 1st Battalion, Gloucestershire Regiment (1st Glosters), and the CCF Spring Offensive that incorporates interviews and later, more detailed assessments, see Mossman, *Ebb and Flow*, pp. 379–429. For a very personal account of the 1st Glosters' fight by a

noted military historian and participant in the operation, see General Sir Anthony ("Tony") Farrar-Hockley, *The Edge of the Sword* (London: Frederick Muller, 1954), which has been reissued several times since its original publication, the most recent being by Pen and Sword in 2007. Farrar-Hockley (8 April 1924–11 March 2006) was a captain and the adjutant of the 1st Glosters during the battle in which he was taken prisoner. He received a Distinguished Service Order (DSO), equivalent to the U.S. DSC, for his actions during this fight. Even before retiring in 1983 from a distinguished military career dating back to 1941, he established himself as a prolific and gifted military historian and commentator with a number of publications to his name. Of these, the two-volume official history *The British Part in the Korean War*, comprising vol. 1, *A Distant Obligation* (London: HMSO, 1990), and vol. 2, *An Honourable Discharge* (London: HMSO, 1995), was one of his most important. The operations of the Glosters and British 29th Brigade along the Imjin are covered in vol. 2, pp. 111–37. For more on Tony Farrar-Hockley, see "General Sir Anthony Farrar-Hockley," in Obituary Archive of the London *Times* at www .timesonline,co.uk/tol/comment/obituaries/article740668.ece. An excellent detailed recent account of the British forces along the Imjin River in 1951 is Andrew Salmon, *To the Last Round: The Epic British Stand on the Imjin River, Korea 1951* (London: Aurum Press, 2009).

2. "Jock columns" were small British units that conducted reconnaissance and raids behind enemy lines. The name derives from their founder, Lt. Col. (later Maj. Gen.) John C. "Jock" Campbell, then commander of the 4th Royal Horse Artillery of the famous British 7th Armoured Division ("The Desert Rats"), who first used them in the fighting against the Italians and then the Germans in the western desert in 1941–1942. Gordon L. Rottman, *FUBAR: Soldier Slang of World War II* (London: Osprey, 2007), p. 164.

3. Review of the Battle of the Imjin Fought by 29 BDE on 22–25 Apr 51, n.d.; copy in Award Case File, Lt. Col. James P. Carne (DSC), box 1385, Eighth U.S. Army AG Section, RG 338, NARA. Although there is no indication of the source of this document, from its contents it is apparent that it was prepared by the staff of the 29th Brigade immediately following the fighting; initials on the document reducing its classification from Secret to Restricted are dated 7 May 1951.

4. Lt. Col. Ned B. Broyles, Assistant Chief of Staff, G-2, Headquarters, 3d Infantry Division, Summary of Enemy Operations in the 29th BIB Sector during the Period 211800 to 251800 April 1951, 9 May 1951, enclosure no. 7 to Frank W. Milburn, Commanding General, I

Corps, to Commanding General, Eighth U.S. Army, 15 May 1951; Subj.: Report of Gloucestershire Battalion, 22–25 April 1951, Ms. 8-5.1A BA97, Report of Gloucestershire Battalion, 22–25 April 1951, CMH. Unless otherwise noted, all citations in this chapter are from Ms. 8.5-1A BA97.

5. Lt. Col. Nathaniel R. Hoskot, Assistant Chief of Staff, G-3, Headquarters, 3d Infantry Division, G-3 Summary on 29th BIB Action, 22–25 April 1951, Inclusive, 15 May 1951, enclosure no. 9 in Milburn to Commanding General, Eighth U.S. Army.

6. Milburn to Commanding General, Eighth U.S. Army.

7. Review of the Battle of the Imjin.

8. Broyles, Summary of Enemy Operations.

9. Colonel James P. Carne (11 April 1906–19 April 1986) was captured by Chinese Communist Forces on 25 April 1951 with the remnants of his battalion. He spent the remainder of the Korean War as a prisoner of war, often in solitary confinement and poorly treated. Following his repatriation, he was awarded a Victoria Cross (VC) for heroism as well as the Distinguished Service Order (DSO) and received a Distinguished Service Cross (DSC) from the U.S. Army. Mossman, *Ebb and Flow*, pp. 411–29; Farrar-Hockley, *An Honourable Discharge*, passim.

10. Results of Interviews with Survivors of the Gloster Battalion Action 22–25 April 51, enclosure no. 8 in Milburn to Commanding General, Eighth U.S. Army, 15 May 1951; Subj.: Report of Gloucestershire Battalion, 22–25 April 1951. The survivors who were interviewed were from only D Company and the Support Company. The sole company commander who escaped was Capt. Maurice G. "Mike" Harvey of D Company.

11. Review of the Battle of the Imjin.

12. Broyles, Summary of Enemy Operations.

13. Milburn to Commanding General, Eighth U.S. Army; Subj.: Report of Gloucestershire Battalion.

14. Personal Account, Col. O. P. Newman, chief of staff, 3d Infantry Division, n.d., enclosure no. 5 in Milburn to Commanding General, Eighth U.S. Army; Subj.: Report of Gloucestershire Battalion. The commander of the 1st Battalion, 7th Infantry, Frederick (Fred) C. Weyand, later served as commander of the Military Assistance Command Vietnam (MACV) and then Chief of Staff, U.S. Army, from 3 October 1974 to 1 October 1976.

15. Hoskot, G-3 Summary.

16. Reserves Available to 29th BIB and CG 3d Division, enclosures

nos. 2 and 3 in Milburn to Commanding General, Eighth U.S. Army; Subj.: Report of Gloucestershire Battalion.

17. Results of Interviews with Survivors of the Gloster Battalion.

18. Review of the Battle of the Imjin.

19. Broyles, Summary of Enemy Operations.

20. The M24 Chaffee light tank was designed to replace the M3/ M5 series light tanks that had proven to be inadequate in combat. Armed with a 75mm gun, one .50 and two .30 caliber machine guns, the M24 Chaffee was introduced late in the war in Europe and saw little action. It was used extensively in Korea in a reconnaissance role. Jackson, *Tanks and Armored Fighting Vehicles,* p. 165; Tucker, *Encyclopedia of the Korean War,* p. 47.

21. Hoskot, G-3 Summary.

22. Milburn to Commanding General, Eighth U.S. Army.

23. Results of Interviews with Survivors of the Gloster Battalion.

24. Review of the Battle of the Imjin.

25. Broyles, Summary of Enemy Operations.

26. Hoskot, G-3 Summary.

27. Brig. Gen. A. D. Mead, Assistant Division Commander, 3d Division, memo to Commanding General, enclosure no. 6 in Milburn to Commanding General, Eighth U.S. Army.

28. O. P. Newman, personal account.

29. Mead memo.

30. The M4A3E8 Sherman tank was the principal version of the standard U.S. medium tank to see combat in Europe during the final months of World War II. It mounted a long-barreled 76mm gun and added a revised suspension system. Along with the M46 Patton, the M4A3E8 Sherman was used extensively in Korea. Jackson, *Tanks and Armored Fighting Vehicles,* pp. 138–39; Alexander Lüdeke, *Weapons of World War II* (Bath, U.K.: Parragon Publishing, 2007), pp. 132–33; Tucker, *Encyclopedia of the Korean War,* p. 45.

31. Milburn to Commanding General, Eighth U.S. Army.

32. The 1st Glosters had a strength of 28 officers and 671 enlisted men when the CCF offensive began on 22 April 1951. The 29th Brigade's initial casualty report listed 622 officers and men killed, wounded, or missing in action, including supporting units. Subsequent accounting following the war indicated that the 1st Glosters had 21 officers and 509 men taken prisoner, of whom eight officers and 145 men were wounded. The Glosters lost 56 men killed in action. Two officers and 24 men died while imprisoned. The other British units engaged suffered the following losses killed in action: Royal Ulster Rifles,

36; Royal Northumberland Fusiliers, 30; Royal Artillery, 10; Royal Engineers, 6; 8th Royal Irish Hussars, 2; Royal Army Medical Corps, 1. All together the British casualties on the Imjin River totaled 1,091, of whom 141 were killed in action. The 1st Glosters' losses represented the largest single unit loss by the British Army since World War II. Mossman, *Ebb and Flow,* p. 428; Salmon, *To the Last Round,* p. 318.

33. Headquarters, Eighth U.S. Army, Korean (EUSAK), General Orders No. 286, "Battle Honors—Citation of Units," 8 May 1951, reproduced at www.nationalarchives.gov.uk/battles/korea/popup/presidential.htm.

34. Headquarters, Department of the Army, General Orders No. 3, 20 January 1954, CMH; see also an early draft for a DSC in Award Case File, Lt. Col. James P. Carne (DSC), box 1385, Eighth U.S. Army AG Section, RG 338, NARA.

35. Headquarters, Department of the Army, General Orders No. 54, 29 May 1952, CMH.

36. Headquarters, Department of the Army, General Orders No. 28, 13 March 1952 (1st Lt. Artiaga), and No. 107, 14 December 1951 (Capt. Yap), CMH.

37. Results of Interviews with Survivors of the Gloster Battalion.

38. Review of the Battle of the Imjin.

39. Milburn to Commanding General, Eighth U.S. Army; Subj.: Report of Gloucestershire Battalion.

40. Lt. Gen. James A. Van Fleet to Commander-in-Chief, Far East Command, 26 May 1951; Subj: Report of Gloucestershire Battalion, 22–25 April 1951.

41. Salmon, *To the Last Round,* pp. 313–14.

42. See Arnold Schwartzman, "Gloster Memorial, Korea, 1957," at www.britains-smallwars.com/korea/gloster_memorial/gloster_memorial.html.

8. Action along the No Name Line

1. 1st Lt. Martin Blumenson, Narrative, n.d., Ms. No. 8-5.1A BA36, Task Force Lindy Lou, CMH.

2. Interview, Lt. Col. Forrest W. Duff by 1st Lt. Martin Blumenson, 19 May 1951, Ms. No. 8-5.1A BA36, Task Force Lindy Lou, CMH. Lt. Blumenson conducted all interviews in manuscripts BA36, 40, and 35 that are used in this chapter. All excerpts are drawn from Blumenson's notes of his interviews as transcribed and reported by him in these documents.

3. Interview, Lt. Col. Leon F. Lavoie, 8 June 1951, Ms. 36.

4. Interview, 1st Lt. Leroy B. Mattingly, 9 June 1951, Ms. 36.

5. Interview, Capt. John F. Gerrity, 8 June 1951, Ms. 36.

6. Lavoie interview.

7. Mattingly interview.

8. Lavoie interview.

9. Interview, Lt. Col. Robert J. Natzel, 18 June 1951, Ms. 36.

10. Interview, Capt. Irving C. Hughes, 13 June 1951, Ms. 40, "Action on the General Defense Line: Company A, 19th Infantry Regiment, 17–18 May 1951," Ms. No. 8-5.1A BA40, CMH.

11. Interview, 1st Lt. Warren E. Clark, 13 June 1951, Ms. 40.

12. Ibid.

13. "Roy A. Hagen," "Korean War Casualty Files," at http://aad.archives.gov/aad.

14. Interview, 1st Lt. Roy A. Hagen, 13 June 1951, Ms. 40.

15. Interview, Sgt. George I. Carr and Cpl. Rufus Cloud, 13 June 1951, Ms. 40.

16. Interview, PFC Willie C. Hales and PFC John W. Cox, 13 June 1951, Ms. 40.

17. "Fred C. Berry, Jr.," "Korean War Casualty Files," at http://aad.archives.gov/aad.

18. Interview, Cpl. Fred Berry, 13 June 1951, Ms. 40.

19. Interview, Sgt. John A. Tipton, 13 June 1951, Ms. 40.

20. Interview, Sgt. Richard A. Rotanz and Cpl. Frank Billemeyer, 13 June 1951, Ms. 40.

21. Interview, Cpl. Jerome Goldberg, 13 June 1951, Ms. 40.

22. Interview, 1st Lt. Harold L. Benskin, 13 June 1951, Ms. 40.

23. Extract, IX Corps, G-3 Telephone Journal, including After-Action Report, 1st Battalion, 19th RCT, May 1951, in Ms. No. 8-5.1A BA40.

24 Clark interview.

25. Interview, 1st Lt. Dale N. Johnson, 13 June 1951, Ms. 40.

26. Hales and Cox interview.

27. Benskin interview.

28. Interview, PFC William L. Johnson and PFC John H. Annacost, 13 June 1951, Ms. 40.

29. Tipton interview.

30. D. Johnson interview.

31. Berry interview.

32. Carr and Cloud interview.

33. Hagen interview.

34. Clark interview.

35. Extract, IX Corps, G-3 Telephone Journal.

36. Narrative, "Action on the General Defense Line: Company A, 19th Infantry Regiment, 17–18 May 1951," Ms. 40.

37. Gen. William Hoge, CG IX Corps, to CG 24th Division, CG 7th Division, CG 2d ROK Division, and CG 6th ROK Division, IXC-CG-100, 182100 May 1951, in 1st Lt. Martin Blumenson, Task Force Byorum, n.d., Ms. No. 8-5.1A BA35, CMH.

38. Maj. (later Col.) Henry M. Byorum (28 March 1914–16 March 2002) joined the Officers' Reserve Corps (ORC) as a 2d lieutenant of infantry in 1936 when he graduated from Minot State University, Minot, N.D. He was called to active duty in 1940 and served as an armor officer during World War II. He remained in the Army and rose to the rank of colonel, retiring in 1966, after serving as armor advisor to the Shah of Iran's armored force and then as chief of staff, U.S. Training Mission in Iran (July 1959–March 1966). See "Byorum" at *Texas Obituaries,* www.obitcentral.com/obitsearch/obits/tx/tx-coryell1.htm; Department of the Army, *U.S. Army Register,* vol. 1, *United States Army Active and Retired Lists, 1 January 1960* (Washington, D.C.: U.S. Government Printing Office, 1960), p. 153.

39. After-Action Report, Task Force Byorum, 6th Medium Tank Battalion, 20 May 1951, in Ms. No. 8-5.1A BA35. The After-Action Report states that the order from 24th Division G-3 directing the establishment of the task force was received at 2200 hours on 17 May; however, the 6th Tank Battalion's S-2/S-3 journal states that the directive was received at 0315 hours on 17 May; see Extract, 6th Medium Tank Battalion, S-2, S-3 Journal, 170001 May 51 to 172400 May 51, in Ms. 35.

40. After-Action Report, Task Force Byorum.

41. Interview, 1st Lt. Tom S. Groseclose, 22 May 1951, Ms. 35.

42. After-Action Report, Task Force Byorum.

43. Interview, Lt. Col. Robert J. Natzel, 23 May 1951, Ms. 35.

44. After-Action Report, Task Force Byorum.

45. Interview, Lt. Col. Henry M. Byorum, 21 May 1951, Ms. 35.

46. Beginning in July 1950 single-engine North American T-6 aircraft from what later became the Fifth U.S. Air Force's 6132d Air Control and Warning Squadron, with an Army observer onboard, provided airborne observation and coordinated tactical air support for ground forces through the Tactical Air Control Center (TACC) while Tactical Air Control Parties (TACPs) accompanied ground units. The aircraft used the nickname of "Mosquito" as their basic call sign,

which was highly appropriate considering their ability to harass the enemy at every turn. See Robert F. Futrell, *The United States Air Force in Korea, 1950–1953* (New York: Duell, Sloan and Pearce, 1961), pp. 78, 98–102, 169–70; John Schlight, *Help from Above: Air Force Close Air Support of the Army, 1946–1973* (Washington, D.C.: Air Force History and Museums Program, 2003), pp. 149–53; Tucker, *Encyclopedia of the Korean War,* pp. 26, 156, 216–17, 514.

47. After-Action Report, Task Force Byorum.

48. Byorum interview.

49. Interview, Capt. John A. LaMontia and SFC Russell W. Underhill, 21 May 1951, Ms. 35.

50. After-Action Report, Task Force Byorum.

51. Byorum interview.

52. Interview, SFC Callen C. Burris, n.d., Ms. 35.

53. Interview, Cpl. Albert Vergara, 21 May 1951, Ms. 35.

54. LaMontia and Underhill interview.

55. After-Action Report, Task Force Byorum.

56. Interview, Capt. James F. McIntosh, 21 May 1951, Ms. 35.

57. LaMontia and Underhill interview.

58. Byorum interview.

9. Anything but Peaceful Valley

1. Bevin R. Alexander, "Artillery Retrograde down 'Peaceful Valley,'" n.d., in Ms. No. 8-5.1A BA56, Peaceful Valley, CMH.

2. Interview, Capt. Henry M. M. Starkey, 1st Lt. Horace D. Nalle, 1st Lt. Joseph Greenes, and SFC Allen D. Knapp Jr., by 2d Lt. Bevin R. Alexander, 6 July 1951, Ms. No. 8-5.1 BA56. Lt. Alexander conducted all the interviews in Ms. 56 that are used in this chapter. All cited excerpts are drawn from Alexander's notes of his interviews as transcribed and reported in this document by him and his assistant, PFC Eugene S. Smykowski.

3. The M16 AAA (Multiple-Gun Motor Carriage, MGMC) mount was a World War II development that featured an M45 quadruple mount for the M2 .50 caliber heavy machine guns on a standard M3 half-track. Better known as the quad 50, these guns were effective in both antiaircraft and antipersonnel operations because of their high rate of fire and killing capabilities. Quad 50s were used through the Vietnam conflict in a ground role. See "Multiple Gun Motor Carriage M16/M17," *Antiaircraft Command,* at www.antiaircraft.org/M16 .htm; "Quad-50 M2 .50 cal. Machine Gun," *Olive-Drab,* at www .olive-drab.com/od_other_firearms_mg_m2_quad50.php.

4. The M19 AAA mount was a modified M24 Chaffee light tank chassis mounting twin 40mm Bofors guns in an open turret. The M19 dual 40 was effective against both air and ground targets. *Tanks and Armored Fighting Vehicles Visual Encyclopedia* (London: Amber Books, 2009), p. 181.

5. Interview, 1st Lt. Donald L. Kelley, 1st Lt. Albert C. Fischer, 1st Lt. Kenneth M. Head, M. Sgt. Glen G. Kimes, and Sgt. Warren J. Lynch, 10 July 1951 (hereafter cited as Kelley et al. interview).

6. Interview, Capt. Lawrence R. Daly, 2d Lt. Frank R. Garner, M. Sgt R. G. Virgil Baker, and Cpl. William J. Elliott, 10 July 1951 (hereafter cited as Daly et al. interview).

7. Interview, SFC Allen D. Knapp Jr., 6 July 1951.

8. Interview, 1st Lt. Paul G. Gonzales, 8 July 1951.

9. Starkey interview.

10. Gonzales interview.

11. Starkey interview.

12. Nalle interview.

13. Kelley et al. interview.

14. Ibid.

15. Ibid.

16. Ibid.

17. Ibid.

18. Ibid.

19. Ibid.

20. Ibid.

21. Daly et al. interview.

22. Ibid.

23. Ibid.

24. Ibid.

25. 1st Lt. Albert B. Gentry, as cited in Daly et al. interview.

26. Daly et al. interview.

27. Starkey interview.

28. Daly et al. interview.

10. The Battle below the Soyang River

1. Interview, Maj. George R. Von Halban by 1st Lt. John Mewha, 8 July 1951, Ms. No. 8-5.1A BA75, Battle of the Soyang, CMH. Lt. Mewha conducted all of the interviews in Ms. 75 that are used in this chapter. All excerpts are drawn from Mewha's notes of his interviews as transcribed and reported by him and his assistant, Cpl. Lensey B. Bennett, in this document. See also Mossman, *Ebb and Flow*, p. 448 and map 36.

2. Interview, Capt. Orlando Ruggerio, 9 July 1951. See also Moss-man, *Ebb and Flow,* p. 448 and map 36.

3. Interview, 2d Lt. Richard P. Kenney, SFC Earl K. Pointdexter, SFC Charles R. Brown, Sgt. William G. Gates, Cpl. Robert L. Krim-minger, Sgt. Donald J. Myers, Sgt. Wilfred J. Jokerst, 7 July 1951 (hereafter referred at as Company C group interview).

4. Ruggerio interview.

5. Interview, 1st Lt. Fred W. Rodgers, 8 July 1951.

6. Company C group interview.

7. A tree burst is a round fired to explode in the top of a tree so that deadly wooden fragments as well as the metal shell fragments will hit those sheltering below. These wooden fragments are as deadly as the metal shrapnel.

8. Ruggerio interview.

9. Company C group interview.

10. Rodgers interview.

11. Interview, 1st Lt. Thomas W. Fife, 26 July 1951.

12. Ruggerio interview.

13. Company C group interview.

14. Fife interview.

15. Rodgers interview.

16. Ruggerio interview.

17. Company C group interview.

18. Ruggerio interview.

19. Company C group interview.

20. Ruggerio interview.

21. Interview, Capt. W. J. Richard, 8 July 1951.

22. Interview, Capt. Perry Sager, 24 July 1951.

23. Rodgers interview.

24. Company C group interview.

25. Fife interview.

26. Ruggerio interview.

27. Company C group interview.

28. Ruggerio interview. According to U.S. Army casualty records, during this action the 72d Medium Tank Battalion lost four men killed in action (Cpl. Rudolph W. Soellner, Pvts. Leo L. Kasselman and Arlo L. White, and M. Sgt. Thomas W. Blanchard), five men wounded in action, four men taken prisoner, one of whom returned on 24 May 1951 and one of whom, M. Sgt. James Goodin, died in captivity on 15 October 1951. See "Rudolph W. Soellner, Leo L. Kasselman, Thomas W. Blanchard, Arlo L. White, and James L. Goodin" and 72d Medium

Tank Battalion casualty files, 16–18 May 1951, "Korean War Casualty Files," at http://aad.archives.gov/aad.

29. Mossman, *Ebb and Flow*, p. 459; Department of the Army General Orders No. 72, 9 August 1951, CMH.

11. The Supply Battle of the Soyang River

1. 1st Lt. John Mewha, Narrative, n.d., in Ms. No. 85.1A BA62, Supply Battle of the Soyang River, CMH.

2. Interview, Capt. Davis L. Mathews by 1st Lt. John Mewha, 7 August 1951, Ms. 62. Lt. Mewha conducted all of the interviews in Ms. 62 that are used in this chapter. All excerpts are drawn from Mewha's notes of his interviews as transcribed and reported by him and his assistant, Cpl. Lensey B. Bennett, in this document.

3. Interview, Maj. Herman C. Hinton, 5 August 1951.

4. Interview, Col. J. K. McCormick, 4 August 1951.

5. Interview, Maj. Harry J. Dodd, 7 August 1951.

6. Hinton interview.

7. McCormick interview.

8. Interview, Maj. William H. Barker, 5 August 1951.

9. Interview, Capt. Jasper N. Erskine, 5 August 1951.

10. Dodd interview.

11. Barker interview.

12. McCormick interview.

12. Task Force Gerhart

1. First Lt. John Mewha, Narrative, Task Force Gerhardt [Gerhart], n.d., Ms. No. 8-5.1A BA54, Task Force Gerhardt, May 1951, CMH. A summary of this action can be found in Russell A. Gugeler, "Task Force Gerhardt," in *Combat Actions in Korea* (Washington: Combat Forces Press, 1954), pp. 183–92. Gugeler's work was originally published by the Association of the United States Army (AUSA) in 1954 and subsequently reprinted several times by the Center of Military History. Lt. Mewha incorrectly recorded the name of the Task Force commander as Col. William Gerhardt, executive officer of the 187th RCT (Abn), whereas the commander was actually Col. George H. Gerhart, commander of the 1st Battalion, 187th RCT (Abn), and former executive officer, deputy commander, and commander of the 187th RCT (Abn), 1950–1951. This error has been repeated in numerous histories of the Korean War, including Mossman, *Ebb and Flow*, pp. 481–83, and Gugeler, *Combat Actions in Korea*, which is based on

Mewha's report. Appleman followed this incorrect spelling but questioned whether it was William or George Gerhardt—see *Ridgway
Duels for Korea,* pp. 536–38, 539, 540, and especially 537n68. Clay
Blair had it correct in his *The Forgotten War: America in Korea,
1950–1953* (New York: Times Books, 1987), pp. 894–96. In this chapter Gerhart's name is spelled correctly in the text except for the incorrect use of his name in the first excerpt from Capt. William R. Ross.
The original incorrect spelling has been retained for all citations in the
footnotes in which it was used, as in Lt. Mewha's report.

2. Mewha, Narrative, Task Force Gerhardt.

3. George H. Gerhart (22 September 1912–5 November 2009)
graduated from the U.S. Military Academy in 1934 and was commissioned in the infantry. He served as S-3 and executive officer, 354th
Infantry Regiment, 89th Infantry Division (1942–1943), and then as
G-3, 89th Infantry Division (1943–1945). Later Gerhart was executive
office, deputy commander, and commander of the 187th RCT (Abn) in
the U.S. and Korea (1950–1951), and commander of the 1st Battalion,
187th RCT, in Korea and Japan (1951). He retired from active duty in
1962 as a colonel. Association of Graduates, U.S. Military Academy,
*Register of Graduates and Former Cadets of the United States Mili-
tary Academy West Point, New York, 2000* (West Point, N.Y.: Association of Graduates, 2000), pp. 4–172.

4. Interview, Maj. William E. Ross, 13 August 1951, with 1st Lt.
John Mewha. Ms. No. 8-5.1A BA BA54, Task Force Gerhardt. Lt.
Mewha conducted all of the interviews in Ms. 54 that are used in this
chapter. All excerpts are drawn from Mewha's notes of his interviews
as transcribed and reported by him and his assistant, Cpl. Lensey B.
Bennett, in this document.

5. Interview, Maj. James H. Spann, 12 August 1951.

6. Ross interview.

7. Interview, Capt. W. J. Richard, 12 August 1951.

8. Ross interview.

9. Spann interview.

10. Interview, Maj. Charles A. Newman, 12 August, 1951.

11. Interview, 2d Lt. (then M. Sgt.) Edwell D. Clements, 13 August
1951.

12. Spann interview.

13. Ross interview.

14. Richard interview.

15. Interview, SFC Glen M. Poppler, 14 August 1951.

16. Newman interview.

17. Clements interview.

18. Newman interview.

19. Clements interview.

20. Interview, SFC Michael R. Kuhel, 14 August 1951.

21. Clements interview.

22. Kuhel interview.

23. Poppler interview.

24. Ross interview.

25. Spann interview.

26. Newman interview.

27. Clements interview.

28. Kuhel interview.

29. Poppler interview.

30. Seventy-second Tank Battalion, Supplemental Report, "Task Force Gerhardt," enclosure to Ms. No. 8-5.1A BA54, reported that a driver of an armored jeep from the reconnaissance platoon was severely wounded on the night of 24–25 May 1951 in an ambush at a Chinese roadblock after he had killed four of the attackers. PFC Irvin A. Rackley was the only man from the 72d who was reported killed in action or died of wounds in this action. He was wounded on 25 May and died on 26 May. See "Irvin A. Rackley," "Korean War Casualty Files," at http://aad.archives.gov/aad.

31. Ross interview.

32. Headquarters X Corps formed Task Force Baker on 25 May 1951 at Umyang-ni on the Soyang River under Brig. Gen. Frank Bowen, commander, 187th RCT (Abn). Task Force Baker was built around Task Force Gerhart and augmented with an armored field artillery battalion, a signal detachment, a naval gunfire team, and two truck companies. Its mission was to push quickly northeast over Route 24 to take Inje and then Kansong on the east coast. After hard fighting, Task Force Baker took Inje on 27 May, but it was stopped far short of Kansong in heavy fighting on 30 May and was then disbanded. See Mossman, *Ebb and Flow,* pp. 482, 484–85; Appleman, *Ridgway Duels for Korea,* pp. 539, 541, 548–49.

33. Spann interview.

34. Newman interview.

35. Gugeler, *Combat Actions in Korea,* pp. 191–92.

13. Task Force Hazel

1. First Lt. Martin Blumenson, Narrative, Task Force Hazel, n.d., Ms. No. 8-5.1A BA38, Task Force Hazel, CMH.

2. Interview, Capt. Chester C. Myers by 1st Lt. Martin Blumen-

son, 9 June 1951, Ms. No. 8-5.1A BA38. Lt. Blumenson conducted all of the interviews in Ms. 38 that are used in this chapter. All excerpts are drawn from Blumenson's notes of his interviews as transcribed and reported by him and his assistant, Cpl. Thomas G. Morgan, in this document.

3. Interview, 1st Lt. Henry H. Parr, 3 June 1951.

4. Interview, 1st Lt. Clifford C. Nunn, 3 June 1951.

5. Interview, Capt. N. L. James, 9 June 1951.

6. Parr interview.

7. See chap. 8, note 46.

8. Interview, Capt. Charles E. Hazel, 8 June 1951.

9. Parr interview.

10. Interview, 1st Lt. Israel J. Miller, 3 June 1951.

11. Interview, SFC George N. Dorn, 4 June 1951.

12. Interview, Sgt. George D. Reeves, 4 June 1951.

13. Interview, SFC Henry A. Campbell, 9 June 1951.

14. Interview, SFC James E. Jubert, 9 June 1951.

15. Interview, Sgt. Joseph J. Blaskiewicz, 9 June 1951.

16. Nunn interview.

17. Interview, PFC Richard I. Winslow, 4 June 1951.

18. Hazel interview.

19. Dorn interview.

20. Reeves interview.

21. Winslow interview.

22. Jubert interview.

23. Campbell interview.

24. Blaskiewicz interview.

25. Hazel interview.

26. Dorn interview.

27. Reeves interview.

28. Winslow interview.

29. Blaskiewicz interview.

30. Campbell interview.

31. Jubert interview.

32. Parr interview.

33. Nunn interview.

34. Interview, SFC J. D. Stiles, 4 June 1951.

35. "Robert M. Handy" and "Oscar D. Martin," "Korean War Casualty Files," at http://aad.archives.gov/aad. Cpls. Handy and Martin were the only MP personnel reported killed in action on 24 May 1951.

36. Captain Chandler, aide de camp, Report of Ambush of General Ferenbaugh, n.d., in Ms. 38.

37. Interview, 1st Lt. Ivan G. Stanaway, 9 June 1951.

38. 32d Infantry Regiment POR #49, 222400 May 1951 and Delayed Activity, Periodic Opns Rpt, dated 26 May 1951, both in Ms. 38.

39. Statement made in conversation, 22 June 1951, with 1st Lt. Martin Blumenson by an officer who preferred to remain unidentified, in Ms. 38.

40. Hazel interview.

41. Interview, Sgt. Robert L. Kammerer, 9 June 1951.

42. James interview.

43. Hazel interview.

44. Stanaway interview.

45. "Sherman P. Cruts, Jr.," "Korean War Casualty Files," at http://aad.archives.gov/aad.

46. James interview.

47. Nunn interview.

48. Interview, 1st Lt. Max R. Stallcup, 9 June 1951.

49. Interview, Capt. Edgar N. Anderson, 4 June 1951.

50. Hazel interview.

51. Ibid.

52. James interview.

53. Interview, Maj. Edward F. Dudley, 4 June 1951.

54. Evaluation prepared by Lt. Col. George B. Pickett, n.d., in Ms. 38; emphasis in original.

55. Interview, Lt. Gen. William M. Hoge, 27 June 1951.

Conclusion

1. Eighth Army Report of Operations, May 1951, NARA, RG 407, entry 429, box 1192, pp. 1–3.

2. Eighth Army Periodic Intelligence Report, No. 285, April 23, 1951, NARA, RG 407, entry 429, box 1181, p. 9.

3. Appleman, *Ridgway Duels for Korea,* pp. 449–55. Appleman estimates the total CCF and NKPA force for all phases at 650,000–700,000 men. Enemy divisions numbered no more than 8,000 men per division.

4. Shu Guang Zhang, *Mao's Military Romanticism,* pp. 145–47.

5. Headquarters, Far East Command, *Terrain Handbook No. 66, Northern Korea,* 17 April 1951, pp. 38–39, map plate VI-I. The formal

name for the entire length of Route 3 is the Wonsan–Seoul Road, though the local valleys lent more precise understanding: thus the usage of "Ch'orwon valley," or "Uijongbu corridor."

6. Between Kansas and final defense were lines Delta, Golden, and Nevada, which presumed the abandonment of Seoul. Waco finalized the defense north of Seoul and rolled up Waco, Golden, and Nevada into a contiguous line. A new plan, Obstinate, defined this and defensive measures. See Eighth Army Command Report, May 1951, pp. 1–5.

7. Eighth Army Command Report, April 1951, NARA, RG 407, entry 429, box 1179, pp. 1–5.

8. Ibid.

9. Eighth Army Command Report, May 1951, book 3, G-2, pp. 1–2.

10. Ibid., p. 3.

11. Peng Dehuai, *Memoirs of a Chinese Marshal: The Autobiographical Notes of Peng Dehuai (1898–1974)*, trans. Zheng Longpu (1984; repr., Honolulu, University Press of the Pacific, 2005), passim; Eighth Army Command Report, April 1951, p. 21.

12. Eighth Army Command Report, May 1951, pp. 7–10, accompanying a map, "Position Changes of 1 May."

13. Eighth Army Command Report, Narrative, May 1951, p. 18.

14. Eighth Army Command Report, May 1951, book 3, pp. 4–5, and map plates 1 and 2, Situation 31 May and Historical Gains and Losses, May 1951.

15. Eighth Army monograph, *Enemy Tactics,* p. 39.

16. Ibid., p. 40.

17. Korea Institute of Military History, *The Korean War,* 3 vols. (Lincoln: University of Nebraska, 1998), vol. 2, chap. 7, passim.

18. Eighth Army Command Report, April 1951, Narrative, p. 27, and chart, "UN Casualties April 1951."

19. Eighth Army Command Report, May 1951, Narrative, p. 33, and chart, "UN Casualties, May 1951."

20. Eighth Army Command Report, April 1951, Narrative, p. 21; Eighth Army Command Report, May 1951, book 3, part 1, G-2 narrative, p. 8.

21. Korea Institute of Military History, *The Korean War,* 2:714–15. The War History Compilation Commission of the Ministry of National Defense, Republic of Korea, produced six volumes of *The History of the United Nations Forces in the Korean War* (Seoul: War History Compilation Commission, 1967–1975), which provides de-

tailed information on all UN forces' actions, divided by country. See also Zhang, *Mao's Military Romanticism*, pp. 153–55n82.

22. Peng, *Memoirs,* p. 481.

23. Zhang, *Mao's Military Romanticism*, chap. 7.

24. Peng, *Memoirs,* p. 480.

BIBLIOGRAPHICAL ESSAY

This volume is based primarily on the interviews, documents, and detailed operational resumes that U.S. Army military historians assigned to the historical detachments of the Military History Section, Headquarters, Eighth U.S. Army Korea (EUSAK), U.S. Army Forces, Far East, collected during the Korean War. The various historical detachments completed their interviews and studies within weeks or months of the operations covered and submitted them as Section IV: After Action Interviews of EUSAK's Command Reports. These reports were then collected at Headquarters, U.S. Army Forces, Far East, and also sent to the Office of the Chief of Military History, Department of the Army, in Washington, D.C., for use in preparing the official history of U.S. Army in the Korean War. Today the Historical Resources Branch, Field Programs and Historical Services Division, U.S. Army Center of Military History (CMH), at Fort McNair in Washington, D.C., holds copies of these interviews and studies. These sources are listed at the end of this essay.

The Center of Military History holds the entire unpublished manuscript of Gen. Matthew Ridgway's manuscript "Korea: The First Year" in its Special Collections. This manuscript forms the basis for the early chapters of Ridgway's *The Korean War* (see below). The manuscript version is superior for its military detail; its final commercial form is more critical of personalities and events.

Other primary sources were used to supplement the interviews in the Center of Military History's Korean War holdings. These sources include unit historical files and reports from Record Group (RG) 407 and award case files from Record Group 500, all held by the National Archives at College Park, Md. Among these records, the Command Reports, Reports of Operations, Periodic Intelligence Reports, and

War Diaries of Headquarters, Eighth U.S. Army, in RG 407, are the most critical for obtaining the details of operations at that level. Other primary sources are noted in the chapter endnotes.

There is a substantial and growing body of secondary material on the Korean War. Only a few of the major titles are noted here as a starting point for those readers who desire to explore additional material about this conflict. For an introduction to the historiography of the war and a bibliography, see Allan R. Millett, "The Korean War: A 50-Year Critical Historiography," *Journal of Strategic Studies* 24 (March 2001): 188–224; *The Korean War: The Essential Bibliography* (Washington, D.C.: Potomac Books, 2007); and "Bibliographical Essay" in his *War for Korea, 1950–1951: They Came from the North* (Lawrence: University Press of Kansas, 2010), pp. 577–610. Millett should also be consulted on the background of the war; see his *War for Korea, 1945–1950: A House Burning* (Lawrence: University Press of Kansas, 2005) and his *War for Korea, 1950–1951: They Came from the North*, which covers the period June 1950–July 1951.

For information on the U.S. Army in the years between the conclusion of World War II and the beginning of the Korean War, see William W. Epley, *America's First Cold War Army, 1945–1950* (Arlington, Va.: Association of the U.S. Army, Land Warfare Paper No. 15, 1993), and Thomas D. Boettcher, *First Call: The Making of the Modern U.S. Military, 1945–1953* (Boston: Little, Brown, 1992).

The U.S. Army published a number of excellent official histories covering military operations. These include the series United States Army in the Korean War, consisting of the following volumes: Roy E. Appleman, *South to the Naktong, North to the Yalu (June–November 1950)* (Washington, D.C.: U.S. Army Center of Military History, 1961); James F. Schnabel, *Policy and Direction: The First Year* (Washington, D.C.: U.S. Army Center of Military History, 1972); Billy C. Mossman, *Ebb and Flow, November 1950–July 1951* (Washington, D.C.: U.S. Army Center of Military History, 1990); and Walter G. Hermes, *Truce Tent and Fighting Front* (Washington, D.C.: U.S. Army Center of Military History, 1992).

The U.S. Army also published a number of monographs on the Korean War. Of special interest for small-unit combat actions is Russell A. Gugeler, *Combat Actions in Korea* (Washington, D.C.: U.S. Army Center of Military History, 1987). A work covering the background on the U.S. Army in Japan before the war and the experiences in the war of one regiment, the 24th Infantry, the last segregated infantry regiment in the U.S. Army, is William T. Bowers, William M. Hammond, and George L. MacGarrigle, *Black Soldier, White Army: The 24th Infantry Regiment in Korea* (Washington, D.C.: U.S. Army Center of Military History, 1996). For an outline of U.S. efforts to develop the Republic of Korea Army (ROKA) before and during the conflict, see Robert K. Sawyer, *Military Advisors in Korea: KMAG in Peace and War* (Washington, D.C.: U.S. Army Center of Military History, 1988).

The U.S. Marine Corps official history is covered in Lynn Montross et al., *History of U.S. Marine Operations in Korea, 1950–1953*, 5 vols. (Washington, D.C.: Marine Corps Historical Branch, 1954–1972). The other services published one-volume histories of their service during the Korean War; see James A. Field Jr., *History of United States Naval Operations in Korea* (Washington, D.C.: Director of Naval History, 1962), and Robert F. Futrell, *The United States Air Force in Korea, 1950–1953*, rev. ed. (Washington, D.C.: Office of the Chief of Air Force History, 1983). The important subject of U.S. Air Force close air support for U.S. and UN ground forces in Korea is well covered in John Schlight, *Help from Above: Air Force Close Air Support of the Army, 1946–1973* (Washington, D.C.: Air Force History and Museums Program, 2003), pp. 113–77.

The first two volumes of this series, William T. Bowers, ed., *The Line: Combat in Korea: January–February 1951* (Lexington: University Press of Kentucky, 2008) and *Striking Back: Combat in Korea, March–April 1951* (Lexington: University Press of Kentucky, 2010), provide important personal perspectives of the American soldier in combat in Korea during the critical early months of 1951. Based on combat interviews with participants and historical reports, these volumes provide unique firsthand experiences of soldiers in combat in the most stressful situations and demanding conditions.

At the higher echelons of command, Gen. Matthew B. Ridgway's *The Korean War* (Garden City, N.Y.: Doubleday, 1967) provides his perspective as commanding general of the Eighth U.S. Army and then of U.S. Far East Command (FECOM), U.S. Army Forces Far East, and the United Nations Command during the operations covered in this volume. Paul Braim provides an important perspective on the leadership and policies of Ridgway's successor as Eighth U.S. Army commander, Lt. Gen. James A. Van Fleet, in his *The Will to Win: The Life of General James A. Van Fleet* (Annapolis: U.S. Naval Institute Press, 2001). Gen. J. Lawton Collin in his *War in Peacetime: The History and Lessons of Korea* (Boston: Houghton Mifflin, 1969) provides the needed view from Washington, where he served as Chief of Staff of the

U.S. Army and a member of the Joint Chiefs of Staff. Omar N. Bradley and Clay Blair, *A General's Life* (New York: Simon and Schuster, 1983), provides the views and experiences of the chairman of the Joint Chiefs of Staff during this period.

On Gen. Douglas MacArthur and his role in the Korean War, there are numerous sources. The general's own *Reminiscences* (New York: McGraw-Hill, 1964) is a beginning point. D. Clayton James provides coverage of Gen. MacArthur's actions in Korea and the Far East in the third volume of his biography, *The Years of MacArthur,* vol. 3, *Triumph and Disaster, 1945–1964* (Boston: Houghton Mifflin, 1985). Two officers who worked closely with MacArthur penned biographies that were published in the mid-1950s: Maj. Gen. Charles A. Willoughby and John Chamberlain, *MacArthur, 1941–1951* (New York: McGraw-Hill, 1954), and Maj. Gen. Courtney Whitney, *MacArthur: His Rendezvous with History* (New York: Alfred A. Knopf, 1955). MacArthur's G-2 for many years, Willoughby, and his primary assistant, Whitney, used excerpts of message traffic and reproduced intelligence reports to make MacArthur's case concerning his pursuit to the Yalu River. President Harry S. Truman's *Memoirs by Harry S. Truman,* vol. 2, *Years of Trial and Hope* (Garden City, N.Y.: Doubleday, 1956) recounts the president's actions and thoughts throughout the Korean War and his sparring with MacArthur.

After Gen. Douglas MacArthur's relief in the Far East in April 1951, he returned to the United States amid great controversy and adulation. From 3 May to 25 June 1951, the U.S. Senate, Committees on Armed Services and on Foreign Relations, 82d Congress, 1st sess., held hearings, appropriately called the MacArthur Hearings, on his removal and U.S. military and foreign policies in Korea and the Far East. The committees released the transcript of the hearings, which was published as *Inquiry into the Military Situation in the Far East and the Facts Surrounding the Relief of General of the Army Douglas MacArthur from His Assignment in That Area.* (Washington, D.C.: U.S. Government Printing Office, 1951).

Among the plentiful secondary works covering the military aspects of the war that are not part of the official histories, of particular note are the four works of Roy E. Appleman that carry the war from his official volume, *South to the Naktong, North to the Yalu,* to the summer of 1951: *Disaster in Korea: The Chinese Confront MacArthur* (College Station: Texas A&M University Press, 1989); *East of the Chosen: Entrapment and Breakout in Korea, 1950* (College Station: Texas A&M University Press, 1990); *Escaping the Trap: The US Army X*

Corps in Northeast Korea, 1950 (College Station: Texas A&M University Press, 1990); and especially *Ridgway Duels for Korea* (College Station: Texas A&M University Press, 1990). The last volume provides considerable detail on the period covered by the combat interviews in this work. T. R. Fehrenbach's classic *This Kind of War: A Study in Unpreparedness* (New York: Macmillan, 1962) remains a must. Steven Hugh Lee, *The Korean War,* Seminar Studies in History (Harlow, U.K.: Pearson Education, 2001), is useful. Also of note is Clay Blair, *The Forgotten War: America in Korea, 1950–1953* (New York: Times Books, 1987), which is based on numerous interviews with commanders at the regimental level and above and provides a unique view of the war from those levels. Other works drawn largely from personal accounts of the war include Rod Paschall, *Witness to War: Korea* (New York: Berkley, 1995); Allan R. Millett, *Their War for Korea: American, Asian, and European Combatants and Civilians, 1945–53* (Washington, D.C.: Brassey's, 2002); John Toland, *In Mortal Combat: Korea, 1950–1953* (New York: William Morrow, 1991); Richard A. Perry and Xiaobing Li, *Voices from the Korean War: Personal Stories of American, Korean, and Chinese Soldiers* (Lexington: University Press of Kentucky, 2004); and David Halberstam, *The Coldest Winter: America and the Korean War* (New York: Hyperion, 2007). A retired U.S. Army historian, Col. Kenneth E. Hamburger, has provided the best detailed operational study of the pivotal fights at the Twin Tunnels and Chip'yong-ni in his *Leadership in the Crucible: The Korean War Battles of Twin Tunnels and Chipyong-ni* (College Station: Texas A&M University Press, 2003).

Spencer C. Tucker, ed., *Encyclopedia of the Korean War* (New York: Checkmark Books/Facts on File, 2002), and Stanley Sandler, *The Korean War: An Encyclopedia* (New York: Garland, 1995), provide a wealth of information on the war in Korea.

S. L. A. Marshall, the noted military historian and analyst, provides a close look at the effect on the Eighth U.S. Army of the entry of Chinese Communist Forces into the Korean War in *The River and the Gauntlet: Defeat of the Eighth Army by the Chinese Communist Forces, November, 1950, in the Battle of the Chongchon River, Korea* (1953; repr., New York: Time Inc., 1962). He also completed a detailed study for the Operations Research Office, Johns Hopkins University, *Commentary on Infantry Operations and Weapons Usage in Korea, Winter of 1950–51* (Report ORO-R-13) (Chevy Chase, Md.), based on his personal observations and interviews in Korea. This report was originally printed in October 1951 for distribution in the Department of Defense and U.S. Army and then reprinted in June 1953. It was subsequently republished as *Infantry Operations and Weapons Usage in Korea* (London: Greenhill Press, 1988) and fills in some important gaps in the story of infantry combat.

James A. Huston, *Guns and Butter, Powder and Rice: U.S. Army Logistics in the Korean War* (Selinsgrove, Pa.: Susquehanna University Press, 1989), draws heavily on historical documents and reports of the Eighth U.S. Army and U.S. Army Forces, Far East, to tell the important story of the Army's logistical support. Charles R. Schrader provides a sound introduction to the far greater logistical challenges that the Communist forces faced in *Communist Logistics in the Korean War* (Westport, Conn.: Greenwood Press, 1995).

The British Commonwealth's military involvement in Korea is covered comprehensively in the two volumes of Field Marshal Sir Anthony Farrar-Hockley's official history, *The British Part in the Korean War;* vol. 1, *A Distant Objective* (London: Her Majesty's Stationery Office, 1990), covers the period up to the end of 1950, and vol. 2, *An Honourable Discharge* (London: Her Majesty's Stationery Office, 1995), treats the remainder of the war, including the battles on the Imjin River during April–May 1951. The operations and tragic loss of the 1st Battalion, the Gloucestershire Regiment, are covered in the second volume as well as in Farrar-Hockley's *The Edge of the Sword* (London: Frederick Muller, 1954). Farrar-Hockley was the adjutant of the 1st Battalion and spent several years as a prisoner of war after he was captured on Hill 235 (Gloster Hill). Andrew Salmon has retold the story of the British forces in the spring of 1951 and especially of the Glosters in his recently published *To the Last Round: The Epic British Stand on the Imjin River, Korea 1951* (London: Aurum Press, 2009). Bob Breen recounts the role of the 3d Battalion, Royal Australian Regiment, in *The Battle of Kapyong: 3rd Battalion, The Royal Australian Regiment, Korea, 23–24 April 1951* (Sydney: Headquarters, Australian Army Training Command, 1992).

Works covering the South Korean perspective of the war include the three volumes published by the Institute of Military History of the Republic of Korea's Ministry of National Defense, *The Korean War* (Lincoln: University of Nebraska Press, 2001). The War History Compilation Commission, Ministry of National Defense, Republic of Korea, has produced six volumes of *The History of the United Nations Forces in the Korean War* (Seoul: War History Compilation Commission, 1967–1975) that cover all of the UNC's national military elements in the Korean War. The memoirs of the South Korean general, Gen.

Paik Sun Yup, *From Pusan to Panmunjom* (Washington, D.C.: Brassey's, 1992), give the perspective of the Republic of Korea's most illustrious commander of the Korean War, who was deeply involved in the operations covered in this volume as commanding general first of the ROK 1st Division until mid-April 1951 and then of the ROK I Corps.

The story of the war from the view of North Korea and its allies is gradually becoming more complete, but there is still much that remains unclear. A good portion of the material is from the Chinese perspective; see for example, Sergei N. Goncharov, John W. Lewis, and Xue Litai, *Uncertain Partners: Stalin, Mao, and the Korean War* (Stanford: Stanford University Press, 1993); Xiaoming Zhang, *Red Wings over the Yalu: China, the Soviet Union, and the Air War in Korea* (College Station: Texas A&M University Press, 2002); Xiaobing Li, *A History of the Modern Chinese Army* (Lexington: University Press of Kentucky, 2007); Shu Guang Zhang, *Mao's Military Romanticism: China and the Korean War, 1950–1953* (Lawrence: University Press of Kansas, 1995); Patrick C. Roe, *The Dragon Strikes: China and the Korean War, June–December 1950* (Novato, Calif.: Presidio Press, 2000); and Russell Spurr, *Enter the Dragon: China's Undeclared War against the U.S. in Korea, 1950–51* (New York: Newmarket Press, 1988). Kevin Mahoney provides a good look at the Chinese and North Korean soldiers in his *Formidable Enemies: The North Korean and Chinese Soldier in the Korean War* (Novato, Calif.: Presidio Press, 2001).

Personal accounts of Chinese Communist commanders in Korea have slowly begun to appear. Of particular interest are the memoirs of Marshal Peng Dehuai (Peng Te-huai), the Communist Chinese commander throughout the Korean War and the architect of the Chinese Spring Offensive (April–May 1951), that were published in Beijing in 1984 following his rehabilitation from Mao's purge during the Cultural Revolution. See Peng Dehuai, *Memoirs of a Chinese Marshal: The Autobiographical Notes of Peng Dehuai (1898–1974)* (1984; repr., Honolulu: University Press of the Pacific, 2005). On Marshal Peng Dehuai himself, see also Jürgen Domes, *Peng Te-huai: The Man and the Image* (Stanford: Stanford University Press, 1985). On other Chinese commanders, see Xiaobing Li, Allan R. Millett, and Bin Yu, trans. and eds., *Mao's Generals Remember Korea* (Lawrence: University Press of Kansas, 2001).

This volume is based on the following Eighth U.S. Army operational interviews and studies in the U.S. Army Center of Military History: No. 8-5.1A BA13, Combat Outpost, Capt. Pierce W. Briscoe, 13 July 1951; No. 8-5.1A BA14, Hill 902, 3d Battalion, 32d Infantry

Regiment, Capt. Pierce W. Briscoe, n.d.; No. 8-5.1A BA33, Tanks above Kap'yong, 1st Lt. Martin Blumenson, 9 May 1951; No. 8-5.1A BA 35, Task Force Byorum, 1st Lt. Martin Blumenson, May 1951, also cited as Ms. 35; No. 8-5.1A BA 36, Task Force Lindy Lou, 1st Lt. Martin Blumenson, n.d., also cited as Ms. 36; No. 8-5.1A BA37, Artillery in Perimeter Defense, 1st Lt. Martin Blumenson, n.d.; No. 8-5.1A BA38, Task Force Hazel, 1st Lt. Martin Blumenson, n.d., also cited as Ms. 38; No. 8-5.1A BA40, Action on the General Defense Line, 1st Lt. Martin Blumenson, n.d., also cited as Ms. 40; No. 8-5.1A BA54, Task Force Gerhardt [Gerhart], May 1951, 1st Lt. John Mewha, n.d., also cited as Ms. 54; No. 8-5.1A BA56, Peaceful Valley, 2d Lt. Bevin R. Alexander, n.d., also cited as Ms. 56; No. 8-5.1A BA62, Supply Battle of the Soyang River, 1st Lt. John Mewha, n.d., also cited as Ms. 62; No. 8-5.1A BA67, Pobwon-ni, Capt. Edward C. Williamson, n.d.; No. 8-5.1A BA68, Hill 128: Forward Observation by Battery B, 999th Armored Field Artillery Battalion (155mm howitzers, self-propelled) during the April Chinese offensive on Seoul, Capt. Edward C. Williamson, n.d., also cited as Ms. 68; No. 8-5.1A BA75, Battle of the Soyang, 1st Lt. John Mewha, n.d., also cited as Ms. 75; No. 8-5.1A BA97, Report of Gloucestershire Battalion, 22–25 April 1951, n.d.; No. 8-5.1A BA99, Action on Hill 628, 8th Ranger Infantry Company (Airborne), Capt. Martin Blumenson, n.d., also cited as Ms. 99.

Internet Sources

"General Sir Anthony Farrar-Hockley," in Obituary Archive of London *Times*, at www.timesonline.co.uk/tol/comment/obituaries /article740668.ece.

Korean War Project is an invaluable source for information on all U.S. Armed Services personnel killed during the Korean War. These files are drawn from the databases of the National Archives and Records Administration, often augmented with personal information. The site contains many of the original Army Map Service's topographical maps from the Korean War era, the L552 series of 1:250,000 maps and L751 series of 1:50,000 maps. These can be viewed online or downloaded as PDF files at www.koreanwar.org/index.html.

"Multiple Gun Motor Carriage M16/M17," *Antiaircraft Command,* at www.antiaircraft.org/M16.htm.

"Quad-50 M2 .50 cal. Machine Gun," *Olive-Drab,* at www.olive drab.com/od_other_firearms_mg_m2_quad50.php.

Schwartzman, Arnold. "Gloster Memorial, Korea, 1957," at www

.britains-smallwars.com/korea/gloster_memorial/gloster_memorial .html.

United States, National Archives and Records Administration, Access to Archival Databases, Record Group 407, Records of the U.S. Army Adjutant General's Office, "Korean War Casualty File, 2/13/1950–12/31/1953," at http://aad.archives.gov/aad. It takes some time to learn how to use the AAD's Korean War databases, but they provide fairly complete information on U.S. Army personnel killed in action, died of wounds, wounded in action, missing in action, and prisoners of war.

INDEX

airfields, corps logistics and, 296
Albaugh, Paul, 83
Alexander, Bevin R., 223–26
Allen, George H., 26
Almond, Edward M.
    battle below the Soyang River
        and, 256, 262, 295, 296
    counteroffensive ordered by,
        297
    Task Force Gerhart and, 298,
        306–11, 329–30
Ames, Richard C., 332, 342,
    344, 345, 348–51, 353,
    363–66
ammunition resupply, during the
    battle below the Soyang Riv-
    er, 285–92, 294
Ammunition Supply Point #50,
    287–89
Anderson, Edgar N., 366, 369–70
Anderson, Herbert, 46–47
Andrews, Reece, 41
Andrews, Robert, 57
Annacost, John H., 204–5
Appleman, Roy E., 383n1
Araedamu-ri, 317
Argent, Lieutenant A., 61, 76

armored personnel carriers, 93,
    389n6
armored tank recovery vehicles,
    220
armored vehicles, 93
Arnett, Captain, 107, 115
Arredondo, Mariano, 394n36
Artiaga, Jose M., Jr., 176
artillery
    resupply during the battle be-
        low the Soyang River, 285–
        92, 294
    significance in the Korean
        War, 385n15
    Van Fleet's policies for opera-
        tions, 6
"Artillery in Perimeter Defense"
    (Blumenson), 115–16
"artillery war," 385n15

B-29 bombers, 262
Baker, R. G. Virgil, 240
Barker, William H., 293,
    295–96
Battery A, 92d Armored Field
    Artillery Battalion, 182,
    184, 186–88, 192

Battery A, 987th Armored Field
    Artillery Battalion, 182,
    184, 186, 192
Battery B, 27th ROK Field Artil-
    lery Battalion, 182, 184,
    186, 192
Battery B, 999th Armored Field
    Artillery
    ambush of, 47–58
    attacked on 22–23 April, 39–46
Beebe, John H., 26
Belgian UN Battalion
    Distinguished Service Cross
        awarded to Lt. Col. Crahay,
        176
    opening of the Chinese offen-
        sive, 149–51
    situation before the Chinese
        offensive, 143, 146, 147, 149
    situation on 23 April, 152–58
    situation on 24 April, 161–64
    situation on 25 April, 166–69,
        172
Bell, George, 281, 282
Bell, Timothy, 50, 58
Bennett, Clemmett, 58
Benskin, Harold L., 202, 204
Benton, Daniel F., 34
Berg, Louis, 73–74
Berry, Fred, 201, 205
Bessler, Captain, 107–9
Bigger, Irvin B., 30
Billemeyer, Frank, 201
Black, Don W., 63–64
Black, Robert W., 132, 396–97n26
Blaskiewicz, Joseph J., 342, 348–
    49, 352–53, 363
"Blue Boys," 249
Blumenson, Martin
    on the actions on Hills 628
        and 1010, 117, 141–42

on Company A, 19th Infantry
    Regiment, 207
interview with Lt. Col. Lavoie,
    88
promoted to captain, 395n1
on Task Force Hazel, 331–33
on Task Force Lindy Lou,
    182–83
Boswell, James, 170
Bowen, Frank, 302, 309, 409n32
Bowman, Maxwell B., 83
Boyle, Thomas, 27
Bragg, Otho C., 77
Bralley, Allan, 358–60
Briscoe, Pierce W., 20
Brodie, Thomas, 155, 156, 169–73
Brooks, Orn G., 239
Brown, Charles, 58
Brown, Charles R., 260, 282
Brown, Edward, 97–98, 108–9
Brown, Robert B., 66, 68
Brubaker, Elbridge, 301–11 passim
Bryan, Blackshear M., 140
Buonocore, George A., 41, 43,
    46, 47, 49
Burnett, Snowden Dale, 19
Burris, Callen C., 217–18
Burros, Harold, 77, 80
Byorum, Henry M., 208–17 pas-
    sim, 220, 403n38

Campbell, Henry A., 341–42,
    348, 353
Carne, James P., 151, 175–76,
    399n9
Carr, George I., 200, 205
Carter, Jessie D., 98
Catalon, Frank, 54–56
Chagnon, Paul O., 129
Chajang-ni ferry, 41
Chandler, Malcolm W., 357–62

Changnam-ni, 247
Chaun-ni
  battle below the Soyang River, 247, 249, 252, 261, 264–65, 268–72, 274–75, 278–79, 281
  Task Force Gerhart and, 306–8, 320
Chech'on, 290
Chinese Communist Forces (CCF)
  entry into the war, 2–3
  Fifth Chinese Offensive (see Fifth Chinese Offensive)
  "Flexible Warfare" tactics, 8
Chinese People's Volunteer Armies (CPVA), 2
Chip'yong-ni, 290, 291
Chmielewski, Alban, 70, 71, 83
Chogutan, 301
Ch'onggu-ri, 315
Ch'ongp'yong dam, 191, 195, 196
Ch'orwon, 6, 148, 377
Choygang-gang (Choygang River), 252
Chudong-ni, 294
Chuktun-ni, 61
Ch'unch'on, 188
  advance of Task Force Hazel to, 335–43
  significance to IX Corps, 331–32
  situation of Task Force Hazel in, 343–49
  in Task Force Hazel's mission, 333
  Task Force Hazel's second advance to, 362–63, 366–70
Cisneros, Jesse, 132
Civilian Transportation Corps (South Korean), 249, 290
Clark, Warren E., 198–99, 202–3, 206, 207

Clements, Edwell D., 306–7, 312–13, 316–20, 326–27
Cloud, Rufus, 200, 205
Combat Actions in Korea (Gugeler), 329–30
Company A, 19th Infantry Regiment, 24th Infantry Division, 118, 196–207
Company A, 32d Infantry Regiment, 31, 38
Company A, 72d Tank Battalion
  Army Presidential Unit Citation award, 87
  in the Cheryong-ni–Kap'yong actions, 59, 61–76, 83–87
  commanded by Lt. Koch, 392n53
  evacuation of wounded soldiers, 78–83
Company B, 2d Chemical Mortar Battalion, 61, 76, 79–80, 82
Company B, 64th Tank Battalion, 304–5, 308–10, 324
Company B, 72d Tank Battalion
  battle below the Soyang River, 261–62, 265–66, 268, 271, 273–76
  Task Force Gerhart, 298, 301, 304–5, 308, 320–23 (see also Task Force Gerhart)
Company C, 6th Medium Tank Battalion, 137
Company C, 72d Tank Battalion
  actions on 17–18 May, 256–67
  awarded the Presidential Unit Citation, 284
  Chinese attacks on 16–17 May, 249–56
  situation prior to the Chinese offensive, 246–49

Company C, King's Shropshire Light Infantry, 209–10, 213
Company I, 32d Infantry Regiment, 20, 22–24, 34–37
Company K, 32d Infantry Regiment
  on Hill 902, 20, 24–31, 33, 36–38
  outpost near Hill 902, 22–23, 31–33
Company L, 21st Infantry Regiment, 120, 121
Company L, 32d Infantry Regiment, 20, 35
Company M, 32d Infantry Regiment, 35–36
corridors, naming of, 386n31
Cox, John W., 200–201, 204
Cox, William R., 131, 133–35, 138, 142
Crahay, Albert, 176
Craig, Charles R., 139
Crawford, Charles, 23, 32
Cruts, Sherman P., Jr., 368
C Squadron, 8th King's Royal Irish Hussars, 143, 160–61, 163, 167, 401n32

Daly, Lawrence, R., 226, 228, 239–42, 243
Daywalt, Kenneth L., 19
deep patrolling, 8
Deramus, Willie M., 46
DeWalt, Kenneth, 56
DiMartino, Peter P., 65–70, 74, 83–85
Distinguished Service Cross (DSC), 87, 175–76, 399n9
Distinguished Service Order (DSO), 175, 399n9
Dodd, Harry J., 290–92, 295

Dorn, George N., 340–41, 346–47, 351–52
Dougherty, John, 267
Drum, Connie M., 123–24
Dudley, Edward F., 371–72
Duff, Forrest W., 183–84
Dunnway, Charles, 321
Dutch Battalion, 256, 262, 284

18th ROK Field Artillery Battalion, 183
8th King's Royal Irish Hussars, 143, 160–61, 163, 167, 401n32
8th Ranger Infantry Company (Airborne)
  actions on Hill 628, 126–33, 140–42
  assigned to Task Force Plumley, 141
  assigned to the U.S. 24th Infantry Division, 117
  Cpl. Black's account of, 397n26
  casualties sustained by, 139, 140
  commanded by Capt. James Herbert, 395n2
  on Hill 1010, 120, 123–26
  reconnoiter of Hill 1168, 120–22
  situation on 22–24 April, 118–20
  Task Force Byorum, 208, 210, 213 (see also Task Force Byorum)
  withdrawal from Hill 628, 133–39
8th ROK Division, 262
Eighth U.S. Army
  anticipation of the Fifth Chinese Offensive, 8–12, 376
  casualties in the Fifth Chinese Offensive, 381
  counterattacks in May, 380

deep patrolling, 8
defense lines, 7, 376, 378, 412n6
(*see also* No Name Line)
early operations in the war,
1–4
operations following the Fifth
Chinese Offensive, 380–81
operations prior to the Fifth
Chinese Offensive, 6–8
response to the Fifth Chinese
Offensive, 376–79
Ridgway's command of, 4
Ridgway's policies for operations, 5
tactics during the Fifth Chinese Offensive, 10, 11
Van Fleet assumes command
of, 5–6
Van Fleet's policies for operations, 6
89th Infantry Division, 408n3
82d Airborne Division, 395n2
82d Antiaircraft Artillery Battalion, 305
8224th Engineer Construction
Group, 293
Elder, John D., 95–96, 102
"elephant gun," 254
11th Marine Regiment, 115
Elliott, William J., 240
Ensley, George H., 253, 272–74,
282
Erskine, Jasper N., 293–95

Fagg, Thomas D., 234
Fazzino, Jack A., 22–23, 31–33
Ferenbaugh, Claude B.
ambush of, 351, 353, 355–62,
364–65
assessment of Task Force Hazel, 370–71

mission of Task Force Hazel,
331
Fields, Joe, 53
Fife, Thomas W., 261–62, 265–
66, 275–76, 309, 321, 326–
27
15th Field Artillery Battalion, 2d
Infantry Division
actions in "Peaceful Valley,"
223, 230–43
ammunition on hand, 286
initial deployment and preparations for Chinese attacks,
226–30
15th Infantry Division, 148, 164,
169
15th Regimental Combat Team,
3d Infantry Division, 294–
95
5th Regimental Combat Team,
24th Infantry Division
actions on 16–17 May, 189,
191, 200
fight on Hill 628 and, 136,
140
withdrawal on 15 May, 187
withdrawal on 17 May, 197
5th ROK Division, 230, 246,
248–49, 256, 297
Fifth Chinese Offensive
American and UN casualties,
381
American tactics during, 10,
11
anticipation by American and
UN forces, 376
attacks in the 7th Infantry Division sector, 13
Chinese casualties, 378, 381
Chinese preparations, 7–8
Chinese tactics during, 10

Fifth Chinese Offensive
    (*continued*)
  Chinese tactics following, 380
  Eighth Army anticipation of,
      8–12
  Eighth Army counterattacks in
      May, 380
  First Impulse, 377
  main axes of advance, 9, 377–78
  Mao's intent for, 10–11
  Peng's planned attacks, 9–12
  Second Impulse, 378–80
Fifth U.S. Air Force, 7, 377,
    403n46
55th Field Squadron, Royal Engi-
    neers, 167, 401n32
52d Antiaircraft Artillery Bat-
    talion, 209–10
  See also Task Force Byorum
52d Field Artillery Battalion,
    140, 397n44
52d Transportation Truck Bat-
    talion, 290–92, 294–95
57mm antitank gun, 254
1st Battalion, 7th Infantry Regi-
    ment, 3d Infantry Division,
    155–58, 162
1st Battalion, Middlesex Regi-
    ment, 59, 76, 81, 85
1st Battalion, Royal Northum-
    berland Fusiliers
  losses killed in action, 401n32
  opening of the Chinese offen-
      sive, 149–51
  situation before the Chinese
      offensive, 143, 146, 149
  situation on 23 April, 152–54,
      157–58
  situation on 24 April, 160–63
  situation on 25 April, 166–69,
      171–72

1st Battalion, Royal Ulster Rifles
  losses killed in action, 400–
      401n32
  opening of the Chinese offen-
      sive, 151
  situation before the Chinese
      offensive, 143, 149
  situation on 23 April, 152,
      154, 157–58
  situation on 24 April, 160–63
  situation on 25 April, 166–69,
      171–72
1st Battalion, the Gloucestershire
    Regiment
  Chinese methods against, 176–78
  Distinguished Service Cross
      awarded to Lt. Col. Carne,
      175–76
  losses in action, 377, 400n32
  opening of the Chinese offen-
      sive, 149–51
  Andrew Salmon on, 179
  situation before the Chinese
      offensive, 143, 147–49
  situation on 23 April, 151–55,
      158
  situation on 24 April, 159–64
  situation on 25 April, 164–73
      passim
  U.S. commanders on the ac-
      tions of, 178
  U.S. Presidential Unit Citation,
      173–75
1st Marine Division
  6th ROK Division and, 59, 88
  counteroffensive toward Line
      Topeka, 331
  in preparations for the Second
      Impulse, 379
  replaces 9th Infantry Regi-
      ment on 18 May, 242

Rocket Battery, 114
situation on 16 May, 226
Task Force Gerhart and, 298
1st MASH Hospital, 293
1st Medium Maintenance Company, 292
I North Korean Corps, 44
I ROK Corps, 180, 379
1st ROK Infantry Division
attack on 4 May, 379
Chinese assaults on, 39, 44, 143
situation on 23–25 April, 153, 164, 173
See also 12th ROK Infantry Regiment
1st U.S. Cavalry, 7
I U.S. Corps
Chinese attacks on 17 May, 256
counterattacks by, 284, 297, 331
operations prior to the Fifth Chinese Offensive, 8
withdrawal on 25 April, 180
Fischer, Albert C., 236–39
515th Medium Automotive Maintenance Company, 292
555th Field Artillery Battalion, 188
559th Regiment, 187th CCF Division, 147
560th Regiment, 187th CCF Division, 147
561st Regiment, 187th CCF Division, 147
503d Field Artillery Battalion, 231, 235, 243, 286
520th Quartermaster Battalion, 293
Five Offensives, 381

Fleets, Charles, 50
"Flexible Warfare" tactics, 8
Forrest, Nathan Bedford, 373–74
48th Field Artillery Battalion, 26, 337, 362
45th Field Regiment, Royal Artillery, 147, 167, 401n32
45th North Korean Division, 13, 15
fougasses, 198
4th Signal Battalion, 293
Fowler, Frederick, 72
French, Harry W., 22, 24, 26–27
French Battalion, 244, 253, 256, 262, 267, 271, 284

Gardiner, Douglas L., 307, 311–15, 317, 328
Gates, William G., 250, 255, 258, 264–65
Gayles, Arthur Lee, 78
general defense line. See No Name Line
Gentry, Albert B., 241
Gerhardt, William, 298, 407–8n1
Gerhart, George H.
formation of Task Force Gerhart, 298, 301–3
military career, 408n3
operations of Task Force Gerhart, 305–6, 309, 325
Gerrity, John F.
actions of Battery A, 92d Armored Field Artillery Battalion on 22–24 April, 93–94, 98–99, 106, 111, 114–15
with Task Force Lindy Lou, 187–88

Giacherine, Alfred J.
  on the 8th Ranger Infantry
    Company, 118–20, 140–41
  actions on Hill 628, 126–27,
    129–30, 140
  Lt. Blumenson on the efforts
    of, 142
  on events leading up to the ac-
    tions on Hill 628, 122–23
  withdrawal from Hill 628,
    135–38
Gillmore, William N., 88, 183,
    186, 188
Girtz, Charles, 24, 37
"Gloster Hill," 179
Glosters. See 1st Battalion, the
    Gloucestershire Regiment
Goad, William A., 70–71
Goff, Roy, 312, 326
Goldberg, Jerome, 201
Gonzales, Paul G., 229–33, 235,
    239
Grant, Calvin C., 394n36
grease gun, 71
Green, Amos, 52
Green, James, 35
Groseclose, Tom S., 209–10
Gugeler, Russell A., 329–30

Hach-ilchon, 368
Hach'onjon-ni, 367
Hackey, Douglas M., 50–51
Hagen, Roy A., 199–200, 205–6
Haines, Charles, 242
Hajin, 291
Hales, Willie C., 200–201, 204
half-tracks, 93
"handie-talkie," 396n5
Handy, Robert M., 358
Han'gye, 280, 283, 298, 301–3
Harris, James C., 58

Harrison, Charles L., 369
Harvey, Maurice G., 159, 163,
    399n10
Hatley, Theral J., 103–4
Hazel, Charles E.
  advance of Task Force Hazel
    to Ch'unch'on, 336–38,
    340–43, 354
  assessment of Task Force Ha-
    zel, 370–71
  command of Task Force Ha-
    zel, 332
  night move of Task Force Ha-
    zel from Ch'unch'on, 349–52
  release of American POWs,
    370
  second advance of Task Force
    Hazel to Ch'unch'on, 362–
    63, 366
  situation of Task Force Hazel
    in Ch'unch'on, 343–46, 349
Head, Kenneth M., 238
Hearin, Joseph N., 94–95, 101,
    103–5, 110
Heavy Tank Company, 32d In-
    fantry Regiment
  advance to Ch'unch'on, 335–
    38, 341–42
  night move from Ch'unch'on,
    350, 352–54
  second advance to Ch'unch'on,
    362–63, 366–69
  situation in Ch'unch'on, 344–
    45, 347–49
  Task Force Hazel, 332
Hector, Artie E., 52, 53, 56
Henley, Eldrich J., 50, 57
Henry, Maurice, 50, 58
Herbert, James A.
  actions of 8th Ranger Infantry
    Company on Hill 628,

119–20, 122–23, 126–27, 131–33, 135–36, 140
military career, 395n2
Hill 63, 214–15
Hill 98, 214, 222
Hill 99, 354
Hill 128, 39–42, 214–15, 219, 221
Hill 129, 211, 215–20
Hill 148, 149
Hill 150, 149
Hill 152, 149
Hill 174, 189, 191
Hill 182, 149, 151
Hill 217, 149
Hill 235 ("Gloster Hill"), 151, 154–55, 159, 163, 166, 179
Hill 257, 155–58
Hill 276, 47
Hill 292, 155
Hill 302, 344–45, 354, 366, 368
Hill 307, 126
Hill 314, 149, 151
Hill 317, 339
Hill 322, 320
Hill 325, 214–15
Hill 336, 339
Hill 341, 137
Hill 342, 199
Hill 343, 337, 339, 343
Hill 347, 337, 339
Hill 387, 336–37, 339–40
Hill 398, 339
Hill 402, 248, 263
Hill 410, 276
Hill 426, 339, 343, 356
Hill 452, 298
Hill 466, 257, 259
Hill 472, 339
Hill 483, 226, 233
Hill 496, 45

Hill 504, 61
Hill 545, 337, 350, 356
Hill 598, 226
Hill 601, 34, 35
Hill 610, 23, 24, 36–37
Hill 628
    actions of the 8th Ranger Infantry Company, 117, 126–33, 140–42
    casualties sustained by the 8th Ranger Infantry Company, 139–40
    objective of the 8th Ranger Infantry Company, 119–22
    withdrawal of the 8th Ranger Infantry Company, 133–39
Hill 635, 246
Hill 638, 231–32
Hill 645, 343
Hill 652, 339
Hill 657, 156
Hill 675, 155, 158, 163, 166
Hill 677, 61
Hill 680, 24, 34, 35
Hill 682, 320
Hill 704, 327
Hill 705, 226
Hill 709, 226
Hill 770, 15–20
Hill 775, 240
Hill 777, 256–57
Hill 830, 121
Hill 899, 226, 229–31
Hill 902, 20, 24–31, 33, 37–38
Hill 914, 262
Hill 915, 15
Hill 925, 246
Hill 1010, 117, 119–20, 123–26, 138
Hill 1051, 246, 252, 262
Hill 1168, 119, 120–22

Hinton, Herman C., 288–89, 292
Hoengsong, 287, 294–95
Hoge, William M., 186, 207–8, 331–32, 362, 374–75
Hongch'on, 287, 288, 290–94
Hongch'on River valley, 224
Hooks, Harold J., 131–32
Hopkins, Wayne D., 88–91
Hotopp, Raymond F., 96–97, 105, 109
Howe, Robert L., 46, 48, 53–54
Hughes, Irving, 196–98
Hutchin, Claire E., Jr., 301

Imjin River, 8
Imjin River, battle of
    actions on 23 April, 151–58
    actions on 24 April, 159–64
    actions on 25 April, 164–73
    Chinese methods in, 176–78
    situation before the Chinese offensive, 143, 145–49
Inch'on, 2
Inje, 409n32
Iron Triangle, 6, 376, 380
Ivanhoe Security Force, 246, 248, 252

Jackson, Anthony, 51
James, N. L., 335–36, 364–66, 368, 371
Jenkins, Lloyd M., 49, 51–52
Jensen, Lloyd K., 257–58, 260–61, 267–72 passim
Johnson, Blaine, 64
Johnson, Dale N., 202–5, 207
Johnson, William L., 204–5
Jokerst, Wilfred, 265, 281, 283
Jones, Ralph G., 31
Jubert, James E., 342, 347–49, 353–54

Kaam-ni, 340
Kammerer, Robert L., 352, 363–64, 368
Kansong, 409n32
Kap'yong River, 59
Karamegi, 348
Kearley, John I., 30
Kelly, Donald L., 227–28, 236–39
Kelly, Richard, 322
Kenney, Richard P., 257, 264
Kimes, Glen G., 239
Kimwha, 6
Kim Yung Man, 41
King, Franklin, 281
King's Shropshire Light Infantry, 209–10, 213
Kingston, J. P., 24, 26, 27, 29–31
Knapp, Allen D., 228–29
Koch, Kenneth W.
    in the Cheryong-ni–Kap'yong actions, 61–65, 68–72, 74
    Distinguished Service Cross awarded to, 87
    evacuation of wounded soldiers, 78–79, 81
    military career, 392n53
    summary of the Cheryong-ni–Kap'yong actions, 83–84
Korean Conflict, 1
Korean War
    China's entry into, 2–3
    early turning points in, 1–4
    Eighth Army operations prior to the Fifth Chinese Offensive, 6–8
    Fifth Chinese Offensive (see Fifth Chinese Offensive)
    road conditions in, 6
    role of terrain and weather in, 6
    significance of artillery in, 385n15

Koridwi-gol, 306, 311, 324
Kramer, Kenneth, 31, 32
Krimminger, Robert L., 255, 264
Kuam-ni, 340
Kuhel, Michael R., 307, 316–20,
    326–27
Kumgong-ni, 45, 211–12, 214–
    15, 217, 221
Kumhwa, 6, 9, 11, 376–77, 380
Kungp'yong, 212–13

L19 airstrips, 296
LaMontia, John A., 215, 218–19,
    221
Lash, Frederick F., 38, 333, 335,
    355
Lavoie, Leon F.
    actions with the 92d Armored
        Field Artillery Battalion on
        22–24 April, 88, 91–92, 95,
        96, 105–9, 111, 113–14
    on the artillery perimeter in
        Korea, 116, 393n3
    command of Task Force Lindy
        Lou, 182, 184, 187
    operations with Task Force
        Lindy Lou, 188–91, 193
    reflections on Task Force Lin-
        dy Lou, 193–95
    on task forces, 194–95
Laws, Henry D., 50, 51, 57
Lees, William, 23
Lenz, Charles N., 123, 127, 129,
    134
Lewis, Johnnie L., 80–81
Lewis, Oscar, 46–47
L'Heureux, Gerald L., 396n3
liaison aircraft strips, 296
light airfields, 296
Light Aviation Section, 369
Limomura, Saburo S., 369

Linder, Charles R., 100, 113
Line Delta, 7, 378, 412n6
Line Golden, 7, 180, 412n6
Line Kansas, 8, 376, 378, 412n6
Line Nevada, 7, 412n6
Line Roger, 226, 227
Line Topeka, 331, 333
Line Waco, 378, 412n6
Line Wyoming, 376
logistics, during the battle below
    the Soyang River, 285–96
Lottman, Marvin F., 22, 23, 31–32

M3A1 personnel carriers, 93
M3/M5 light tanks, 400n20
M3 machine pistol, 71
M4A3E8 Sherman tank, 63, 173,
    220, 249, 305, 355, 368,
    400n30
M16 AAA mount, 404n3
    See also quad 50s
M18 motor gun carriage, 389n6
M19 AAA mount, 405n4
    See also twin 40s
M24 Chaffee light tank, 162,
    390, 400n20, 405n4
M26 Pershing tank, 389n5
M32s, 220
M39 Armored Utility Vehicle
    (AUV), 48–58, 389n6
M41 155mm self-propelled how-
    itzers, 93, 94, 182, 187–88,
    390n11
M46 medium (Patton) tank, 47,
    158, 171–72, 208, 219–20,
    329, 389n5, 400n3
M47 heavy tank, 389n5
M48 heavy tank, 389n5
Mabry, Hiram T., 31, 32
MacArthur, Douglas, 1, 3–4, 11
machine pistols, 71

maintenance companies, 292
maintenance road teams, 292
Mann, Orville, 281–82
Manning, William R., 22, 23, 31–32
Mao Zedong, 9–10, 381
Marchant, G. H., Jr., 37
Marshall, S. L. A., 7
Martin, Erman W., 234
Martin, Oscar D., 358
Masogu-ri, 212
Mathews, Davis L., 287–88
Matthews, Clarence, 22, 23, 31, 32
Mattingly, Leroy B., 186–87, 191–93
Mazyck, John L., 77
McCall, Thomas, 41, 43, 44
McCord, Robert E., 101–2, 110
McCormick, J. K., 289–90, 292–93, 296
McFadin, Billy, 22–23, 31–33
McGhee, Sam, 240
McGregor, Joseph P., 124–25, 132, 134
McIntosh, James F., 220–21
McNeely, James, 120–21, 123, 127–29, 133–34, 142
M Company, 32d Infantry Regiment, 24
Mead, A. D., 169–73
Meadows, Byron D., 24, 35–37
Meeks, Thomas, 50
Mewha, John, 285–87, 297–98
Middlesex Regiment, 59, 76, 81, 85
"MIG Alley," 377
Milburn, Frank W., 178
military police, 295
Miller, Wallace, 24
Miller, Wilfred D., 63, 66–70, 72–74, 81–82, 87, 392n53

Miller, Israel J., 337, 339–40, 366, 370
Molmegi, 315, 318, 322
Moore, Myles P., 82
Moore, Philip D., 121–22, 132, 133
Morae-kogae, 336, 340, 343, 351
"Mosquito" aircraft, 214, 215, 218, 337, 403–4n46
Mount, Charles McN., Jr., 339
Munbong-ni, 246–49
Munsan-ni, 331
Munsan-ni corridor, 378
Murphy, Thomas A., 63, 87
Musumak, 229, 233, 234, 238, 239
Myers, Chester C., 333
Myers, Donald, 283

Naasz, Wilbert A., 71–72
Nalle, Horace D., 234–36
napalm, 198
Naptu-ri, 48
Natzel, Robert J., 195–96, 212
Newman, Charles A.
  actions of Task Force Gerhart at the Soyang River, 325–26
  advance of Task Force Gerhart to the Soyang River, 311–17, 320, 325
  assessment of Task Force Gerhart, 328–29
  command of the point of Task Force Gerhart, 304–8
Newman, O. P., 155–57, 169–70
Nicholson, James, 42, 46–48
987th Armored Field Artillery Battalion, 88, 90, 182, 184
  See also Task Force Lindy Lou
955th Field Artillery, 209, 213
999th Armored Field Artillery
  ambush of Battery B, 47–58

attacks on Battery B, 22–23
    April, 39–46
Battery A, 49, 52
937th Field Artillery Battalion,
    192, 243
19th CCF Army Group, 44, 147
19th Infantry Regiment, 24th In-
    fantry Division, 118, 196–207
19th Medium Maintenance
    Company, 292
19th Regimental Combat Team,
    191
IX CCF Army Group, 188
IX Corps
    Chinese attacks on 17 May, 256
    counterattacks by, 284, 297, 331
    Hoge's guidance to division
        commanders, 207–8
    No Name Line, 180 (see also
        No Name Line)
    significance of Ch'unch'on ba-
        sin, 331–32
    Task Force Byorum, 207–22
    Task Force Lindy Lou, 182–96
    Van Fleet's preparations for
        the Second Impulse, 379
9th Infantry Division, 392n53
9th Infantry Regiment, 2d Infan-
    try Division
    artillery support from 15th
        Field Artillery Battalion,
        223, 243
    Chinese attacks on, 223, 230
    lateral movement on 18 May,
        242, 262
    No Name Line, 226, 227
    Roger Line on 16 May, 226
92d Armored Field Artillery Bat-
    talion
    actions of Battery A, 92–94,
        98–101, 111–14

actions of Battery C, 92–96,
    101–6, 109–10, 114–15
actions of Headquarters Bat-
    tery, 92–94, 96–98, 106–9
Battery B, 92
Lt. Martin Blumenson's as-
    sessment of, 115–16
casualties sustained and in-
    flicted by, 114–15, 394n36
enemy attacks on the 2d Rock-
    et Field Artillery Battery,
    88–91
Lt. Col. Lavoie's assessment
    of, 115
organizational weapons, 195
Service Battery, 115
situation on 20 April, 88
situation on 22 April, 92
situation on 23 April, 91–92
Task Force Lindy Lou, 182,
    184, 186 (See also Task
    Force Lindy Lou)
96th Field Artillery Battalion,
    231, 243, 251
No Name Line
    9th Infantry Regiment and,
        226–27
    15th Field Artillery Battalion's
        withdrawal to, 223, 227,
        233–43
    actions of Company A, 19th
        Infantry Regiment, 196–207
    Company C, 72d Tank Bat-
        talion on, 246
    establishment of, 180, 378
    operations of Task Force Lin-
        dy Lou, 182–96
    Task Force Byorum, 207–22
    withdrawal of the 5th and 7th
        ROK Divisions to, 256
North Taebaek Range, 6

Nunn, Clifford C., 335, 342–43, 356–57, 366, 368, 370
Nurupchong, 322
Nutting, Wallace H., 281–82

O'Brien, Lawrence, 361–362
Odums, Luther, 58
Ogumal, 306, 313
"Old Gold Mine Road," 268, 276
Olga, Karl, 34
O'Neal, James D., 57
188th CCF Division, 153
189th CCF Division, 151, 161
187th Airborne Infantry Regiment, 395n2
187th Airborne Regimental Combat Team
  attached to 2d Infantry Division, 297
  attack north on 23 May, 298
  commanded by Col. Gerhart, 408n3
  moved to Han'gye on 22 May, 295
  moved to IX Corps sector, 379
  Task Force Gerhart, 304–7
187th CCF Division, 145, 147, 150, 153, 161
194th Engineer Combat Battalion, 182, 184
Operation Audacious, 7, 376, 378
Operation Chromite, 1–2
Operation Courageous, 4
Operation Dauntless, 4, 376
Operation Killer, 4
Operation Piledriver, 380
Operation Ripper, 4
Operation Roundup, 4
Operation Rugged, 4, 376
Operation Swing, 4

Operation Thunderbolt, 4
Operation Tomahawk, 4
Oron-ni, 246, 313–14, 316–17, 321, 324–25
Oui-dong, 43

Padgett, Wade H., 76–77
Paeng-ni, 333, 340
Parr, Henry H., 333–36, 338–39, 354–56, 362
Patton (M46) tank. See M46 medium (Patton) tank
"Peaceful Valley"
  actions of the 15th Field Artillery Battalion in, 223, 230–43
  initial deployment and preparations of the 15th Field Artillery Battalion, 226–30
  naming of, 226
  physical description of, 223–26
Peng Dehuai, 9–11, 297, 377–79, 381
Perkins, Otto T., 140, 397n44
Pershing tank, 389n5
Petro, Mike, 255
Phase Line 1, 343, 356
Philippine 10th Battalion Combat Team
  Distinguished Service Crosses awarded to, 176
  opening of the Chinese offensive, 150
  situation before the Chinese offensive, 143
  situation on 23 April, 153, 156–58
  situation on 24 April, 160–64
  situation on 25 April, 168, 170, 172
Pickett, George B., 63, 74, 84, 372–74

Piercefield, Freemont, 15
Plan Obstinate, 412n6
Pobwon-ni, 47, 48
Pointdexter, Earl K., 275, 281–82
P'oltang-ni, 212
Poppler, Glen M., 310–11, 320–23, 327–28
Porter, Oliver, 112
Powell, George T., 102, 105
Presidential Unit Citation, 33, 87, 284, 393n4
Princess Patricia's Canadian Light Infantry, 59, 61, 87
prisoners of war
    Lt. Col. James Carne as, 399n9
    released by Task Force Hazel, 366, 368–70
Psychological Warfare Loudspeaker Team, 361
Puch'aedol, 256, 262, 265, 271, 303, 306–7
Pukhan River, 354
Pukpang-ni, 229, 234
P'ungam-ni, 293, 295, 302
Pusan perimeter, 1, 2
Pusawon-ni, 334
P'yonggang, 6

quad 50s, 227, 359–60, 404n3
Quander, Clarence C., 45, 51

Rackley, Irvin A., 328, 409n30
radios
    SCR300, 17, 386–87n1
    SCR536, 396n5
Raftery, Bernard G., 92, 101–4, 106, 109–10, 114
Ragen, Paul W., 66, 73, 83
Randolph, James W., 250, 254–55
Ranger companies, 140–41

Ranger Company, 2d Infantry Division, 244
Reconnaissance Platoon, 187th Airborne Regimental Combat Team, 304–7
Reed, David R., 39, 41–45
Reeves, George D., 341, 346–47, 352
Richard, W. J., 249, 271, 302–3, 310
Richardson, Beverly, 268, 272
Ridgway, Matthew Bunker, 4–7, 9, 376–77
Ritchotte, Leroy W., 65, 69–70
Rivera, Eugene C., 131, 134–38, 396n24
Roberts, Austin E., 100–101, 112
Roberts, Paul T., 102–3, 106, 110
Rocket Battery, 1st Marine Division, 114
rocket launchers, 86
Rodgers, Fred W., 252–54, 260–61, 266–67, 270, 272–74
Rodriguez, Jerardo, 71
Roger Line, 226–27
Rogers, Willard B., 29–31, 37–38
Rosen, Michael, 122
Ross, William E.
    actions of Task Force Gerhart at the Soyang River, 328
    advance of Task Force Gerhart to the Soyang River, 311, 324–25
    formation and start of Task Force Gerhart, 298, 301–4, 306, 309–10
Rotanz, Richard A., 201
Route 1, 377–78
Route 3, 9, 377–78
Route 24, 247, 248, 298, 409n32
Route 33, 9

Route 92, 298
Royal Army Medical Corps, 401n32
Royal Artillery, 147, 167, 401n32
Royal Australian Regiment. *See* 3d Battalion, Royal Australian Regiment
Royal Engineers, 167, 401n32
Ruble, Willis V., Jr., 97, 107–8
Ruffner, Clark L., 308–10, 324
Ruggerio, Orlando
    description of actions on 17–18 May, 256–59, 263–64
    description of preliminary Chinese attacks on 16–17 May, 249–54
    on the situation of the 72d Tank Battalion prior to the Chinese offensive, 246–48
    on the withdrawal of the 72d Tank Battalion, 267–71, 274, 276–84

Sabangu, 351, 355–56
Saemal, 269, 277–78, 305
Sager, Perry, 271–72
Sagol, 226, 229, 232–36, 238
Salmon, Andrew, 179
Samgo-ri, 260, 263
Sanders, Lemmie F., 55
Sapuppo, Joseph J., 17–19
Sarangch'on, 226, 233–34
Scott, Enoch, 48, 49, 54–57
Scott, Mason F., 77–78
SCR300 radios, 17, 386–87n1
SCR536 radios, 396n5
2d Battalion, Princess Patricia's Canadian Light Infantry, 59, 61, 87
2d Battalion, 21st Infantry Regiment, 24th Infantry Division

8th Ranger Company and, 119, 123, 126, 135–36, 138
Task Force Lindy Lou, 182, 184, 186 (*see also* Task Force Lindy Lou)
2d Battalion, 23d Infantry Regiment, 2d Infantry Division, 244, 258, 260–61, 267–68, 270–72, 274, 284
2d Chemical Mortar Battalion, 61, 76, 79, 80, 82, 90
2d Infantry Division
    187th Regimental Combat Team attached to, 297
    Ammunition Supply Point #50, 288
    awarded the Presidential Unit Citation, 284
    Chinese attacks on, 223, 244, 256, 262
    in Eighth Army reserves, 7
    Ivanhoe Security Force, 246, 248, 252
    Task Force Gerhart (*see* Task Force Gerhart)
    Task Force Zebra, 244 (*see also* Task Force Zebra)
    See also 15th Field Artillery Battalion; *individual regiments*
2d Magazine Platoon, 69th Ordnance Ammunition Company, 287–89
2d MASH Hospital, 293
2d Ranger Company, 356
2d Regiment, 6th ROK Division, 63, 64
2d Rocket Field Artillery Battery, 88–91, 110, 393n4
2d ROK Infantry Division, 182–96 *passim*

2d ROK Regiment, 6th ROK Division, 90
self-propelled howitzers, 93, 390n11
Seoul, 378
715th Transportation Truck Company, 290
17th Field Artillery Battalion, 192
17th ROK Field Artillery Battalion, 45, 46
7th Infantry Division
    moved to IX Corps sector, 379
    North Korean attacks on in the Spring Offensive, 13
    in reserve on 22 April, 148
    Task Force Hazel, 331–33 (see also Task Force Hazel)
    See also 32d Infantry Regiment
7th Infantry Regiment, 3d Infantry Division
    situation on 23 April, 154–58
    situation on 24 April, 162
    situation on 25 April, 167–8, 170
7th Marine Regiment, 344
7th Reconnaissance Company
    advance to Ch'unch'on, 336–43
    attached to 32d Infantry Regiment, 332
    night move from Ch'unch'on, 350–52
    second advance to Ch'unch'on, 362–63, 366–68
    situation in Ch'unch'on, 346–47
    Task Force Hazel, 332–35
7th ROK Division, 256, 289, 297
7th ROK Regiment, 6th ROK Division, 63
74th Engineer Combat Battalion
    actions on 23–24 April, 76–82

support of 27th British Commonwealth Brigade, 59, 61
Task Force Lindy Lou, 182, 184, 186
72d Tank Battalion
    actions on 17–18 May, 256–67
    initial Chinese attacks on 16–17 May, 249–56
    situation prior to the Chinese offensive, 246–49
    Task Force Gerhart, 298, 301–3, 320–23, 325–29 (see also Task Force Gerhart)
    Task Force Zebra, 244
    See also individual companies
73d Heavy Tank Battalion, 166
Sherman tank. See M4A3E8 Sherman tank
Shields, Don, 274
Signal Corps Radio (SCR) 300, 17, 386–87n1
Signal Corps Radio (SCR) 536, 396n5
Silka, Henry P., 121–22
Sims, Deward, 41
Sinchon, 366
Sindae ferry, 41
Sinjom-ni, 336–37, 340, 342–43, 350–51, 355–56, 360
Sink, Ernest L., 281
674th Airborne Field Artillery Battalion, 305
16th New Zealand Field Regiment, 61, 63, 64
6th Medium Tank Battalion, 137, 208–10, 213–14
    See also Task Force Byorum
6th ROK Division
    artillery support by Task Force Lindy Lou, 182–96 passim

6th ROK Division (*continued*)
  disintegration on 22–23 May,
    63–64, 67, 70, 88, 90, 92,
    117
  situation prior to the Chinese
    offensive, 59
60th Indian Field Ambulance, 69
65th Infantry Regiment, 3d In-
    fantry Division
  situation on 22 April, 143,
    148, 150
  situation on 23 April, 153–54,
    157
  situation on 24 April, 162–64
  situation on 25 April, 166,
    168–70
64th CCF Army, 153
64th Medium Tank Battalion
  in 3d Infantry Division re-
    serves, 158
  actions on 24 April, 162–63
  Gloucestershire Battalion and,
    171
  Task Force Gerhart, 304–5,
    308–10, 323–24, 327
69th Ordnance Ammunition
    Company, 287–89
69th Ordnance Battalion, 293
6132d Air Control and Warning
    Squadron, 403n46
63d CCF Army, 145, 147, 161
Smith, Cecil G., 15
Smith, Edward D., 128–29
Smith, Keith W., 124, 134, 138
Snavely, Paul E., Jr., 139
Soch'i-ri, 314
Soellner, Rudolph W., 277
Sojae, 228, 241
Sokchang-ni, 82
*South to the Naktong, North to
  the Yalu* (Appleman), 383n1

Soyang-gang, 246, 367
Soyang River, battle below
  actions of American units on
    17–18 May, 256–67
  initial Chinese attacks on 16–
    17 May, 249–56
  situation before the Chinese
    attacks, 244, 246–49
  withdrawal of American units,
    267–84
Spann, James H., 301–2, 304,
    307–10, 325, 328
Spencer, Lewis E., 18
Spitler, Joseph V., 41, 45–48, 52–
    53, 56
Spraglin, Oscar O., 52
Stallcup, Max R., 366, 368–69
Stanaway, Ivan G., 359–61, 367–68
Starkey, Henry M. M., 227, 230,
    233–34, 242
Staunton, Richard, 53
Steele, Nathan, 58
Stiles, J. D., 356–57
Strocky, Edward, 27
Strong, Berkeley J., 123, 126,
    131–34
Suiter, William O., Jr., 69, 79–80
Surisil-kogae, 336
Sushinko, John, 327

T-6 aircraft, 403–4n46
  See also "Mosquito" aircraft
Tactical Air Control Center
    (TACC), 403n46
Tactical Air Control Parties
    (TACPs), 403n46
Taebaek mountains, 377
Taech'on, 39, 45
tanks
  M3/M5 light tanks, 400n20
  M4A3E8 Sherman tank, 63,

173, 220, 249, 305, 355, 368, 400n30
M24 Chaffee light tank, 162, 390, 400n20, 405n4
M26 Pershing tank, 389n5
M46 medium (Patton) tank, 47, 158, 171–72, 208, 219–20, 329, 389n5, 400n3
M47 heavy tank, 389n5
M48 heavy tank, 389n5
recovering disabled tanks, 220–21
tank tactics, 84, 86–87
Tari-gol, 322, 325
Task Force Baker, 328, 409n32
Task Force Byorum
operations of, 210–22
organization and mission of, 208–10
Task Force Gerhart
actions at the Soyang River, 325–28
advance to the Soyang River, 311–25
assessments of, 328–30
mission of, 298, 303, 305
PFC Rackley killed in action, 409n30
point force, 304–9
problems in the organization and start of, 298, 301–11
Task Force Baker and, 328, 409n32
units in, 298, 305
Task Force Hazel
advance to Ch'unch'on, 335–43
ambush of Gen. Ferenbaugh and, 351, 353, 355–62, 364–65
assessments of, 370–75
equipment of, 335

formation of, 332–35
loss of Lt. Ames's tanks, 363–66
mission of, 332–33
night move from Ch'unch'on, 349–54
Lt. Parr's account of, 354–56
release of American POWs, 366, 368–70
second advance to Ch'unch'on, 362–63, 366–70
situation in Ch'unch'on, 343–49
units in, 332
Task Force Lindy Lou
establishment of, 182–83
Lt. Col. Lavoie's reflections on, 193–95
mission of, 183–84, 187
Lt. Col. Natzel on the importance of, 195–96
operations on 16–19 May, 188–93
preparations for the Chinese offensive, 184, 186–88
units in, 182, 184, 186
Task Force Plumley, 141
task forces, Lt. Col. Lavoie on, 194–95
Task Force Zebra
actions on 17–18 May, 256–67
initial Chinese attacks, 16–17 May, 249–56
mission of, 247
situation prior to the Chinese offensive, 244, 246–49
withdrawal of, 267–84
Taunton, Charles B., 139
telephones, 17, 387n1
10th CCF Army, 168
X Corps
battle below the Soyang River (see Soyang River, battle below)

X Corps (*continued*)
  Chinese assaults in November, 1950, 3–4
  Chinese assaults on 16–18 May, 223, 379
  counteroffensive in May, 284, 297
  logistics, 10 May–7 June, 285–96
  No Name Line, 180
  Operation Chromite, 1–2
  Task Force Baker, 409n32
3d Armored Cavalry Regiment, 392n53
3d Battalion, Royal Australian Regiment
  Army Presidential Unit Citation, 87
  in the Cheryong-ni–Kap'yong actions, 59, 61–63, 67–68, 70, 72–73, 75–76, 84–85
  evacuation of wounded soldiers, 78–79, 81–82
3d Battalion, 23d Infantry Regiment, 2d Infantry Division, 264, 270–72
3d Battalion, 32d Infantry Regiment, 7th Infantry Division, 20–38
3d Battalion, 65th Infantry Regiment, 3d Infantry Division, 162–63, 168
III CCF Army Group, 188
3d Engineer Combat Battalion, 198, 210, 213
3d Infantry Division
  15th Regimental Combat Team, 294–95
  air section, 146
  Imjin River actions, 143, 154–57, 167–73

movement into the X Corps area, 18–20 May, 293–95, 297
reserve units available to, 157–58
situation on 17 May, 262
Van Fleet's use of during the Second Impulse, 379
See also individual regiments
3d Ranger Company, 158, 162
3d Recon Company, 158, 162, 168, 172
III ROK Corps, 180, 256, 379
XIII CCF Army Group, 188
13th Engineer Combat Battalion, 332, 340, 343
13th Field Artillery Battalion, 199
38th Field Artillery Battalion, 286
38th Infantry Regiment, 2d Infantry Division
  in the battle below the Soyang River, 244, 256, 262, 267, 284
  Chinese attacks on, 231, 242
  fire support from the 15th Field Artillery Battalion, 234, 240
  situation on 16 May, 226, 234, 244
31st Infantry Regiment, 7th Infantry Division, 334
31st ROK Infantry Regiment, 2d ROK Infantry Division, 190–91, 194
32d Heavy Mortar Company, 26, 33
32d Infantry Regiment, 7th Infantry Division
  attacks on Company B, 13–20

attacks on 3d Battalion at Hill
902, 20–38
7th Reconnaissance Company
attached to, 332
Task Force Hazel, 333–35,
338–39 (see also Task Force
Hazel)
32d Tank Company. See Heavy
Tank Company, 32d Infan-
try Regiment
37th Field Artillery Battalion,
250, 286
36th ROK Infantry Regiment,
5th ROK Division, 246,
248–49, 261
Thompson, Allen, 53
Thompson, Robert J., 53–55
354th Infantry Regiment, 89th
Infantry Division, 408n3
300th Field Artillery Battalion,
243
328th Medium Maintenance
Company, 292
Tipton, John A., 201, 205
Tojang-dong, 44
Tok-kogae, 228
Toksim-ni, 220
Tolmoru, 228, 241, 243
Tomlinson, Bert, 65–66, 69
To the Last Round (Salmon), 179
traffic control, during the battle
below the Soyang River,
292–93
transportation, during the battle
below the Soyang River,
289–93
Triscik, Rudolph, 73, 82
Trout, Henry C., Jr., 139
"truck bank," 289, 293–94
Truman, Harry, 4
Tuman-ni, 56

Tungmudae, 79
Turkish Brigade, 148, 150
12th North Korean Division, 13
12th ROK Infantry Regiment, 1st
ROK Division, 41, 57, 149,
166
20th CCF Army, 117
25th Infantry Division, 148, 173
21st Infantry Regiment, 24th Infantry Division
2d Battalion in Task Force
Lindy Lou, 182, 184, 186
(see also Task Force Lindy
Lou)
8th Ranger Company and,
118–21, 123, 126, 135–36,
138
actions of 2d Battalion on 23–
25 April, 135–36
Task Force Plumley, 141
24th Infantry Division
Chinese attacks on, 117, 173
Company A, 19th Infantry
Regiment, 118, 196–207
situation on 4 May, 182
situation on 16–19 May, 188–
90, 192
situation prior to the Chinese
offensive, 59
Task Force Byorum, 208–22
See also 5th Regimental Combat Team; 21st Infantry
Regiment
24th Reconnaissance Company,
209–10
29th British Independent Infantry Brigade Group
opening of the Chinese offensive, 149–51
reserve units available to,
157–58

29th British Independent Infantry
    Brigade Group (*continued*)
  situation before the Chinese
    offensive, 143, 145–48
  situation on 23 April, 151–57
  situation on 24 April, 161–62
  situation on 25 April, 166–73
29th CCF Division, 167–68
27th British Commonwealth Brigade, 59, 64, 79, 87
27th CCF Army, 117
27th ROK Field Artillery Battalion, 90, 182, 184, 186
23d Infantry Regiment, 2d Infantry Division
  2d Battalion in Task Force Ze-
    bra, 244, 258, 260–61, 267–
    72, 274, 284
  3d Battalion in the battle be-
    low the Soyang River, 264,
    268, 270–72, 284
  Chinese attacks on 16–17
    May, 242
  Company K, 281–82
  in the X Corps counteroffen-
    sive, 298
twin 40s, 177, 228, 405n4
252d Transportation Truck Company, 290
213th Field Artillery Battalion,
  61, 63–64, 67, 88

Uijongbu corridor, 377–78,
  386n31
Umyang-ni, 324, 328
Underhill, Russell W., 215
United Nations Command
  (UNC)
  anticipation of the Fifth Chi-
    nese Offensive, 376

casualties in the Fifth Chinese
    Offensive, 381
  early operations in the war,
    1–4
  operations following the Fifth
    Chinese Offensive, 380–81
U.S. Army Ranger Hall of Fame,
  395n2, 396n24, 396n26
U.S. Military Assistance Command Vietnam, 395n2

Van Fleet, James A.
  anticipation of the Fifth Chi-
    nese Offensive, 8–10, 376
  assumes command of Eighth
    Army, 5–6
  battle below the Soyang River,
    262
  counteroffensive in May, 297,
    331, 380
  deep patrolling and, 8
  on the Gloucestershire Regi-
    ment, 178
  No Name Line created by, 180
  operations following the Fifth
    Chinese Offensive, 380–81
  response to the Fifth Chinese
    Offensive, 378–79
"Van Fleet Day of Fire," 6
Varnell, William A., 132–33
Vergara, Albert, 218
Victoria Cross (VC), 175, 399n9
Von Gerichten, Theodore, 46
Von Halban, George R.
  with Task Force Gerhart, 305,
    306, 309–311
  with Task Force Zebra, 244,
    246, 264

Walker, Walton H., 2–4

"walkie-talkie," 122, 387n1, 396n5

Warren, Carroll, 250, 254–55

Wayson, Manford, Jr., 71

Welden, James W., 39, 43, 45–49, 52, 56–58

western corridor, 377, 386n31

Weyand, Frederick C., 155–56

White, James R., 99–100, 111–12

Wilcox, Curtis, 46–47, 53–54

Williams, Raymond, 50

Williamson, Edward C., 39, 44, 58

Winslow, Richard I., 343, 347, 352

wired field communications, 387n1

Wohlfeil, Carl, 237–38

Wonch'ang-kogae, 333, 338, 354, 363

Wonch'ang-ni valley, 338, 350, 357

Wondong-ni, 248, 251, 259

Won-gol, 333

Wonjin Ferry, 367

Wonju, 288–91, 294

Wonsan, 2

Wonsan–Seoul corridor, 386n31

Woodhouse, Guy E., 27, 29

Word, Joseph, 51–52

Workman, Robert E., 17

Wright, Robert, 24, 34, 37

Yalu River, 3

Yap, Conrado D., 176

Zagursky, Harry, 125–26, 133, 135

Zayat, Arthur, 258

CPSIA information can be obtained at www.ICGtesting.com
Printed in the USA
BVOW041405180911

271463BV00001B/5/P